AN EXAMINATION
OF PRIME TIME NETWORK TELEVISION
SPECIAL PROGRAMS, 1948 TO 1966

This is a volume in the
Arno Press collection

DISSERTATIONS IN BROADCASTING

Advisory Editor
Christopher H. Sterling

See last pages of this volume
for a complete list of titles.

AN EXAMINATION
OF PRIME TIME NETWORK TELEVISION
SPECIAL PROGRAMS, 1948 TO 1966

Robert Lee Bailey

NYT

ARNO PRESS
A New York Times Company
New York • 1979

Editorial Supervision: Andrea Hicks

First publication 1979 by Arno Press Inc.

Reproduced from a copy in the University of Wisconsin Library

DISSERTATIONS IN BROADCASTING
ISBN for complete set: 0-405-11754-X
See last pages of this volume for titles.

Manufactured in the United States of America

Library of Congress Cataloging in Publication Data

Bailey, Robert Lee.
An examination of prime time network television special programs, 1948 to 1966.

(Dissertations in broadcasting)
Originally presented as the author's thesis, University of Wisconsin, 1967.
1. Television specials--United States. I. Title. II. Series.
PN1992.8.S64B34 1979 791.45'5 78-21716
ISBN 0-405-11755-8

AN EXAMINATION OF PRIME TIME NETWORK TELEVISION SPECIAL PROGRAMS, 1948 to 1966

BY

ROBERT LEE BAILEY

A thesis submitted in partial fulfillment of the requirements for the degree of

DOCTOR OF PHILOSOPHY
(Speech)

at the

UNIVERSITY OF WISCONSIN

1967

ACKNOWLEDGEMENTS

This study is the result of a research project begun by the author at the University of Wisconsin in 1963 under the direction of Dr. Joseph M. Ripley II, who conceived the project. Many people contributed considerable time and effort in supplying source materials, information necessary to the study, and machine data processing. The author wishes to express his appreciation to the following persons and institutions:

ABC-TV, CBS-TV, and NBC-TV were each extremely cooperative in granting the author access to program records. Mr. Gene Klimek of ABC, Miss Rose Marie O'Reilly, Manager of Ratings at CBS, and Miss Miriam Hoffmeir, Director of Program Analysis at NBC, cordially assisted the author.

The A. C. Nielsen Company of Chicago, through Laurence Frerk, Promotion Director, generously provided program ratings and permission to include them in this study.

WHA-TV, the University of Wisconsin educational television channel, and WMTV, Madison, supplied many back issues of TV Guide magazine. The balance of this material was obtained from Mr. John Lovell of TV Guide's Milwaukee office.

The data for this study were machine processed at Wisconsin State University--Eau Claire's Data Processing Center under the supervision of Mr. Rudolf Polenz, Director of the Center. Mr. Polenz' contribution in terms of personnel, hardware and software was substantial.

Finally, the author's patient wife spent many hours at the tedious chore of verifying the data as they were transferred to punch cards for computer analysis in addition to lending moral support to the project.

TABLE OF CONTENTS

LIST OF TABLES

Table | Page

Table Page

Table		Page

LIST OF ILLUSTRATIONS

Figure		Page

Figure | Page

CHAPTER I

INTRODUCTION

A marked characteristic of national network[1] television broadcasting in the United States is the concept of regular programming. Programs appearing regularly at specified times on certain weekdays on a daily, bi-weekly, weekly, or monthly basis comprise by far the bulk of network television offerings. However, network telecasting does not consist wholly of regularly scheduled programs. Since the early days of television networking, regular schedules have been interrupted from time to time for the presentation of one-time only or occasionally produced programs. A portion of these programs was the subject of this inquiry.

The term "special" is generally used in referring to occasional or one-time only programs. However, a search of trade magazine articles on non-regular programming made in preparing this study revealed there was no universal definition for "special" programs. The terms "special" and "spectacular" were often used interchangeably, and precisely what was meant by either was often unclear. This lack of a uniform definition for television "special" programs was reflected in statements such as the following from an article in <u>Advertising Age</u>:

---

[1]Hereafter, the term "network" will refer only to a national network capable of simultaneous transmission on a regular basis.

> Definitions are so loose as to be almost meaningless for the type of programming which once was called spectaculars and is now generally referred to as specials. But, in general, they are the tv dessert, as distinguished from the week-in-week-out regular fare.[2]

A later item in the same periodical stated,

> Defining this type of programming becomes more difficult with the passage of time. In the old days, when specials were called spectaculars, they generally were 90-minute live color shows and (in aim at least) of a blockbusting nature.[3]

The television networks themselves disagreed on what programs should be labeled "specials":

> An NBC spokesman said the news, public affairs and sports shows weren't counted in his network's totals [of special programs scheduled for the 1959-1960 season]. 'The way CBS counts,' he said, 'we could include every game of the World Series as a special.'
>
> A CBS spokesman commented: 'NBC counts weekly programs as specials. This year we're not counting 'Playhouse 90' as a special and that's presented on an every week basis. Meanwhile, NBC is counting regular Sunday, Tuesday and Friday shows as specials. . . .'[4]

At one point, NBC vice president Richard Linkroum offered a set of criteria to distinguish "specials" from other programs:

> Linkroum described a 'real special' as having three specific characteristics: (1) The feeling that its an 'event'--such as Sir Lawrence Olivier's first performance on TV . . . (2) it tends to

---

[2]"Fifty-five Advertisers Set TV Specials for '59-'60," Advertising Age, August 3, 1959, p. 1.

[3]Maurine Christopher, "Honeymoon Over for TV Specials," Advertising Age, September 12, 1960, p. 114.

[4]"TV Networks Differ on Specials Count," Printer's Ink, July 31, 1959, p. 10.

> interrupt the normal schedule of programming: (3) money if often related to a special, in the sense of extra creative effort, more careful planning, more rehearsal time, better talent.[5]

Such vague definitions, which wedded "special" and "spectacular" programs, do not account for the "specials" which are not "spectacular," such as the occasional news program, documentary, political talk, and others. Clearly, other criteria are needed to discriminate between "special" and regular programs.

Obvious criteria exist in a program's frequency and regularity of appearance. This study's concept of a "special" program is based on the quality of non-regularity as opposed to the regularity of most television programming. Such a basis for discrimination avoids subjective evaluations of program content as determinants of "special" programs, hinging instead on a characteristic that can be determined objectively--non-regularity. Moreover, a definition so based includes all instances of non-regular programming, not just those which qualify on an impressionistic basis.

"Specials," then, as conceived by this study, are programs which pre-empt other programs, but not on a regular basis. Some network programs, notably the "spectaculars" which began during the 1954-1955 season, shared certain time periods with other programs and appeared regularly--usually once a month--over entire seasons. These programs were excluded as specials on the rationale that programs scheduled at regular intervals eight or more times during a winter season and three

---

[5] "Are Sponsors Disenchanted by Specials?" Printer's Ink, June 24, 1960, p. 12.

or more times during a summer season were actually regulars, not pre-emptive programs. The number eight eliminated programs regularly scheduled on a monthly basis, which would normally appear nine times during a winter season, allowing for one pre-emption in the series. The figure three eliminated programs scheduled regularly monthly during each summer season month.

Many studies of radio and television programming, programs, and program content exist.[6] In 1928, sociologist George Lundberg[7] undertook what Professor Lawrence W. Lichty calls "probably the first serious study of broadcasting's content."[8] However, apparently only one earlier study of television special programming has been made: in 1961, the A. C. Nielsen Company, an audience and market research organization, analysed the rating performance of some network television special programs and the effect these specials had on the ratings of regular programs.[9] This analysis was limited to special

---

[6]For a bibliography of such studies see Francis Barcus, "A Bibliography of Studies of Radio and Television Program Content, 1928-1958," Journal of Broadcasting, 4:4, Fall, 1960, p. 335. For a listing of many studies on individual programs and program types see Lawrence W. Lichty, "The Nation's Station, A History of Radio Station WLW," unpublished Ph.D. dissertation, Ohio State University, 1964, pp. 841-842.

[7]George Lundberg, "The Content of Radio Programs," Social Forces, 8:1, September, 1928, p. 58.

[8]Lawrence W. Lichty, "Who's Who on Firsts: A Search for Challengers," Journal of Broadcasting, 10:1, Winter, 1965-66, p. 78.

[9]C. W. Besosa, "The Performance of Television Specials," Chicago, A. C. Nielsen Company, August, 1961. (Released only to Nielsen clients.) For a report on this study see, "The TV Special: It's No Gamble," Sponsor, September 11, 1961, p. 36; or "Are Specials Only for Special Viewers?" Broadcasting, September 11, 1961, p. 94.

programs appearing on the air for most of one season, 1960-1961, and offered no information on trends or patterns in special programming. Thus, the present work apparently stands as the only survey to date dealing with total prime time special programming.

There is a two-fold purpose to this study: (1) to provide a basic, systematic, descriptive analysis of trends and changes in network television prime time special programming and to point out some of its fundamental characteristics, and (2) to document and to provide a written record of pre-emptive prime time network television programs. Dr. Harrison B. Summers of Ohio State University began work in recording a history of network regular radio programs.[10] Dr. Lawrence W. Lichty is currently working on a study of network television regular programs at the University of Wisconsin. Thus, the present effort will partially fill a gap in the written history of American broadcast programming.

A thorough understanding of the television medium is not possible without knowledge of its ultimate product--programming. Moreover, knowledge of the medium's output is incomplete without consideration of total programming, including special programs. With the exception of the Besosa study for Nielsen, all published network programming analyses to date have dealt with regular programs, carefully selecting samples as free of special programs as possible to obtain "typical" data. However, in recent years the "typical" television week has contained one or more non-regular programs. By concentrating on the area

---

[10] Harrison B. Summers, Radio Programs Carried on National Networks, 1926-1956 (Columbus: Speech Department, Ohio State University, 1958).

of special programming, this study provides information heretofore unavailable as a unique contribution to the literature.

Results of studies such as this provide a basis for action. In introducing his analysis of radio programming made in 1946, Kenneth Baker wrote, ". . . the results of such . . . [analyses] can be and have been used for . . . guidance in programming."[11] A series of seven television programming studies supervised by the National Association of Educational Broadcasters (NAEB) was prefaced with the thought that they "should be useful in identifying trends in television broadcasting and should provide a basis for more intelligent planning by commercial and educational broadcasters alike."[12]

Inquiries into the nature and composition of television programming have also been found useful by the Federal Communications Commission. Specifically, early studies in the NAEB series mentioned previously were accorded some weight by the FCC during the early 1950's in determining that commercial television broadcasting should be augmented with educational channels.[13]

Dallas Smythe, conductor of the NAEB television content studies, indicates that quantitative studies of what has been broadcast

---

[11]Kenneth Baker, "An Analysis of Radio's Programming," in Paul F. Lazarsfeld and Frank N. Stanton, Communications Research 1948-1949 (New York: Harper and Brothers, 1949), p. 51.

[12]Dallas M. Smythe and Angus Campbell, Los Angeles Television May 23-29, 1951 (Urbana: National Association of Educational Broadcasters, 1951), p. iii.

[13]Dallas M. Smythe, "The Content and Effects of Broadcasting," in Harry B. Nelson, ed., Mass Media and Education. The Fifty-Third Yearbook of the National Society of Education, Part II (Chicago: University of Chicago Press, 1954), p. 195.

represent the first step toward ultimate critical analysis of broadcasting.[14]

National network television's entire history, from the 1948-1949 season in which significant TV networking began,[15] to the end of the 1966 summer season, comprised the period under study. Within this period, the universe of programs considered consisted of all discovered prime time national network television special programs.

National network programming was selected for study because its national characteristic makes it particularly significant. Presently, there are television receivers in 95 per cent of United States homes,[16] all having access to one or more national networks. Hence, a national network program has the theoretical potential of reaching virtually the entire population simultaneously. This massive distribution seems a cogent motivation for descriptive studies designed to ascertain the precise nature of broadcast programming and learn to what types of programs the populace is being exposed through television.

Included in this study are only prime time programs, i.e., those appearing on the air between the hours of 7:30 and 11:00 p.m. New York City time, whence the programs originate. No attempt was made to convert daylight to standard time since the hours considered "prime" remain the same according to New York City clock time regardless of the time system used. This limitation on the programs included was designed to conform to that natural segment of the broadcast day during

---

[14]"Telestatus," Broadcasting-Telecasting, January 28, 1952, p. 74.

[15]Sydney Head, Broadcasting in America (Boston: Houghton-Mifflin Co., 1956), p. 153.

[16]Broadcasting, October 17, 1966, p. 66.

which the greatest number of people are available to view television, and hence the period when the networks offer their most attractive programs.

A further limitation on the study concerned program length. Only special programs lasting 15 minutes or longer were included in the analysis. Material shorter than 15 minutes duration broadcast during prime time has been either brief news bulletins or five-minute political programs,[17] neither of which pre-empt regular programs but merely interrupt them briefly or shorten them somewhat. The five-minute political programs generally occurred in the final five-minute period usually occupied by regular programs. The regular programs were deliberately designed to be 25 or 55 minutes long to accommodate the political announcement and thus remained complete programs.

Special programming data from all national networks were included: the American Broadcasting Company (ABC-TV), the Columbia Broadcasting System (CBS-TV), the DuMont Television Network, and the National Broadcasting Company (NBC-TV).

The research design of this study required that a schedule of prime time special programs televised by all national networks from the fall of 1948 to the fall of 1966 be compiled. As each special program was listed, it was classified according to a pre-determined classification system described in the following pages. Raw data on the final

---

[17] The five-minute political broadcasts of the 1960 and 1964 presidential campaigns are included in an analysis by Lawrence W. Lichty, Joseph M. Ripley II, and Harrison B. Summers, "Political Programs on National Television Networks: 1960 and 1964," Journal of Broadcasting, 9:3, Summer, 1965, p. 217.

schedule of 2,671 special programs were transferred to punch cards and analysed by machine for several pre-determined characteristics. The result was a quantitative description of network television prime time special programming according to these characteristics.

In studying the data prior to designing the final analysis, many variables became apparent, some seemingly of primary interest and importance, others of less significance. The ultimate analysis was confined to what appeared to be the primary variables: the categorical composition and growth of prime time special programming, including trends and changes in this area; patterns in the scheduling of the programs by time, weekdays, and months; competitive scheduling of specials against specials; sponsorship and rating characteristics of prime time special programs; and apparent function, entertainment or information, of special programming. In each of these areas, to which the following chapters of this study are devoted, notable characteristics were observed.

The first objective, to ascertain the kinds of prime time specials broadcast by the networks, required devising a system for classifying the programs. Using a modified version of a classification scheme employed by several programming researchers[18] the programs were first distributed into four broad categories: drama, talks, variety, and

---

[18] Cf. Don C. Smith, "A Study of Programming of the Three Major Radio Networks Between October, 1931 and July, 1935," unpublished Master's thesis, Ohio State University, 1949, p. 8. Robert H. Stewart, "The Development of Network Television Program Types to January, 1953," unpublished Ph.D. dissertation, Ohio State University, 1954, p. 201. Henry L. Ewbank and Sherman P. Lawton, Broadcasting: Radio and Television (New York: Harper and Brothers, 1952), pp. 129-131.

non-classifiable, then further distributed into sub-types. While music potentially represents a fifth broad class, all music offerings could be treated as part of one of the above.

Prior studies of broadcast programming, radio and television alike, have pointed out the difficulty of devising sharply delineated categories defining program content. Most programs contain various elements which cut across categorical boundaries. To devise rigorous categories defining such content can produce ludicrous results. The extent of the problem is suggested in an article written by Neil Postman:

> As the number of different types of programs increased through the years, the problem of establishing recognizable 'genres' became more difficult. A humorous example of the unwieldy proportions of the problem was provided in 1957 when an award was given for the 'Best Continuing Performance (Male) in a Series by a Comedian, Singer, Host, Dancer, M.C., Announcer, Narrator, Panelist, or Any Person Who Essentially Plays Himself.' Although this extraordinary award was never repeated, its appearance--even once--suggests the difficulties involved in classifying television programs.[19]

Baker, in his 1946 radio programming study, attempted to solve the problem by permitting programs to be classified into more than one category.[20] Robert Stewart suggests in his dissertation:

> To set up a list of program types to provide for the many variations between programs would require a list of program types and sub-types nearly as long as the list of programs itself.[21]

---

[19]Neil Postman, "The Literature of Television," in Charles Steinberg, ed., Mass Media and Communication (New York: Hastings House, Publishers, 1966), p. 259.

[20]Baker, loc. cit., p. 57.

[21]Stewart, loc. cit., p. 200.

However, a satisfactory classification system can be based on the dominant characteristics of television programs as indicated by available program information or actual observation. This method of using predominant content to determine program classification is typical of broadcast programming studies.[22]

Definitions of the categories into which the special programs of this study were distributed follow:

Drama

Dramatic programs portray stories through spoken or sung dialog and action. Sub-types under this heading were structured to approximate the carefully worked-out categories in Dallas Smythe's study of New York television.[23]

Action and adventure drama. In these programs action and adventure are the dominant dramatic elements; however, two program types composed essentially of action and adventure have been granted separate standing for they have become recognizable genres in their own rights: *western drama* and *crime, mystery, spy, detective drama*. The *western* is a distinct drama type in American (and other) culture, recognizable in the setting, type of action, and costuming. *Crime, mystery,*

---

[22]Cf. Don C. Smith, *loc. cit.*, p. 8. Herman S. Hettinger, *A Decade of Radio Advertising* (Chicago: University of Chicago Press, 1933), p. 213. Roger W. Forster, "Trends in Radio Programming," unpublished Master's thesis, University of Wisconsin, 1952, p. 10. Dallas W. Smythe and Angus Campbell, *Los Angeles Television, May 23-29, 1951* (Urbana: NAEB, 1951), p. 40.

[23]Dallas W. Smythe, *Three Years of New York Television, 1951-1953* (Urbana: NAEB, 1953), p. 130.

spy, detective dramas are a separate sub-type characterized primarily by plot.

Comedy dramas are dramatic programs emphasizing humorous themes. This includes "situation comedy" plots in which the humor derives from incongruous situations, and light romantic themes in which the humor involves romantic entanglements.

Crime, mystery, spy, detective drama includes programs in which crime, suspense, mystery, murder, horror, spy, and detective work are primary elements.

Dramatic readings are defined as simply readings of dramatic works or other literature, with no attempt to portray the action.

Fairy tales and puppet/cartoon drama. This category includes tales from folklore and children's literature such as "Snow White and the Seven Dwarfs," "Jack and the Beanstalk," etc., presented by human performers or animated cartoons, puppets, marionettes, or combination thereof. In some cases television adaptations of traditional folklore tales relied on music in telling the story to such an extent that the programs became musical dramas and were so categorized.

Historical and biographical drama are those plays depicting real historical events, or events in the life of an actual person.

Motion picture drama pertains to all films originally produced for exhibition in motion picture theatres regardless of content.

Musical drama includes all dramatic presentations in which music plays an integral part in telling the story and dialog becomes primarily lyrics set to music as in operas, operettas, musical comedies, and special musical adaptations of other stories.

Prestige drama refers to dramatic works that have become part of the permanent literature of the theatre, plays based on classic novels, and contemporary plays which have appeared on the stage with notable success and have been adapted to television. Included in this category are the works of such authors as Shakespeare, Ibsen, Eugene O'Neill, and Arthur Miller.

Western drama is the typical "cowboy" melodrama.

Unclassifiable drama. To categorize plays accurately, something must be known of their content or plot. For some television dramas, not enough information was available to permit a justifiable classification. In these cases, the plays were distributed in this category.

Talks

Talks programs are those in which the primary communication takes the form of oral discourse, or in which a verbal explanation is necessary to the full understanding of what is being presented visually.

Actualities. Programs broadcast live from on-the-spot locations of events not necessarily designed especially as television shows, but which have interest in their newsworthiness, are termed actualities. Immediacy is included in this definition. Edited films and tapes of prior occurrences do not qualify for this category, but rather constitute news reports or documentaries. Reports on events occurring simultaneously with the commentary but not capable of presenting the event visually are also excluded from this category, i.e., a verbal description from a television studio of what is occurring during a space flight, although having immediacy, is not an actuality broadcast. However, a live report on the launching of a space vehicle from an on-the-spot location is an actuality broadcast.

Awards and pageants. Programs designed to present awards and/or pageantry and spectacles fall into this classification. Included are such programs as the Motion Picture Academy Awards, all beauty contests, fashion showings, parades, non- or quasi-religious ceremonies and rituals such as the British Queen's coronation.

Documentary. Documentary programs are defined as those dealing with significant historical, social, scientific, or economic subjects,[24] or presenting biographical information in non-dramatic form, using such visual and oral documentation as pictures, film clips, interviews, sound recordings, and other evidence. This implies extensive editing of materials so immediacy is definitely not a part of documentary programs. Television tours through famous places, such as the White House or Louvre Museum, and through various cities, were also classified under this heading. Fictionalized or highly dramatized presentations are not documentaries but belong instead to the drama classification.

Instructional programs are those which present information in a manner to suggest a teacher-pupil relationship between the communicator(s) and viewers. Their primary intent is apparently to convey a certain amount of information that the viewers are intended to learn. The Bell Science Series is an example of this type of special; Watch Mr. Wizard affords another example, although it was a regular series.

---

[24] This definition is a modified version of the description of documentary films used by the Academy of Motion Picture Arts and Sciences, quoted by A. William Bluem in Documentary in American Television (New York: Hastings House Publishers, 1965), p. 33.

News and news analysis programs include news reports and analyses of newsworthy events, together with presidential news conferences and occasional year-end "news roundups."

Panel discussions are round table discussions, interviews, forums, symposiums, and non-political debates, i.e., all programs in which an interchange of ideas and/or opinions between two or more persons takes place.

Political programs refer to all programs relating to political campaigns, regardless of form. Political speeches by or on behalf of a candidate, political convention coverage, election returns coverage, political rallies, and other programs generated by a political campaign designed to examine candidates, provide background information, or preview political conventions are included.

Religious programs refer to actual church services, religious rallies, and talks by recognized religious representatives on religious subject matter.

Speeches includes all speeches of a non-political nature.

Sports and sports news specials include all play-by-play descriptions of sports events, interviews with sports personalities, and sports news programs.

Variety

Variety programs are those designed to present entertainment of a mixed character and are classified according to their most dominant element.

Circus variety programs present circus acts in the traditional manner of the circus. This category includes aquatic performances by trained marine creatures also.

Comedy variety uses various forms of comedy as the primary program content. Characteristic of these programs are a cast and featured personality noted for their comic talent, although other types of performers may appear on the program in roles subordinate to those performed by the comedians.

Musical variety programs are those in which music is the predominant program content, excluding musical drama programs. Such programs are characterized by a cast and featured performer noted for their musical ability. Other types of performers may appear on the program in roles ancillary to those played by the musical artists.

Although music may seem to deserve a separate classification with sub-types of its own, as has been done, for example, in studies of radio programming, the use of music in network television prime time special programming did not warrant this treatment at this time. The musical specials in this study always included other types of content as well, such as comedy, or the Leonard Bernstein lectures on music in the Young People's Concert specials, which gave them a variety characteristic.

Vaudeville variety programs present a series of various "acts," none of which are related so as to form continuity. These programs are usually presided over by a non-performing host who functions primarily to introduce the various performers.

Non-classifiable

Some special programs, such as an occasional auto show introducing new model automobiles, experimental programs like the first satellite transmissions of 1962, the coverage of the aftermath of President Kennedy's assassination, and others, did not fit into any of these categories. In a few instances, programs with ambiguous titles and for which no program information could be located could not be accurately classified. So long as the number of programs defying categorization remained small, it was deemed best to group them in a non-classifiable category rather than devise unique categories for each program, or merely guess at classifications.

To summarize briefly the classification system used to categorize the special programs comprising the corpus of data for this study, the following outline is presented:

Drama

Action and adventure drama
Comedy drama
Crime, mystery, spy, detective drama
Dramatic readings
Fairy tales and puppet/cartoon drama
Historical and biographical drama
Motion picture drama
Musical drama
Prestige drama
Western drama
Unclassified drama

Talks

Actualities
Awards and pageants
Documentary
Instructional
News and news analysis
Panel discussions
Political
Religious
Speeches
Sports and sports news

Variety

Circus variety
Comedy variety
Musical variety
Vaudeville variety

Non-classifiable

Aside from recording program titles and categorizing the specials according to the above classification scheme, other bits of information about the programs were noted: starting time, expressed in New York City time, and length of the programs; date and weekday on which the specials appeared; whether they were sustaining or sponsored and if sponsored, by whom; the average audience rating and share of audience figures according to the A. C. Nielsen National Television Index where available; and program notes regarding content to aid in categorization.

Primary source materials examined to obtain this information and compile a schedule of prime time national network special programs included all issues of TV Guide magazine from volume two, number seven (February 12, 1954) to volume 14, number 37 (September 10, 1966). Apparently no library in the United States maintains this periodical and it was impossible to obtain copies of volume one and the early numbers of volume two even from the publisher.

In addition, a page-by-page search of Broadcasting-Telecasting (originally, and now again titled Broadcasting) was made in issues dating from September, 1948 through December, 1957. From 1958 through the end of the study, Broadcasting's quarterly "Showsheets" feature giving advance listings of special programs was examined. Additional information was obtained from Sponsor, Advertising Age, and the New York Times.

All three existing networks, ABC-TV, CBS-TV, and NBC-TV furnished a great deal of information on their respective special programming. This material was an invaluable supplement to the published sources cited.

Program ratings for many specials were obtained directly from the A. C. Nielsen Company, which granted permission for their inclusion in this study. Other Nielsen ratings data were found in Broadcasting and Variety.

With information gathered from various sources, it was possible to cross-check the specials schedule being compiled for accuracy. The systematic search of the periodicals noted yielded data that were cross-checked against network program records and Nielsen ratings lists. The result was believed to be a highly complete and accurate list of national network television prime time special programs broadcast between September 15, 1948 and September 14, 1966. However, due to inconsistencies in reporting, particularly during the years 1948 through 1953, some programs undoubtedly were not recorded in print and may remain undiscovered here. In later years, some "instant specials," especially sustaining one-time programs, televised with only a few hours advance notice and therefore not appearing in printed program lists, possibly may have escaped discovery. The number of such omissions should not be large enough to bias findings.

For the analysis, some provision had to be made for specials beginning prior to 7:30 p.m. N.Y.T. and running into prime time, or beginning in the prime time segment and continuing past 11:00 p.m. N.Y.T., since the study was concerned only with prime time specials.[25] In such

---

[25]The significance of the prime time limitation was discussed on page 7, supra.

cases, only that portion of a program appearing in prime time was credited to the appropriate category. For example, in the case of a musical variety program beginning at 7:00 p.m. N.Y.T. and continuing to 8:00 p.m. N.Y.T., only 30 minutes would be credited to the musical variety category; however, the program would be counted as one show (not one-half of a program).

Finally, the data were divided into television seasons and each network's prime time special programming examined separately by seasons. Since the national networks begin charging sponsors winter rates near mid-September[26] and generally introduce their new fall shows at this time also, the date September 15th was chosen as the beginning date for each winter television season. Network contracts are usually drawn up for 13-week periods. Three 13-week periods comprise the entire winter season. Beginning on September 15th, therefore, the winter season would continue until mid-June the following year, with the remaining 13-week period comprising the summer television season. Hence, the winter television season is here defined as the period between September 15th and June 14th; the summer season as the period between June 15th and September 14th. The analysis of network television prime time special programming in the succeeding chapters is structured to conform to this seasonal pattern.

---

[26]"NBC Falls in Step on Rates," Broadcasting, December 19, 1966, p. 34.

CHAPTER II

GROWTH AND COMPOSITION OF NETWORK TELEVISION PRIME TIME SPECIAL PROGRAMMING

This chapter traces the growth of prime time network television special programming from the fall of 1948 through the summer of 1966, and analyzes the categorical structure of that programming.

ABC-TV

Between September 15, 1948 and September 14, 1966, ABC-TV broadcast 629 programs totaling 583 hours and 25 minutes qualifying as prime time specials under the definition employed in this study. The time figure represented 2.53 per cent of total prime time during that period. Table 1, page 22, presents the seasonal breakdown of ABC-TV's prime time pre-emptive programming. Winter and summer seasons are listed separately to illustrate their individual characteristics more clearly.

ABC-TV did little prime time special programming during winter seasons until 1956-1957. In that season, the number of nighttime specials nearly doubled over any previous season. The 1956-1957 season was also the first in which ABC-TV devoted more than one per cent of total prime time to special programs: 1.4 per cent. Subsequent to the 1956-1957 season, ABC-TV special programming during the evening hours has always amounted to more than one per cent of total prime time.

Although the growth pattern has been somewhat erratic, the number of pre-emptive prime time programs on ABC-TV has increased over the years reaching a peak in the 1960-1961 season that was nearly matched again in 1964-1965. Most of ABC-TV's prime time special programming has taken place since 1959-1960.

TABLE 1

ABC-TV PRIME TIME SPECIAL PROGRAMS BY SEASONS

Winter Seasons				Summer Seasons			
Season	No. Sp.[a]	No. Hrs.[b]	% Prime Time	Season	No. Sp.	No. Hrs.	% Prime Time
48-49	3	8:00	-1[c]	1949	-	-	-
49-50	1	0:30	-1	1950	2	1:00	-1
50-51	3	1:15	-1	1951	2	1:00	-1
51-52	6	4:00	-1	1952	12	25:00	7.7
52-53	12	10:30	-1	1953	3	2:00	-1
53-54	10	5:45	-1	1954	5	3:00	-1
54-55	4	4:00	-1	1955	6	5:30	1.4
55-56	8	6:00	-1	1956	13	30:00	9.2
56-57	23	15:00	1.4	1957	2	2:30	-1
57-58	24	13:55	1.1	1958	10	7:20	2.1
58-59	18	13:30	1.1	1959	11	8:15	2.3
59-60	40	29:30	2.8	1960	17	35:30	10.9
60-61	72	49:00	4.6	1961	6	4:00	1.1
61-62	52	38:10	3.6	1962	14	10:30	2.9
62-63	55	40:15	3.7	1963	13	10:30	2.9
63-64	35	44:30	4.4	1964	38	54:00	16.7
64-65	53	46:45	4.6	1965	11	8:30	2.4
65-66	39	38:15	3.6	1966	6	6:00	1.8
Total	458	368:50		Total	171	214:35	

[a]Indicates number of prime time special programs.

[b]Indicates number of hours devoted to prime time special programs.

[c]The symbol "-1" indicates the number of hours constituted less than one per cent of total prime time during that season.

Summer season special programming during the prime time hours displayed a different pattern than winter seasons on ABC-TV. Instead

1962-1963			1963-1964			1964-1965			1965-1966		
Hours		%	Hours		%	Hours		%	Hours		%
1:00(	1)	2.5	-		-	-		-	1:00(	1)	2.6
-		-	-		-	-		-	0:30(	1)	1.3
0:30(	1)	1.3	-		-	-		-	1:30(	1)	3.9
-		-	-		-	-		-	-		-
-		-	-		-	-		-	1:00(	1)	2.6
-		-	-		-	-		-	-		-
-		-	-		-	-		-	-		-
-		-	-		-	-		-	0:30(	1)	1.3
-		-	-		-	-		-	-		-
-		-	-		-	-		-	-		-
-		-	-		-	3:00(	2)	6.5	-		-
-		-	-		-	-		-	1:30(	1)	3.9
2:30(	3)	6.2	4:00(	3)	8.9	3:00(	3)	6.5	3:00(	3)	7.8
11:30(	12)	28.5	11:30(	11)	25.9	15:30(	16)	33.1	19:00(	19)	49.7
-		-	-		-	-		-	-		-
2:45(	5)	6.8	1:30(	2)	3.3	0:45(	1)	1.6	3:45(	4)	9.9
3:00(	5)	7.5	2:00(	3)	4.5	-		-	1:00(	1)	2.6
3:30(	1)	8.6	-		-	11:30(	17)	24.5	-		-
-		-	-		-	-		-	-		-
0:30(	2)	1.3	-		-	3:00(	4)	6.5	1:00(	1)	2.6
3:00(	3)	7.5	9:00(	9)	20.3	2:30(	2)	5.3	-		-
-		-	-		-	-		-	-		-
5:30(	10)	13.6	1:00(	1)	2.2	-		-	-		-
6:00(	11)	14.9	1:30(	2)	3.4	7:30(	8)	16.0	4:30(	5)	11.8
-		-	-		-	-		-	-		-
0:30(	1)	1.3	14:00(	4)	31.5	-		-	-		-
40:15	55	100.0%	44:30	35	100.0%	46:45	53	100.0%	38:15	39	100.0%

of the more-or-less gradual growth trend evident in winter season preemptive programming, summer seasons were given to rather extreme fluctuations. From almost no summer prime time specials up to 1952, the total suddenly jumped to 25 hours and 12 programs. The explanation for this abrupt increase lies in ABC-TV's coverage of the 1952 political conventions (note that the 1952-53, 1956-57, 1960-61, and 1964-65 winter seasons, which included the autumn political campaigns and November presidential elections, also showed significant increases over other seasons).

Summer season prime time special programming peaked sharply every fourth year on ABC-TV. Subsequent categorical analysis will show this pattern was due to the quadrennial influence of presidential election campaigns. As with the winter season trend, more summer specials have appeared on ABC-TV in recent years; however, the pattern has been erratic.

Special programming's general nature can be noted by examining the program types of which it is composed. Table 2 breaks down the gross number of ABC-TV prime time special programs into categories, and indicates the percentage of total <u>special</u> hours (not total prime time hours) devoted to each category each winter season. Table 3 does the same for ABC-TV's summer prime time specials.

Throughout the period under study the categorical composition of ABC-TV's special programming changed considerably. These changes are apparent from a careful study of Tables 2 and 3. <u>Drama</u> programs played a minor role in ABC-TV's prime time special programming during winter seasons. Five drama specials appeared during the final season, 1965-1966,

1958-1959			1959-1960			1960-1961			1961-1962		
urs		%	Hours		%	Hours		%	Hours		%
-		-	-		-	1:00(	1)	2.0	-		-
-		-	1:30(	1)	5.1	-		-	-		-
-		-	-		-	-		-	2:00(	2)	5.3
-		-	-		-	-		-	-		-
-		-	-		-	0:30(	1)	1.0	-		-
-		-	-		-	-		-	-		-
-		-	-		-	-		-	-		-
-		-	-		-	-		-	2:00(	2)	5.3
-		-	-		-	-		-	-		-
-		-	-		-	-		-	-		-
-		-	2:00(	2)	6.7	-		-	-		-
-		-	-		-	-		-	-		-
-		-	0:30(	1)	1.6	0:30(	1)	1.0	1:30(	2)	3.9
:30(	6)	33.3	3:30(	4)	11.8	17:00(	24)	34.7	12:25(	17)	32.5
-		-	-		-	-		-	-		-
:00(	1)	7.4	9:00(	17)	30.6	3:45(	8)	7.7	2:00(	3)	5.3
-		-	1:00(	2)	3.4	0:30(	1)	1.0	1:00(	2)	2.6
:00(	1)	7.4	-		-	12:00(	17)	24.5	-		-
:00(	2)	7.4	-		-	-		-	-		-
:00(	4)	14.8	1:00(	2)	3.4	0:30(	1)	1.0	-		-
:00(	1)	7.4	1:00(	1)	3.4	5:00(	6)	10.3	2:45(	4)	7.2
:00(	1)	7.4	1:00(	1)	3.4	-		-	-		-
-		-	-		-	2:00(	3)	4.0	5:30(	9)	14.4
:00(	2)	14.8	9:00(	9)	30.6	5:45(	8)	11.8	8:00(	10)	20.9
-		-	-		-	-		-	1:00(	1)	2.6
-		-	-		-	0:30(	1)	1.0	-		-
:30	18	99.9%	29:30	40	100.0%	49:00	72	100.0%	38:10	52	100.0%

1955	1955-1956			1956-1957			1957-1958		
%	Hours		%	Hours		%	Hours		%
-	-		-	-		-	-		-
-	-		-	-		-	-		-
-	-		-	-		-	-		-
-	-		-	-		-	-		-
-	-		-	-		-	-		-
-	-		-	-		-	-		-
-	-		-	-		-	-		-
-	-		-	-		-	-		-
-	-		-	-		-	-		-
-	1:00(	1)	16.7	-		-	-		-
1) 50.0	-		-	-		-	-		-
-	-		-	-		-	-		-
1) 25.0	1:00(	1)	16.7	1:00(	1)	6.6	-		-
1) 12.5	-		-	-		-	2:30(	4)	17.9
-	-		-	-		-	-		-
-	-		-	-		-	1:25(	2)	10.2
-	0:30(	1)	8.2	-		-	0:30(	1)	3.6
-	1:30(	2)	25.0	8:30(	13)	56.7	2:30(	5)	17.9
-	-		-	0:30(	1)	3.3	1:00(	2)	7.2
1) 12.5	1:00(	2)	16.7	-		-	3:00(	6)	21.6
-	-		-	-		-	2:30(	3)	17.9
-	-		-	-		-	-		-
-	-		-	-		-	-		-
-	1:00(	1)	16.7	3:00(	5)	20.0	-		-
-	-		-	-		-	-		-
-	-		-	2:00(	3)	13.4	0:30(	1)	3.6
100.0%	6:00	8	100.0%	15:00	23	100.0%	13:55	24	99.9%

	1951-19 52			1952-1953			1953-1954			1954
%	Hours		%	Hours		%	Hours		%	Hours
-	-		-	-		-	-		-	-
-	-		-	-		-	-		-	-
-	-		-	-		-	-		-	-
-	-		-	-		-	-		-	-
-	-		-	-		-	-		-	-
-	-		-	-		-	-		-	-
-	-		-	-		-	-		-	-
-	-		-	-		-	-		-	-
-	-		-	-		-	-		-	-
-	-		-	-		-	-		-	-
-	-		-	-		-	-		-	2:00(
-	-		-	-		-	-		-	-
-	-		-	3:30(	3)	33.3	0:30(	1)	8.7	1:00(
-	-		-	-		-	0:30(	1)	8.7	0:30(
-	-		-	-		-	-		-	-
-	-		-	1:00(	1)	9.6	-		-	-
-	0:30(	1)	12.5	0:30(	1)	4.7	-		-	-
-	1:00(	1)	25.0	4:45(	5)	45.3	-		-	-
-	-		-	-		-	-		-	-
.0	1:30(	3)	37.5	0:45(	2)	7.1	2:45(	6)	47.9	0:30(
-	-		-	-		-	0:30(	1)	8.7	-
-	-		-	-		-	-		-	-
-	-		-	-		-	-		-	-
-	-		-	-		-	1:30(	1)	26.0	-
-	-		-	-		-	-		-	-
-	1:00(	1)	25.0	-		-	-		-	-
.0%	4:00	6	100.0%	10:30	12	100.0%	5:45	10	100.0%	4:00

rams in

TABLE 2

COMPOSITION OF ABC-TV'S PRIME TIME SPECIAL PROGRAMMING (WINTERS

Category	1948-1949		1949-1950		1950-1951	
Drama	Hours*	%**	Hours	%	Hours	
Action	-	-	-	-	-	
Comedy	-	-	-	-	-	
Crime	-	-	-	-	-	
Readings	-	-	-	-	-	
Fairy Tales	-	-	-	-	-	
Historical	-	-	-	-	-	
Motion Picture	-	-	-	-	-	
Musical	3:00(1)	37.6	-	-	-	
Prestige	-	-	-	-	-	
Western	-	-	-	-	-	
Unclassified	-	-	-	-	-	
Talks						
Actualities	-	-	-	-	-	
Pageants	-	-	-	-	-	
Documentary	-	-	0:30(1)	100.0	-	
Instructional	-	-	-	-	-	
News	-	-	-	-	-	
Panel	-	-	-	-	-	
Political	3:30(1)	43.7	-	-	-	
Religious	-	-	-	-	-	
Speeches	-	-	-	-	1:15(3)	10
Sports	-	-	-	-	-	
Variety						
Circus	-	-	-	-	-	
Comedy	-	-	-	-	-	
Musical	-	-	-	-	-	
Vaudeville	-	-	-	-	-	
Non-classifiable	1:30(1)	18.7	-	-	-	
Totals	8:00(3)	100.0%	0:30 1	100.0%	1:15 3	10

* In parentheses following the hours figure is the number of pro
each category

** Indicates percentage of total special prime time hours.

963	Summer 1964			Summer 1965			Summer 1966		
%	Hours		%	Hours		%	Hours		%
-	-		-	0:30(	1)	5.9	-		-
-	-		-	-		-	-		-
-	-		-	-		-	-		-
-	-		-	-		-	-		-
-	-		-	-		-	1:00(	1)	16.7
-	-		-	-		-	-		-
-	-		-	-		-	-		-
-	-		-	-		-	-		-
-	-		-	-		-	-		-
-	-		-	-		-	-		-
-	-		-	1:00(	1)	11.8	-		-
-	-		-	-		-	-		-
-	-		-	-		-	-		-
) 33.3	2:00(	2)	3.7	2:30(	3)	29.4	2:00(	2)	33.3
-	-		-	-		-	-		-
) 19.1	-		-	0:30(	1)	5.9	-		-
-	-		-	1:00(	2)	11.8	-		-
-	34:30(	20)	63.9	-		-	-		-
-	-		-	-		-	-		-
-	-		-	-		-	-		-
) 42.9	15:30(	14)	28.7	3:00(	3)	35.2	3:00(	3)	50.0
-	-		-	-		-	-		-
-	-		-	-		-	-		-
) 4.7	2:00(	2)	3.7	-		-	-		-
-	-		-	-		-	-		-
-	-		-	-		-	-		-
100.0%	54:00	38	100.0%	8:30	11	100.0%	6:00	6	100.0%

Summer 1960			Summer 1961			Summer 1962			Summer
Hours		%	Hours		%	Hours		%	Hours
-		-	-		-	-		-	-
-		-	-		-	-		-	-
-		-	-		-	-		-	-
-		-	-		-	-		-	-
-		-	-		-	-		-	-
-		-	-		-	-		-	-
-		-	-		-	-		-	-
-		-	-		-	-		-	-
-		-	-		-	-		-	-
-		-	-		-	-		-	-
-		-	-		-	-		-	-
-		-	-		-	-		-	-
-		-	-		-	-		-	-
3:00(	3)	8.4	1:00(	2)	25.0	2:30(	3)	23.9	3:30(
-		-	-		-	-		-	-
-		-	-		-	0:30(	1)	4.7	2:00(
-		-	-		-	0:30(	1)	4.7	-
30:00(	11)	84.5	-		-	-		-	-
-		-	-		-	-		-	-
-		-	0:30(	1)	12.5	-		-	-
1:30(	2)	4.2	1:00(	1)	25.0	2:30(	3)	23.9	4:30(
-		-	-		-	-		-	-
-		-	0:30(	1)	12.5	1:00(	1)	9.5	-
1:00(	1)	2.9	1:00(	1)	25.0	2:00(	2)	19.0	0:30(
-		-	-		-	-		-	-
-		-	-		-	1:30(	3)	14.3	-
35:30	17	100.0%	4:00	6	100.0%	10:30	14	100.0%	10:30

r 1956		Summer 1957			Summer 1958			Summer 1959		
	%	Hours		%	Hours		%	Hours		%
	-	-		-	-		-	-		-
	-	-		-	-		-	-		-
	-	-		-	-		-	-		-
	-	-		-	-		-	-		-
	-	-		-	-		-	-		-
	-	-		-	-		-	-		-
	-	-		-	-		-	-		-
	-	-		-	-		-	-		-
	-	-		-	-		-	-		-
	-	-		-	-		-	-		-
	-	-		-	-		-	-		-
	-	-		-	-		-	-		-
1)	1.6	-		-	-		-	-		-
	-	-		-	2:30(	4)	34.1	1:30(	2)	18.1
	-	-		-	-		-	-		-
	-	-		-	1:20(	2)	18.2	1:00(	2)	12.2
	-	-		-	-		-	-		-
11)	91.7	-		-	-		-	-		-
	-	-		-	-		-	-		-
	-	-		-	1:00(	2)	13.6	1:45(	4)	21.3
1)	6.7	2:30(	2)	100.0	2:30(	2)	34.1	1:30(	1)	18.1
	-	-		-	-		-	-		-
	-	-		-	-		-	-		-
	-	-		-	-		-	1:00(	1)	12.2
	-	-		-	-		-	-		-
	-	-		-	-		-	1:30(	1)	18.1
13	100.0%	2:30	2	100.0%	7:20	10	100.0%	8:15	11	100.0%

1952	Summer 1953			Summer 1954			Summer 1955			Sum
%	Hours		%	Hours		%	Hours		%	Hour
-	-		-	-		-	-		-	-
-	-		-	-		-	-		-	-
-	-		-	-		-	-		-	-
-	-		-	-		-	-		-	-
-	-		-	-		-	-		-	-
-	-		-	-		-	-		-	-
-	-		-	-		-	-		-	-
-	-		-	-		-	-		-	-
-	-		-	-		-	-		-	-
-	-		-	-		-	-		-	-
-	-		-	-		-	-		-	-
-	-		-	-		-	-		-	-
2.0	-		-	0:30(	1)	16.7	1:30(	1)	27.3	0:3
-	-		-	-		-	-		-	-
-	-		-	-		-	-		-	-
-	1:00(	1)	50.0	-		-	0:15(	1)	4.6	-
-	-		-	-		-	-		-	-
98.0	-		-	-		-	-		-	27:3
-	-		-	-		-	-		-	-
-	0:30(	1)	25.0	1:00(	2)	33.3	0:15(	1)	4.6	-
-	-		-	1:30(	2)	50.0	2:00(	1)	36.4	2:0
-	-		-	-		-	-		-	-
-	-		-	-		-	-		-	-
-	-		-	-		-	-		-	-
-	0:30(	1)	25.0	-		-	1:00(	1)	18.1	-
-	-		-	-		-	0:30(	1)	9.0	-
100.0%	2:00	3	100.0%	3:00	5	100.0%	5:30	6	100.0%	30:

TABLE 3

COMPOSITION OF ABC-TV'S PRIME TIME SPECIAL PROGRAMMING (SUMMERS)

Category	Summer 1949		Summer 1950		Summer 1951		Summer	
Drama	Hours*	%**	Hours	%	Hours	%	Hours	
Action	-	-	-	-	-	-	-	
Comedy	-	-	-	-	-	-	-	
Crime	-	-	-	-	-	-	-	
Readings	-	-	-	-	-	-	-	
Fairy Tales	-	-	-	-	-	-	-	
Historical	-	-	-	-	-	-	-	
Motion Picture	-	-	-	-	-	-	-	
Musical	-	-	-	-	-	-	-	
Prestige	-	-	-	-	-	-	-	
Western	-	-	-	-	-	-	-	
Unclassified	-	-	-	-	-	-	-	
Talks								
Actualities	-	-	-	-	-	-	-	
Pageants	-	-	-	-	-	-	0:30(	1
Documentary	-	-	-	-	-	-	-	
Instructional	-	-	-	-	-	-	-	
News	-	-	-	-	-	-	-	
Panel	-	-	-	-	-	-	-	
Political	-	-	-	-	-	-	24:30(	11
Religious	-	-	-	-	-	-	-	
Speeches	-	-	1:00(2)	100.0	1:00(2)	100.0	-	
Sports	-	-	-	-	-	-	-	
Variety								
Circus	-	-	-	-	-	-	-	
Comedy	-	-	-	-	-	-	-	
Musical	-	-	-	-	-	-	-	
Vaudeville	-	-	-	-	-	-	-	
Non-classifiable	-	-	-	-	-	-	-	
Totals			1:00 2	100.0%	1:00 2	100.0%	25:00	12

* In parentheses following the hours figure is the number of programs in each category.

** Indicates percentage of total special prime time hours.

more than had appeared in any one previous season. During summer seasons, no prime time drama specials appeared at all on ABC-TV until 1965 and 1966. Non-regular talks programs accounted for most of ABC-TV's nighttime specials schedule, followed by programs in the variety category.

The trends and changes in the composition of ABC-TV's prime time special programming were more apparent when the data were summarized. The eighteen winter and summer seasons were combined and divided into three equal blocks, each containing six winter and six summer seasons. With the data thus arranged, each six-year period was noted to contain figures pertaining to one-and-a-half Presidential election campaigns, i.e., the fall campaign of one election plus the summer political conventions and fall campaign of another Presidential election year. This circumstance is noted here since political programs played a powerful role in prime time special programming on all national networks.

Table 4, then, summarizes the data into equal six-season periods with summer seasons included.

During the initial six-year period of television networking, ABC-TV's prime time programming was dominated by only two program types: speeches and political programs. Together, these sub-categories accounted for just over 70 per cent of all pre-emptive hours scheduled in prime time by ABC-TV from September, 1948 to September, 1954.

The relatively large number of hours accruing to the political programs sub-category, which alone made up over half the total special prime time hours programmed by ABC-TV in this period, was due primarily to coverage of the 1952 national political conventions. Characteristically, whole evenings have been given over to this coverage for the

TABLE 4

COMPOSITION OF ABC-TV'S PRIME TIME SPECIAL PROGRAMMING
BY SIX-YEAR PERIODS

Category	1948-1949 Through Summer, 1954		1954-1955 Through Summer, 1960		1960-1961 Through Summer, 1966	
Drama	Hours*	%**	Hours	%	Hours	%
Action	-	-	-	-	3:30(4)	1.0
Comedy	-	-	1:30(1)	0.9	0:30(1)	0.1
Crime	-	-	-	-	4:00(4)	1.1
Readings	-	-	-	-	-	-
Fairy Tales	-	-	-	-	2:30(3)	0.7
Historical	-	-	-	-	-	-
Motion Picture	-	-	-	-	-	-
Musical	3:00(1)	4.8	-	-	2:30(3)	0.7
Prestige	-	-	-	-	-	-
Western	-	-	1:00(1)	0.6	-	-
Unclassified	-	-	4:00(3)	2.3	4:00(3)	1.1
Talks						
Actualities	-	-	-	-	1:30(1)	0.4
Pageants	5:00(6)	8.1	5:30(6)	3.2	14:30(15)	4.1
Documentary	1:00(2)	1.6	18:00(24)	10.5	100:25(115)	28.8
Instructional	-	-	-	-	-	-
News	2:00(2)	3.2	14:00(25)	8.2	17:30(29)	5.0
Panel	1:00(2)	1.6	2:00(4)	1.2	9:00(15)	2.6
Political	33:45(18)	54.5	71:00(43)	41.5	61:30(55)	17.5
Religious	-	-	2:30(5)	1.5	-	-
Speeches	9:45(21)	15.8	10:30(22)	6.2	5:30(9)	1.6
Sports	2:00(3)	3.2	16:30(14)	9.6	51:45(52)	14.8
Variety						
Circus	-	-	2:00(2)	1.2	-	-
Comedy	-	-	-	-	15:30(25)	4.4
Musical	1:30(1)	2.4	17:00(19)	9.9	38:45(50)	11.1
Vaudeville	0:30(1)	0.8	1:00(1)	0.6	1:00(1)	0.3
Non-classifiable	2:30(2)	4.0	4:30(6)	2.6	16:30(9)	4.7
Totals	62:00 59	100.0%	171:00 176	100.0%	350:25 394	100.0%

* In parentheses following the hours figure is the number of programs in each category.

** Indicates percentage of total special prime time hours.

entire run of both national political parties' conventions every fourth year (in the summer of 1948, the four national networks covered the Progressive party convention in addition to the Democratic and Republican conventions). Another significant element in the total hours devoted to political programs was election night coverage. Election nights were also marked by network television coverage generally extending over entire evenings. (As noted in Chapter I,[1] those portions of programs which extended beyond prime time hours, or began prior to prime time, as many convention and election night specials did, were not counted in the total hours figure.)

Political specials also included speeches by candidates and their supporters, and other programs relative to election campaigns; however, these programs accounted for a relatively small proportion of the total time spent on political programs.

The other predominant sub-category in the first six-year span, speeches, consisted mostly of addresses by the President of the United States. Of 21 speeches carried by ABC-TV in prime time during this period, 16 were talks by Presidents Truman and Eisenhower, the remaining five were addresses by other political figures. President Truman delivered nine speeches on ABC-TV in this period, using four hours and 30 minutes of prime time; President Eisenhower spoke seven times using three hours and 15 minutes of prime time. Thus, Presidential pronouncements accounted for 78.8 per cent of all prime time speeches on ABC-TV in this first six-year period, while fully 100 per cent was comprised of talks by political figures, domestic and foreign.

---

[1] Page 20, supra.

Ranking third in the initial six-year period of ABC-TV's prime time special programming, the awards and pageants sub-category included film coverage of England's Queen Elizabeth II's coronation and the first telecast of a "Miss America" beauty pageant on September 11, 1954.

During the second six-year period, ABC-TV scheduled almost exactly three times as many prime time specials as in the first period. Total number of hours devoted to these non-regular programs also nearly tripled. In addition to increasing the amount of time devoted to special programs, ABC-TV employed more types of specials. Comedy and western drama, religious programs and circus variety were added to ABC-TV's prime time specials schedule.

Political programs remained the dominant element in ABC-TV's nighttime special programming, still comprising nearly half the total non-regular program hours; however, significant increases in the use of other categories developed during the period 1954-1955 through the summer of 1960. Documentary, a previously little-used program type, expanded to command second place among ABC-TV's nighttime non-regular programs. A large increase in the number of news and news analysis programs occurred also. The news specials increase began during the fall of 1959, generated by a visit the then Russian Premier Nikita S. Khrushchev paid to the United States. ABC-TV reported on Khrushchev's tour of the U. S. in a non-regular series of prime time news programs entitled "Khrushchev Abroad" during September, 1959. In December of that year, President Eisenhower embarked on a tour of middle eastern nations, and the following May journeyed to Paris for an ill-fated summit conference which ended in chaos when a U-2 American reconnaissance aircraft was shot down over the Soviet Union. ABC-TV covered these events in a series of "Presidential Mission" specials, then televised highlights of emergency United Nations sessions created by the collapse of the Paris Summit Conference.

Speeches remained a frequently scheduled special program type during the second six-year period. Twenty-two prime time speeches appeared on ABC-TV during these years, 14 of which were delivered by President Eisenhower. The remainder were also addresses by political figures, including a speech by Britain's Queen Elizabeth II delivered while visiting Canada in the fall of 1957, carried on U. S. TV by ABC.

A trend toward more musical variety programs occurred in this second period from 1954-1955 through the summer of 1960, and an increase in the number of sports programs took place.

Special program trends which developed in the second six-year period continued during the final span of seasons from 1960-1961 through summer, 1966. The trend toward more prime time special programming continued apace on ABC-TV. The number of specials broadcast during evening hours in this period more than doubled the previous six-year block, which in turn had trebled the initial period. The strong trend toward more documentary specials on ABC-TV gained impetus and this category replaced political programs as the dominant non-regular program type, although political programs also continued to increase in number. About twice as many documentary as political specials appeared on ABC-TV in prime time during the final period. Together, these two sub-categories made up 46.3 per cent of ABC-TV's prime time special programming from 1960-1961 through the following six winter and summer seasons.

A decided surge in the number of prime time special documentary programs scheduled by ABC-TV occurred in the 1960-1961 season when this sub-category accounted for over 34 per cent of all non-regular evening special program time. That was also the season in which ABC-TV broadcast more prime time pre-emptive programs than in any other season before or since. In each winter season since the 1960-1961 season, documentary programs have made up more than one-fourth of all ABC-TV's prime time special programming.

Sports became an important element in ABC-TV's prime time special programming in this final six-year period. Most sports specials were scheduled in 1963-1964 and summer, 1964 when ABC-TV covered the Olympic games. In January and February, 1964, ABC scheduled nine hours of prime time sports specials devoted to the Winter Olympics in Innsbruck, Austria. The following summer, ABC telecast nine and one-half hours of U. S. Olympic trials from New York and Los Angeles, plus three hours of a U. S.-Russian track and field meet and a few other sports specials.

Time devoted to awards and pageants programs, after having remained nearly constant during the first two periods, suddenly increased by almost three times, largely due to ABC-TV's telecasting of Hollywood's Motion Picture Academy Awards. This annual spring special moved from NBC-TV to ABC-TV in 1961, where it has remained since.

Time devoted to ABC-TV news specials continued to increase in the third period, in response to a plethora of national and international events. ABC-TV covered the opening sessions of the 15th General Assembly of the United Nations in September, 1960, at which many world leaders spoke including President Dwight D. Eisenhower and Soviet Premier

Nikita S. Khrushchev. The United States space exploration program made notable achievements during this period which ABC-TV noted in prime time news specials. President John F. Kennedy made an historic journey to Europe during the summer of 1963, covered by ABC-TV in a series of specials titled "Presidential Mission." Later that year, ABC-TV produced a prime time news special noting the transition in government occasioned by President Kennedy's assassination. These and other events helped swell the total of news and news analysis specials on ABC-TV.

Panel discussions achieved some importance as a prime time special program form after 1960, with most such programs televised during the 1962-1963 season.

ABC-TV scheduled about three times as many drama specials in prime time during the final six-year period as in the previous period. Drama types appearing for the first time included action and adventure drama, crime, mystery, spy, detective drama, and fairy tale and puppet/cartoon drama.

Comedy variety, a sub-category unused in earlier periods, became an important part of ABC-TV's nighttime special programming for four seasons beginning in 1960-1961. Use of this program-type on ABC reached a peak in the 1962-1963 season after which it declined, then disappeared completely following the 1963-1964 season.

The rather large percentage of non-classifiable programs appearing in the final six-year period resulted from ABC-TV's coverage of President John F. Kennedy's assassination. This coverage consisted of such disparate elements--actuality, news reports, documentary films, and even classical music--that it defied classification, and was placed in the non-classifiable category.

Table 5, on the following page, presents the total composite picture of ABC-TV's prime time special programming from mid-September, 1948 to mid-September, 1966. Some important characteristics of that programming become apparent from a study of this table. Sub-types comprising the talks classification made up the great majority of ABC-TV's non-regular evening programming--78.2 per cent. Within this grouping, political programs, documentary, and sports and sports news were the dominant types accounting for 61 per cent of total evening special hours programmed by ABC-TV. The instructional category was the only program type within the talks classification not used at all by ABC as a form of prime time special. Religious specials were rare.

Variety programs comprised the next most frequently scheduled special program type on ABC-TV. Of total prime time special hours programmed by ABC, 13.3 per cent were devoted to variety programs. Within this classification, musical variety appeared most often, accounting for 10 per cent of total special prime time hours.

Drama specials were definitely not an important part of ABC-TV's non-regular programming during evening hours, totaling only 4.5 per cent of all special prime time. Four drama sub-categories were not employed at all: dramatic readings, historical and biographical, motion picture, and prestige drama.

CBS-TV

An analysis of the growth trends and composition of CBS-TV's non-regular programming is offered next. Table 6 presents a seasonal

TABLE 5

COMPOSITION OF ABC-TV'S TOTAL PRIME TIME SPECIAL PROGRAMMING

Category	No. Sp.	No. Hrs.	Per Cent of Total Special Prime Time
Drama			
Action/Adventure	4	3:30	0.6%
Comedy	2	2:00	0.3
Crime, Mystery, Spy	4	4:00	0.7
Dramatic Readings	-	-	-
Fairy Tale, Puppet/Cartoon	3	2:30	0.4
Historical/Biographical	-	-	-
Motion Picture	-	-	-
Musical	4	6:00	1.0
Prestige	-	-	-
Western	1	1:00	0.2
Unclassified Drama	6	8:00	1.3
Talks			
Actualities	1	1:30	0.3
Awards and Pageants	27	25:00	4.3
Documentary	141	119:25	20.5
Instructional	-	-	-
News and News Analysis	56	33:30	5.7
Panel Discussions	21	12:00	2.1
Political	116	166:15	28.5
Religious	5	2:30	0.4
Speeches	52	25:45	4.4
Sports and Sports News	69	70:15	12.0
Variety			
Circus	2	2:00	0.3
Comedy	25	15:30	2.6
Musical	70	57:15	10.0
Vaudeville	3	2:30	0.4
Non-classifiable	17	23:30	4.0
Totals	629	583:25	100.0%

TABLE 6

CBS-TV PRIME TIME SPECIAL PROGRAMMING BY SEASONS

Winter Seasons				Summer Seasons			
Season	No. Sp.[a]	No. Hrs.[b]	% Prime Time	Season	No. Sp.	No. Hrs.	% Prime Time
48-49	30	41:15	3.9	1949	2	1:00	-1[c]
49-50	27	15:50	1.2	1950	9	4:20	1.1
50-51	27	13:40	1.0	1951	8	4:15	1.1
51-52	16	8:45	-1[c]	1952	16	25:30	7.9
52-53	25	17:30	1.5	1953	6	5:30	1.5
53-54	12	7:00	-1	1954	5	2:00	-1
54-55	11	10:30	-1	1955	4	2:00	-1
55-56	17	13:00	1.0	1956	13	23:45	7.1
56-57	24	20:40	2.0	1957	1	0:30	-1
57-58	37	39:00	3.6	1958	14	9:45	2.8
58-59	52	55:00	5.2	1959	15	7:00	2.0
59-60	85	86:30	8.3	1960	38	49:00	15.0
60-61	67	65:00	6.2	1961	15	11:30	3.2
61-62	51	45:00	4.3	1962	19	14:45	4.3
62-63	53	45:55	4.3	1963	23	18:30	5.4
63-64	37	45:00	4.3	1964	36	52:00	15.7
64-65	59	50:50	4.9	1965	6	6:00	1.7
65-66	45	47:10	4.4	1966	12	13:00	3.9
Total	675	627:35			242	250:20	

[a]Indicates number of prime time special programs.

[b]Indicates number of hours devoted to prime time special programs.

[c]The symbol "-1" indicates the number of hours constituted less than one per cent of total prime time during that season.

breakdown of CBS-TV's prime time pre-emptive programming.

In the years under study, CBS-TV broadcast 917 prime time special programs totaling 877 hours and 55 minutes. The total hours figure represented 3.8 per cent of all prime time between September 15, 1948 and September 14, 1966.

During the 1948-1949 season, CBS-TV scheduled more hours of prime time special programs than at any other time before the 1958-1959 season. In that first season, 3.9 per cent of all prime time hours were filled with non-regular programs on CBS. Falling back from that point, there was little change in the amount of special prime time hours scheduled during the succeeding seven winter seasons. The percentage of prime time devoted to non-regular programs each winter season from 1949-1950 through 1955-1956 ranged only a few points above or below one per cent, with the average exactly one per cent. Beginning with the 1956-1957 season, however, a decided trend toward more nighttime special programming began on CBS-TV. This trend reached a peak in the 1959-1960 season when a total of 8.3 per cent of the network's prime time was composed of special programs. Nighttime CBS-TV special programming receded from this high point the following season, dropping back to an average of 4.4 per cent of total prime time during winter seasons from 1961-1962 through 1965-1966.

The summer seasons of 1952, 1956, 1960, and 1964 clearly reflected the influence of the political parties' national conventions. The figures for these summers indicated a great deal more special programs were generated by the conventions of 1960 and 1964 than previous ones.

Beginning in 1958, summer time special programming on CBS-TV increased somewhat, consistently remaining at a higher level thereafter than during the pre-1958 summers. Thus, the trend has been towards more summer season prime time specials on CBS-TV with a sharp increase every Presidential election year.

Tables 7 and 8 further break CBS-TV's prime time special programming into categories. Then, in order to illustrate more clearly the growth of CBS-TV's special programming and trends in its categorical makeup, Table 9 summarizes the data into three equal blocks of six years each.

TABLE 8

COMPOSITION OF CBS-TV'S PRIME TIME SPECIAL PROGRAMMIN

Category	Summer 1949			Summer 1950			Su
Drama	Hours*		%**	Hours		%	Hou
Action	-		-	-		-	-
Comedy	-		-	-		-	-
Crime	-		-	-		-	-
Readings	-		-	-		-	-
Fairy Tales	-		-	-		-	-
Historical	-		-	-		-	-
Motion Picture	-		-	-		-	-
Musical	-		-	-		-	1:
Prestige	-		-	-		-	-
Western	-		-	-		-	-
Unclassified	-		-	-		-	-
Talks							
Actualities	-		-	-		-	-
Pageants	-		-	-		-	-
Documentary	-		-	0:45(	1)	17.4	2:
Instructional	-		-	-		-	-
News	-		-	0:30(	1)	11.5	-
Panel	-		-	1:30(	3)	34.6	0:
Political	-		-	-		-	-
Religious	-		-	-		-	-
Speeches	0:30(	1)	50.0	1:35(	4)	36.5	0:
Sports	-		-	-		-	-
Variety							
Circus	-		-	-		-	-
Comedy	-		-	-		-	-
Musical	-		-	-		-	-
Vaudeville	-		-	-		-	-
Non-classifiable	0:30(	1)	50.0	-		-	-
Totals	1:00	2	100.0%	4:20	9	100.0%	4:1

* In parentheses following the hours figure is the numbe each category.

** Indicates percentage of total special prime time hours

1963-1964			1964-1965			1965-1966		
Hours		%	Hours		%	Hours		%
-		-	-		-	-		-
1:00	(1)	2.3	-		-	0:30	(1)	1.1
-		-	1:00	(1)	2.0	-		-
-		-	1:00	(1)	2.0	2:00	(2)	4.3
-		-	1:30	(1)	3.0	3:30	(4)	7.4
-		-	-		-	-		-
0:30	(1)	1.1	1:30	(1)	3.0	1:30	(1)	3.1
3:00	(2)	6.6	2:30	(2)	5.0	-		-
1:30	(1)	3.3	-		-	2:00	(1)	4.3
-		-	-		-	-		-
0:30	(1)	1.1	1:00	(1)	2.0	-		-
-		-	-		-	2:30	(1)	5.3
1:00	(1)	2.3	2:00	(2)	4.0	3:00	(3)	6.3
4:30	(4)	10.0	10:00	(12)	19.6	9:30	(9)	20.2
-		-	-		-	-		-
3:30	(4)	7.8	1:55	(3)	3.7	6:00	(5)	12.7
2:30	(3)	5.5	-		-	1:00	(1)	2.1
3:30	(5)	7.8	11:55	(16)	23.4	-		-
-		-	-		-	-		-
-		-	3:30	(5)	6.8	2:10	(3)	4.4
-		-	-		-	-		-
0:30	(1)	1.1	0:30	(1)	0.9	0:30	(1)	1.1
2:00	(2)	4.4	1:00	(1)	2.0	2:00	(2)	4.3
7:00	(7)	15.5	11:30	(12)	22.6	10:00	(10)	21.3
-		-	-		-	1:00	(1)	2.1
14:00	(4)	31.2	-		-	-		-
45:00	37	100.0%	50:50	59	100.0%	47:10	45	100.0%

(SUMMERS)

mer 1951		Summer 1952		Summer 1953		Summer 1954	
s	%	Hours	%	Hours	%	Hours	%
	-	-	-	-	-	-	-
	-	-	-	-	-	-	-
	-	-	-	-	-	-	-
	-	-	-	-	-	-	-
	-	-	-	-	-	-	-
	-	-	-	-	-	1:00(2)	50.0
	-	-	-	-	-	-	-
o(2)	23.6	-	-	-	-	-	-
	-	-	-	-	-	-	-
	-	-	-	-	-	-	-
	-	-	-	-	-	-	-
	-	-	-	-	-	-	-
	-	-	-	-	-	-	-
)(3)	47.0	-	-	-	-	-	-
	-	-	-	-	-	-	-
	-	-	-	1:00(1)	18.2	-	-
(1)	11.7	-	-	0:30(1)	9.1	-	-
	-	25:30(16)	100.0	-	-	-	-
	-	-	-	-	-	-	-
(2)	17.7	-	-	-	-	1:00(3)	50.0
	-	-	-	-	-	-	-
	-	-	-	-	-	-	-
	-	-	-	0:30(1)	9.1	-	-
	-	-	-	-	-	-	-
	-	-	-	2:30(2)	45.4	-	-
	-	-	-	1:00(1)	18.2	-	-
8	100.0%	25:30 16	100.0%	5:30 6	100.0%	2:00 5	100.0%

of programs in

	1959-1960			1960-1961			1961-1962			1962-1963		
	Hours		**%**	**Hours**		**%**	**Hours**		**%**	**Hours**		**%**
	9:00	(6)	10.5	3:00	(2)	4.7	-		-	-		-
	4:00	(3)	4.7	1:30	(1)	2.4	4:30	(5)	10.0	-		-
	5:30	(4)	6.3	1:30	(1)	2.4	-		-	-		-
	-		-	-		-	-		-	0:30	(1)	1.0
	-		-	-		-	1:00	(1)	2.2	-		-
	3:00	(2)	3.4	-		-	1:00	(1)	2.2	-		-
	0:30	(1)	0.5	0:30	(1)	0.7	0:30	(1)	1.1	0:30	(1)	1.0
	1:00	(1)	1.1	-		-	1:00	(1)	2.2	-		-
	6:00	(4)	6.9	10:30	(10)	16.2	6:00	(5)	13.4	1:00	(1)	2.2
	-		-	-		-	1:00	(1)	2.2	-		-
	10:30	(8)	12.2	3:00	(2)	4.7	-		-	1:00	(1)	2.2
	-		-	-		-	-		-	-		-
	-		-	-		-	-		-	1:25	(2)	3.0
	10:30	(10)	12.2	14:00	(15)	21.5	2:30	(4)	5.6	6:30	(8)	14.2
	-		-	-		-	-		-	-		-
	12:00	(22)	13.8	3:30	(6)	5.3	3:30	(5)	7.8	8:00	(12)	17.5
	2:00	(2)	2.4	-		-	7:00	(10)	15.6	3:30	(6)	7.7
	-		-	11:30	(13)	17.7	1:00	(1)	2.2	5:00	(3)	10.9
	-		-	-		-	-		-	-		-
	0:30	(1)	0.5	1:00	(2)	1.5	-		-	0:30	(1)	1.0
	3:30	(4)	4.0	-		-	-		-	-		-
	2:00	(2)	2.4	2:00	(2)	3.0	0:30	(1)	1.1	-		-
	12:00	(11)	13.8	8:30	(8)	13.0	3:00	(3)	6.6	2:00	(2)	4.4
	4:30	(4)	5.3	4:30	(4)	6.9	11:30	(11)	25.6	16:00	(15)	34.9
	-		-	-		-	-		-	-		-
	-		-	-		-	1:00	(1)	2.2	-		-
%	86:30	85	100.0%	65:00	67	100.0%	45:00	51	100.0%	45:55	53	100.0%

Summer 1955 ours		%	Summer 1956 Hours		%	Summer 1957 Hours		%	Summer 1958 Hours		%
-		-	-		-	-		-	-		-
-		-	-		-	-		-	-		-
-		-	-		-	-		-	-		-
-		-	-		-	-		-	-		-
-		-	-		-	-		-	-		-
-		-	-		-	-		-	-		-
-		-	-		-	-		-	-		-
:00(	1)	50.0	-		-	-		-	-		-
-		-	-		-	-		-	-		-
-		-	-		-	-		-	-		-
-		-	-		-	-		-	-		-
-		-	-		-	-		-	1:45(	1)	17.
-		-	-		-	0:30(	1)	100.0	1:00(	1)	10.
-		-	-		-	-		-	1:30(	3)	15.
-		-	-		-	-		-	-		
-		-	0:30(	1)	2.1	-		-	3:00(	6)	30.
-		-	-		-	-		-	1:30(	2)	15.
-		-	22:30(	10)	94.7	-		-	-		-
-		-	-		-	-		-	-		-
:30(	2)	25.0	0:15(	1)	1.1	-		-	-		-
-		-	0:30(	1)	2.1	-		-	-		-
-		-	-		-	-		-	-		-
-		-	-		-	-		-	-		-
-		-	-		-	-		-	1:00(	1)	10.
30(	1)	25.0	-		-	-		-	-		-
-		-	-		-	-		-	-		-
00	4	100.0%	23:45	13	100.0%	0:30	1	100.0%	9:45	14	100.

1955-1956		1956-1957		1957-1958		1958-1959	
rs	%	Hours	%	Hours	%	Hours	%
	-	-	-	4:30(3)	11.6	1:30(1)	2.
	-	-	-	9:45(8)	25.0	10:30(9)	19.
	-	-	-	-	-	3:00(3)	5.
	-	-	-	-	-	-	-
	-	-	-	-	-	-	-
	-	-	-	-	-	-	-
	-	2:00(1)	9.7	-	-	-	-
	-	1:30(1)	7.3	1:30(1)	3.9	7:00(5)	12.
	-	-	-	4:30(3)	11.6	6:00(4)	10.
	-	-	-	-	-	-	-
	-	-	-	-	-	1:30(1)	2.
	-	-	-	-	-	-	-
	-	-	-	1:30(1)	3.9	0:30(1)	0.
00(3)	23.0	-	-	8:00(8)	20.6	9:00(11)	16.
	-	2:00(2)	9.7	-	-	-	-
2(1)	5.4	-	-	0:30(1)	1.2	1:30(2)	2.
	-	0:30(1)	2.4	-	-	-	-
18(1)	2.4	7:40(11)	37.0	-	-	2:30(2)	4.
	-	-	-	-	-	-	
00(4)	15.4	1:00(2)	4.8	2:45(6)	7.0	1:00(2)	1
	-	-	-	1:00(1)	2.5	-	
00(2)	15.4	-	-	-	-	-	
00(3)	23.0	2:00(2)	9.7	2:00(2)	5.1	3:00(3)	5
30(2)	11.6	4:00(4)	19.4	3:00(3)	7.6	6:00(6)	10.
	-	-	-	-	-	2:00(2)	3.
30(1)	3.8	-	-	-	-	-	-
00 17	100.0%	20:40 24	100.0%	39:00 37	100.0%	55:00 52	100.

Summer 1959 Hours	Summer 1959 %	Summer 1960 Hours	Summer 1960 %	Summer 1961 Hours	Summer 1961 %	Summer 1962 Hours	Summer 1962 %
-	-	-	-	-	-	-	-
-	-	-	-	0:30(1)	4.4	-	-
-	-	-	-	-	-	-	-
-	-	-	-	-	-	2:00(2)	13.6
-	-	-	-	-	-	-	-
-	-	-	-	-	-	-	-
-	-	-	-	-	-	-	-
-	-	-	-	-	-	-	-
-	-	-	-	1:00(1)	8.6	-	-
-	-	-	-	-	-	-	-
-	-	-	-	-	-	1:00(1)	6.8
-	-	-	-	-	-	-	-
2:00(3)	28.5	2:00(3)	4.1	2:30(2)	21.8	2:30(2)	16.9
1:00(2)	14.3	2:00(2)	4.1	2:30(3)	21.8	-	-
-	-	-	-	-	-	-	-
2:15(6)	32.1	2:00(4)	4.1	1:30(3)	13.0	-	-
-	-	2:00(2)	4.1	3:00(4)	26.0	5:00(8)	33.9
-	-	31:00(12)	63.3	-	-	-	-
-	-	-	-	-	-	-	-
1:45(5)	25.1	0:30(1)	1.0	0:30(1)	4.4	-	-
-	-	7:30(12)	15.3	-	-	1:00(1)	6.8
-	-	-	-	-	-	-	-
-	-	1:00(1)	2.0	-	-	-	-
-	-	1:00(1)	2.0	-	-	2:00(2)	13.6
-	-	-	-	-	-	-	-
-	-	-	-	-	-	1:15(3)	8.4
7:00 15	100.0%	49:00 38	100.0%	11:30 15	100.0%	14:45 19	100.0%

51-	1952	1952-1953			1953-1954			1954-1955			
	%	Hours		%	Hours		%	Hours		%	Ho
	-	-		-	-		-	-		-	
	-	-		-	-		-	-		-	
	-	-		-	-		-	-		-	
	-	-		-	-		-	-		-	
	-	-		-	-		-	-		-	
	-	-		-	-		-	1:00(	2)	9.6	
	-	-		-	-		-	-		-	
	-	-		-	-		-	-		-	
	-	-		-	-		-	1:00(	1)	9.6	
	-	-		-	-		-	-		-	
	-	-		-	-		-	2:00(	1)	19.0	
	-	-		-	-		-	-		-	
	-	1:30(	2)	8.6	0:30(	1)	7.2	-		-	
2)	11.4	-		-	-		-	-		-	3
	-	-		-	-		-	-		-	
2)	14.2	1:00(	1)	5.7	-		-	-		-	0
	-	1:30(	2)	8.6	-		-	-		-	
1)	5.7	8:30(	12)	48.5	-		-	3:30(	4)	33.3	0
	-	-		-	-		-	-		-	
3)	17.2	1:30(	3)	8.6	2:45(	6)	39.2	-		-	2
	-	-		-	-		-	-		-	
	-	-		-	-		-	-		-	2
3)	17.1	1:00(	2)	5.7	-		-	-		-	3
	-	-		-	2:30(	3)	35.7	3:00(	3)	28.5	1
	-	1:00(	1)	5.7	-		-	-		-	
5)	34.4	1:30(	2)	8.6	1:15(	2)	17.9	-		-	0
16	100.0%	17:30	25	100.0%	7:00	12	100.0%	10:30	11	100.0%	13

TABLE 7

COMPOSITION OF CBS-TV'S PRIME TIME SPECIAL PROGRAMMING (WINTERS)

Category	1948-1949			1949-1950			1950-1951			
Drama	Hours*		%**	Hours		%	Hours		%	Hour
Action	-		-	-		-	-		-	-
Comedy	-		-	-		-	-		-	-
Crime	-		-	-		-	-		-	-
Readings	-		-	-		-	-		-	-
Fairy Tales	0:25(	1)	1.0	-		-	-		-	-
Historical	-		-	-		-	-		-	-
Motion Picture	-		-	-		-	-		-	-
Musical	-		-	-		-	-		-	-
Prestige	-		-	-		-	0:30(	1)	3.7	-
Western	-		-	-		-	-		-	-
Unclassified	-		-	-		-	-		-	-
Talks										
Actualities	-		-	-		-	-		-	-
Pageants	-		-	2:50(	5)	17.8	0:30(	1)	3.7	-
Documentary	-		-	0:30(	1)	3.1	4:15(	8)	31.0	1:0
Instructional	-		-	-		-	-		-	-
News	-		-	0:45(	1)	4.7	0:30(	1)	3.7	1:1
Panel	4:30(	3)	10.9	-		-	-		-	-
Political	5:40(	5)	13.8	1:00(	1)	6.4	1:00(	2)	7.3	0:3
Religious	-		-	-		-	-		-	-
Speeches	1:30(	2)	3.7	4:15(	8)	26.8	1:40(	4)	12.2	1:3
Sports	23:25(	12)	56.8	1:30(	3)	9.5	0:30(	2)	3.7	-
Variety										
Circus	-		-	-		-	-		-	-
Comedy	-		-	-		-	2:45(	4)	20.0	1:3
Musical	2:00(	3)	4.8	-		-	-		-	-
Vaudeville	-		-	1:30(	2)	9.5	-		-	-
Non-classifiable	3:45(	4)	9.0	3:30(	6)	22.2	2:00(	4)	14.6	3:0
Totals	41:15	30	100.0%	15:50	27	100.0%	13:40	27	100.0%	8:4

* In parentheses following the hours figure is the number of programs in each category.

** Indicates percentage of total special prime time hours.

Summer 1963			Summer 1964			Summer 1965			Summer 1966		
Hours		%	Hours		%	Hours		%	Hours		%
-		-	-		-	-		-	-		-
-		-	-		-	-		-	-		-
-		-	-		-	-		-	-		-
-		-	-		-	1:00(	1)	16.7	-		-
-		-	-		-	-		-	-		-
-		-	-		-	-		-	-		-
-		-	-		-	-		-	-		-
-		-	-		-	-		-	-		-
-		-	-		-	-		-	-		-
-		-	-		-	-		-	-		-
0:30(	1)	2.7	-		-	-		-	-		-
-		-	-		-	-		-	-		-
2:00(	2)	10.8	2:00(	2)	3.9	2:00(	2)	33.3	1:00(	1)	7.7
6:00(	7)	32.5	6:00(	6)	11.5	1:00(	1)	16.7	1:00(	1)	7.7
-		-	-		-	-		-	-		-
4:30(	7)	24.3	1:30(	2)	2.9	0:30(	1)	8.3	2:00(	3)	15.4
4:30(	5)	24.3	1:30(	3)	2.9	-		-	2:00(	2)	15.4
-		-	31:30(	13)	60.5	-		-	-		-
-		-	-		-	-		-	-		-
-		-	-		-	-		-	-		-
-		-	0:30(	1)	0.9	-		-	7:00(	5)	53.8
-		-	-		-	-		-	-		-
-		-	2:00(	2)	3.9	-		-	-		-
1:00(	1)	5.4	7:00(	7)	13.5	1:30(	1)	25.0	-		-
-		-	-		-	-		-	-		-
-		-	-		-	-		-	-		-
18:30	23	100.0%	52:00	36	100.0%	6:00	6	100.0%	13:00	12	100.0%

TABLE 9

COMPOSITION OF CBS-TV'S PRIME TIME SPECIAL PROGRAMMING
BY SIX-YEAR PERIODS

Category	1948-1949 Through Summer, 1954		1954-1955 Through Summer, 1960		1960-1961 Through Summer, 1966	
Drama	Hours*	%**	Hours	%	Hours	%
Action	-	-	15:00(10)	4.7	3:00(2)	0.7
Comedy	-	-	24:15(20)	7.7	8:00(9)	1.9
Crime	-	-	8:30(7)	2.7	2:30(2)	0.6
Readings	-	-	-	-	6:30(7)	1.6
Fairy Tales	0:25(1)	0.3	-	-	6:00(6)	1.4
Historical	1:00(2)	0.7	4:00(4)	1.3	1:00(1)	0.2
Motion Picture	-	-	2:30(2)	0.8	5:00(6)	1.2
Musical	1:30(3)	1.0	12:00(9)	3.8	6:30(5)	1.6
Prestige	-	-	17:30(12)	5.5	22:00(19)	5.3
Western	-	-	-	-	1:00(1)	0.2
Unclassified	-	-	14:00(10)	4.4	7:00(7)	1.6
Talks						
Actualities	-	-	1:45(1)	0.6	2:30(1)	0.6
Pageants	5:20(9)	3.6	7:30(10)	2.4	19:25(19)	4.7
Documentary	8:30(15)	5.8	35:00(38)	11.1	63:30(70)	15.3
Instructional	-	-	2:00(2)	0.6	-	-
News	5:00(7)	3.4	22:27(43)	7.1	36:25(51)	8.8
Panel	8:30(10)	5.8	6:00(7)	1.9	30:00(42)	7.2
Political	42:10(37)	28.8	67:28(40)	21.0	64:25(51)	15.7
Religious	-	-	-	-	-	-
Speeches	17:00(36)	11.6	10:15(24)	3.2	7:40(12)	1.8
Sports	25:25(17)	17.4	12:30(18)	3.9	8:30(7)	2.1
Variety						
Circus	-	-	4:00(4)	1.3	4:00(6)	1.0
Comedy	5:45(10)	3.9	23:00(22)	7.2	20:30(20)	4.9
Musical	4:30(6)	3.1	24:00(24)	7.7	72:00(70)	17.5
Vaudeville	5:00(5)	3.4	2:30(3)	0.8	1:00(1)	0.2
Non-classifiable	16:30(25)	11.2	0:30(1)	0.3	16:15(8)	3.9
Totals	146:35 183	100.0%	316:40 311	100.0%	414:40 423	100.0%

* In parentheses following the hours figure is the number of programs in each category.

** Indicates percentage of total special prime time hours.

The pattern displayed by CBS-TV prime time special programming was one of growth both in numbers and variety. During the first six years, political programs, sports, and speeches dominated CBS-TV's evening pre-emptive programming. The political programs, of course, dealt primarily with the 1948 and 1952 Presidential elections. Sports specials, which played a more important part in CBS-TV's special programming during this first period than in any other, consisted of several full evenings of roller derbys, in addition to horse shows, rodeos, boxing matches, football games, and other sports events. Sports predominated as a prime time special program type primarily during the 1948-1949 season; thereafter its use was limited. Speeches were very nearly evenly divided between Presidential addresses and addresses by other notables. Presidents Truman and Eisenhower accounted for 47.1 per cent of the time allotted to this category. Whereas on ABC-TV all speeches were delivered by political figures, CBS-TV presented speakers representing the fields of science, religion, education, and communications; however, 89.7 per cent of the prime time speeches on CBS-TV were delivered by persons connected with government, both U. S. and foreign.

The second period, 1954-1955 through the summer of 1960, saw the number of prime time hours CBS-TV devoted to pre-emptive programming increase by about two and one-half times over the first period. This compared with an increase of about three times for the same period on ABC-TV. The makeup of this programming also changed considerably. To be sure, political programs continued to dominate CBS-TV's prime time special programming; however, previously little-used program forms began to assume importance. Documentary specials replaced sports as CBS's second most frequently scheduled special type. A program form completely unused during the first period, comedy drama, became the third most popular type of special with CBS-TV programmers, sharing that position with musical variety. Nearly identical amounts of time were spent on news and news analysis and prestige drama.

Speeches fell from a position of prominence during the first six-year period to relative obscurity in the second. This was due both to a decline in the number of speeches televised, and an increase in the employment of other program types. President Eisenhower used 70.7 per cent of all hours CBS-TV allotted this category from September, 1954 to September, 1960. All but one of the prime time speeches for which CBS pre-empted regular programs were delivered by political figures; the exception was an address by a member of the military.

Drama specials began to assume importance as prime time specials on CBS-TV during the second period. This trend can be identified in Table 7 as having begun in earnest during the 1957-1958 season. Previously unused drama types employed by CBS-TV as prime time specials during and after the 1954-1955 season were action and adventure drama, comedy drama, crime, mystery, spy, detective drama, motion picture drama and prestige drama. During the entire period under study, CBS-TV was the only national network to schedule motion picture films as prime time specials; moreover, the only picture CBS scheduled in this manner was "The Wizard of Oz." The film was first televised in November, 1956, and became an annual event appearing at least partially in prime time with the 1959-1960 season. Thus, while feature length films have become a staple of regular television fare on all the networks, their use as a prime time special form during the period of this study was strictly limited.

A marked increase in the number of CBS-TV news specials in the second period reflected events of the times. About half all news specials scheduled in prime time during this period appeared in the 1959-1960 season. Nikita S. Khrushchev's visit to the United States in September, 1959, was reported by CBS-TV in a series of news specials titled "Khrushchev in the United States." "Eyewitness to History" followed President Dwight D. Eisenhower on a tour of middle eastern countries later that year. Early in 1960, Eisenhower traveled to Latin America followed by CBS-TV news cameras on "Eyewitness to History." Khrushchev visited France in March, 1960 to confer with French Premier DeGaulle, after which DeGaulle came to the United States to meet with President Eisenhower. "Eyewitness to History" recorded these events. The purpose of this activity was to arrange a summit meeting of the Big Four world powers, the United States, Russia, Britain, and France. In May, 1960, the principles gathered in Paris for the conference, but before any fruitful work could be accomplished the famous U-2 incident disrupted proceedings. CBS-TV's "Eyewitness to History" specials covered these historic occurrences.

The growth rate of pre-emptive programming in prime time on CBS-TV slowed considerably during the final six-year period, increasing by about one-third over the middle six years. Trends emerging in the previous period continued into the third period, carrying musical variety to the fore as the predominant prime time special form on

CBS-TV. The number of documentary programs continued to increase also until they nearly equaled political programs in hours scheduled. (Although political programs were fewer in number than documentaries, they accounted for more time. This occurred because political programs, particularly convention and election night coverage, frequently lasted entire evenings.) These three program types, musical variety, political programs, and documentaries, comprised nearly half--48.2 per cent--of the total prime time special hours on CBS-TV in the final six-year period.

Although CBS-TV made use of all sub-categories under the drama classification, adding several dramatic readings and a western drama, the total number of drama specials declined somewhat during the last six years. Prestige drama dominated this category, including such non-regular programs as "Family Classics," "Hallmark Hall of Fame," "Breck Golden Showcase," "Westinghouse Presents," and others.

Speeches continued to dwindle as a special program form on CBS-TV during the last six years. All twelve speeches in this period were delivered by political figures. Presidents Eisenhower, Kennedy, and Johnson were the speakers on ten of these occasions.

Domestic and foreign events continued to supply an abundance of material for news specials. CBS-TV reported on President John F. Kennedy's European trip in the summer of 1961, his South American trip that same winter, and his extensive European tour of summer, 1963. The United States entered the space age in 1962 when John Glenn piloted the spacecraft "Friendship 7" into orbit. This and subsequent experiments in orbital space flight were reported by CBS-TV during the final six-year period. Civil rights disputes occasioned several specials, notable among them the programs reporting on integration problems at the University of Mississippi in the fall of 1962. The Bay of Pigs disaster and the Cuban Crisis of October, 1962 were covered in CBS news specials, as was the first explosion of a nuclear device by Red China in October, 1964. Lately, the war in Vietnam has generated news specials.

The non-classifiable category in this final period was inflated by 14 hours devoted to coverage of events subsequent to the Kennedy assassination in November, 1963.

From the foregoing tables illustrating CBS-TV's evening pre-emptive programming since September, 1948, Table 10 was drawn giving an overall picture of this network's special broadcasting.

The overall categorical breakdown of CBS-TV's prime time non-regular programming since September, 1948, indicates the talks category predominated by far. Various types of talks programs accounted for 57.4 per cent of CBS-TV's total evening special hours. Within the general talks classification, the leading sub-categories were political programs and documentaries. These two sub-categories combined made up just over 31 per cent of CBS-TV's total special time, nearly one-third.

Variety programs ranked second in number of hours scheduled. The variety classification comprised 23.1 per cent of total special prime time on CBS-TV, with musical variety scheduled about twice as often as its nearest competitor, comedy variety. Nearly equal amounts of time were devoted to circus variety and vaudeville variety, although these two sub-categories combined only accounted for two per cent of total special prime time on CBS.

TABLE 10

COMPOSITION OF CBS-TV'S TOTAL PRIME TIME SPECIAL PROGRAMMING

Category	No. Sp.	No. Hrs.	Per Cent of Total Special Prime Time
Drama			
Action/Adventure	12	18:00	2.2%
Comedy	29	32:15	3.7
Crime, Mystery, Spy	9	11:00	1.4
Dramatic Readings	7	6:30	0.7
Fairy Tale, Puppet/Cartoons	7	6:25	0.7
Historical/Biographical	7	6:00	0.7
Motion Picture	8	7:30	0.8
Musical	17	20:00	2.3
Prestige	31	39:30	4.5
Western	1	1:00	0.1
Unclassified Drama	17	21:00	2.4
Talks			
Actualities	2	4:15	0.6
Awards and Pageants	38	32:15	3.7
Documentary	123	107:00	12.3
Instructional	2	2:00	0.2
News and News Analysis	101	63:52	7.3
Panel Discussions	59	44:30	5.2
Political	128	174:03	18.8
Religious	-	-	-
Speeches	72	34:55	3.9
Sports and Sports News	42	46:25	5.4
Variety			
Circus	10	8:00	0.9
Comedy	52	49:15	5.7
Musical	100	100:30	11.5
Vaudeville	9	8:30	1.1
Non-classifiable	34	33:15	3.9
Totals	917	877:55	100.0%

Drama specials were third-ranked in number of hours, comprising 19.5 per cent of total CBS special prime time. Prestige and comedy drama were most frequently scheduled.

Program categories employed little or not at all by CBS-TV as prime time specials included religious programs, western drama, actualities, and instructional talks.

NBC-TV

Table 11 indicates NBC-TV broadcast 1,053 specials during the years covered by this study, pre-empting 1,070 hours and 20 minutes of prime time. Thus, NBC-TV has done more prime time special programming than any other network. Nighttime hours pre-empted for specials on NBC-TV amounted to 4.65 per cent of prime time over the priod of the study. Corresponding figures for the other networks were 2.53 per cent for ABC-TV, and 3.8 per cent for CBS-TV.

NBC-TV's evening special programming exhibited an erratic growth pattern during the early years from the 1948-1949 season through the 1955-1956 season. A period of steady growth during winter seasons began in 1956-1957 which carried NBC-TV's non-regular programming to a peak in the 1960-1961 season. Following the 1960-1961 season the pattern once again became erratic.

Data for NBC-TV's summer season prime time special programming again pointed out the extent to which non-regular programming was influenced by political activity. In each Presidential election year, NBC-TV's summer specials schedule showed a great increase over other years. The trend has been toward more political specials each fourth year, as evidenced by the figures for 1960 and 1964. Except for

TABLE 12

COMPOSITION OF NBC-TV'S PRIME TIME SPECIAL PROGRAMMING (WI

Category	1948-1949			1948-1950			1950-
Drama	Hours*		%**	Hours		%	Hours
Action	-		-	-		-	-
Comedy	-		-	-		-	-
Crime	-		-	-		-	-
Readings	-		-	-		-	-
Fairy Tales	-		-	-		-	-
Historical	-		-	-		-	-
Motion Picture	-		-	-		-	-
Musical	1:00(	1)	7.3	-		-	-
Prestige	-		-	-		-	-
Western	-		-	-		-	-
Unclassified	-		-	-		-	-
Talks							
Actualities	-		-	-		-	-
Pageants	-		-	0:30(	1)	100.0	-
Documentary	-		-	-		-	-
Instructional	-		-	-		-	-
News	-		-	-		-	-
Panel	0:30(	1)	3.6	-		-	-
Political	3:00(	1)	21.6	-		-	-
Religious	-		-	-		-	-
Speeches	-		-	-		-	1:15(
Sports	-		-	-		-	-
Variety							
Circus	-		-	-		-	-
Comedy	-		-	-		-	-
Musical	1:00(	1)	7.3	-		-	1:00(
Vaudeville	3:30(	1)	25.3	-		-	3:30(
Non-classifiable	4:50(	5)	34.9	-		-	-
Totals	13:50	10	100.0%	0:30	1	100.0%	5:45

* In parentheses following the hours figure is the number of each category.

** Indicates percentage of total special prime time hours.

TERS)

951	1951-	1952		1952-1953			1953-1954			
%	Hours		%	Hours		%	Hours		%	Ho
-	-		-	-		-	-		-	
-	-		-	-		-	1:00(	1)	13.8	
-	-		-	-		-	-		-	
-	-		-	-		-	-		-	
-	-		-	-		-	-		-	
-	-		-	-		-	-		-	
-	-		-	-		-	-		-	
-	-		-	-		-	-		-	
-	-		-	-		-	-		-	
-	-		-	-		-	-		-	
-	-		-	-		-	-		-	2
-	-		-	-		-	-		-	
-	-		-	1:00(	2)	8.9	1:00(	2)	13.8	2
-	-		-	-		-	0:30(	1)	6.9	1
-	-		-	-		-	-		-	
-	-		-	-		-	-		-	
-	-		-	1:00(	2)	8.9	-		-	
-	-		-	8:45(	15)	77.8	-		-	3
-	-		-	-		-	-		-	
) 21.8	1:00(	2)	33.3	0:30(	1)	4.4	1:45(	4)	24.1	(
-	0:30(	1)	16.7	-		-	-		-	(
-	-		-	-		-	-		-	1
-	-		-	-		-	-		-	5
) 17.3	-		-	-		-	2:30(	2)	34.5	1
) 60.9	-		-	-		-	-		-	1
-	1:30(	2)	50.0	-		-	0:30(	1)	6.9	1
100.0%	3:00	5	100.0%	11:15	20	100.0%	7:15	11	100.0%	2(

programs in

1954-1955			1955-1956			1956-1957			1957-1958		
urs		%	Hours		%	Hours		%	Hours		
		-	-		-	-		-	-		
		-	-		-	1:30(	1)	4.7	-		
		-	-		-	1:30(	1)	4.7	1:30(	1)	
		-	-		-	-		-	-		
		-	-		-	-		-	6:00(	6)	1:
		-	-		-	1:30(	1)	4.7	-		
		-	-		-	-		-	-		
		-	1:00(	1)	7.5	-		-	4:00(	3)	8
		-	-		-	6:00(	4)	18.6	3:00(	3)	6
		-	0:30(	1)	3.8	-		-	-		
00(	1)	10.0	-		-	1:30(	1)	4.7	-		
		-	-		-	-		-	-		
30(	3)	12.5	2:00(	2)	15.0	2:00(	2)	6.2	1:30(	2)	3
30(	3)	7.5	6:00(	8)	45.3	6:30(	6)	20.1	2:00(	2)	4
		-	-		-	-		-	2:00(	2)	4
		-	-		-	-		-	-		
		-	-		-	-		-	-		
00(	4)	15.0	0:30(	1)	3.8	5:00(	7)	15.5	-		
		-	-		-	-		-	-		
30(	1)	2.5	0:30(	1)	3.8	0:15(	1)	0.7	2:00(	4)	4
30(	1)	2.5	1:15(	2)	9.5	1:00(	1)	3.1	1:00(	1)	2
00(	1)	5.0	-		-	-		-	-		
30(	6)	27.5	1:00(	1)	7.5	-		-	12:30(	13)	25
30(	2)	7.5	0:30(	1)	3.8	5:30(	6)	17.0	10:30(	10)	21
30(	1)	5.0	-		-	-		-	2:00(	1)	4
00(	1)	5.0	-		-	-		-	0:30(	1)	1
00	24	100.0%	13:15	18	100.0%	32:15	31	100.0%	48:30	49	100

1958-1959 Hours		%	1959-1960 Hours		%	1960-1961 Hours		%	1961-1962 Hours	
-		-	-		-	2:30(	2)	2.2	-	
-		-	1:00(	1)	1.2	2:30(	2)	2.2	2:00(	2)
0:30(	1)	0.9	5:00(	5)	6.3	5:00(	5)	4.5	5:30(	5)
-		-	-		-	-		-	-	
5:00(	5)	8.8	-		-	2:00(	1)	1.9	-	
-		-	1:00(	1)	1.2	7:00(	9)	6.3	1:30(	1)
-		-	-		-	-		-	-	
4:30(	3)	7.8	3:00(	3)	3.8	1:30(	1)	1.4	-	
6:00(	4)	10.6	7:30(	5)	9.4	2:00(	3)	1.9	3:00(	2)
-		-	-		-	1:30(	1)	1.4	-	
-		-	3:30(	4)	4.3	-		-	-	
-		-	-		-	1:30(	1)	1.4	-	
1:30(	2)	2.6	4:00(	5)	4.9	3:00(	3)	2.7	1:00(	1)
2:00(	3)	3.5	5:00(	5)	6.3	25:30(	26)	23.3	35:00(	37)
2:00(	2)	3.5	-		-	1:00(	1)	0.9	1:00(	1)
2:00(	2)	3.5	20:00(	30)	24.8	13:45(	24)	12.5	8:30(	10)
-		-	0:30(	1)	0.6	1:30(	2)	1.4	2:00(	3)
2:00(	1)	3.5	-		-	10:30(	11)	9.5	-	
-		-	-		-	1:30(	1)	1.4	-	
-		-	0:30(	1)	0.6	0:30(	1)	0.5	-	
3:30(	4)	6.2	3:30(	4)	4.3	-		-	-	
-		-	-		-	3:00(	3)	2.7	-	
11:00(	11)	19.3	11:00(	11)	13.7	9:00(	9)	8.2	5:00(	5)
13:00(	13)	22.8	14:00(	14)	17.4	13:00(	13)	11.8	15:00(	15)
4:00(	4)	7.0	1:00(	1)	1.2	2:00(	2)	1.9	-	
-		-	-		-	-		-	-	
57:00	55	100.0%	80:30	91	100.0%	109:45	121	100.0%	79:30	82

%	1962-1963 Hours		%	1963-1964 Hours		%	1964-1965 Hours		%	1965-1966 Hours		%
-	-		-	-		-	-		-	-		-
.6	3:00	(2)	3.9	1:30	(1)	1.8	-		-	1:00	(1)	1.5
.9	-		-	-		-	-		-	-		-
-	-		-	-		-	-		-	-		-
-	1:00	(1)	1.4	1:00	(1)	1.3	1:00	(1)	1.0	1:00	(1)	1.5
.8	1:30	(1)	1.9	3:00	(2)	3.7	3:00	(2)	3.1	4:30	(3)	6.4
-	-		-	-		-	-		-	-		-
-	1:30	(1)	1.9	1:00	(1)	1.3	1:00	(1)	1.0	2:00	(1)	2.9
.8	1:30	(1)	1.9	-		-	-		-	1:30	(1)	2.1
-	-		-	-		-	-		-	-		-
-	-		-	-		-	-		-	-		-
-	-		-	1:30	(1)	1.8	-		-	3:30	(1)	5.0
.3	2:00	(2)	2.7	2:00	(2)	2.5	2:00	(2)	2.1	3:30	(4)	5.0
ı.0	30:30	(32)	40.5	27:30	(26)	33.7	25:30	(26)	26.9	9:00	(9)	12.9
.3	-		-	1:00	(1)	1.3	1:00	(1)	1.0	-		-
).6	7:30	(8)	10.0	4:00	(4)	4.9	9:45	(13)	10.3	6:30	(6)	9.3
.6	1:30	(2)	1.9	1:30	(2)	1.8	1:30	(2)	1.5	-		-
-	6:30	(6)	8.7	2:00	(3)	2.5	13:30	(16)	14.3	0:30	(1)	0.7
-	-		-	-		-	-		-	-		-
-	-		-	-		-	3:00	(4)	3.1	1:00	(1)	1.5
-	4:00	(4)	5.3	1:00	(1)	1.3	8:45	(8)	9.3	4:45	(2)	6.8
-	-		-	-		-	-		-	2:00	(2)	2.9
.3	7:00	(7)	9.3	3:30	(3)	4.2	13:30	(13)	14.3	5:30	(5)	7.8
.8	8:00	(8)	10.6	17:00	(17)	20.8	11:00	(11)	11.6	18:30	(19)	26.5
-	-		-	-		-	-		-	2:00	(2)	2.9
-	-		-	14:00	(4)	17.1	0:30	(1)	0.5	3:00	(3)	4.3
).0%	75:30	75	100.0%	81:30	69	100.0%	95:00	101	100.0%	69:45	62	100.0%

TABLE 11

NBC-TV PRIME TIME SPECIAL PROGRAMMING BY SEASONS

Winter Seasons				Summer Seasons			
Season	No. Sp.[a]	No. Hrs.[b]	% Prime Time	Season	No. Sp.	No. Hrs.	% Prime Time
48-49	10	13:50	1.3	1949	-	-	-
49-50	1	0:30	-1[c]	1950	2	1:00	-1
50-51	5	5:45	-1	1951	2	1:30	-1
51-52	5	3:00	-1	1952	18	28:00	8.6
52-53	20	11:15	1.1	1953	4	4:00	1.1
53-54	11	7:15	-1	1954	6	5:30	1.5
54-55	24	20:00	1.7	1955	6	3:45	-1
55-56	18	13:15	1.1	1956	12	28:00	8.6
56-57	31	32:15	2.9	1957	2	2:00	-1
57-58	49	48:30	4.7	1958	8	6:00	1.7
58-59	55	57:00	5.5	1959	12	11:30	3.4
59-60	91	80:30	7.8	1960	31	45:30	13.8
60-61	121	109:45	10.6	1961	18	13:30	3.9
61-62	82	79:30	7.8	1962	22	18:15	5.4
62-63	75	75:30	7.3	1963	19	15:00	4.5
63-64	69	81:30	8.0	1964	30	47:30	14.6
64-65	101	95:00	9.6	1965	15	13:45	4.0
65-66	62	69:45	6.6	1966	16	21:30	6.5
Total	830	804:05			223	266:15	

[a]Indicates number of prime time special programs.

[b]Indicates number of hours devoted to prime time special programs.

[c]The symbol "-1" indicates the number of hours constituted less than one per cent of total prime time during that season.

political programs, NBC apparently scheduled very few prime time specials during summer seasons throughout the first half of the period under study. In 1959, NBC-TV's summer specials schedule showed a distinct increase over previous non-election year summers. Although the trend has been somewhat erratic, the tendency was toward more summer time pre-emptive programming on NBC-TV during evening hours.

The categorical composition of NBC-TV's prime time special programming is noted in Tables 12 and 13. These tables show NBC-TV's

63	Summer 1964			Summer 1965			Summer 1966		
%	Hours		%	Hours		%	Hours		%
-	-		-	-		-	-		-
-	-		-	-		-	-		-
-	-		-	-		-	-		-
-	-		-	-		-	1:00(	1)	4.7
-	-		-	-		-	-		-
-	-		-	-		-	-		-
-	-		-	-		-	-		-
-	-		-	-		-	-		-
-	-		-	-		-	-		-
-	-		-	-		-	-		-
-	-		-	-		-	-		-
-	-		-	-		-	-		-
6.7	1:00(	1)	2.1	2:00(	2)	14.6	1:00(	1)	4.7
26.6	6:00(	6)	12.6	4:30(	2)	32.8	5:30(	3)	25.5
-	-		-	-		-	-		-
53.3	4:00(	5)	8.4	3:45(	7)	27.2	1:30(	2)	6.9
-	-		-	-		-	-		-
-	36:30(	18)	76.9	-		-	-		-
-	-		-	-		-	-		-
-	-		-	-		-	-		-
-	-		-	-		-	6:30(	3)	30.2
-	-		-	-		-	-		-
6.7	-		-	3:30(	4)	25.4	-		-
6.7	-		-	-		-	2:00(	2)	9.4
-	-		-	-		-	4:00(	4)	18.6
-	-		-	-		-	-		-
100.0%	47:30	30	100.0%	13:45	15	100.0%	21:30	16	100.0%

	Summer 1960			Summer 1961			Summer 1962			Summer 1
%	Hours		%	Hours		%	Hours		%	Hours
-	-		-	-		-	-		-	-
8.7	-		-	1:00(	1)	7.4	-		-	-
-	-		-	1:00(	1)	7.4	-		-	-
-	-		-	-		-	-		-	-
-	-		-	-		-	-		-	-
-	-		-	-		-	-		-	-
-	-		-	-		-	-		-	-
-	-		-	-		-	-		-	-
-	-		-	-		-	-		-	-
-	-		-	-		-	-		-	-
-	-		-	-		-	-		-	-
-	-		-	-		-	-		-	-
-	1:30(	1)	3.3	-		-	1:00(	1)	5.5	1:00(
17.4	1:30(	2)	3.3	4:30(	5)	33.3	11:00(	12)	60.2	4:00(
-	-		-	-		-	-		-	-
47.8	6:00(	8)	47.3	4:30(	8)	33.3	1:30(	2)	8.3	8:00(1
-	-		-	1:00(	1)	7.4	1:30(	2)	8.3	-
-	33:00(	16)	38.4	-		-	0:30(	1)	2.7	-
-	-		-	-		-	-		-	-
4.3	0:30(	1)	1.1	0:30(	1)	3.7	-		-	-
21.8	1:00(	1)	2.2	-		-	2:00(	2)	10.9	-
-	-		-	-		-	-		-	-
-	1:00(	1)	2.2	1:00(	1)	7.4	-		-	1:00(
-	1:00(	1)	2.2	-		-	-		-	1:00(
-	-		-	-		-	-		-	-
-	-		-	-		-	0:45(	2)	4.1	-
00.0%	45:30	31	100.0%	13:30	18	100.0%	18:15	22	100.0%	15:00

mer 1956		Summer 1957		Summer 1958		Summer 19
s	%	Hours	%	Hours	%	Hours
	-	-	-	-	-	-
	-	-	-	-	-	1:00(1)
	-	-	-	1:00(1)	16.7	-
	-	-	-	-	-	-
	-	-	-	3:00(3)	50.0	-
00(1)	3.6	-	-	-	-	-
	-	-	-	-	-	-
	-	-	-	-	-	-
	-	-	-	-	-	-
	-	-	-	-	-	-
	-	-	-	-	-	-
	-	-	-	-	-	-
	-	-	-	-	-	-
	-	1:00(1)	50.0	1:00(2)	16.7	2:00(2)
	-	-	-	-	-	-
	-	-	-	-	-	5:30(7)
	-	-	-	0:30(1)	8.3	-
00(10)	92.8	-	-	-	-	-
	-	-	-	-	-	-
	-	-	-	0:30(1)	8.3	0:30(1)
	-	1:00(1)	50.0	-	-	2:30(1)
	-	-	-	-	-	-
	-	-	-	-	-	-
00(1)	3.6	-	-	-	-	-
	-	-	-	-	-	-
	-	-	-	-	-	-
00 12	100.0%	2:00 2	100.0%	6:00 8	100.0%	11:30 12

	1952	Summer 1953			Summer 1954			Summer 1955			S
	%	Hours		%	Hours		%	Hours		%	Ho
	-	-		-	-		-	-		-	
	-	-		-	-		-	-		-	
	-	-		-	-		-	-		-	
	-	-		-	-		-	-		-	
	-	-		-	-		-	-		-	
	-	-		-	-		-	-		-	1
	-	-		-	-		-	-		-	
	-	-		-	-		-	-		-	
	-	-		-	-		-	-		-	
	-	-		-	-		-	-		-	
	-	-		-	-		-	-		-	
	-	-		-	-		-	-		-	
	-	-		-	0:30(	1)	9.0	-		-	
	-	0:30(	1)	12.5	1:30(	2)	27.3	-		-	
	-	-		-	-		-	-		-	
	-	1:30(	2)	37.5	-		-	1:00(	1)	26.6	
	-	-		-	-		-	0:30(	1)	13.4	
.8)	100.0	-		-	-		-	-		-	26
	-	-		-	-		-	-		-	
	-	-		-	1:00(	2)	18.2	0:15(	1)	6.6	
	-	-		-	2:30(	1)	45.5	1:30(	2)	40.0	
	-	-		-	-		-	-		-	
	-	-		-	-		-	0:30(	1)	13.4	
	-	-		-	-		-	-		-	I
	-	2:00(	1)	50.0	-		-	-		-	
	-	-		-	-		-	-		-	
	100.0%	4:00	4	100.0%	5:30	6	100.0%	3:45	6	100.0%	2

concentration on talks specials, the development of variety specials in 1954-1955 and succeeding seasons, and the introduction of several drama types in 1956-1957 followed by increased use of drama specials in later seasons. NBC-TV's summer season prime time special programming consisted mostly of talks programs with very few drama or variety shows.

When the data on NBC-TV's prime time special programming were summarized into six-year periods in Table 14, political programs were shown to comprise nearly half the total special hours scheduled in the first period. As on the other networks, political programs played a central role in NBC-TV's prime time special programming.

The nine hours of vaudeville variety televised on a special basis by NBC in this initial period from 1948-1949 through the summer of 1954 consisted of two Milton Berle "telethons" for the Damon Runyon Cancer Fund, one on April 9, 1949 and another on June 9, 1951, and a two-hour Ford "Golden Anniversary" program on June 15, 1953.

Although NBC-TV apparently did not televise as many speeches as ABC or CBS, this category was still a prominent part of NBC's prime time special programming in the early period. Of the 15 speeches which appeared on NBC during the first six years, 13 were addresses by Presidents Truman and Eisenhower, the others were talks by Adlai Stevenson and Vice President Richard Nixon.

The number of prime time specials and hours devoted to them on NBC-TV during the second period more than quadrupled over the first six years, a greater relative increase than on any other network. A strong trend toward more variety specials developed on NBC during this period

TABLE 13

COMPOSITION OF NBC-TV'S PRIME TIME SPECIAL PROGRAMMING (SUMMERS)

Category	Summer 1949			Summer 1950			Summer 1951			Summ
Drama	Hours*		%**	Hours		%	Hours		%	Hours
Action	-		-	-		-	-		-	-
Comedy	-		-	-		-	-		-	-
Crime	-		-	-		-	-		-	-
Readings	-		-	-		-	-		-	-
Fairy Tales	-		-	-		-	-		-	-
Historical	-		-	-		-	-		-	-
Motion Picture	-		-	-		-	-		-	-
Musical	-		-	-		-	-		-	-
Prestige	-		-	-		-	-		-	-
Western	-		-	-		-	-		-	-
Unclassified	-		-	-		-	-		-	-
Talks										
Actualities	-		-	-		-	-		-	-
Pageants	-		-	-		-	-		-	-
Documentary	-		-	-		-	-		-	-
Instructional	-		-	-		-	-		-	-
News	-		-	-		-	-		-	-
Panel	-		-	-		-	-		-	-
Political	-		-	-		-	-		-	28:00(
Religious	-		-	-		-	-		-	-
Speeches	-		-	1:00(	2)	100.0	0:30(	1)	33.3	-
Sports	-		-	-		-	-		-	-
Variety										
Circus	-		-	-		-	-		-	-
Comedy	-		-	-		-	-		-	-
Musical	-		-	-		-	1:00(	1)	66.6	-
Vaudeville	-		-	-		-	-		-	-
Non-classifiable	-		-	-		-	-		-	-
Totals	-	-	-	1:00	2	100.0%	1:30	2	99.9%	28:00

* In parentheses following the hours figure is the number of programs in each category.

** Indicates percentage of total special prime time hours.

TABLE 14

COMPOSITION OF NBC-TV'S PRIME TIME SPECIAL PROGRAMMING
BY SIX-YEAR PERIODS

Category	1948-1949 Through Summer, 1954			1954-1955 Through Summer, 1960			1960-1961 Through Summer, 1966		
Drama	Hours*		%**	Hours		%	Hours		%
Action	-		-	-		-	2:30(	2)	0.4
Comedy	1:00(	1)	1.1	3:30(	3)	1.0	11:00(	9)	1.7
Crime	-		-	9:30(	9)	2.7	11:30(	11)	1.8
Readings	-		-	-		-	1:00(	1)	0.1
Fairy Tales	-		-	14:00(	14)	4.0	6:00(	5)	0.9
Historical	-		-	3:30(	3)	1.0	20:30(	18)	3.3
Motion Picture	-		-	-		-	-		-
Musical	1:00(	1)	1.1	12:30(	10)	3.6	7:00(	5)	1.1
Prestige	-		-	22:30(	16)	6.5	8:00(	7)	1.2
Western	-		-	0:30(	1)	0.1	1:30(	1)	0.2
Unclassified	-		-	7:00(	6)	2.0	-		-
Talks									
Actualities	-		-	-		-	6:30(	3)	1.0
Pageants	3:00(	6)	3.7	15:00(	17)	4.3	19:30(	20)	3.0
Documentary	2:30(	4)	3.1	28:30(	34)	8.3	188:30(	186)	29.5
Instructional	-		-	4:00(	4)	1.1	4:00(	4)	0.6
News	1:30(	2)	1.8	34:30(	48)	9.9	73:15(	103)	11.5
Panel	1:30(	3)	1.8	1:30(	3)	0.4	10:30(	14)	1.6
Political	39:45(	34)	48.9	69:30(	39)	19.9	70:00(	56)	10.9
Religious	-		-	-		-	1:30(	1)	0.2
Speeches	7:00(	15)	8.6	5:30(	12)	1.5	5:00(	7)	0.8
Sports	3:00(	2)	3.7	16:45(	18)	4.9	27:00(	20)	4.3
Variety									
Circus	-		-	1:00(	1)	0.3	5:00(	5)	0.8
Comedy	-		-	42:30(	44)	12.3	49:00(	48)	7.7
Musical	5:30(	5)	6.7	47:00(	48)	13.6	85:30(	86)	13.4
Vaudeville	9:00(	3)	11.0	8:00(	7)	2.2	8:00(	8)	1.2
Non-classifiable	6:50(	8)	8.5	1:30(	2)	0.4	18:15(	10)	2.8
Totals	81:35	84	100.0%	348:15	339	100.0%	640:30	630	100.0%

* In parentheses following the hours figure is the number of programs in each category.

** Indicates percentage of total special prime time hours.

with large increases in the number of comedy and musical variety programs. Notable increases were made in the number of documentary and news specials, while the amount of time devoted to political programs increased appreciably. NBC-TV also began to develop drama as a special form, although not to the extent CBS-TV did.

The large increase in the number of news specials on NBC-TV during this period corresponded to similar increases on the other networks in response to world events. NBC-TV's "Journey to Understanding" specials reported President Eisenhower's European trip in the fall of 1959, Khrushchev's U. S. visit that same year, Eisenhower's middle eastern tour early in 1960, DeGaulle's April, 1960 trip to the U. S., and the abbreviated Paris Summit Conference of May, 1960. Also during this period, "Journey to Understanding" covered Eisenhower's tour of the Pacific and a planned visit to Japan which had to be cancelled because of violent protests by Japanese students.

Musical variety and comedy variety ranked second and third behind political programs in amount of special prime time devoted to each by NBC-TV in the second six-year period. Comedy variety made its strongest showing on NBC-TV as a prime time special program form in the 1957-1958 season, when it led all other sub-categories.

During the middle six years, the number of documentary programs appearing as prime time specials on NBC-TV underwent large seasonal variations. Documentaries predominated in the 1955-1956 season and the 1956-1957 season. In 1958-1959, however, documentaries ranked near the bottom in number of hours scheduled per category, and remained relatively insignificant for the remainder of the second period.

Growth of NBC-TV's nighttime special programming slowed in the final six years, not quite doubling over the previous period which had quadrupled over the initial period. The documentary came into its own as a special program form during this period when it appeared far more frequently than any other non-regular program type on NBC-TV. Nearly 30 per cent of all special prime time hours on NBC in this final period was devoted to documentary specials.

The amount of time spent on prime time news specials more than doubled over the middle period. NBC-TV displayed a greater sensitivity to current events than the other networks, pre-empting twice as many prime time hours as CBS-TV and four times as many as ABC-TV for news specials during the final six years.

Musical variety, which had always been an important element in NBC-TV's prime time special programming, gained strength in the final period, while time devoted to comedy variety increased only slightly.

The unclassified category was inflated in this period since it contained NBC-TV's coverage of the Kennedy assassination, which, as noted earlier, defied simple categorization.

Table 15 presents a total composite picture of NBC-TV's prime time special programming combining the foregoing data.

Talks programs comprised by far the largest share of NBC-TV's prime time special programming during the period under study; 59.7 per cent of all hours NBC pre-empted for evening special programs were devoted to various kinds of talks shows. Within the talks classification, three sub-categories stood out: documentary, news and news analysis, and political programs. Nearly half of all NBC-TV's prime

TABLE 15

COMPOSITION OF NBC-TV'S TOTAL PRIME TIME SPECIAL PROGRAMMING

Category	No. Sp.	No. Hrs.	Per Cent of Total Special Prime Time
Drama			
Action/Adventure	2	2:30	0.2%
Comedy	13	15:30	1.4
Crime, Mystery, Spy	20	21:00	2.0
Dramatic Readings	1	1:00	0.1
Fairy Tale, Puppet/Cartoons	19	20:00	1.9
Historical/Biographical	21	24:00	2.2
Motion Picture	-	-	-
Musical	16	20:30	1.9
Prestige	23	30:30	2.9
Western	2	2:00	0.2
Unclassified Drama	6	7:00	0.7
Talks			
Actualities	3	6:30	0.6
Awards and Pageants	43	37:30	3.5
Documentary	224	219:30	20.5
Instructional	8	8:00	0.8
News and News analysis	153	109:15	10.2
Panel Discussions	20	13:30	1.3
Political	129	179:15	16.7
Religious	1	1:30	0.1
Speeches	34	17:30	1.6
Sports and Sports News	40	46:45	4.4
Variety			
Circus	6	6:00	0.6
Comedy	92	91:30	8.5
Musical	139	138:00	12.9
Vaudeville	18	25:00	2.3
Non-Classifiable	20	26:35	2.5
Totals	1053	1070:20	100.0%

time pre-emptions between September, 1948 and September, 1966, were for programs in these categories--47.4 per cent.

Variety was the next largest classification in numbers of programs and hours scheduled by NBC-TV. This category accounted for 24.3 per cent of NBC-TV's prime time special offerings. Most NBC variety specials were of the musical type, with comedy variety running second.

Drama programs comprised 13.5 per cent of NBC-TV's total prime time special programming and constituted the least used special program form on this network.

Four program categories stood out dominantly in NBC-TV's evening non-regular programming: documentary (20.5 per cent), political programs (16.7 per cent), musical variety (12.9 per cent), and news and news analysis (11.7 per cent). Together, these four sub-categories accounted for 61.8 per cent of all the prime time hours NBC-TV pre-empted for special programming between September, 1948 and September, 1966.

DuMont

The DuMont Television Network[2] operated as a national network until September 15, 1955.[3] During the seven winter and seven summer seasons DuMont operated, the network scheduled a total of 72 prime specials, pre-empting 74 hours and 20 minutes of regular programs.

---

[2]For a history of the DuMont Television Network see Gary Newton Hess, "An Historical Study of the DuMont Television Network," unpublished Ph.D. dissertation, Northwestern University, 1960.

[3]"FCC Filing Signifies End of DuMont TV Network," Broadcasting-Telecasting, September 5, 1955, p. 7. See also Broadcasting-Telecasting, February 13, 1956, p. 106.

TABLE 16

DuMONT PRIME TIME SPECIAL PROGRAMMING BY SEASONS

Winter Seasons				Summer Seasons			
Season	No. Sp.[a]	No. Hrs.[b]	% Prime Time	Season	No. Sp.	No. Hrs.	% Prime Time
48-49	1	1:30	-1[c]	1949	-	-	-
49-50	1	1:30	-1	1950	2	1:00	-1
50-51	5	2:35	-1	1951	3	1:45	-1
51-52	3	2:00	-1	1952	13	24:00	7.3
52-53	18	14:30	1.3	1953	4	2:30	-1
53-54	7	4:00	-1	1954	1	0:30	-1
54-55	12	18:00	1.7	1955	2	0:30	-1
	47	44:05			25	30:15	

[a]Indicates the number of prime time special programs.

[b]Indicates the number of hours devoted to prime time special programs.

[c]The symbol "-1" indicates the number of hours constituted less than one per cent of total prime time during that season.

The majority of DuMont's specials were political programs and sports shows.

In only three seasons did the amount of hours DuMont devoted to special prime time programming amount to more than one per cent of total prime time. Political campaign coverage during the summer of 1952 resulted in the most hours of special programming on DuMont. Again the following winter season, 1952-1953, political programs boosted DuMont's special programming. In DuMont's last full season, 1954-1955, sports programs were the major factor in its special programming.

DuMont's prime time special programming consisted almost entirely of talks programs. Of all DuMont's nighttime pre-emptive program time, 91.1 per cent consisted of various talks specials, the most prominent

TABLE 17

COMPOSITION OF DuMONT'S PRIME TIME SPECIAL PROGRAMMING (WINTERS)

Category	1948-1949			1949-1950			1950-1951			
Drama	Hours*		%**	Hours		%	Hours		%	Ho
Action	-		-	-		-	-		-	-
Comedy	-		-	-		-	-		-	-
Crime	-		-	-		-	-		-	-
Readings	-		-	-		-	-		-	-
Fairy Tales	-		-	-		-	-		-	-
Historical	-		-	-		-	-		-	-
Motion Picture	-		-	-		-	-		-	-
Musical	-		-	-		-	-		-	-
Prestige	-		-	-		-	-		-	-
Western	-		-	-		-	-		-	-
Unclassified	-		-	-		-	-		-	-
Talks										
Actualities	-		-	-		-	-		-	-
Pageants	-		-	-		-	-		-	-
Documentary	-		-	1:30(	1)	100.0	-		-	-
Instructional	-		-	-		-	-		-	-
News	-		-	-		-	1:20(	2)	51.6	-
Panel	-		-	-		-	-		-	-
Political	-		-	-		-	-		-	-
Religious	-		-	-		-	-		-	-
Speeches	-		-	-		-	1:15(	3)	48.4	1
Sports	-		-	-		-	-		-	-
Variety										
Circus	-		-	-		-	-		-	-
Comedy	-		-	-		-	-		-	-
Musical	-		-	-		-	-		-	-
Vaudeville	-		-	-		-	-		-	-
Non-classifiable	1:30(	1)	100.0	-		-	-		-	1
Totals	1:30	1	100.0%	1:30	1	100.0%	2:35	5	100.0%	2

* In parentheses following the hours figure is the number of programs in each category.

** Indicates percentage of total special prime time hours.

...mmer	1952	Summer 1953		Summer 1954		Summer 1955	
...rs	%	Hours	%	Hours	%	Hours	%
-	-	-	-	-	-	-	-
-	-	-	-	-	-	-	-
-	-	-	-	-	-	-	-
-	-	-	-	-	-	-	-
-	-	-	-	-	-	-	-
-	-	-	-	-	-	-	-
-	-	-	-	-	-	-	-
-	-	-	-	-	-	-	-
-	-	-	-	-	-	-	-
-	-	-	-	-	-	-	-
-	-	-	-	-	-	-	-
-	-	-	-	-	-	-	-
30(1)	2.1	-	-	-	-	-	-
-	-	-	-	-	-	-	-
-	-	-	-	-	-	-	-
-	-	1:00(1)	40.0	-	-	0:15(1)	50.0
-	-	-	-	-	-	-	-
30(12)	97.9	-	-	-	-	-	-
-	-	-	-	-	-	-	-
-	-	0:30(1)	20.0	0:30(1)	100.0	0:15(1)	50.0
-	-	0:30(1)	20.0	-	-	-	-
-	-	-	-	-	-	-	-
-	-	-	-	-	-	-	-
-	-	-	-	-	-	-	-
-	-	0:30(1)	20.0	-	-	-	-
-	-	-	-	-	-	-	-
00 13	100.0%	2:30 4	100.0%	0:30 1	100.0%	0:30 2	100.0%

TABLE 18

COMPOSITION OF DuMONT'S PRIME TIME SPECIAL PROGRAMMING (SUMMERS)

Category	Summer 1949		Summer 1950		Summer 1951		S
Drama	Hours*	%**	Hours	%	Hours	%	Ho
Action	-	-	-	-	-	-	
Comedy	-	-	-	-	-	-	
Crime	-	-	-	-	-	-	
Readings	-	-	-	-	-	-	
Fairy Tales	-	-	-	-	-	-	
Historical	-	-	-	-	-	-	
Motion Picture	-	-	-	-	-	-	
Musical	-	-	-	-	-	-	
Prestige	-	-	-	-	-	-	
Western	-	-	-	-	-	-	
Unclassified	-	-	-	-	-	-	
Talks							
Actualities	-	-	-	-	-	-	
Pageants	-	-	-	-	-	-	0
Documentary	-	-	-	-	-	-	
Instructional	-	-	-	-	-	-	
News	-	-	-	-	-	-	
Panel	-	-	-	-	-	-	
Political	-	-	-	-	-	-	23
Religious	-	-	-	-	-	-	
Speeches	-	-	1:00(2)	100.0	1:00(2)	57.2	
Sports	-	-	-	-	0:45(1)	42.8	
Variety							
Circus	-	-	-	-	-	-	
Comedy	-	-	-	-	-	-	
Musical	-	-	-	-	-	-	
Vaudeville	-	-	-	-	-	-	
Non-classifiable	-	-	-	-	-	-	
Totals	-	-	1:00 2	100.0%	1:45 3	100.0%	24

* In parentheses following the hours figure is the number of programs in each category.

** Indicates percentage of total special prime time hours.

1951-1952			1952-1953			1953-1954			1954-1955		
rs		%	Hours		%	Hours		%	Hours		%
		-	-		-	-		-	-		-
		-	-		-	-		-	-		-
		-	-		-	-		-	-		-
		-	-		-	-		-	-		-
		-	-		-	-		-	-		-
		-	-		-	-		-	-		-
		-	-		-	-		-	-		-
		-	-		-	-		-	-		-
		-	-		-	-		-	-		-
		-	-		-	-		-	-		-
		-	-		-	-		-	2:00(	1)	11.1
		-	-		-	-		-	-		-
		-	1:30(	1)	10.4	-		-	-		-
		-	-		-	0:30(	1)	12.5	-		-
		-	-		-	-		-	-		-
		-	1:00(	1)	6.9	-		-	0:30(	1)	2.8
		-	0:30(	1)	3.5	-		-	-		-
		-	7:30(	11)	51.7	-		-	1:00(	2)	5.6
		-	-		-	-		-	-		-
00(	2)	50.0	1:00(	2)	6.9	2:00(	5)	50.0	0:30(	1)	2.8
		-	3:00(	3)	20.6	-		-	14:00(	7)	77.7
		-	-		-	-		-	-		-
		-	-		-	-		-	-		-
		-	-		-	1:30(	1)	37.5	-		-
		-	-		-	-		-	-		-
00(	1)	50.0	-		-	-		-	-		-
00	3	100.0%	14:30	18	100.0%	4:00	7	100.0%	18:00	12	100.0%

of which were political, sports and sports news, and speeches. Thus, specials were not an important part of the DuMont Television Network's evening programming. No trends in DuMont's special programming were discernible, and no real patterns emerge since the network was active only during the first seven years of the period under study.

Table 19 summarizes DuMont's total special programming from September, 1948 to September, 1955.

Comparative Analysis

With the prime time special programming of the national networks categorized and quantified in some detail, these data were used to compare growth trends and patterns in this programming. Of first interest was a comparison of the simple growth patterns in special programming on each network. Using the percentage of prime time pre-empted for special programming as an index, Figure 1 graphically portrays the prime time special programming of ABC-TV, CBS-TV, and NBC-TV. The DuMont network was not represented since its special programming was for the most part near the zero level. Further, summer season special programming was not included in Figure 1 but was illustrated separately in order to point out more clearly its unique characteristics.

Figure 1 illustrates an interesting similarity in the growth patterns of prime time special programming on the national networks. During the early years, between the 1948-1949 and the 1955-1956 seasons, the amount of time pre-empted for occasional programs apparently fluctuated randomly. Prime time special programming on all the networks declined in 1949-1950 from the previous season. Some of the non-regular programming during the initial season of television networking was

TABLE 19

COMPOSITION OF DuMONT'S TOTAL PRIME TIME SPECIAL PROGRAMMING

Category	No. Sp.	No. Hrs.	Per Cent of Total Special Prime Time
Drama			
Action/Adventure	-	-	-
Comedy	-	-	-
Crime, Mystery, Spy	-	-	-
Dramatic Readings	-	-	-
Fairy Tale, Puppet/Cartoons	-	-	-
Historical/Biographical	-	-	-
Motion Picture	-	-	-
Musical	-	-	-
Prestige	-	-	-
Western	-	-	-
Unclassified Drama	1	2:00	2.7
Talks			
Actualities	-	-	-
Awards and Pageants	2	2:00	2.7
Documentary	2	2:00	2.7
Instructional	-	-	-
News and News Analysis	6	4:05	515
Panel Discussions	1	0:30	0.7
Political	25	32:00	43.0
Religious	-	-	-
Speeches	20	9:00	12.1
Sports and Sports News	11	18:15	24.5
Variety			
Circus	-	-	-
Comedy	-	-	-
Musical	1	1:30	2.0
Vaudeville	1	0:30	0.7
Non-classifiable	2	2:30	3.4
Totals	72	74:20	100.0%

FIGURE 1

GROWTH PATTERN OF WINTER SEASON NETWORK TELEVISION PRIME TIME SPECIAL PROGRAMMING

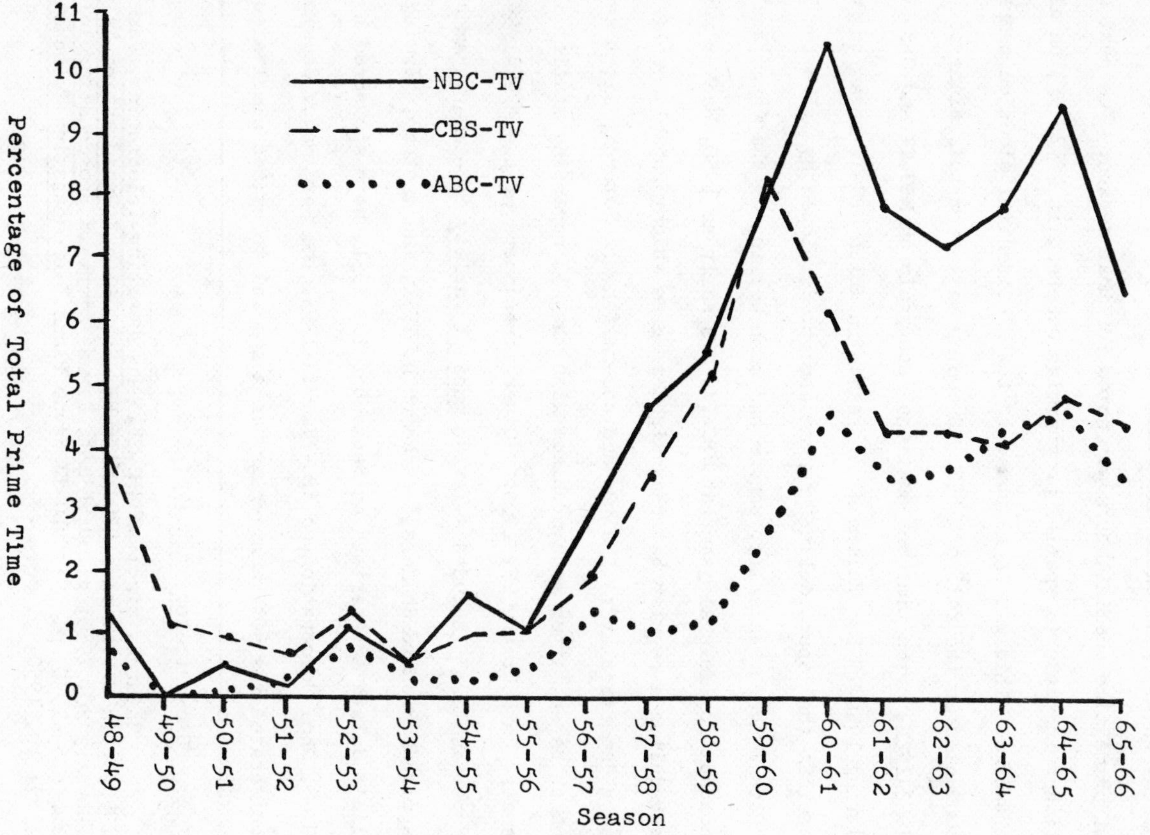

probably due to the rather chaotic situation existing regarding programming that year. Stewart suggests network program schedules did not become regularized until the winter of 1959,[4] and a drop in the number of prime time special hours was noted for that season. The next significant increase in special programming occurred in 1952-1953 on all networks. This was in response to the Presidential election campaign conducted in the fall of 1952. Dropping back from this minor peak in 1953-1954, prime time pre-emptions rose again on NBC-TV and CBS-TV during 1954-1955. This was the season in which NBC-TV began to fully exploit the "spectacular" program concept developed by Sylvester L. "Pat" Weaver. Actually, Weaver had been working on the "spectacular" concept for several years at NBC-TV. As early as 1950, Weaver was scheduling a regular Saturday night program which probably qualified as a "spectacular": the two-and-one-half hour "Saturday Night Revue" which began, after some problems with the FCC regarding station clearances, on February 25, 1950.[5] Other forerunners of the 1954-1955 "spectaculars" included a lavish <u>musical</u> <u>variety</u> one-timer, "America Applauds Richard Rodgers," on March 4, 1951, and another, "Irving Berlin's Salute to America" on September 12, 1951, both sponsored by the U. S. Shoe Corporation on NBC-TV. In 1953, the Ford Motor Company celebrated its 50th anniversary in a special televised simultaneously

---

[4]Stewart, <u>loc</u>. <u>cit</u>., p. 198.

[5]"Saturday Night on NBC-TV," <u>Broadcasting-Telecasting</u>, January 2, 1950, p. 45. See also "FCC Hits NBC Sat. Plan," <u>Broadcasting-Telecasting</u>, February 20, 1950, p. 68; "'Sat. Revue' Starts," <u>Broadcasting-Telecasting</u>, March 6, 1950, p. 65; "NBC-TV Revue Plans," <u>Broadcasting-Telecasting</u>, April 10, 1950, p. 66.

by NBC-TV and CBS-TV, "The American Road." General Foods used the facilities of all four national networks on March 28, 1954, clearing 255 stations for a musical variety 25th anniversary program. Movie producer David O. Selznick dazzled television on October 24, 1954 with a program observing the 75th anniversary of Thomas Edison's invention of the electric light, "Light's Diamond Jubilee." The program, estimated to cost in the neighborhood of one million dollars,[6] was sponsored by the Electric Companies of America, and appeared on a total of 425 stations affiliated with all four networks. These and other elaborate programs presaged the "spectaculars" which began on NBC-TV in 1954-1955 and appeared for the most part on a regular basis, hence are not included in this study's data. However, the "spectaculars" were no doubt a prime influence in the rise of pre-emptive programming which began with the 1956-1957 season on CBS-TV and NBC-TV, and in 1959-1960 on ABC-TV.

The marked trend toward more prime time pre-emptions on NBC and CBS which began with the 1956-1957 season carried through for five seasons on NBC-TV and four seasons on CBS-TV. ABC-TV significantly increased its nighttime special programming in 1959-1960, hitting a peak the following season. ABC-TV was apparently a reluctant competitor in the area of special programming. ABC-TV president Oliver Treyz believed regular programming had audience-building power. "We believe television is a habit medium" he said, adding, "We think you should interrupt those habits only when what you are presenting is superior to the regular fare. . . ."[7] There were probably other reasons for

---

[6]"The New Season," TV Guide, September 25, 1954, p. 4.

[7]"Strategy for a Program Battle," Broadcasting, August 17, 1959, p. 27.

ABC-TV's delayed entrance into prime time pre-emptive programming on a large scale. The network was having problems with station clearances during the 1950's and, as a partial result, found little or no advertiser demand for special programming through its facilities.[8] However, by 1959-1960 ABC-TV had solved some of its problems and planned an increase in special programming.[9]

After the peak seasons (1959-1960 for CBS and 1960-1961 for NBC and ABC) prime time pre-emptions declined on each network then rose on all networks during the 1964-1965 season, however, not equaling the previous high points. In the last season analyzed for this study, nighttime pre-emptions were on the decline at all networks.

Although CBS-TV led in the number of prime time hours pre-empted for special programs until the 1953-1954 season, NBC-TV was the overall leader in this field. With the exception of one season--1959-1960--NBC has led in prime time pre-emptions since the 1954-1955 season, the year in which the "spectacular" arrived. Since the 1960-1961 season, NBC-TV has scheduled a much greater number of prime time specials than ABC-TV or CBS-TV.

Figures 2 through 4 show each network's summer season prime time special programming. Since the patterns displayed were so nearly identical, separate graphs were prepared for each network to avoid the confusion of many overlapping lines.

---

[8]Fred Silverman, "An Analysis of ABC Television Network Programming From February 1953 to October 1959," unpublished Master's thesis, Ohio State University, 1959, p. 148.

[9]*Ibid.*, p. 329.

FIGURE 2

ABC-TV'S SUMMER SEASON PRIME TIME SPECIAL PROGRAMMING

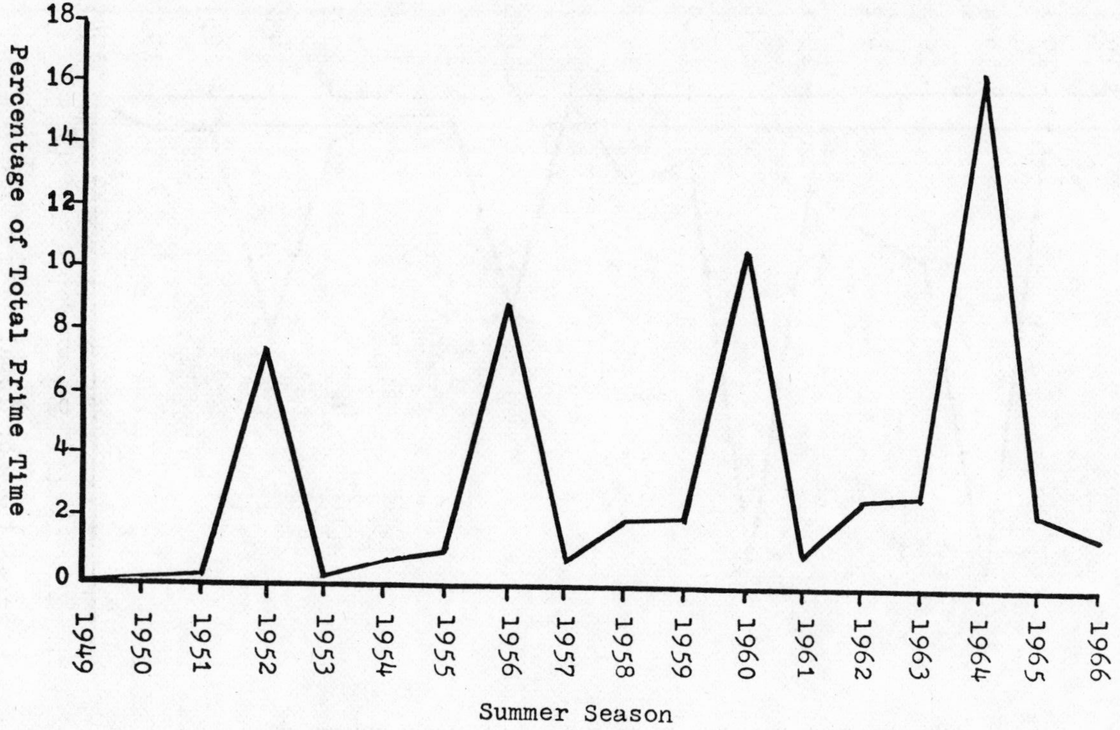

FIGURE 3

CBS-TV'S SUMMER SEASON PRIME TIME SPECIAL PROGRAMMING

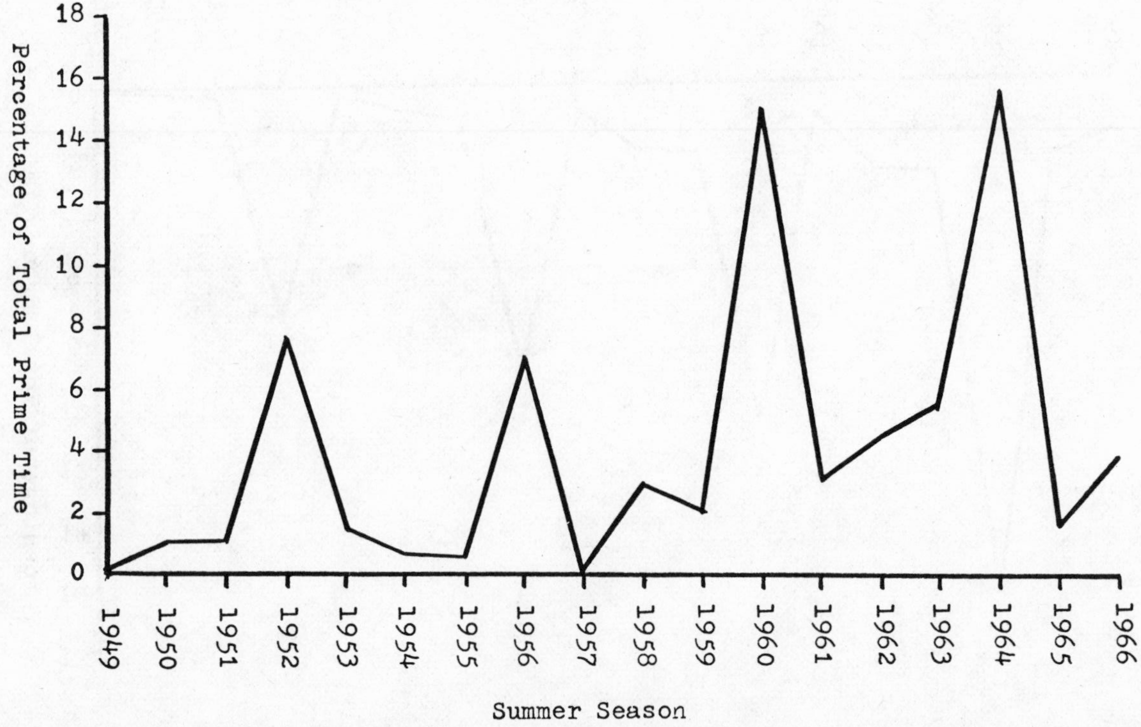

FIGURE 4

NBC-TV'S SUMMER SEASON PRIME TIME SPECIAL PROGRAMMING

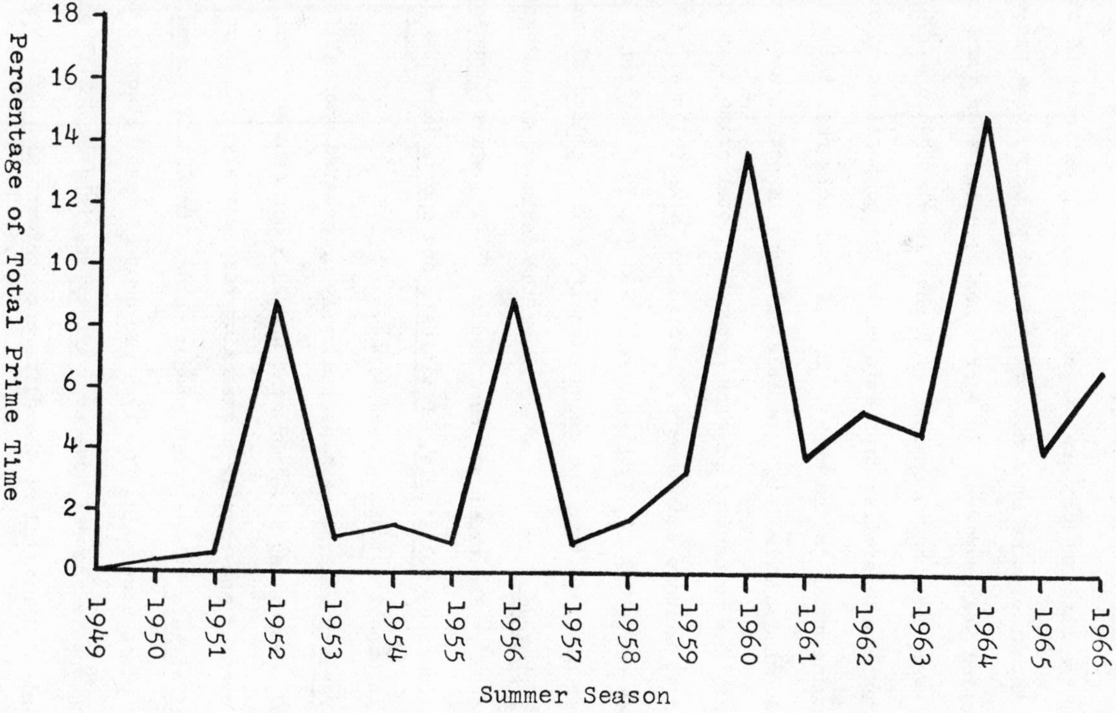

The cyclical fluctuations in summer time special programming were obvious. The quadrennial national political conventions, always fully covered by each network, resulted in sharp peaks every fourth year. Besides the standard pattern, there is also a great deal of similarity in the amount of time each network devoted to prime time pre-emptions in election year summers. In recent non-election year summers, prime time pre-emptions have remained at higher levels than pre-1957 summers.

Remarkable similarities existed in the composition of non-regular programming among the networks. On all four networks, talks comprised the predominant prime time specials category in both winter and summer seasons. The percentage of each network's total prime time special offerings, winters and summers, devoted to talks follows: ABC-TV, 78.2 per cent; CBS-TV, 57.4 per cent; NBC-TV, 59.7 per cent; DuMont, 91.2 per cent. Within the talks classification, political and documentary programs, in that order, were the dominant sub-categories on ABC and CBS. The order was reversed on NBC-TV, where documentaries led followed by politicals. Politicals and sports were the prime elements in DuMont's talks pre-emptions.

Variety was the next most heavily programmed special form on ABC and NBC, comprising 13.3 per cent and 24.3 per cent of those networks' total evening non-regular programming respectively. In each case the musical variety sub-category predominated. On CBS-TV, drama fell into second place accounting for 19.5 per cent of that network's total evening special hours; however, variety specials on CBS-TV made up 19.2 per cent of the total so the difference between drama and variety was hardly significant. Drama and variety shared second place on DuMont, each comprising 2.7 per cent of all DuMont's prime time pre-emptions.

Drama was a little-used special program form on ABC-TV, making up only 4.5 per cent of that network's total nighttime special programming. On NBC-TV, 13.5 per cent of all prime time pre-emptions were for drama specials.

The preceeding graphs illustrated total prime time special programming on the national networks. The following graphs depict trends and changes in certain categories and sub-categories. Represented are the major classifications into which the programs in this study were distributed: drama, talks, and variety.[10] Other graphs portray important sub-categories: documentary, politicals, news and news analysis, and musical variety. The index again was percentage of total prime time devoted to each category.[11]

In overall appearance, the graphs illustrating the several categories indicated have the major characteristic of sharp fluctuations rather than gradual changes. High peaks and deep valleys predominate the line graphs in nearly all instances. A few trends endured for several seasons, but all such trends eventually disappeared into random variations. The only category which displayed regularity and durability in its pattern was political programs.

Talks, the largest prime time specials classification, is shown in Figure 5. Notable similarities among the networks in scheduling

---

[10]The non-classifiable category was not illustrated since this classification represented only a small proportion of total special programming.

[11]Due to the small number of prime time special programs scheduled by the DuMont Television Network, no representation of that network's pre-emptive programming needed to be made.

FIGURE 5

PATTERNS IN PRIME TIME SPECIAL TALKS PROGRAMMING

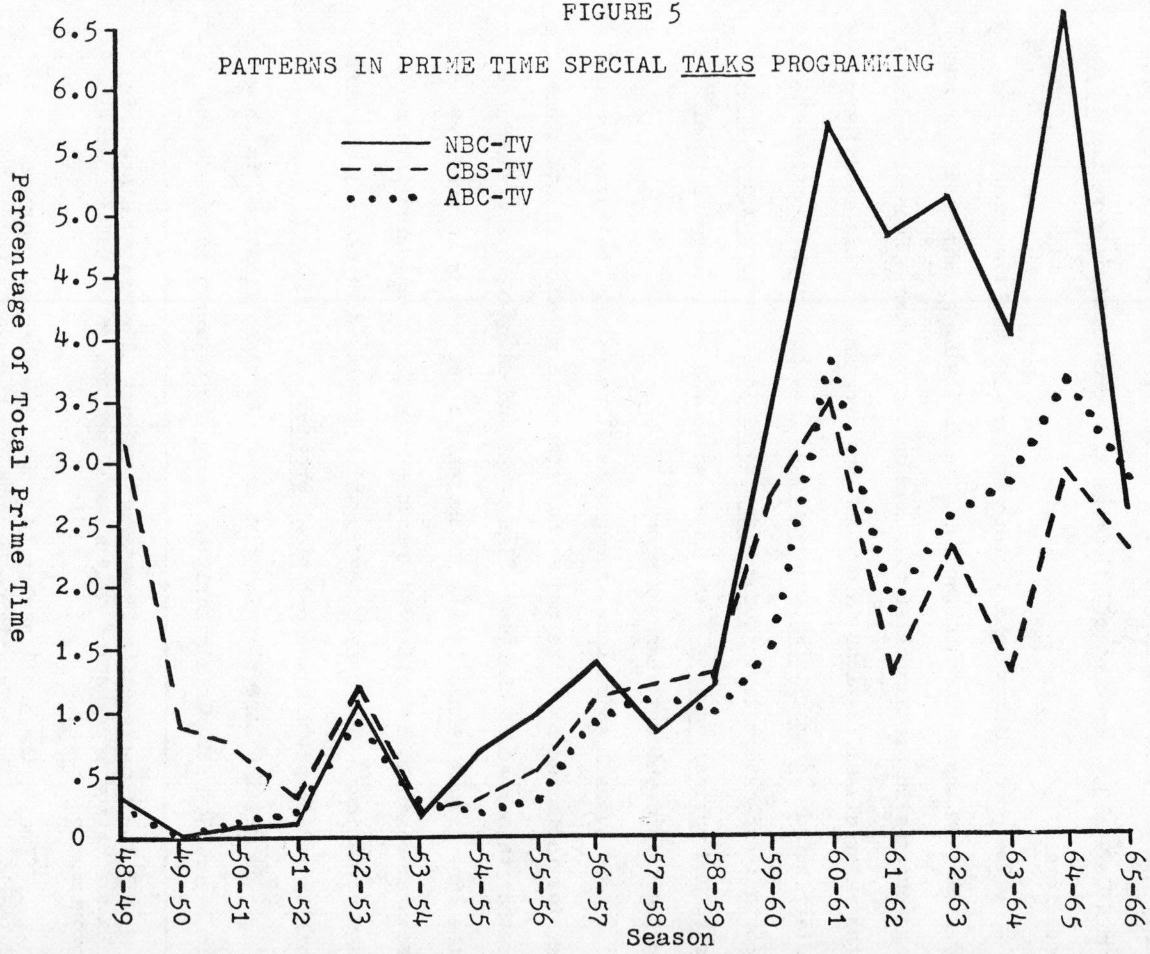

talks specials were readily apparent here. Talks shows on the three networks illustrated peaked in 1952-1953 (influenced by the 1952 Presidential election campaign), fell back the following season, then rose in concert through the 1956-1957 season. Each network increased the time devoted to talks shows greatly in 1960-1961, with strong emphasis on documentary, political, and news specials. The talks category declined on all networks the following season, then rose again in 1962-1963. ABC-TV's schedule of talks continued to increase from 1961-1962 through 1964-1965, while on NBC-TV and CBS-TV this category declined again in 1963-1964, then rose together during 1964-1965. In the final winter season of this study, talks had declined once again on all three networks.

Figure 6 charts the growth of variety programs. The pattern here did not reflect the degree of similarity among the networks apparent in talks specials; however, each network inclined toward scheduling more prime time variety specials during the latter 1950's and early 1960's.

Prime time special drama programming departed somewhat from the patterns produced by talks and variety programs. Here, only one significant peak appeared on the chart for NBC-TV and CBS-TV. ABC-TV's offerings in this category remained minimal throughout the entire period, never amounting to even one-half of one per cent of total prime time. Peak years for special nighttime drama began with the 1956-1957 season, culminating in 1959-1960 on CBS-TV and in 1960-1961 on NBC-TV. Between 1957-1958 and 1959-1960, CBS scheduled a great deal more prime time hours of special drama than NBC. From 1960-1961

FIGURE 6

PATTERNS IN PRIME TIME SPECIAL VARIETY PROGRAMMING

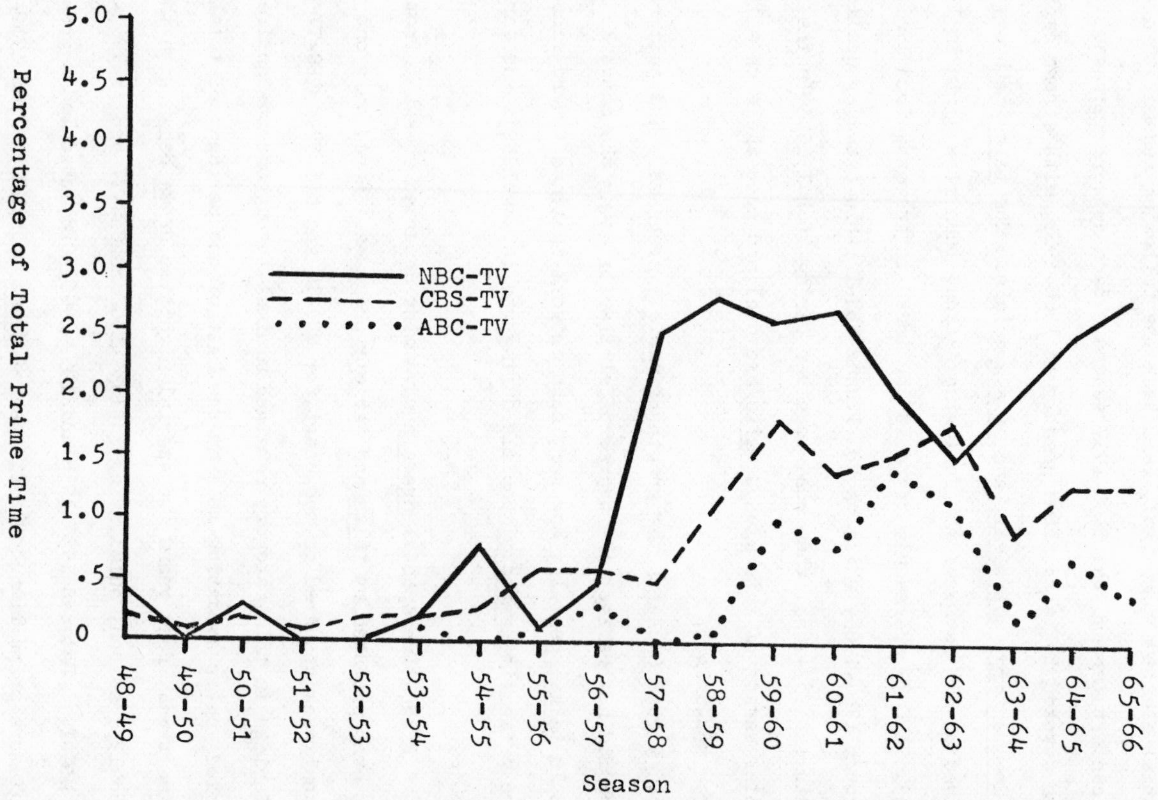

FIGURE 7

PATTERNS IN PRIME TIME SPECIAL <u>DRAMA</u> PROGRAMMING

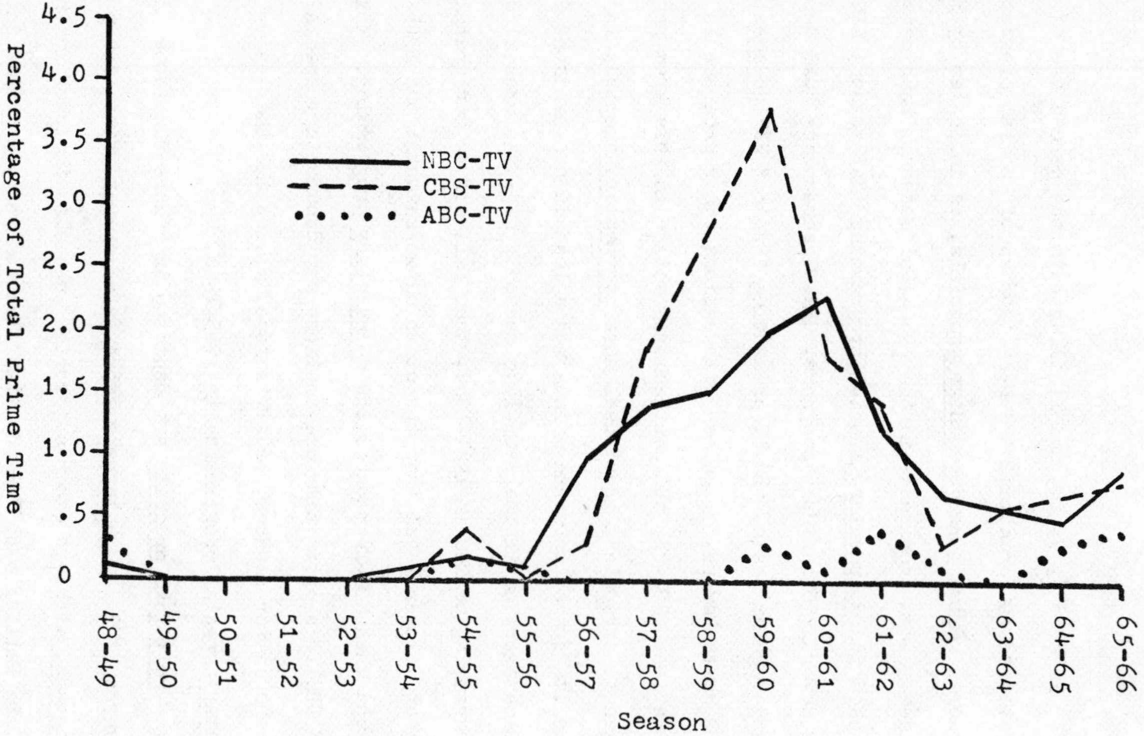

through the end of the period, only slight differences occurred between CBS's and NBC's evening pre-emptions for drama specials. In the final year included in this study, a minor upturn in this category was apparent.

Figures 8, 9, 10, and 11 illustrate the percentage of prime time devoted to the predominant sub-categories of special programs on each network. Prime time documentary specials, as indicated by Figure 8, gained sudden prominence in the 1960-1961 season. Each network increased its documentary special programming that season, ABC-TV offering several "Close-Up!" programs, CBS-TV scheduling "CBS Reports" on a non-regular basis, NBC-TV presenting "Project XX" documentaries and "NBC White Papers," together with various other programs in this classification. NBC-TV, not particularly active in this area previously, began to schedule a great deal more documentary specials in prime time than its competitors and maintained a lead in pre-emptions for this sub-category until the 1965-1966 season. CBS-TV's special documentary programming peaked in 1961-1962, then fell off rather sharply, remaining at a lower level than the other networks until the 1965-1966 season when NBC-TV reduced its documentary programming. While NBC-TV's and CBS-TV's prime time pre-emptions for documentary specials declined in the latter seasons, ABC-TV's rose, making ABC the leader in documentary special programming in 1965-1966.

Political programs are depicted in Figure 9. (Note also that Figures 2, 3, and 4 largely represented summer prime time political programs, although other categories were also included in these graphs.) In the fall of each Presidential election year, a marked increase in

FIGURE 8

PATTERNS IN PRIME TIME SPECIAL DOCUMENTARY PROGRAMMING

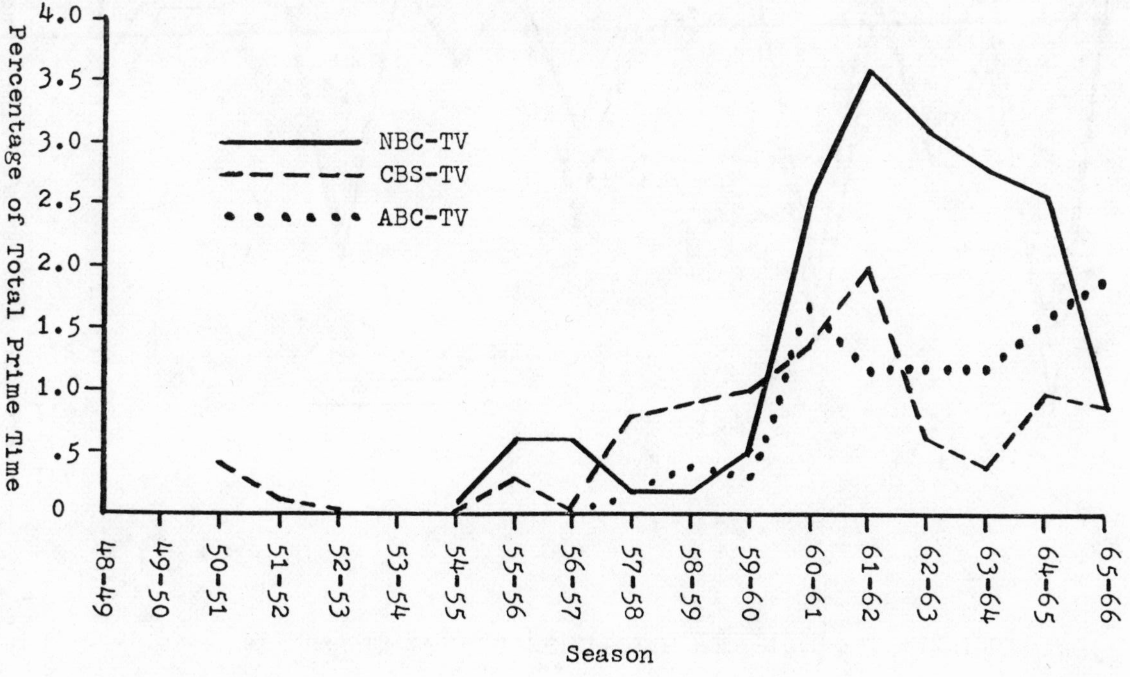

FIGURE 9

PATTERNS IN PRIME TIME SPECIAL <u>POLITICAL</u> PROGRAMMING

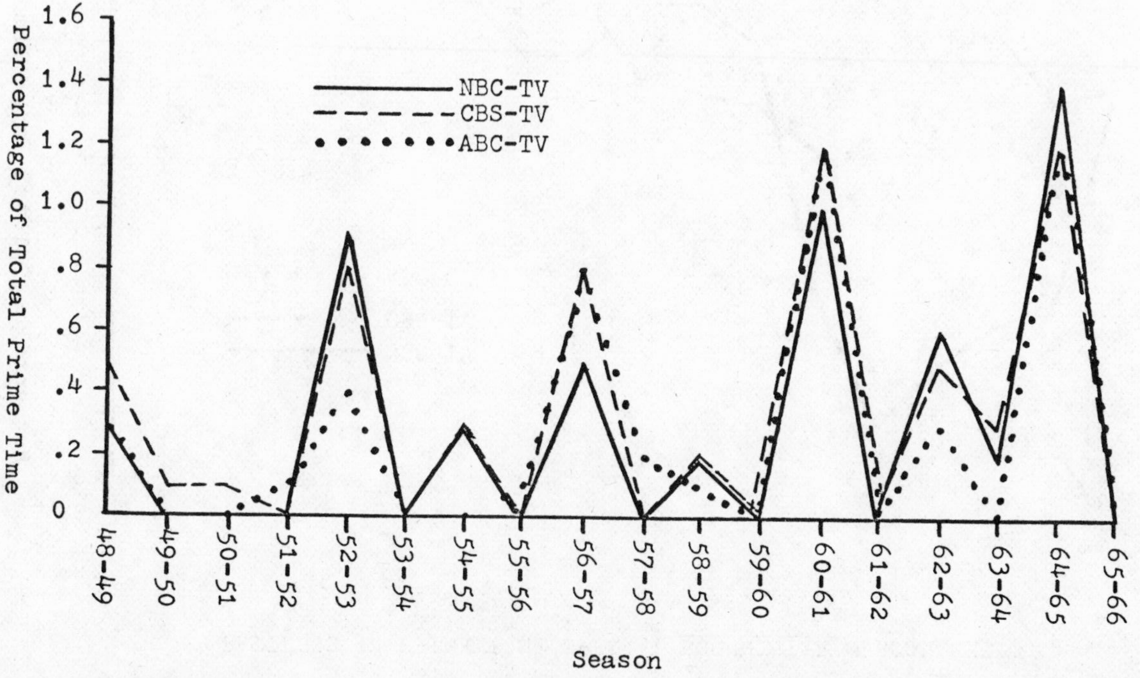

pre-emptions for political specials occurred. Definite increases of lesser magnitude occurred during each Congressional election year. Two characteristics set the pattern of political special programming apart from other categories of prime time non-regular programming: the measured regularity of the fluctuations, and the strong similarity among the networks in their patterns of scheduling this sub-category. Although remarkable similarities existed regarding the use of other categories, in none was the percentage of prime time expended on a program type by the various networks so nearly identical as in the case of political specials.

The development of news and news analysis as a prime time special program form is shown in Figure 10. Until the 1959-1960 season, news specials played virtually no part in evening special program schedules on the networks. Beyond the common sharp incline of news specials in 1959-1960, there was little similarity among the networks in their employment of this type. ABC-TV has been least active in this area, NBC-TV most active. As noted earlier in this chapter, the usual subjects of news specials have been the travels of world leaders, the space exploration program, disasters, the civil rights movement, deaths of prominent persons, unusual international developments such as the U-2 incident, Khrushchev's ouster from the Russian government, or Red China's atomic explosion, and the Vietnam war.

Figure 11 illustrates musical variety, another prominent subcategory, NBC-TV led in programming musical variety specials from 1956-1957 through 1961-1962. This trend followed a relatively smooth ascendancy on NBC-TV through those six seasons, after which pre-emptions

FIGURE 10

PATTERNS IN PRIME TIME SPECIAL NEWS PROGRAMMING

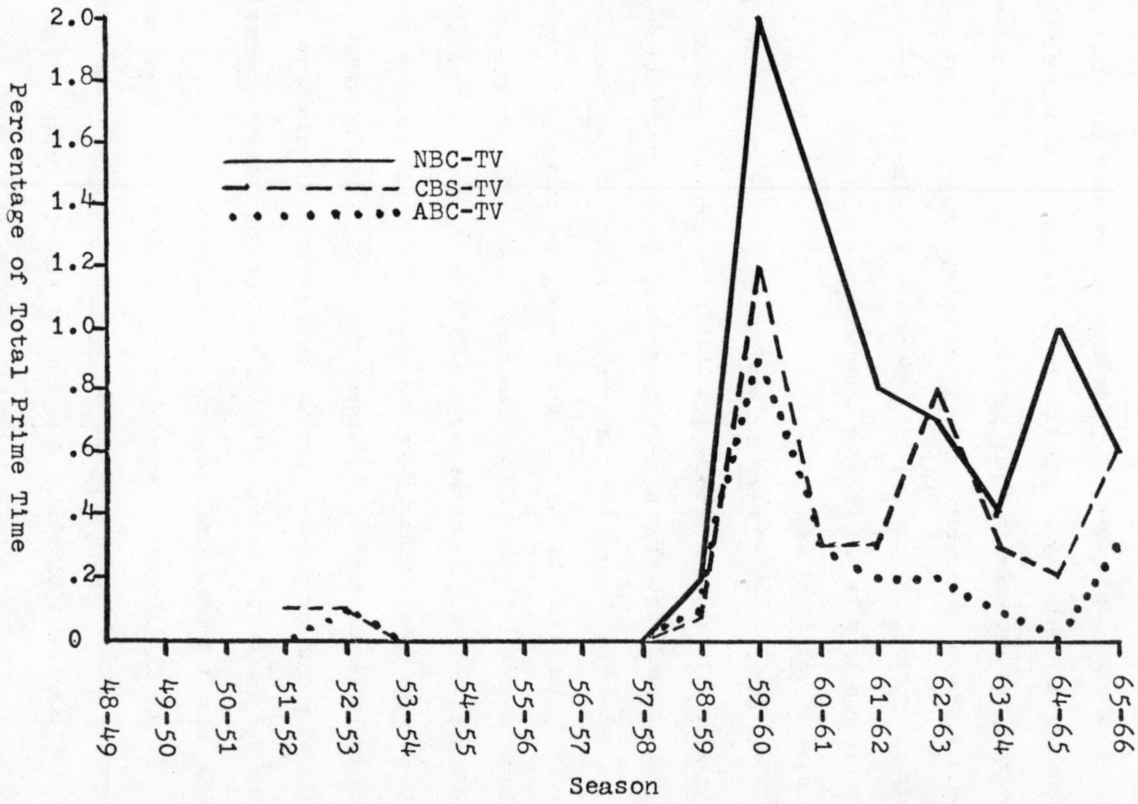

FIGURE 11

PATTERNS IN PRIME TIME SPECIAL MUSICAL VARIETY PROGRAMMING

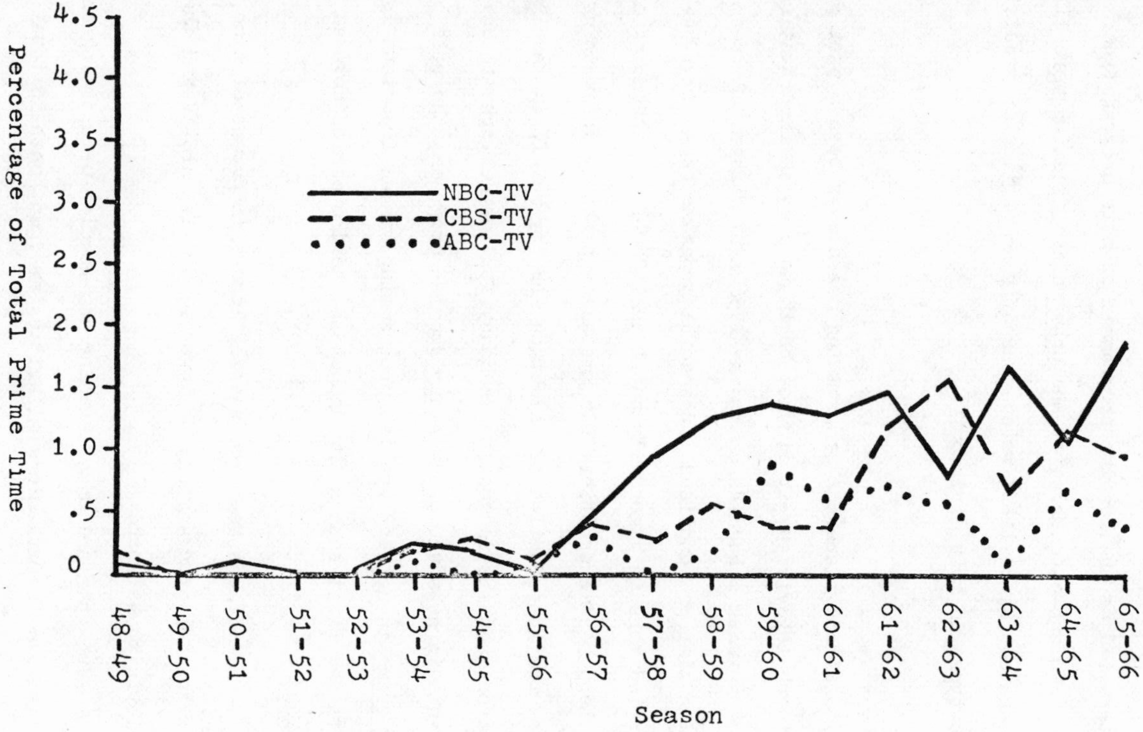

for this sub-category fell off into an uneven pattern more characteristic of most network television prime time special programming. For the final four seasons, 1962-1963 through 1965-1966, NBC-TV and CBS-TV alternated as the leading programmer of this program type.

No sub-categories of the drama classification were illustrated separately since there were apparently no particularly outstanding sub-types in this division.

Summary

Although special programming has always been a part of national network television, it did not begin to play an important role in prime time network schedules until the 1956-1957 season. A trend toward more prime time pre-emptions for special programs began in 1956-1957 and carried through vigorously until the 1960-1961 season, after which the pattern became erratic. Circumstances probably influencing this trend were the introduction of "spectaculars" by NBC-TV in the 1954-1955 season, and the increasing tendency for the networks to cover world events in news and documentary special programs; the role of political programs in network special programming was an important influence from the first season throughout the entire period covered by this study.

NBC-TV has been the overall leader in amount of time pre-empted for special programming, followed by CBS-TV, ABC-TV and the DuMont Television Network.

In a comparison of evening non-regular programming on the networks, some remarkable similarities emerged, both in total special programming, and in the scheduling of certain program types. Talks programs comprised the dominant specials classification on all networks. Within this broad category, political programs and documentaries were the most programmed sub-types on all networks. The strongest similarities appeared in patterns of summer season special programming and in the scheduling of political specials.

The pattern displayed by summer season prime time special programming was decidedly different from winter seasons. Summer season special programming varied with cyclical regularity, influenced by national political activity. Winter season special programming exhibited no cyclical characteristics, but appeared to vary randomly.

CHAPTER III

SCHEDULING OF NETWORK TELEVISION PRIME TIME SPECIAL PROGRAMS

This study's second objective was to determine if any patterns existed in the scheduling of network television prime time pre-emptive programs. To that end, the data were examined with regard to which categories appeared with what frequency during which months on each network. In addition, the data were searched to determine which days of the week were favored for pre-emptive evening specials, what times these programs were generally offered, and how long they were. Data for each network are presented separately, then a comparative analysis is offered.

ABC-TV

Table 20 indicates the amount and composition of ABC-TV's prime time special programming by months. The months were listed consecutively beginning with September since that is the month the winter television season begins. The percentage of total prime time indicated for each month was based on ABC-TV's total amount of pre-empted time for the entire period: 583 hours and 25 minutes.

Table 20 pointed out the extent to which ABC-TV's non-regular prime time programming was sensitive to United States politics. Although major political campaign activity occurred only every four years, more prime time was pre-empted for political programs than

TABLE 20

MONTHLY DISTRIBUTION OF ABC-TV'S PRIME TIME SPECIAL PROGRAMMING

Category	Septembers*	Octobers	Novembers	Decembers	Januaries
Drama	Hours**	Hours	Hours	Hours	Hours
Action	1:30(2)	-	1:00(1)	-	-
Comedy	-	-	-	-	-
Crime	2:00(2)	-	-	-	-
Readings	-	-	-	-	-
Fairy Tales	1:00(1)	-	-	-	-
Historical	-	-	-	-	-
Motion Picture	-	-	-	-	-
Musical	-	1:00(1)	3:30(2)	1:00(1)	-
Prestige	-	-	-	-	-
Western	-	-	-	-	-
Unclassified	1:30(2)	2:00(1)	-	1:30(1)	-
Talks					
Actualities	-	1:30(1)	-	-	-
Pageants	2:30(3)	-	1:00(2)	6:00(7)	2:00(2)
Documentary	8:25(10)	5:30(7)	11:00(13)	10:00(11)	9:00(11)
Instructional	-	-	-	-	-
News	6:30(13)	0:30(1)	0:45(2)	9:00(12)	2:45(5)
Panel	0:30(1)	0:30(1)	0:30(1)	0:30(1)	2:00(4)
Political	7:30(14)	15:45(30)	23:30(15)	-	-
Religious	1:00(2)	-	-	1:30(3)	-
Speeches	3:15(7)	2:00(4)	1:00(2)	0:30(1)	4:30(7)
Sports	9:00(10)	2:30(4)	-	3:15(4)	8:00(8)
Variety					
Circus	-	-	-	-	-
Comedy	2:30(4)	2:00(3)	1:00(2)	1:00(2)	1:00(2)
Musical	3:00(3)	9:00(10)	5:00(6)	7:15(11)	4:00(7)
Vaudeville	-	-	-	-	-
Non-classifiable	1:00(1)	0:30(1)	14:00(4)	-	2:00(2)
Totals	51:10 75	42:45 64	62:15 50	41:30 54	35:15 48
Percentage of Special Time	8.7%	7.3%	10.7%	7.2%	6.1%

* The months of October through December are represented for the years 1948 through 1965; all other months for the years 1949 through 1966.

** In parentheses following the hours figure is the number of programs in each category.

Februaries Hours		Marches Hours		Aprils Hours		Mays Hours		Junes Hours		Julys Hours		Augusts Hours	
-		-		1:00(	1)	-		-		-		-	
-		-		2:00(	2)	-		-		-		-	
-		-		1:30(	1)	-		0:30(	1)	-		-	
-		-		-		-		-		-		-	
-		1:00(	1)	0:30(	1)	-		-		-		-	
-		-		-		-		-		-		-	
-		-		-		-		-		-		-	
-		-		-		-		-		-		-	
-		-		-		-		-		-		-	
1:00(	1)	-		-		-		-		-		-	
3:00(	2)	-		-		-		-		-		-	
-		-		-		-		-		-		-	
0:30(	1)	-		8:00(	8)	2:00(	2)	2:30(	1)	-		0:30(	1)
12:00(	14)	14:30(	15)	16:30(	21)	10:30(	13)	12:30(	14)	2:00(	3)	7:30(	9)
-		-		-		-		-		-		-	
0:25(	1)	2:00(	1)	-		4:30(	8)	2:30(	5)	3:35(	6)	1:00(	2)
1:00(	1)	1:00(	2)	-		3:30(	5)	2:30(	5)	-		-	
0:30(	1)	-		-		3:30(	5)	1:00(	2)	70:45(	30)	43:45(	19)
-		-		-		-		-		-		-	
0:30(	2)	2:45(	5)	2:30(	5)	3:00(	6)	1:15(	3)	1:45(	4)	2:45(	6)
6:00(	6)	4:30(	4)	-		1:30(	2)	5:30(	5)	10:00(	9)	20:00(	17)
-		2:00(	2)	-		-		-		-		-	
1:30(	2)	0:30(	1)	2:00(	3)	2:00(	3)	1:00(	2)	-		1:00(	1)
6:30(	7)	6:00(	6)	6:30(	8)	4:30(	6)	2:30(	3)	-		3:00(	3)
-		-		1:00(	1)	-		1:00(	1)	0:30(	1)	-	
-		0:30(	1)	1:00(	1)	0:30(	1)	2:00(	2)	2:00(	4)	-	
32:55	38	34:45	38	42:30	52	35:30	51	34:45	44	70:35	57	79:30	58
5.7%		5.9%		7.3%		6.1%		5.9%		15.5%		13.6%	

any other sub-category. When the composite months were ranked by the number of hours of prime time special programming, those months in which national political party conventions have been held and presidential campaigns have been waged ranked first: July, August, November, September, and October, in that order. In each of these months except September, the political sub-category was dominant. Sports predominated in September.

The prominent role documentary has played in ABC-TV's prime time pre-emptive programming was also underscored in Table 20. No seasonal aspect was apparent with regard to this sub-category; a considerable number of documentaries has appeared during each month of the year. More special prime time has been devoted to documentaries on ABC-TV than any other sub-category in all months except those in which politicals and sports were dominant.

ABC-TV confined its little drama special programming to the winter season months, and scheduled no prime time drama specials in the months of January, May, July, and August.

Talks and variety specials appeared during all months of the year; however, except for politicals, these classifications became sparse in the summer months.

Figure 12 presents the pattern displayed when all prime time ABC-TV specials for the period under study were distributed by months. July and August were the months in which the most prime time was preempted for specials, influenced by political programs. To discover the pattern underlying political programming, all political specials were removed from the data and Figure 13 constructed. With political

FIGURE 12

MONTHLY DISTRIBUTION PATTERN OF ABC-TV'S PRIME TIME SPECIAL PROGRAMMING

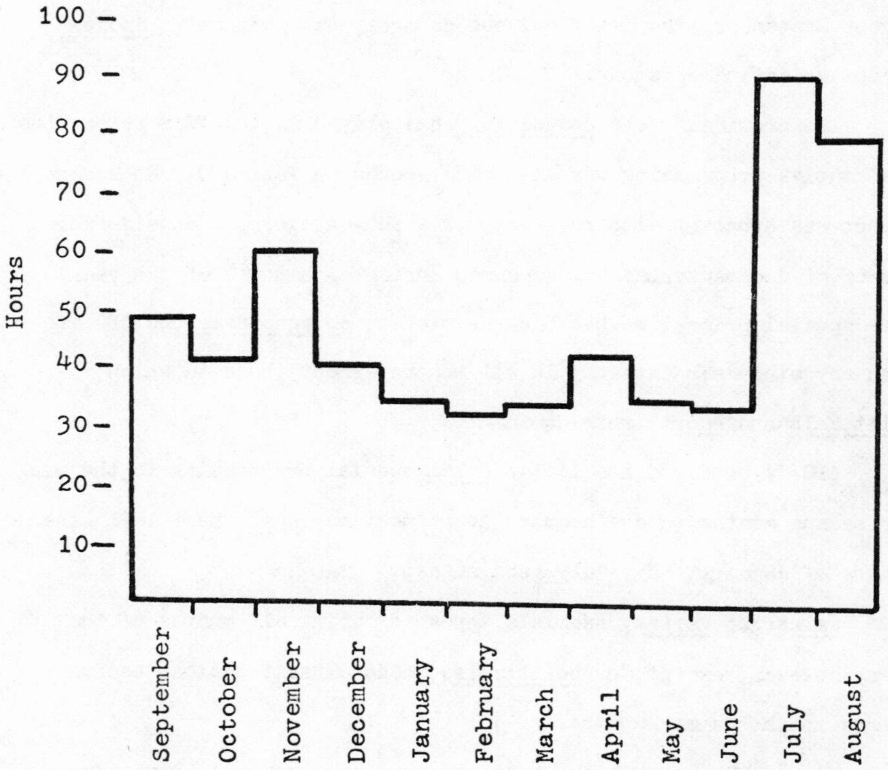

FIGURE 13

MONTHLY DISTRIBUTION PATTERN OF ABC-TV'S PRIME TIME SPECIAL PROGRAMMING, POLITICAL PROGRAMS REMOVED

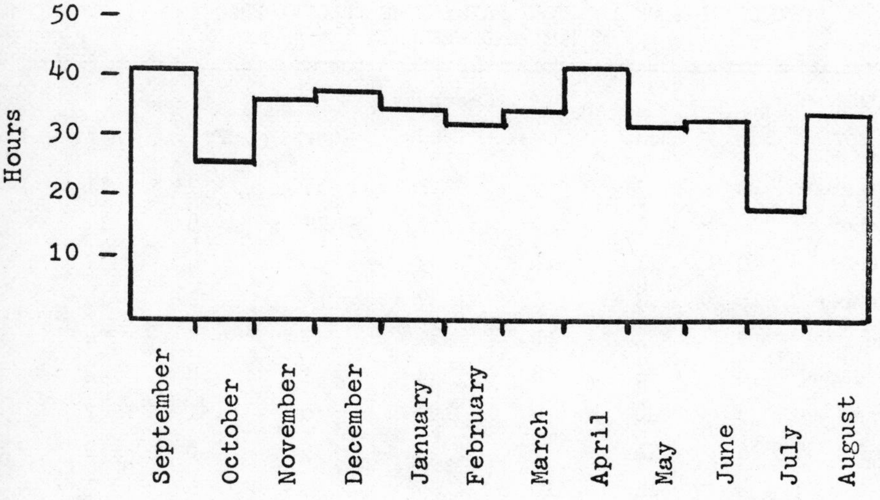

programming removed, July moved from the month of most to the month of least prime time hours pre-empted. Emerging as months in which most ABC-TV evening special programming occurred, other than political, were September, April, December, and November, each with more than 35 hours of prime time non-regular programs.

While ABC-TV's prime time special programs tended not to be distributed evenly throughout the year, they did tend to be fairly evenly distributed throughout days of the week. Table 21 plotted the number of specials which have appeared on ABC-TV each night of the week for

TABLE 21

DISTRIBUTION OF ABC-TV'S PRIME TIME SPECIAL PROGRAMS BY MONTHS AND WEEKDAYS

Month	Weekday						
	Sun.	Mon.	Tues.	Wed.	Thurs.	Fri.	Sat.
September	13	3	15	11	15	7	11
October	5	7	9	9	15	8	11
November	10	11	10	7	6	4	2
December	16	7	6	7	2	2	14
January	9	3	11	11	3	7	4
February	6	6	8	3	3	8	4
March	6	8	4	9	8	1	2
April	6	14	7	6	9	8	2
May	4	14	10	5	8	6	4
June	8	7	10	4	7	3	5
July	6	7	12	8	8	8	8
August	5	9	5	5	5	21	8
	94	96	107	85	89	83	75

each month of the year. Translated into percentages, Table 21 indicated that 14.7 per cent of all ABC-TV's evening special programs appeared on Sunday nights, 15.3 per cent on Monday nights, 17.0 per cent on Tuesday nights, 13.6 per cent on Wednesday nights, 14.2 per cent on Thursday nights, 13.3 per cent on Friday nights, and 11.9 per cent on Saturday nights. Most ABC-TV prime time pre-emptions occurred on Tuesday nights, least on Saturday nights, although the difference between these extremes is only 5.1 per cent; thus, there was only slight variation in the distribution of prime time specials by weekdays on ABC-TV.

The data were further examined to note the days of the week on which the various sub-categories appeared. Table 22 presents this information. In only a few instances were definite patterns apparent. Awards and pageants appeared most frequently on Monday, Saturday, and Tuesday nights on ABC-TV. Documentary, a large category, appeared every night of the week, but most frequently on Wednesdays, least frequently on Saturdays; however, documentary was spread fairly evenly Sundays through Fridays. News and news analysis appeared most frequently on Sunday nights, least frequently on Monday nights. Panel discussions were generally televised Tuesdays, Fridays, and Sundays on ABC-TV, not at all on Saturdays. Political programs appeared every night of the week, but there were markedly fewer such specials on Sunday nights than during the remainder of the week. Most political specials on ABC-TV were televised on Monday nights, the day on which the political conventions began, and the day preceeding the November elections. Thus, Mondays would include last-minute campaign appearances of presidential candidates. Friday, Saturday, and Sunday were

TABLE 22

DISTRIBUTION OF ABC-TV'S PRIME TIME SPECIAL PROGRAM CATEGORIES BY WEEKDAYS

Category	Weekday						
Drama	Sun.	Mon.	Tue.	Wed.	Thur.	Fri.	Sat.
Action	1	1	1	-	1	-	-
Comedy	-	-	-	1	-	1	-
Crime	-	-	1	-	-	1	2
Readings	-	-	-	-	-	-	-
Fairy Tales	-	-	1	1	1	-	-
Historical	-	-	-	-	-	-	-
Motion Picture	-	-	-	-	-	-	-
Musical	1	1	-	-	1	-	1
Prestige	-	-	-	-	-	-	-
Western	-	-	-	-	-	-	1
Unclassified	1	1	-	1	1	2	-
Talks							
Actualities	-	1	-	-	-	-	-
Awards	1	9	5	2	1	1	8
Documentary	21	18	21	26	22	23	10
Instructional	-	-	-	-	-	-	-
News	14	3	11	9	7	5	7
Panel	5	1	6	2	2	5	-
Political	4	24	21	18	23	12	14
Religious	3	-	-	2	-	-	-
Speeches	5	16	9	7	9	5	1
Sports	15	2	5	7	4	19	17
Variety							
Circus	-	1	-	-	1	-	-
Comedy	2	2	10	-	7	2	2
Musical	15	13	10	8	9	6	9
Vaudeville	1	-	2	-	-	-	-
Non-classifiable	5	3	4	1	-	1	3
Totals	94	96	107	85	89	83	75

the nights on which ABC-TV televised most of their sports specials, although no weekday was neglected for this category. Weekends, however, appeared to be sports oriented including not only most sports specials, but regularly scheduled sports programs also. Comedy variety, which never appeared on a Wednesday night on ABC-TV, was most often televised on Tuesday and Thursday evenings. The largest variety sub-category, musical variety, pre-empted time on each week night, with most pre-emptions occurring on Sunday nights, fewest on Friday nights.

The sub-categories with few entries, notably the drama types, of course displayed no patterns.

A tally of the starting times of ABC-TV's prime time pre-emptions revealed a more definite pattern. Table 23 divides prime time into half-hour segments and indicates the number of programs which began at each time listed for each month. The column labeled "Other" includes programs that began prior to prime time and ran into it, plus a small number of specials which began at 10:15 and 10:45.

ABC-TV apparently exercised a preference for scheduling specials to begin at 10:00 p.m. Of the 629 ABC-TV prime time non-regular programs in this study, 16.7 per cent began at 7:30 p.m., New York time, 6.9 per cent began at 8:00, 7.9 per cent began at 8:30, 9.7 per cent at 9:00, 12.9 per cent began at 9:30, 22.6 per cent at 10:00, 16.5 per cent began at 10:30, and 6.8 per cent began at other times. The rather large numbers of programs in the "Other" column for July and August represent political convention programs which frequently began prior to 7:30 p.m. November includes four evenings devoted to coverage of the Kennedy assassination which began during the day and continued until sign-off.

TABLE 23

ABC-TV'S PRIME TIME SPECIAL PROGRAMS DISTRIBUTED BY STARTING TIME

Month	New York City Time							
	7:30	8:00	8:30	9:00	9:30	10:00	10:30	Other*
September	13	4	3	12	13	13	15	2
October	8	5	7	6	7	16	13	2
November	3	3	4	-	5	17	9	9
December	5	-	6	4	9	14	13	3
January	12	-	3	6	10	8	9	-
February	5	2	8	3	3	10	5	2
March	6	3	2	4	7	12	4	-
April	8	2	3	11	2	18	7	1
May	12	10	3	2	2	10	10	2
June	11	5	2	-	8	6	11	1
July	13	5	2	7	8	6	5	11
August	9	5	7	6	7	12	3	9
Totals	105	44	50	61	81	142	104	42

* Includes programs which began prior to the prime time segment and ran into it, plus a few specials which began at 10:15 and 10:45.

Programs which began at 10:00 and 10:30 p.m. in most cases filled the final hour or half-hour of prime time. Thus, nearly 40 per cent of all ABC-TV's nighttime non-regular programs were scheduled to conclude the prime time segment. On the other hand, 16.7 per cent of these programs were scheduled to begin the prime time hours, commencing at 7:30 p.m. Thus, the most frequently used special programming tactics by ABC-TV were to schedule special programs as lead-ins to the regular prime time shows, or as lead-outs of the prime time period. Subsequent analyses will show the same tactics were employed to a conspicuous degree by the other networks also.

In Table 24, categories of ABC-TV's prime time special programs are distributed by starting times to reveal patterns in the schedules of categories. Table 24 shows that most specials scheduled to begin the prime time hours at 7:30 consisted of documentary, politicals, sports, news, and musical variety shows, all but the latter in the talks classification. Essentially the same program types were also heavily scheduled during the closing hour of prime time: documentary, sports, politicals, and musical variety beginning at 10:00 p.m., and politicals, news, speeches, comedy and musical variety at 10:30 p.m.

ABC-TV expressed a definite preference for scheduling its documentary specials either early or late; of 141 ABC-TV documentaries, 22.7 per cent were scheduled at 7:30, while 27.7 per cent were scheduled to begin at 10:00 p.m. This represented just over half all ABC-TV prime time documentary specials. The same pattern emerged with respect to news specials; 17.9 per cent of the 56 ABC-TV news specials began at 7:30 p.m., 35.8 per cent began at 10:30 p.m., representing nearly 54 per cent of all news pre-emptions.

Political specials also tended to begin either early or late, although the pattern with regard to this category was not as marked as with documentary and news specials.

Most sports programs were scheduled to begin at 10:00, 9:30 and 7:30 p.m.

TABLE 24

DISTRIBUTION OF ABC-TV'S PRIME TIME SPECIAL PROGRAM CATEGORIES BY STARTING TIMES

Category	New York City Time							
Drama	7:30	8:00	8:30	9:00	9:30	10:00	10:30	Other*
Action	1	-	-	-	1	1	-	1
Comedy	-	-	1	1	-	-	-	-
Crime	3	-	-	-	-	-	1	-
Readings	-	-	-	-	-	-	-	-
Fairy Tales	1	1	-	-	-	-	-	1
Historical	-	-	-	-	-	-	-	-
Motion Picture	-	-	-	-	-	-	-	-
Musical	1	1	1	-	-	-	-	1
Prestige	-	-	-	-	-	-	-	-
Western	1	-	-	-	-	-	-	-
Unclassified	-	1	1	1	2	1	-	-
Talks								
Actualities	-	-	1	-	-	-	-	-
Awards	2	3	2	1	4	8	6	1
Documentary	32	9	9	17	16	49	9	-
Instructional	-	-	-	-	-	-	-	-
News	10	5	2	2	6	6	20	5
Panel	4	-	1	-	4	2	9	1
Political	17	14	12	9	6	14	22	22
Religious	-	-	-	1	2	1	1	-
Speeches	5	4	4	10	6	9	11	3
Sports	13	2	2	5	14	29	2	2
Variety								
Circus	2	-	-	-	-	-	-	-
Comedy	-	-	4	3	2	5	11	-
Musical	9	1	7	7	18	16	11	1
Vaudeville	-	2	-	1	-	-	-	-
Non-classifiable	4	1	2	2	1	1	1	5
Totals	105	44	49	60	82	142	104	43

* Includes programs which began prior to the prime time segment and ran into it, plus a few specials which began at 10:15 and 10:45.

Most variety specials appeared after 8:30 p.m. on ABC-TV, with the 10:00 to 11:00 p.m. time period containing the most variety shows.

With ABC-TV's evening special program schedule distributed by months, weekdays, and starting times, these programs are next considered in another dimension: length. Nearly half all ABC-TV's evening non-regular programs were half-hour presentations, with hour-long shows next. Expressed as percentages of ABC-TV's total 629 prime time special programs, 2.5 per cent were 15 minute shows, 46.6 per cent were 30 minutes long, 0.5 per cent ran 45 minutes, 38.6 per cent were hour-long shows, 3.7 per cent ran one-and-one half hours, 1.6 per cent were two-hour specials, 1.4 per cent lasted two-and-one-half hours, 0.5 per cent were three hours long, and 4.6 per cent were three-and-one-half hour programs. The longest specials, those over 90 minutes in length, were usually political programs consisting of convention and election night coverage. Because of this variation in program length, some seasons showed a relatively small number of special programs but a relatively large number of hours pre-empted, or vice versa.

To summarize, ABC-TV has done most of its pre-emptive prime time programming during the months of July, August, September, and November, putting a preponderance of pre-emptions into the summer months. This was directly attributable to the coverage ABC-TV afforded national political activity. With the influence of political coverage removed, April, September, November, and December became the months in which the most prime time was pre-empted for special programs, with fewest pre-emptions occurring in July and October.

ABC-TV's nighttime non-regular programming has been spread quite evenly over days of the week with a slight edge going to Tuesday nights. Most such programming was scheduled to begin at 10:00 p.m., New York time, with other favored times being 7:30 and 10:30 p.m. More than half the prime time specials either began or concluded the prime time hours.

Nearly half ABC-TV's prime time special programs were 30-minute shows, and more than a third were hour-long presentations.

CBS-TV

The monthly distribution of CBS-TV's prime time special programming is indicated in Table 25. The percentage of total special time is based on CBS-TV's entire nighttime special schedule for the period under study: 877 hours and 55 minutes.

Pre-emptions favoring political programs have played a major role in CBS-TV's prime time specials schedule. More hours have been pre-empted for political programs than for any other sub-category on CBS-TV. As a result, the months in which political campaigns and conventions were conducted were the months in which the greatest amount of prime time was pre-empted: July, November, September, October, and August, in that order. These are the same months noted as having the most pre-emptions on ABC-TV, although in somewhat different rank order.

While political specials accounted for most of the prime time CBS-TV pre-empted during four months of the composite year, July, August, October, and November, documentary specials led in hours pre-empted during five months: September, December, February, April and

TABLE 25

MONTHLY DISTRIBUTION OF CBS-TV'S PRIME TIME SPECIAL PROGRAMMING

Category	Septembers*	Octobers	Novembers	Decembers	Januaries
Drama	Hours**	Hours	Hours	Hours	Hours
Action	3:00(2)	1:30(1)	1:30(1)	-	3:00(2)
Comedy	3:00(3)	1:00(1)	4:15(3)	5:00(4)	3:30(3)
Crime	1:00(1)	2:00(2)	1:30(1)	-	2:30(2)
Readings	-	-	-	-	0:30(1)
Fairy Tales	-	-	-	1:55(3)	-
Historical	3:00(5)	-	-	-	-
Motion Picture	-	-	2:00(1)	2:00(4)	3:30(3)
Musical	-	2:00(2)	5:00(3)	2:00(2)	1:00(1)
Prestige	1:30(1)	5:30(4)	2:30(2)	6:00(5)	6:00(5)
Western	-	1:00(1)	-	-	-
Unclassified	4:00(5)	5:00(3)	-	-	-
Talks					
Actualities	-	2:30(1)	-	-	-
Pageants	10:30(11)	4:15(5)	2:30(3)	-	2:00(3)
Documentary	16:45(20)	9:30(10)	7:00(8)	11:30(13)	7:00(7)
Instructional	-	-	1:00(1)	-	-
News	6:15(13)	1:55(3)	1:00(2)	8:30(11)	4:45(5)
Panel	5:00(7)	7:00(6)	0:30(1)	1:30(2)	1:00(2)
Political	6:25(12)	17:35(31)	34:15(27)	-	-
Religious	-	-	-	-	-
Speeches	3:40(9)	1:00(2)	1:00(2)	1:25(3)	5:00(8)
Sports	9:45(14)	7:30(4)	7:15(3)	8:10(4)	2:00(2)
Variety					
Circus	-	-	-	2:00(2)	-
Comedy	5:30(6)	9:15(10)	4:30(5)	3:30(4)	3:00(3)
Musical	9:30(9)	4:00(4)	10:00(10)	11:30(11)	15:30(16)
Vaudeville	-	-	2:00(2)	0:30(1)	-
Non-classifiable	1:00(1)	0:30(1)	15:30(6)	2:15(3)	5:15(7)
Totals	89:50 119	83:00 91	103:15 81	67:45 72	65:30 70
Percentage of Special Time	10.2%	9.4%	11.8%	7.7%	7.5%

* The months of October through December are represented for the years 1948 through 1965; all other months for the years 1949 through 1966.

** In parentheses following the hours figure is the number of programs in each category.

Februaries Hours		Marches Hours		Aprils Hours		Mays Hours		Junes Hours		Julys Hours		August Hours
3:00(	2)	6:00(	4)	-		-		-		-		-
2:00(	2)	2:00(	2)	7:30(	7)	1:00(	1)	2:30(	2)	0:30(	1)	-
1:30(	1)	1:00(	1)	-		1:30(	1)	-		-		-
1:00(	1)	-		-		-		4:00(	4)	-		1:00(
3:00(	2)	-		1:00(	1)	-		0:30(	1)	-		-
-		-		1:30(	1)	1:30(	1)	-		-		-
-		-		-		-		-		-		-
1:30(	1)	1:30(	1)	2:00(	1)	-		5:00(	6)	-		-
4:30(	4)	5:30(	4)	1:00(	1)	5:00(	3)	1:00(	1)	-		1:00(
-		-		-		-		-		-		-
2:30(	2)	3:00(	2)	4:00(	3)	1:30(	1)	1:00(	1)	-		-
-		-		-		-		-		1:45(	1)	-
1:00(	1)	0:30(	1)	0:30(	1)	2:30(	3)	1:30(	2)	6:00(	7)	1:00(
10:30(	11)	4:30(	6)	15:30(	19)	8:30(	10)	8:15(	9)	4:00(	6)	4:00(
-		1:00(	1)	-		-		-		-		-
3:27(	6)	7:30(	7)	1:30(	3)	6:00(	10)	8:45(	16)	6:00(	10)	8:15(
1:30(	2)	2:30(	3)	2:30(	3)	4:00(	5)	1:30(	3)	9:30(	13)	8:00(
1:18(	2)	0:30(	1)	-		3:00(	4)	2:00(	3)	71:30(	33)	37:30(
-		-		-		-		-		-		-
3:40(	7)	6:15(	11)	3:30(	7)	3:30(	7)	2:15(	6)	2:10(	6)	1:30(
3:00(	4)	-		-		0:45(	3)	0:30(	1)	-		7:30(
-		0:30(	1)	4:30(	6)	1:00(	1)	-		-		-
5:00(	5)	6:00(	6)	3:30(	4)	5:00(	5)	4:00(	4)	-		-
10:00(	10)	13:30(	13)	7:00(	8)	2:00(	2)	8:30(	8)	4:00(	4)	5:00(
-		1:00(	1)	-		2:00(	2)	2:00(	1)	0:30(	1)	0:30(
1:30(	2)	1:00(	2)	3:00(	6)	0:30(	1)	-		2:45(	5)	-
59:55	65	63:45	67	58:30	71	49:15	60	53:15	68	108:40	87	75:15
6.8%		7.3%		6.6%		5.6%		6.1%		12.4%		8.6%

May. Thus, in five of the nine winter season months on CBS-TV, documentary was the dominant special program type.

During the collective months of January and March, more hours were pre-empted for musical variety than any other sub-category, and in June news and news analysis made up most of the special prime time.

As noted in Chapter II, CBS-TV was the only national network to employ the motion picture sub-category as a special during the period under study, and only repeat showings of the film "The Wizard of Oz" were scheduled as specials in this classification. Table 25 indicated "The Wizard of Oz" only appeared in the mid-winter months of November, December, and January; hence, the film came to be associated with the holiday season. "The Wizard of Oz" was frequently scheduled to begin earlier than 7:30 p.m., New York time, presumably to capture a young audience; thus, the four December telecasts of this film amounted to only two hours of prime time. Also, during at least two seasons, an edited 90-minute version of the two-hour film was presented.

Awards and pageants specials appeared during each month of the composite year except December on CBS-TV; however, most such specials were scheduled in September. The 11 September awards and pageants specials were all "Miss America Pageants" and "Miss America Parades" which CBS-TV televised annually from 1957 through 1965. In 1966, the annual spectacle moved to NBC-TV.

Special circus variety programs appeared more often on CBS-TV than on the other networks. Most circus specials were scheduled for the spring months of March, April, and May, although two such programs were televised in December. CBS-TV's circus specials consisted either of performances by the Ringling Brothers, Barnum and Bailey Circus, or Marineland of the Pacific. The first circus program scheduled as a CBS-TV special was tied in with the Christmas holiday season of 1955 and billed as "Christmas With the Greatest Show on Earth." In later years the program became an annual springtime television special.

Figure 14 is a pictorial translation of the monthly distribution of CBS-TV's prime time special programming. The preponderance of hours pre-empted in the summer and fall months is strikingly apparent, the pattern due, of course, to political convention, campaign, and election coverage. Since most political activity occurs only every fourth year, the pattern exhibited in Figure 14 was not typical of most years, only presidential election years. To arrive at the pattern typical of other years, time CBS-TV devoted to political programming was removed from the data. With political programs suspended, the bulk of CBS-TV's prime time special programming shifted out of the summer months into the fall and winter months. In the absence of politicals, July became the month in which fewest prime time hours were pre-empted rather than the most, and September became the leading month in time pre-empted followed by November, December, January, and October.

With the monthly distribution pattern of CBS-TV's nighttime special programming defined, Table 26 turns to the weekday distribution of this programming.

CBS-TV pre-empted more prime time during mid-week than on weekends to present special programs, with Wednesday night receiving the most pre-emptions, more than twice as many as Saturday night which received the fewest pre-emptions. Translated into percentages, 10.5

FIGURE 14

MONTHLY DISTRIBUTION PATTERN OF CBS-TV'S PRIME TIME SPECIAL PROGRAMMING

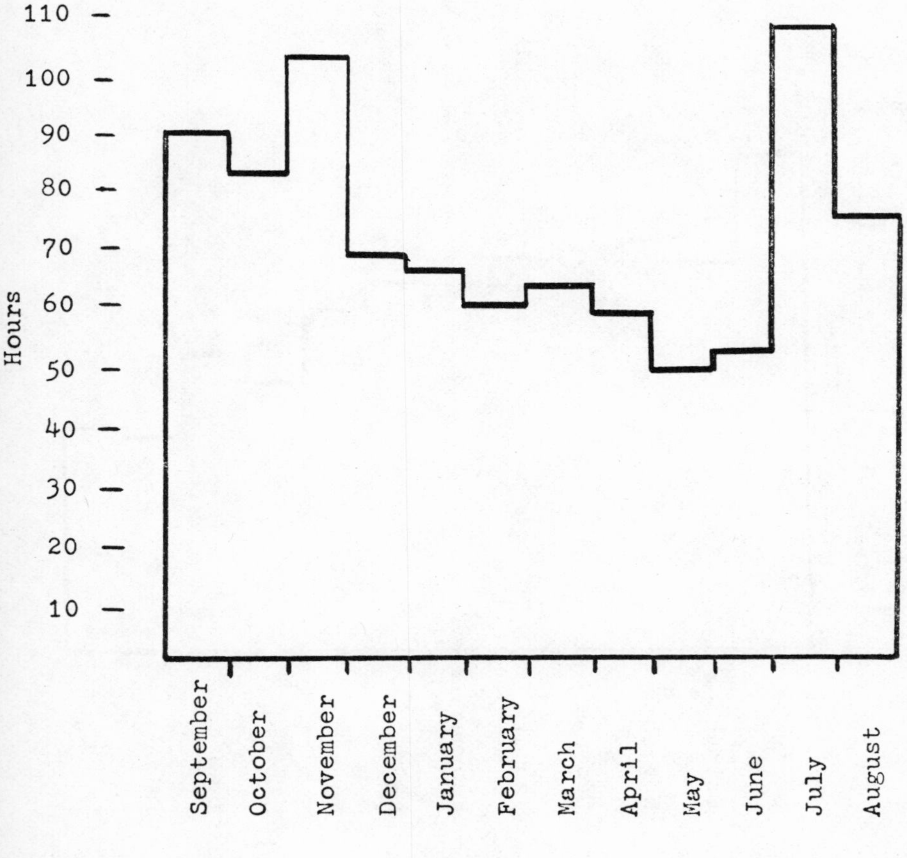

FIGURE 15

MONTHLY DISTRIBUTION PATTERN OF CBS-TV'S PRIME TIME SPECIAL PROGRAMMING, POLITICAL PROGRAMS REMOVED

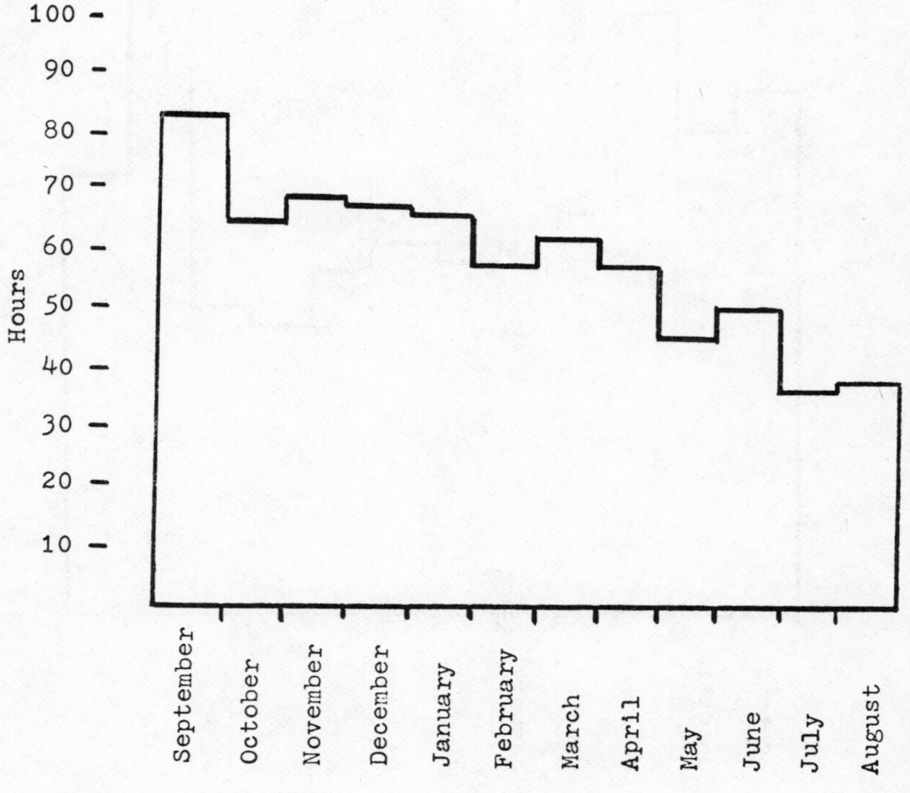

TABLE 26

DISTRIBUTION OF CBS-TV'S PRIME TIME SPECIAL PROGRAMS
BY MONTHS AND WEEKDAYS

Month	Weekday						
	Sun.	Mon.	Tues.	Wed.	Thurs.	Fri.	Sat.
September	15	10	25	23	18	13	15
October	9	11	17	20	16	9	9
November	8	18	14	13	8	9	11
December	10	12	10	11	11	11	7
January	15	6	7	15	12	9	6
February	4	8	13	13	9	12	6
March	4	10	8	15	11	10	9
April	12	7	13	9	13	13	4
May	5	5	6	15	11	10	8
June	4	7	12	15	14	14	2
July	4	8	19	20	16	11	9
August	6	7	11	13	14	14	1
Totals	96	109	155	182	153	135	87

per cent of all CBS-TV prime time special programs appeared on Sunday nights, 11.9 per cent on Monday nights, 16.9 per cent of Tuesday nights, 19.8 per cent on Wednesday nights, 16.7 per cent on Thursday nights, 14.7 per cent on Friday nights, and 9.5 per cent on Saturday nights. Thus, CBS-TV appeared reluctant to distrub its regular weekend programming, preferring to insert pre-emptive shows into its schedule during mid-week evenings.

Table 27 distributes CBS-TV's prime time special program categories by week days. This distribution produced distinct patterns with regard to some sub-categories, none in others.

TABLE 27

DISTRIBUTION OF CBS-TV'S PRIME TIME SPECIAL PROGRAM CATEGORIES BY WEEKDAYS

Category	Weekday						
Drama	Sun.	Mon.	Tue.	Wed.	Thur.	Fri.	Sat.
Action	2	2	5	1	1	1	-
Comedy	2	12	4	2	3	2	4
Crime	1	-	-	3	2	2	1
Readings	1	-	1	1	2	2	-
Fairy Tales	-	2	1	2	1	-	1
Historical	4	1	-	-	2	-	-
Motion Picture	7	-	-	-	-	-	1
Musical	4	-	2	2	2	5	2
Prestige	5	3	1	5	7	6	4
Western	-	-	1	-	-	-	-
Unclassified	2	2	3	5	1	4	-
Talks							
Actualities	-	1	-	-	1	-	-
Awards	1	1	7	-	6	5	18
Documentary	7	11	19	35	21	24	6
Instructional	-	1	-	1	-	-	-
News	12	13	18	24	16	14	4
Panel	3	3	6	20	20	6	1
Political	4	20	33	29	19	17	6
Religious	-	-	-	-	-	-	-
Speeches	4	11	14	12	17	7	7
Sports	1	3	5	2	7	14	10
Variety							
Circus	5	-	1	-	2	2	-
Comedy	13	4	6	12	8	3	6
Musical	16	14	14	22	12	15	7
Vaudeville	-	3	3	-	-	-	3
Non-classifiable	2	2	11	4	3	6	6
Totals	96	109	155	182	153	135	87

When the drama classification was taken as a whole, Table 27 showed that most prime time CBS-TV drama specials appeared on Sunday nights, fewest on Saturday nights, with a fairly even distribution Monday through Friday. Comedy drama was most frequently televised on Monday nights. Motion picture drama appeared seven out of eight times on Sunday, once on Saturday. The only western special CBS-TV presented was seen on a Tuesday night. Other drama sub-categories appeared randomly throughout the composite week.

CBS-TV prime time talks specials exhibited a more marked pattern. Most talks were scheduled on Tuesday, Wednesday and Thursday nights, fewest on Sunday nights; hence, mid-week was preferred by CBS-TV, particularly Wednesday night, for the presentation of talks specials. Awards and pageants and sports specials both were scheduled more frequently on Saturday night than any other week night on CBS. For most other talks sub-categories, Saturday was the night of fewest appearances. Documentary pre-emptions were heaviest on Wednesday nights, as were pre-emptions for news and political specials. Panel discussions appeared with equal frequency Wednesday and Thursday nights. Pre-emptions for speeches were most apt to occur during the week, least apt to occur on weekends.

CBS-TV variety specials appeared most often on Wednesday, Sunday, and Tuesday nights, least often on Saturday nights. Most circus pre-emptions came on Sunday nights, not at all on Monday, Wednesday, or Saturday. Sunday and Wednesday nights were favored for comedy variety by CBS-TV, and Wednesday nights for musical variety.

TABLE 28

CBS-TV'S PRIME TIME SPECIAL PROGRAMS DISTRIBUTED BY STARTING TIMES

Month	New York City Time							
	7:30	8:00	8:30	9:00	9:30	10:00	10:30	Other*
September	23	15	11	14	12	35	5	4
October	11	11	19	10	13	18	7	2
November	15	5	8	12	12	12	8	9
December	21	6	7	8	5	13	6	6
January	15	9	6	14	10	9	4	3
February	12	9	5	6	9	17	4	3
March	8	16	6	7	7	7	15	1
April	14	9	5	12	5	13	9	4
May	7	8	5	9	7	15	7	2
June	10	6	3	9	8	22	8	2
July	19	7	3	9	7	16	15	11
August	16	3	2	5	11	17	3	9
Totals	171	104	80	115	106	194	91	56

* Includes programs that began prior to prime time and ran into the prime time segment, and a few programs that began on quarter-hours.

The hours beginning at 10:00 p.m. New York time were most frequently pre-empted for special programs by CBS-TV, followed by the hour beginning at 7:30 p.m. There were distinctly more CBS-TV specials scheduled to begin at these times than at any others during prime time. The least frequently pre-empted time period was that beginning at 8:30 p.m. Expressed in percentages, 18.6 per cent of all CBS-TV prime time special programs began at 7:30 p.m., New York time, 11.3 per cent began at 8:00 p.m., 8.7 per cent began at 8:30, 12.5 per cent began at 9:00, 11.6 per cent began at 9:30, 21.2 per cent began at 10:00, 9.9 per cent began at 10:30, and 6.2 per cent began at other times, usually prior to 7:30. Thus, nearly half the time--49.7 per cent--CBS-TV specials either led into the prime time hour or led out of it. The percentage would be even greater if those specials beginning prior to 7:30 and running into the prime time segment were included. These tactics in scheduling special programs were similar to those employed by ABC-TV.

To note the types of specials programmed at the various prime time hours, Table 29 was constructed. This table showed CBS-TV drama specials began most frequently at 9:30 p.m., New York time, least frequently at 8:00 p.m. No special drama was scheduled to begin at 10:30 on CBS. Starting time patterns appeared to be random for most categories of drama; however, most motion picture drama (the "Wizard of Oz" film) began earlier than 7:30, probably to insure capturing the young children's attention. Musical drama most frequently pre-empted the hour beginning at 9:00 p.m., and prestige drama began most often at 9:30 and 7:30 p.m.

Most CBS-TV talks specials were scheduled at 10:00, 7:30 and 10:30, in that order. More than half all CBS talks specials were scheduled to lead into or out of prime time, with fewer talks programs scheduled during the middle hours of 8:00, 8:30, 9:00, and 9:30 p.m. Documentary specials followed this pattern closely, most such programs being scheduled at 10:00 and 7:30 p.m. CBS-TV apparently

TABLE 29

DISTRIBUTION OF CBS-TV'S PRIME TIME SPECIAL PROGRAM CATEGORIES BY STARTING TIMES

Category	New York City Time							
Drama	7:30	8:00	8:30	9:00	9:30	10:00	10:30	Other*
Action	1	1	3	1	6	-	-	-
Comedy	2	3	4	5	7	8	-	-
Crime	-	3	1	2	3	-	-	-
Readings	1	-	1	1	-	4	-	-
Fairy Tales	3	1	2	-	-	-	-	1
Historical	-	2	-	1	-	4	-	-
Motion Picture	-	-	-	1	-	-	-	7
Musical	1	1	2	7	3	3	-	-
Prestige	9	2	1	4	11	4	-	-
Western	-	-	-	-	-	1	-	-
Unclassified	1	4	5	5	1	1	-	-
Talks								
Actualities	-	-	1	-	-	-	-	1
Awards	-	4	2	-	2	21	7	2
Documentary	30	15	11	10	7	37	11	2
Instructional	-	-	-	1	-	1	-	-
News	33	12	2	4	7	16	22	5
Panel	21	3	2	3	4	23	3	-
Political	21	11	8	14	28	16	12	18
Religious	-	-	-	-	-	-	-	-
Speeches	4	6	4	12	8	6	26	6
Sports	5	3	10	8	7	2	2	5
Variety								
Circus	2	3	-	1	-	-	-	4
Comedy	10	8	7	10	-	17	-	-
Musical	23	16	10	19	4	28	-	-
Vaudeville	1	2	2	2	-	-	2	-
Non-classifiable	3	4	2	4	8	2	6	5
Totals	171	104	80	115	106	194	91	56

* Includes programs which began prior to 7:30 and ran into the prime time segment, plus a few specials which began on the quarter hour.

preferred a later starting time for most awards and pageants specials; 10:00 and 10:30 p.m. were the usual starting times for these programs, probably because most pageants were beauty contest programs designed for an adult audience. News programs began most often at 7:30 and 10:30, with few news specials scheduled in the middle prime time hours. Political programs were scheduled fairly heavily throughout the prime time period, but most often at 7:30 and 9:30, with a relatively large number beginning before 7:30 and continuing into prime time. Speeches appeared decidedly more often at the end of prime time, beginning at 10:30 p.m.

CBS-TV's variety specials were favored slightly for a 10:00 p.m. starting time, although many were programmed to begin at 7:30, 8:00, 8:30, and 9:00. Least favored times for variety were 9:30 and 10:30. Circus variety generally was scheduled to begin early at 7:30 or 8:00, again possibly to catch a young audience. Comedy variety was most frequently scheduled to begin at 10:00, never at 9:30 or 10:30. Musical variety followed the early-or-late pattern, appearing most often at 10:00 or 7:30 p.m.

CBS-TV special programs were for the most part hour and half-hour presentations: 2.5 per cent were 15 minutes long, 37.8 per cent were 30 minutes long, 1.3 per cent lasted 45 minutes, 42.2 per cent were hour-long presentations, 9.4 per cent ran 90 minutes, 1.9 per cent were two hours long, 1.2 per cent ran two-and-one-half hours, 0.6 per cent lasted three hours, and 3.1 per cent were three-and-one-half hours long. The longer programs were generally political convention coverage and election night coverage.

As with ABC-TV, most CBS-TV prime time special programming was done in the summer and fall months, due to the large amounts of time pre-empted for specials dealing with national political activity. When political programs were subtracted from the data, the pattern shifted and most pre-empted hours then fell into the fall and winter months, months in which television's available audience is largest.

CBS-TV pre-empted fewer week-end prime time hours for non-regular programming, placing most specials at mid-week. CBS-TV interrupted regular programming more frequently on Wednesday nights than on any other week nights, followed by Tuesday and Thursday. Regular Saturday night programming was least interrupted by special offerings on CBS. This was somewhat in contrast to ABC-TV's pre-emptive programming which was spread more evenly over the week, although favoring Tuesday nights slightly.

About half of CBS-TV's prime time special offerings either began the prime time segment at 7:30 p.m., or concluded prime time programming beginning at 10:00 or 10:30 p.m. Fewest CBS specials began at 8:30 p.m., most at 10:00 p.m. This early-or-late scheduling pattern was similar to that discovered for ABC-TV.

About 90 per cent of all CBS-TV evening pre-emptive programs were either 30 minutes, 60 minutes, or 90 minutes long, most being hour-long presentations.

NBC-TV

Table 30 on the following page distributes the categories of NBC-TV's pre-emptive prime time programming by months. The percentage of

TABLE 30

MONTHLY DISTRIBUTION OF NBC-TV'S PRIME TIME SPECIAL PROGRAMMING

Category	Septembers*	Octobers	Novembers	Decembers	Januaries
Drama	Hours**	Hours	Hours	Hours	Hours
Action	-	1:30(1)	-	1:00(1)	-
Comedy	-	2:30(2)	-	1:00(1)	1:00(1)
Crime	3:00(3)	2:00(2)	1:00(1)	1:00(1)	0:30(1)
Readings	-	-	-	-	-
Fairy Tales	1:00(1)	2:00(2)	2:00(2)	7:00(6)	1:00(1)
Historical	1:00(1)	4:30(4)	3:00(2)	1:00(1)	2:30(2)
Motion Picture	-	-	-	-	-
Musical	4:00(3)	1:00(1)	5:00(3)	5:30(5)	2:00(1)
Prestige	-	7:30(5)	6:00(5)	5:00(4)	-
Western	-	-	-	0:30(1)	-
Unclassified	1:00(1)	2:00(1)	-	-	1:00(1)
Talks					
Actualities	1:30(1)	3:30(1)	-	-	-
Pageants	2:30(3)	1:30(2)	1:00(1)	1:30(2)	-
Documentary	21:30(19)	7:30(9)	22:00(21)	23:30(24)	21:00(21)
Instructional	-	2:00(2)	-	1:00(1)	2:00(2)
News	14:30(23)	6:00(6)	-	10:30(14)	9:00(12)
Panel	0:30(1)	0:30(1)	1:00(1)	2:00(2)	2:00(3)
Political	10:15(16)	18:00(30)	26:30(19)	-	-
Religious	-	-	-	1:30(1)	-
Speeches	2:30(5)	1:00(2)	1:00(2)	0:30(1)	4:00(6)
Sports	8:00(6)	4:30(5)	1:00(1)	5:15(7)	9:30(6)
Variety					
Circus	-	1:00(1)	2:00(2)	-	-
Comedy	1:30(2)	9:00(9)	12:30(13)	9:00(9)	16:00(15)
Musical	6:00(6)	11:30(11)	20:30(21)	15:30(16)	11:30(12)
Vaudeville	1:00(1)	1:00(1)	2:00(1)	2:30(3)	-
Non-classifiable	2:00(2)	1:30(2)	14:00(4)	1:50(3)	3:30(3)
Totals	81:45 94	91:30 100	120:30 99	96:35 103	86:30 87
Percentage of Special Time	7.6%	8.6%	11.3%	9.0%	8.1%

* The months of October through December are represented for the years 1948 through 1965; all other months for the years 1949 through 1966.

** In parentheses following the hours figure is the number of programs in each category.

Februaries Hours	Marches Hours	Aprils Hours	Mays Hours	Junes Hours	Julys Hours	Augusts Hours
-	-	-	-	-	-	-
4:30(3)	2:30(2)	2:00(2)	-	1:00(1)	-	1:00(
4:00(3)	2:00(2)	3:30(3)	1:00(1)	3:00(3)	-	-
-	-	-	-	-	-	1:00(
1:00(1)	1:00(1)	1:00(1)	1:00(1)	1:00(1)	1:00(1)	1:00(
3:00(2)	0:30(1)	5:30(5)	2:00(2)	1:00(1)	-	-
-	-	-	-	-	-	-
2:00(2)	-	1:00(1)	-	-	-	-
4:00(3)	5:00(4)	1:30(1)	1:30(1)	-	-	-
-	-	-	1:30(1)	-	-	-
-	-	3:00(3)	-	-	-	-
-	-	1:30(1)	-	-	-	-
6:30(5)	5:30(9)	2:30(4)	9:00(9)	4:00(4)	0:30(1)	3:00(
16:00(17)	31:00(31)	19:00(21)	16:30(18)	19:00(20)	9:00(10)	13:30(1
3:00(3)	-	-	-	-	-	-
7:15(9)	7:00(7)	4:30(7)	13:30(19)	16:15(24)	12:30(19)	8:15(1
0:30(1)	-	0:30(1)	2:00(3)	2:00(3)	1:30(2)	1:00(
0:30(1)	1:00(2)	0:30(1)	0:30(1)	1:00(1)	78:30(41)	42:30(1
-	-	-	-	-	-	-
0:15(1)	1:45(3)	2:15(5)	1:00(2)	1:30(3)	0:45(2)	1:00(
1:00(1)	1:30(1)	0:30(1)	2:30(2)	4:30(5)	3:30(3)	5:00(
-	2:00(2)	1:00(1)	-	-	-	-
11:00(11)	7:00(7)	9:00(9)	9:00(9)	2:30(3)	1:00(1)	4:00(
17:00(17)	16:30(16)	17:00(17)	12:00(12)	6:30(7)	1:00(1)	3:00(
-	3:30(3)	3:30(1)	1:00(1)	7:30(4)	2:00(2)	1:00(
1:00(1)	0:30(1)	1:00(1)	0:30(1)	-	0:45(2)	-
82:30 81	88:15 92	80:15 86	74:30 83	70:45 80	112:00 85	85:15 6
7.7%	8.3%	7.5%	6.9%	6.6%	10.5%	7.9%

special time indicated for each month was figured against NBC-TV's total prime time pre-empted hours: 1,070 hours and 20 minutes.

As with the other networks, political programs had a considerable influence on the monthly pattern displayed by NBC-TV's nighttime pre-emptive programming. Politicals helped make the composite months of November, July, and October the months in which most prime time was pre-empted by NBC-TV during the period under study. However, the prime factor in NBC's pre-emptive programming was documentary, which constituted the largest single sub-category. Documentary was the dominant sub-category during the months of January, March, April, May, June, September, and December. Politicals predominated in the months of July, August, October, and November. During one composite month, February, musical variety was the dominant category.

Figure 16 is a graphic portrayal of NBC-TV's prime time special programming distributed by months. The most obvious features were the prominence of July and November as the months in which NBC has pre-empted most prime time hours.

When political programs were subtracted from NBC-TV's special offerings, as in Figure 17, a seasonal influence on that programming was apparent. The mid-summer months of July and August became the months in which fewest prime time hours were pre-empted. November remained first-ranked in amount of pre-empted prime time, followed most closely by December, March, and January, in that order. A steady and pronounced decline in the amount of prime time pre-emptions between March and August emerged when politicals were removed from the data; thus, NBC-TV's nighttime non-regular programming waxed and waned with

FIGURE 16

MONTHLY DISTRIBUTION PATTERN OF NBC-TV'S PRIME TIME SPECIAL PROGRAMMING

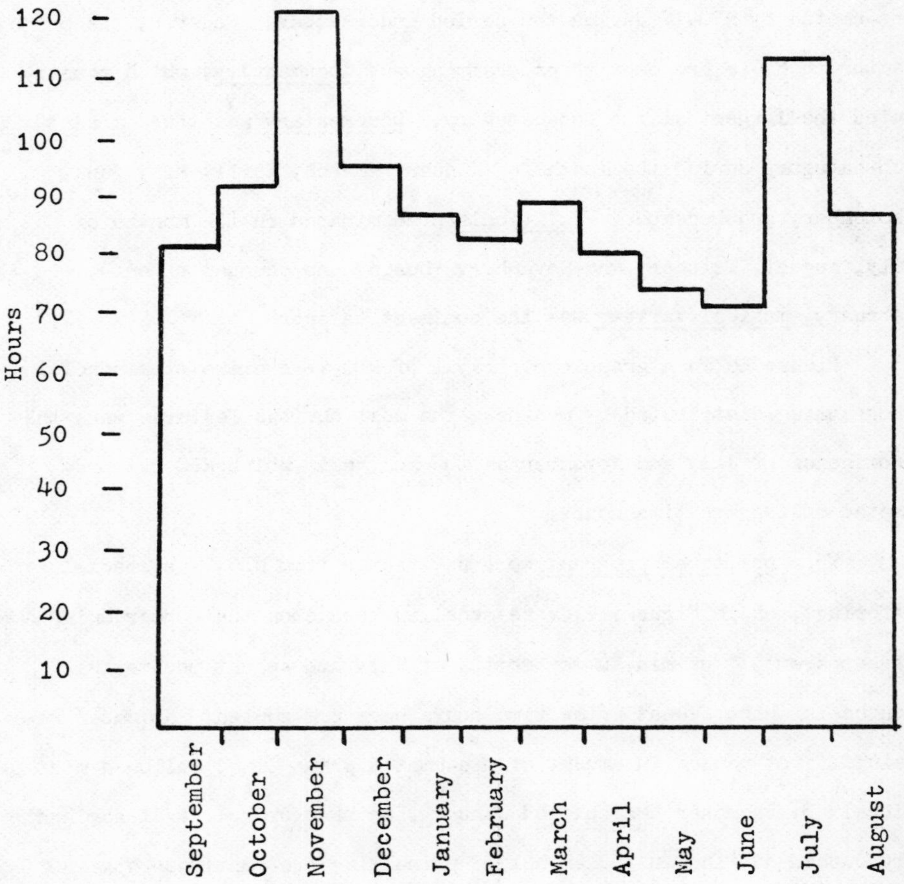

FIGURE 17

MONTHLY DISTRIBUTION PATTERN OF NBC-TV'S PRIME TIME SPECIAL PROGRAMMING, <u>POLITICAL</u> PROGRAMS REMOVED

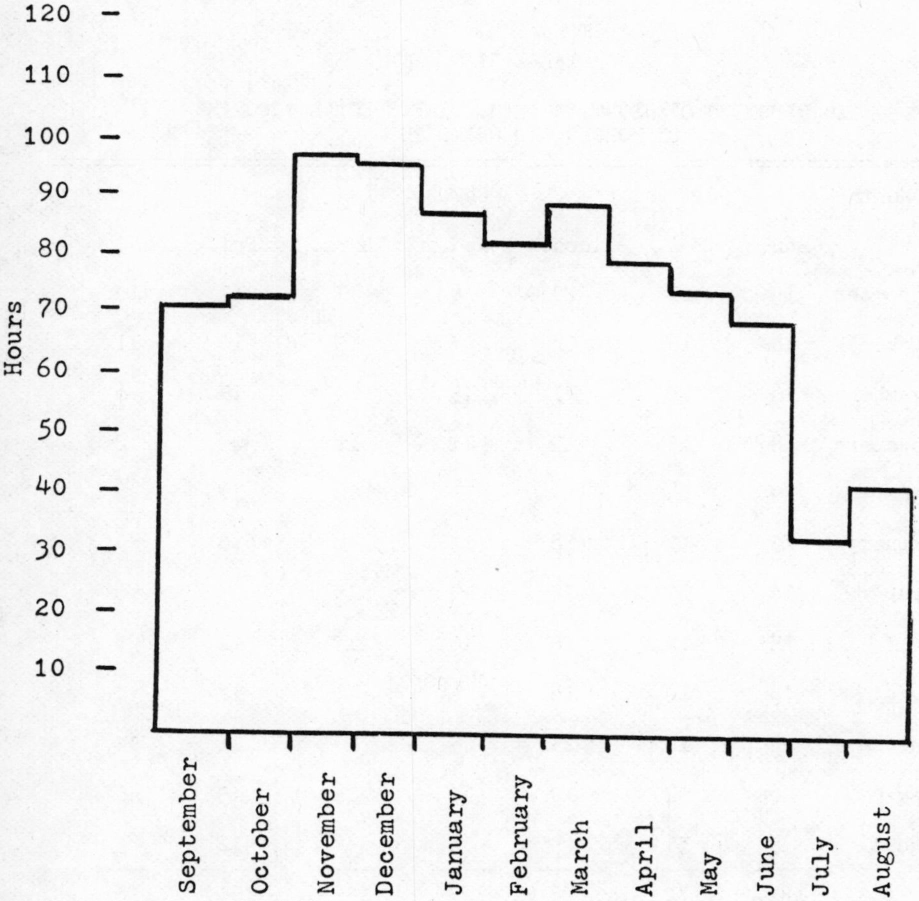

the winter season. This was roughly comparable with CBS-TV's special programming, not so much with ABC-TV's, which exhibited a more even pattern throughout the year when political programs were not considered.

Table 31 shows that NBC-TV offered most special programs on Tuesday nights during the years covered by this study; 21.5 per cent of all nighttime NBC-TV special programs have interrupted the Tuesday night

TABLE 31

DISTRIBUTION OF NBC-TV'S PRIME TIME SPECIAL PROGRAMS BY MONTHS AND WEEKDAYS

Month	Weekday						
	Sun.	Mon.	Tues.	Wed.	Thurs.	Fri.	Sat.
September	10	19	22	8	12	13	10
October	14	16	22	7	15	15	11
November	16	12	21	15	14	15	6
December	18	15	15	11	11	25	8
January	9	14	19	11	8	18	8
February	12	13	18	13	8	8	9
March	16	10	22	14	15	7	8
April	15	10	16	16	10	11	8
May	6	20	18	4	11	17	7
June	4	12	25	5	13	11	10
July	6	14	19	13	14	13	6
August	5	16	9	8	8	12	5
Totals	131	171	226	125	139	165	96

schedule. Saturday nights have sustained the fewest pre-emptions. The percentages of all NBC-TV prime time special programs appearing on the various weeknights are: 12.4 per cent on Sunday, 16.2 per cent on Monday, 21.5 per cent on Tuesday, 11.9 per cent on Wednesday, 13.2 per cent on Thursday, 15.7 per cent on Friday, and 9.1 per cent on Saturday. NBC-TV's fewer pre-emptions on weekends, more pre-emptions during midweek compared to CBS-TV's pattern of scheduling in this respect, while ABC-TV's pre-emptions were more evenly distributed throughout the days of the week.

The categorical weekday distribution of NBC-TV's prime time special programming appears in Table 32. NBC-TV's special drama shows appeared on Sunday night more frequently than on any other night of the week, least frequently on Saturday night. There appeared to be no real pattern of drama programming during the balance of the composite week. Most comedy and prestige drama was televised on Sunday night by NBC-TV; however, no marked scheduling patterns in the drama sub-categories appeared.

NBC-TV talks specials most frequently pre-empted time on Tuesday, Monday, and Friday nights, in that order. Fewest pre-emptions for talks programs were made on Sunday night. Awards and pageants were fairly evenly distributed throughout the week. Tuesdays were definitely favored for documentary specials on NBC. More time on Saturday night was pre-empted for NBC news specials than for any other category; however, no marked weekday preference for news specials was evident. Least political programming was done on Sunday, most on Tuesday. NBC-TV sports shows pre-empted more time on Friday than on any other weeknight.

TABLE 32

DISTRIBUTION OF NBC-TV'S PRIME TIME SPECIAL PROGRAM CATEGORIES BY WEEKDAYS

Category	Weekday						
Drama	Sun.	Mon.	Tue.	Wed.	Thur.	Fri.	Sat.
Action	-	1	1	-	-	-	-
Comedy	6	-	3	3	-	1	-
Crime	5	3	6	2	1	3	-
Readings	-	-	1	-	-	-	-
Fairy Tale	4	1	4	3	2	5	-
Historical	1	1	2	4	4	4	5
Motion Picture	-	-	-	-	-	-	-
Musical	4	-	2	3	2	4	1
Prestige	9	6	2	1	4	1	-
Western	-	-	-	1	-	1	-
Unclassified	4	-	-	1	-	-	1
Talks							
Actualities	-	2	-	1	-	-	-
Awards	5	8	8	6	3	5	8
Documentary	32	35	75	21	24	31	6
Instructional	-	2	-	1	1	4	-
News	14	24	27	15	22	24	27
Panel	2	6	3	2	1	3	3
Political	2	21	35	18	25	16	12
Religious	-	-	-	-	-	-	1
Speeches	1	10	7	4	7	4	1
Sports	2	7	6	1	3	16	5
Variety							
Circus	-	-	1	-	3	1	1
Comedy	10	18	17	18	8	15	6
Musical	21	20	21	16	26	21	14
Vaudeville	5	2	2	-	2	5	2
Non-classifiable	4	4	3	4	1	1	3
Totals	131	171	226	125	139	165	96

Variety special programming on NBC-TV appeared with nearly uniform frequency Sunday through Friday nights; however, there was a marked decline in interruptions for variety shows on Saturday night. The scheduling pattern for variety sub-categories appeared to be random except that fewest such programs were televised on Saturday nights.

TABLE 33

NBC-TV'S PRIME TIME SPECIAL PROGRAMS DISTRIBUTED BY STARTING TIMES

Month	New York City Time							
	7:30	8:00	8:30	9:00	9:30	10:00	10:30	Other*
September	17	9	6	10	15	22	12	3
October	15	9	13	19	10	29	4	1
November	14	6	8	24	8	24	7	8
December	12	14	16	13	9	30	5	4
January	7	8	11	14	12	26	4	5
February	13	7	8	17	9	24	-	3
March	18	9	3	18	14	20	8	2
April	14	4	10	13	10	27	5	3
May	13	6	11	9	9	28	5	2
June	9	9	13	10	12	16	7	4
July	21	7	8	10	8	12	6	13
August	8	5	14	6	4	14	1	11
Totals	161	93	121	163	120	272	64	59

* Includes programs which began prior to 7:30 p.m. and ran into the prime time segment, plus a few specials which began on quarter-hours.

As did ABC-TV and CBS-TV, NBC-TV scheduled most of its prime time special programs to begin at 10:00 p.m. New York City time. The next most frequently pre-empted time periods on NBC-TV were those beginning at 9:00 and 7:30 p.m., the former favored by only 0.1 per cent over the latter. Of NBC-TV's total prime time special programs, 15.3 per cent began at 7:30, 8.8 per cent began at 8:00, 11.5 per cent began at 8:30, 15.4 per cent at 9:00, 11.5 per cent began at 9:30, 25.8 per cent began at 10:00, 6.1 per cent began at 10:30, and 5.6 per cent began at other times. About half the programs--47.2 per cent--either began the prime time period at 7:30, or concluded it beginning at 10:00 or 10:30. In this respect, NBC-TV's scheduling of non-regular programs was highly similar to that of ABC-TV and CBS-TV.

To further refine the analysis of NBC-TV's specials scheduling, Table 34 distributes the categories by starting times.

Special prime time drama on NBC-TV most frequently pre-empted the time periods beginning at 7:30 and 10:00 p.m., New York time. This early-or-late pattern was followed in scheduling comedy drama on NBC-TV. Crime drama was usually scheduled to begin at 10:00 p.m., while fairy tales and puppet/cartoon drama was most frequently televised at 7:30 and 8:00 p.m. probably to collect a youthful audience. Prestige drama, often 90-minutes long and oriented toward an adult audience, began most of the time at 9:30, usually filling the 9:30 to 11:00 time period.

NBC-TV talks specials also exhibited the early-or-late scheduling pattern. The most favored starting time by far for NBC-TV's talks pre-emptions was 10:00 p.m., followed by 7:30 p.m. Talks specials began

TABLE 34

DISTRIBUTION OF NBC-TV'S PRIME TIME SPECIAL PROGRAM CATEGORIES BY STARTING TIMES

Category	New York City Time							
Drama	7:30	8:00	8:30	9:00	9:30	10:00	10:30	Other*
Action	-	-	-	-	1	1	-	-
Comedy	4	1	1	2	-	5	-	-
Crime	-	1	2	2	2	12	-	1
Readings	1	-	-	-	-	-	-	-
Fairy Tale	10	8	1	-	-	-	-	-
Historical	5	1	2	3	7	3	-	-
Motion Picture	-	-	-	-	-	-	-	-
Musical	5	1	3	4	-	1	-	2
Prestige	5	-	1	1	10	3	-	3
Western	-	-	2	-	-	-	-	-
Unclassified	-	-	1	1	1	2	-	1
Talks								
Actualities	2	-	-	1	-	-	-	-
Awards	3	3	4	6	1	17	9	-
Documentary	39	12	25	19	26	93	7	3
Instructional	3	1	1	3	-	-	-	-
News	32	21	16	10	23	20	25	6
Panel Talks	3	4	4	1	2	4	1	1
Political	17	6	20	19	24	15	9	19
Religious	-	-	-	-	1	-	-	-
Speeches	4	-	3	7	4	6	8	2
Sports	4	1	1	3	5	13	2	11
Variety								
Circus	3	1	-	1	-	1	-	-
Comedy	4	13	17	41	3	12	-	2
Musical	11	16	11	34	9	55	3	-
Vaudeville	2	2	5	3	-	3	-	3
Non-classifiable	4	1	1	2	1	6	-	5
Totals	161	93	121	163	120	272	64	59

* Includes programs which began prior to the prime time segment and ran into it, plus a few specials which began at the quarter-hour.

least frequently at 8:00 p.m. Substantially more awards and pageants specials began at 10:00 p.m. on NBC. These late-starting awards programs usually consisted of beauty contests and the Motion Picture Academy Awards presentations. Table 34 indicated NBC-TV exercised a strong preference for scheduling documentary specials to begin at 10:00 p.m. also. Most documentaries began either at 10:00 or 7:30 p.m., following the early-or-late pattern, with substantially fewer offerings at 7:30. News programs seemed to appear randomly at the various time periods on NBC-TV; however, there was a tendency for news specials to begin at 7:30. Political specials most often pre-empted time beginning at 9:30, least often the time beginning at 8:00 p.m., although the pattern with regard to politicals was quite erratic. NBC-TV sports specials were inclined to begin at 10:00 p.m.

The scheduling pattern exhibited by NBC-TV's variety pre-emptions differed from that of drama and talks in that the early-late aspect was not apparent; instead, most variety specials were scheduled to begin at 9:00 and 10:00 p.m. Circus variety, presumably child oriented, appeared early for the most part, usually beginning at 7:30. Comedy variety most frequently pre-empted the 9:00 p.m. period. Musical variety, NBC-TV's largest variety sub-category, set the basic pattern for this classification, usually beginning at 10:00 or 9:00 p.m.

Turning to program length characteristics of NBC-TV's prime time pre-emptive programming, more than half the specials were hour-long presentations, and just over one-fourth were 30-minute shows. On a percentage basis, 1.0 per cent of all NBC-TV's evening pre-emptions lasted 15 minutes, 26.5 per cent were 30-minutes long, 58.9 per cent were one hour shows, 7.4 per cent lasted 90 minutes, 1.8 per cent ran two hours, 0.6 per cent were two-and-one-half hour programs, 0.5 per cent were three hour shows, and 3.3 per cent were three-and-one-half hours long. Most of the longest programs were politicals consisting of convention and election coverage; however, NBC-TV has pre-empted entire evenings for a few other special presentations. In January of 1965 and again in 1966, NBC televised the Orange Bowl football games which took up most of prime time those nights. On March 16, 1966, the Gemini Eight space flight coverage pre-empted the prime time hours. On September 2, 1963, NBC devoted an evening to an examination of the Negroes' struggle for civil rights in a program titled "The American Revolution of '63." In September, 1965, NBC-TV's "American White Paper: United States Foreign Policy" lasted an entire evening. An actuality program covering Pope Paul VI's brief visit to the United States in October, 1965, filled the prime time hours on NBC-TV, and also appeared on the other networks.

To briefly summarize, the monthly distribution pattern of NBC-TV's prime time special programming reflected that network's coverage of national political activity. Months in which such activity occurred showed the greatest amount of pre-empted prime time. This put a large proportion of NBC-TV's special programming into the summer months. When political coverage was removed from the data, the monthly distribution pattern showed the summer months contained the fewest number of pre-empted prime time hours, while the mid-winter months contained the greatest. This would seem to indicate NBC-TV's special programming was keyed to television audience usage patterns (except for political programs), i.e., viewers tend to make greater use of television during fall and winter months, less during spring and summer months.

NBC-TV pre-empted time on Tuesday nights more than on any other weeknight. The network's Saturday night schedule was least frequently interrupted by special programs.

NBC-TV indicated a distinct preference for scheduling specials to begin at 10:00 p.m., New York time; 31.9 per cent of all NBC's prime time specials fell within the 10:00 to 11:00 time period.

Hour-long programs dominated NBC-TV's nighttime non-regular program schedule, comprising 58.9 per cent of all prime time specials. About one-fourth the programs were 30 minute offerings.

DuMont

Prime time special programming on the DuMont Television Network was sparse; for this reason, a monthly distribution table for DuMont did not seem necessary. Most of DuMont's pre-emptive programming occurred in response to political activity, news developments, important speeches, and sports events. The pattern of this programming, as illustrated in Figure 18, showed most prime time pre-emptions on DuMont in the political convention month of July, with October and November receiving somewhat fewer pre-emptions. Spring months contained the fewest pre-emptions. With political specials removed, as in Figure 19, the most conspicuous change occurred in the month of July, while the other months remained relatively unchanged. In the absence of political programs, fall and winter months received the most DuMont pre-emptions, spring and summer months the fewest.

FIGURE 18

MONTHLY DISTRIBUTION PATTERN OF DuMONT TELEVISION'S
PRIME TIME SPECIAL PROGRAMMING

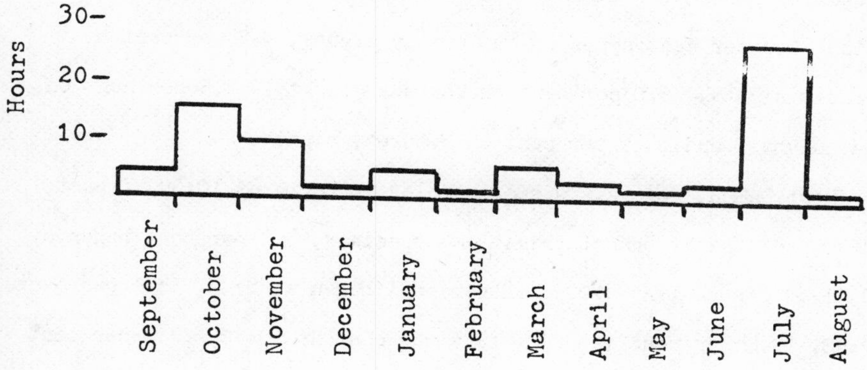

FIGURE 19

MONTHLY DISTRIBUTION PATTERN OF DuMONT TELEVISION'S
PRIME TIME SPECIAL PROGRAMMING,
POLITICAL PROGRAMS REMOVED

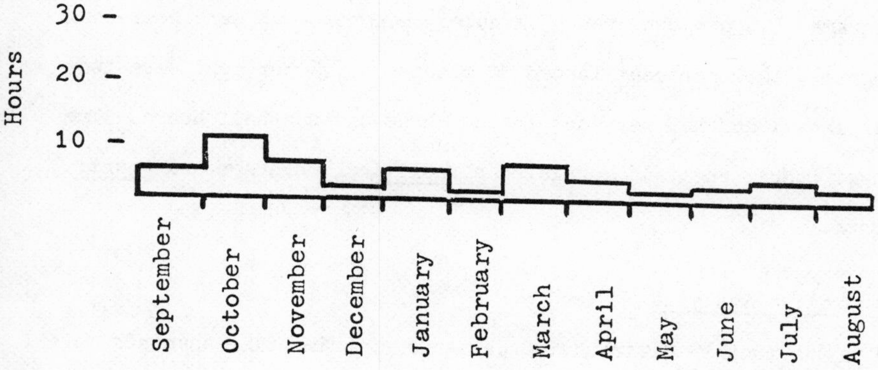

The Thursday and Tuesday evening DuMont schedules were most often interrupted by special programs, while the Sunday night schedule was least disturbed. Seven per cent of all DuMont's nighttime non-regular programming pre-empted time on Sunday nights, 11.1 per cent on Monday nights, 20.8 per cent appeared on Tuesday nights, 9.7 per cent on Wednesday nights, 25.0 per cent on Thursday nights, 12.5 per cent on Friday nights, and 13.9 per cent on Saturday nights.

Most DuMont specials were scheduled to begin at 10:30, fewest at 7:30. Of the 72 DuMont prime time specials, 4.2 per cent began at 7:30, 15.3 per cent at 8:00, 1.4 per cent began at 8:30, 18.1 per cent at 9:00, 19.4 per cent at 9:30, 12.5 per cent at 10:00, 22.2 per cent at 10:30, and 6.9 per cent began at other times.

There were not enough programs in the various classifications to establish any patterns of scheduling by categories.

With regard to the length of DuMont evening special programs, exactly 50 per cent were half-hour shows, 7.0 per cent were 15-minute programs, 3.0 per cent ran 45 minutes, 6.0 per cent were hour-long programs, 14.0 per cent lasted 90 minutes, 15.5 per cent were two-hour shows, and 4.5 per cent lasted three-and-one-half hours. The longer DuMont specials consisted of political coverage and sports events.

Comparative Analysis

The monthly distribution patterns of prime time specials on all the national networks displayed some fundamental similarities. The patterns, in each case reflecting response to national political campaign activity, showed a great number of pre-empted hours in mid-summer and late-fall months, fewer pre-empted hours in mid-winter and spring months. The patterns underlying this political special programming were also similar in each case. When the political influence was removed from the data, the monthly distribution patterns of each network's prime time special programming were restructured to show the fewest number of pre-empted hours in mid-summer and the greatest number in fall and winter months. The latter pattern appeared closely allied to general patterns of television audience usage. Thus, except for political programs appearing in the summer, most specials televised during prime time by all the networks were scheduled during months when the television audience was the largest, i.e., fall and winter.

In Table 35, the percentage of each network's prime time special programming which appeared during each month of the year is listed for purposes of comparison. Political programs were included in the table.

July ranked as the month during which most prime time hours were pre-empted on all networks except NBC-TV where November was the leading month followed by July. July and November appeared among the first three months ranked by amount of prime time pre-empted on all four national networks.

The percentages of pre-empted time appearing in each month on ABC, NBC, and CBS were generally quite alike. The largest difference occurred in the composite months of August when ABC-TV presented a larger proportion of its pre-empted time than the other networks. DuMont's pattern differed markedly during some months, such as October, December, and February, and was quite similar in others, such as September, November, and January.

TABLE 35

COMPARISON OF THE MONTHLY DISTRIBUTION OF PRIME TIME SPECIAL PROGRAMS, ALL NETWORKS

ABC-TV		CBS-TV		NBC-TV		DuMont	
Month	%*	Month	%	Month	%	Month	%
Sept.	8.7	Sept.	10.2	Sept.	7.6	Sept.	6.0
Oct.	7.3	Oct.	9.4	Oct.	8.6	Oct.	20.8
Nov.	10.7	Nov.	11.8	Nov.	11.3	Nov.	12.8
Dec.	7.2	Dec.	7.7	Dec.	9.0	Dec.	0.5
Jan.	6.1	Jan.	7.5	Jan.	8.1	Jan.	5.4
Feb.	5.7	Feb.	6.8	Feb.	7.7	Feb.	0.3
March	5.9	March	7.3	March	8.3	March	7.4
April	7.3	April	6.6	April	7.5	April	4.2
May	6.1	May	5.6	May	6.9	May	2.0
June	5.9	June	6.1	June	6.6	June	2.7
July	15.5	July	12.4	July	10.5	July	35.9
Aug.	13.6	Aug.	8.6	Aug.	7.9	Aug.	2.0
Totals	100.0%		100.0%		100.0%		100.0%

*Indicates percentage of each network's total number of pre-empted prime time hours.

Weekday distribution of special programming is compared in Table 36, with the percentage of each network's total prime time

TABLE 36

COMPARISON OF THE WEEK-DAY DISTRIBUTION OF PRIME TIME SPECIAL PROGRAMMING, ALL NETWORKS

ABC-TV		CBS-TV		NBC-TV		DuMONT	
Day	%*	Day	%	Day	%	Day	%
Sun.	14.7	Sun.	10.5	Sun.	12.4	Sun.	7.0
Mon.	15.3	Mon.	11.9	Mon.	16.2	Mon.	11.1
Tues.	17.0	Tues.	16.9	Tues.	21.5	Tues.	20.8
Wed.	13.6	Wed.	19.8	Wed.	11.9	Wed.	9.7
Thurs.	14.2	Thurs.	16.7	Thurs.	13.2	Thurs.	25.0
Fri.	13.3	Fri.	14.7	Fri.	15.7	Fri.	12.5
Sat.	11.9	Sat.	9.5	Sat.	9.1	Sat.	13.9
Totals	100.0%		100.0%		100.0%		100.0%

*Indicates percentage of prime time special programs.

special programs indicated. On all networks mid-week schedules--Tuesday, Wednesday, and Thursday--were interrupted most frequently for nighttime non-regular programs, while weekend schedules were disturbed the least. DuMont again presented a departure from the pattern offering the fewest number of specials on Sunday nights and Wednesday nights.

Ten p.m., New York time, was the most frequently pre-empted hour for occasional programs on all networks except DuMont, which favored a 10:30 starting time for its specials. Most often, then, specials were scheduled to conclude the network's prime time program feeds to local stations. The next most frequently pre-empted time period was

TABLE 37

COMPARISON OF PRIME TIME SPECIAL PROGRAM STARTING TIMES, ALL NETWORKS

ABC-TV		CBS-TV		NBC-TV		DuMONT	
Time	%*	Time	%	Time	%	Time	%
7:30	16.7	7:30	18.6	7:30	15.3	7:30	4.2
8:00	6.9	8:00	11.3	8:00	8.8	8:00	15.3
8:30	7.9	8:30	8.7	8:30	11.5	8:30	1.4
9:00	9.7	9:00	12.5	9:00	15.4	9:00	18.1
9:30	12.9	9:30	11.6	9:30	11.5	9:30	19.4
10:00	22.6	10:00	21.2	10:00	25.8	10:00	12.5
10:30	16.5	10:30	9.9	10:30	6.1	10:30	22.2
Other**	6.8	Other	6.2	Other	5.6	Other	6.9
Totals	100.0%		100.0%		100.0%		100.0%

* Indicates percentage of special prime time programs.

**Includes programs which began on the quarter-hour and programs which began prior to 7:30, running into prime time.

that beginning at 7:30 p.m. (however, note the difference between 7:30 and 9:00 p.m. on NBC-TV was only 0.1 per cent). Hence, the second most often used scheduling device regarding specials was to use them to lead into the prime time segment. This set up what has been termed in this chapter an early-or-late pattern in each network's special program scheduling.

There are many reasons why special programs were scheduled at particular times on particular nights during particular months. The early-or-late specials scheduling pattern observed in ABC-TV's, CBS-TV's, and NBC-TV's prime time special programming might be explained in part by the fact that a program's rating tends to affect the rating of the following program. For example, a program following a highly rated program is also apt to receive a relatively high rating; conversely, a low rated program is apt to depress the rating of the following program. In view of this, network programmers might tend to schedule specials for which low ratings are anticipated at the end of the prime time period to avoid lowering the ratings of other prime time regular programs. Or, specials for which high ratings are anticipated might be scheduled at the beginning of the prime time hours to boost ratings of following shows.

Type of audience desired for a program also, no doubt, affects the time and possibly the day on which it is scheduled. Programs directed at children would logically be offered early in the evening hours before the youngsters' bedtime. Programs directed at a primarily adult audience could be scheduled later in the evening. Tables 24, 29, and 34 indicated that ABC-TV, CBS-TV, and NBC-TV tended to televise fairy tale and puppet/cartoon drama and circus variety programs, specials with a great deal of appeal to young people, at early hours. CBS-TV's "The Wizard of Oz" was also scheduled early in the evening. On the other hand, specials with little or no appeal for children were most frequently offered late in the evening: prestige drama, awards and pageants, documentary. Of course, the pattern is not without its exceptions. Much documentary programming was scheduled early, as was news, political programs, and other programs of interest primarily to adults.

Clues to some of the factors network program planners consider in scheduling special programs was found in program research material obtained from ABC-TV. In November, 1965, Gene Klimek of ABC-TV's program research department, was investigating various alternatives relative to the scheduling of "Alice in Wonderland," a special which appeared on ABC at 8:00 p.m. Wednesday, March 30, 1966. Klimek's recommendation to schedule the special in the 8:00 to 9:00 time period was based on three primary considerations: 1) sets-in-use figures, 2) rating strength of alternative "lead-in" (preceeding) programs, and 3) competition.[1] Klimek's report stated:

> Scheduled at 8:00PM Wednesday, ALICE IN WONDERLAND will utilize the highest sets-in-use hour of the evening. With 8:00-9:00pm set usage exceeding 67%, ALICE would be slotted in a time period with a potential 5% greater than that available at 7:30-8:30PM (64.1). In addition, the 8:00PM starting time would offer an estimated 4,370,000 viewers above the total number watching between 7:30 and 8:30PM.

---

[1]Interdepartmental correspondence, ABC-TV, letter from Gene Klimek to William Firman, November 24, 1965.

> Slotted at 8:00PM on Wednesday evening, ALICE IN WONDERLAND would benefit greatly from the BATMAN series, a lead-in far more compatible with the Lewis Carrol fantasy than the diverse local offerings leading into a 7:30PM telecast.
> . . . note that CBS competition for both BATMAN and the ALICE IN WONDERLAND special is showing further signs of decline. Lost In Space registered a 29.6 NTI share in the November 1 report, a season low for the program.[2]

Klimek's report pointed out that a lead-in program with a high rating can strengthen the rating of the following program: "Even a strong special, with inherent recruiting power far beyond that of a regularly scheduled series, can add to its rating with a strong lead-in."[3]

Another ABC-TV time period analysis, this one for the 1966 "Miss America Pageant," made a recommendation based primarily on competition and strength of lead-in program. This proposal concluded with the statement,

> . . . the Miss America Pageant will have its greatest chance of capitalizing on the available Saturday evening audience by being scheduled on ABC-TV at 9:30 PM following the Lawrence Welk Show and directly opposite a proven weak program, The Loner [on CBS-TV].[4]

The 1966 "Miss America Pageant," however, was not televised by ABC-TV but appeared on NBC-TV Saturday, September 10, 1966, at 10:00 p.m., New York time.

Another reason for scheduling a television special on a certain weekday at a certain time might be to break up the existing viewing

---

[2] Ibid.

[3] Ibid.

[4] Interdepartmental correspondence, ABC-TV, letter from Joseph Schrier to Jerry Bradouw, November 12, 1965.

pattern for that period. The hope is that the redistributed viewing pattern will favor the network presenting the special. In placing a strong special early in prime time the audience it collects could be expected to flow from the special into the regular programs which follow, bolstering their ratings and perhaps introducing new viewers to them.

Over the scheduling of certain kinds of specials, the networks can exercise little or no control. Live coverage of events must, of course, be scheduled to coincide with the events. Pre-emptions for "instant" news specials are dictated more by the urgency of the news than other considerations. Sponsors may declare preferences for certain time periods over others. In short, not all specials scheduling was strategic.

Probable conclusions that arose from this examination of specials scheduling were that the networks apparently avoided pre-empting their own strong regular programs and avoided scheduling specials against strong competition. (When this study's data can be compared with an examination of regular television programming,[5] firm evidence in this area should appear.) Coupled with the fact that most often, specials were scheduled as lead-outs of prime time, possibly to avoid disturbing regular programs and their audiences as little as possible, the networks appeared to program specials in "safe" time periods, i.e., in time periods where the specials would meet weak competition and have

---

[5]Data on regular network programs that might possibly be used for such a comparison are being compiled by Professor Lawrence W. Lichty of the University of Wisconsin.

a better chance of succeeding in gathering a large audience, or in periods of relatively low sets-in-use when even if the specials did poorly in the ratings the consequences were not serious.

This chapter has demonstrated certain definite patterns existed in the distribution of prime time special programs by years, months, days, and time periods, and further, distinct similarities in these patterns existed among the networks. These patterns and similarities suggested that although special programming was non-regular in nature, its scheduling in large measure followed a certain logic and was not entirely random.

CHAPTER IV

NETWORK TELEVISION PRIME TIME SPECIALS PROGRAMMED AGAINST OTHER PRIME TIME SPECIALS

Part of this study's objective was to determine the extent to which the various networks scheduled evening special programs on the same date and time, thereby pitting special against special in the competition for audience. Criticism has occasionally been directed against the networks for programming specials against specials.[1] TV Guide magazine once reported a proposal offered by ABC-TV president Tom Moore suggesting the networks enter into a gentlemen's agreement not to schedule specials competitively so that viewers would not be forced to choose between two or three attractive programs.[2] However, to this date apparently no such arrangement has been made.

Competitive specials scheduling involves the usual concepts of counter and cross programming, i.e., setting programs of a dissimilar type (counter programming) or a similar type (cross programming) against each other. However, a situation unique to specials programming has arisen in many cases; there has been a tendency for all television networks to cover important events through special programs. This has frequently resulted in simultaneous duplication of program material

---

[1] "Webs Getting More Statesmanlike in Answering Specs with Specs . . . ," Variety, January 18, 1967, p. 31.

[2] "As We See It," TV Guide, Wisconsin Edition, May 29, 1965, p. 4.

on two or more networks, carrying the concept of cross programming to an ultimate degree. Prime examples of simultaneous duplication are the Republican and Democratic national conventions which since 1948 have always been covered by all national television networks. Important Presidential speeches are frequently broadcast simultaneously by two or more networks. Simultaneous duplication is a significant programming phenomenon since it greatly increases the distribution of program material broadcast in this manner.

Programs can be simultaneously duplicated in one of three ways: 1) through separate coverage of an event by each network involved; 2) through "pooled" coverage, whereby one network originates the program and supplies it to participating networks which in turn feed it to their local affiliates, or 3) through a combination of the first two methods, which may be termed a "semi-pooled" arrangement. An example of the third method would be pooled video coverage with separate commentary by each network involved, such as has been the case with many Presidential addresses.

The degree of similarity in the duplicated program material appearing on the networks depends, of course, on the method of duplication employed. Pooled coverage results in absolutely identical offerings by each network carrying the program. Programs televised through a semi-pooled arrangement are very similar but not completely identical. Separate coverage results in the least similar programs; however, in all cases the program subject material is being duplicated simultaneously.

In analyzing the data to ascertain the frequency with which prime time specials were scheduled against other specials, a distinction was made between simultaneously duplicated programs and others. To differentiate between the two groups, one was termed "simultaneously duplicated" and the other "non-duplicated competitive," although, of course, the duplicated specials were also competitive. The term "competitive" as used throughout this chapter refers only to specials versus other specials, disregarding the competitive aspect of specials versus regular programs. Prime time specials which were duplicated but not simultaneously were not included in this analysis since the concern here was with competitive programming. Non-duplicated specials were considered competitive if they overlapped by at least 15 minutes.

ABC-TV

Of the 629 prime time special programs ABC-TV telecast during the period encompassed by this study, 108, or 17.2 per cent, were duplicated simultaneously on one or more other networks. Seventy-one ABC-TV prime time specials, 11.3 per cent, were scheduled against other specials. Thus, over one-fourth of ABC-TV's total prime time special programming--28.5 per cent--competed with special programs on other networks.

With regard to the 108 ABC-TV simultaneously duplicated specials, 87 appeared on all networks (including DuMont while it was in operation), nine received competition from CBS specials, five from DuMont, four from NBC, two from NBC and DuMont, and one was scheduled on all networks except DuMont.

Only certain kinds of specials tended to be duplicated simultaneously by the networks. As indicated in Table 38, nearly all such programs fell into the talks classification, with the most frequently

TABLE 38

ABC-TV SIMULTANEOUSLY DUPLICATED PRIME TIME SPECIAL PROGRAM CATEGORIES

Category	No. of Programs	Percentage of Total Duplicated
Drama		
Unclassified Drama	1	0.9
Talks		
Actualities	1	0.9
Awards and Pageants	2	1.9
Documentary	1	0.9
News and News Analysis	11	10.2
Panel Discussions	1	0.9
Political Programs	51	47.2
Speeches	31	28.7
Variety		
Musical Variety	1	0.9
Non-classifiable*	8	7.5
Totals	108	100.0%

*This classification included programs inaugurating the mid-west coaxial cable on January 11, 1949 and the coast-to-coast microwave facilities on September 30, 1951, two experimental programs telecast via communications satellite on July 10th and 11th, 1962, and coverage of events surrounding the Kennedy assassination in November, 1963.

duplicated sub-types being political programs, speeches, and news. Since 1960, the number of simultaneously duplicated speeches has dropped markedly, probably because of new video recording techniques which permit programs to be recorded easily for presentation at times convenient to each network carrying them.

In Table 39, categories of ABC-TV's non-duplicated competitive prime time specials were noted. More documentaries competed against

TABLE 39

ABC-TV NON-DUPLICATED COMPETITIVE PRIME TIME SPECIAL PROGRAM CATEGORIES

Category	No. of Programs	Percentage of Total Non-duplicated
Drama		
Comedy	1	1.4
Talks		
Awards and Pageants	3	4.2
Documentary	21	29.6
News and News Analysis	10	14.1
Panel Talks	3	4.2
Political Programs	11	15.5
Religious Programs	1	1.4
Speeches	5	7.0
Sports and Sports News	6	8.5
Variety		
Comedy	3	4.2
Musical	2	9.9
Totals	71	100.0%

specials on other networks than any other ABC program category, followed by political programs and news specials. ABC-TV talks specials competed with other prime time specials far more frequently than specials of any other type. This was probably to be expected since nearly 80 per cent of ABC-TV's prime time special programs consisted of talks shows.

ABC-TV non-duplicated competitive specials most often competed against NBC-TV specials. Forty-six nighttime non-regular ABC-TV programs competed against NBC-TV specials, 23 against CBS-TV specials, one against a DuMont special, and one competed against specials on both NBC and CBS.

To illustrate the frequency of counter and cross programming by categories, the 179 ABC-TV simultaneously duplicated and non-duplicated competitive prime time specials were plotted in Table 40. This table, and others like it which follow in this chapter, should not be construed as implying that the cross and counter programming resulted from program strategy employed by the network under discussion. Which network scheduled a special first and which network subsequently decided to schedule a special in competition with it was impossible to determine; moreover, in some cases competitive specials scheduling may have been the result of accident rather than design.

The data in Table 40 were interpreted on two levels: cross and counter programming by gross classification, i.e., drama against drama, or drama against talks, etc., and by sub-categories, i.e., documentary versus documentary or politicals, or comedy variety, etc.

When analyzed by gross classifications, 150 competing ABC-TV nighttime specials were found to have been cross programmed (83.8 per cent), while 29 programs were counter programmed (16.2 per cent). When analyzed by sub-categories only a small change was noted: 127 programs (70.9 per cent of all specials scheduled against other specials) were cross programmed, 52 programs (29.1 per cent) were counter programmed. Hence, by far the majority of ABC-TV's special programs which competed with specials on other networks appeared opposite programs of similar type. This was due in part to the large number of simultaneously duplicated programs (108 of the 179) which appeared in the data.

TABLE 40

CROSS AND COUNTER PROGRAMMING OF ABC-TV PRIME TIME SPECIALS

	Drama						Talks						
	Action	Crime	Historical	Prestige	Western	Unknown	Actualities	Awards	Documentary	Instructional	News	Panel	Political
Drama													
Action	-	-	-	-	-	-	-	-	-	-	-	-	-
Comedy	-	-	-	-	-	-	-	-	-	-	-	-	-
Crime	-	-	-	-	-	-	-	-	-	-	-	-	-
Readings	-	-	-	-	-	-	-	-	-	-	-	-	-
Puppets	-	-	-	-	-	-	-	-	-	-	-	-	-
History	-	-	-	-	-	-	-	-	-	-	-	-	-
Movies	-	-	-	-	-	-	-	-	-	-	-	-	-
Musical	-	-	-	-	-	-	-	-	-	-	-	-	-
Prestige	-	-	-	-	-	-	-	-	-	-	-	-	-
Western	-	-	-	-	-	-	-	-	-	-	-	-	-
Unknown	-	-	-	-	-	1	-	-	-	-	-	-	-
Talks													
Actualities	-	-	-	-	-	-	1	-	-	-	-	-	-
Awards	-	-	-	-	-	-	-	2	-	-	1	-	1
Documentary	-	3	-	1	-	-	-	2	8	1	2	-	1
Instructional	-	-	-	-	-	-	-	-	-	-	-	-	-
News	1	1	-	-	-	1	-	-	1	-	15	-	-
Panel	-	-	-	-	-	-	-	-	1	-	-	1	-
Political	-	-	-	-	-	-	-	1	1	-	1	-	58
Religious	1	-	-	-	-	-	-	-	-	-	-	-	-
Speeches	-	-	-	2	-	-	-	-	-	1	1	-	-
Sports	-	-	-	-	-	-	-	1	1	-	3	-	-
Variety													
Circus	-	-	-	-	-	-	-	-	-	-	-	-	-
Comedy	-	-	-	-	-	-	-	-	3	-	-	-	-
Musical	-	-	1	-	1	1	-	-	1	-	1	-	-
Vaudeville	-	-	-	-	-	-	-	-	-	-	-	-	-
Non-classified*	-	-	-	-	-	-	-	-	-	-	-	-	-

*All eight non-classified programs were simultaneously duplicated and can therefore logically be counted with the cross programmed specials.

Religious	Speeches	Sports	Variety: Circus	Variety: Comedy	Variety: Musical	Non-classified	Total
-	-	-	-	-	-	-	
-	-	-	-	1	-	-	1
-	-	-	-	-	-	-	
-	-	-	-	-	-	-	
-	-	-	-	-	-	-	
-	-	-	-	-	-	-	
-	-	-	-	-	-	-	
-	-	-	-	-	-	-	
-	-	-	-	-	-	-	
-	-	-	-	-	-	-	
-	-	-	-	-	-	-	1
-	-	-	-	-	-	-	1
-	-	-	-	-	1	-	5
-	-	1	-	-	3	-	22
-	-	-	-	-	-	-	
-	-	-	-	2	-	-	21
-	-	-	-	-	2	-	4
-	-	1	-	-	-	-	62
-	-	-	-	-	-	-	1
-	31	-	-	-	1	-	36
1	-	-	-	-	-	-	6
-	-	-	-	-	-	-	
-	-	-	-	-	-	-	3
1	-	-	1	-	1	-	8
-	-	-	-	-	-	-	
-	-	-	-	-	-	8	8
							179

The only sub-category counter programmed more often than cross programmed was musical variety, which appeared opposite diverse other program types in apparently random fashion.

CBS-TV

On CBS-TV during the years covered by this study, 110 prime time specials, representing 12.0 per cent of CBS-TV's 917 nighttime non-regular programs, were duplicated simultaneously on one or more other networks. Sixty programs--6.5 per cent of all CBS prime time specials--were non-duplicated competitive prime time programs. The total of 170 prime time CBS specials programmed against specials on other networks equalled 18.5 per cent of all CBS-TV's nighttime special offerings from September, 1948 to September, 1966.

Table 41 presents the categorical breakdown of CBS-TV's simultaneously duplicated prime time special programming.

Eighty-seven of the 110 simultaneously duplicated CBS-TV prime time specials were available on all other networks (this figure, of course, remains the same for each network except DuMont), 12 appeared on CBS and NBC, nine on CBS and ABC, one on CBS, NBC, and DuMont, and one on CBS, ABC, and NBC (excluding the DuMont network).

The categorical makeup of CBS-TV's simultaneously duplicated prime time special programming was identical to that of ABC-TV except for the addition of one program in the vaudeville variety sub-category. The number of duplicated CBS-TV specials was also nearly the same as for ABC-TV.

The categorical distribution of non-duplicated competitive CBS-TV prime time special programs is displayed in Table 42.

TABLE 41

CBS-TV SIMULTANEOUSLY DUPLICATED PRIME TIME
SPECIAL PROGRAM CATEGORIES

Category	No. of Programs	Percentage of Total Duplicated
Drama		
Unclassified Drama	1	0.9
Talks		
Actualities	1	0.9
Awards and Pageants	1	0.9
Documentary	1	0.9
News and News Analysis	15	13.6
Panel Talks	1	0.9
Political Programs	52	47.3
Speeches	28	25.5
Variety		
Musical Variety	1	0.9
Vaudeville Variety	1	0.9
Non-classifiable*	8	7.3
Totals	110	100.0%

*This classification included programs inaugurating the mid-west coaxial cable on January 11, 1949 and the coast-to-coast microwave facilities on September 30, 1951, two experimental programs telecast via communications satellite on July 10th and 11th, 1962, and coverage of events surrounding the Kennedy assassination in November, 1963.

Although more types of CBS-TV specials were involved in non-duplicated than simultaneously duplicated competition with other specials, the bulk of this programming remained in the talks classification. News, politicals, documentary, and musical variety were the sub-categories most often scheduled against other specials.

TABLE 42

CBS-TV NON-DUPLICATED COMPETITIVE PRIME TIME SPECIAL PROGRAM CATEGORIES

Category	No. of Programs	Percentage of Total Non-duplicated
Drama		
Action/Adventure Drama	3	5.0
Comedy Drama	1	1.7
Crime, Mystery, Spy Drama	1	1.7
Fairy Tale, Puppet/Cartoon	1	1.7
Prestige Drama	3	5.0
Unclassified Drama	1	1.7
Talks		
Awards and Pageants	4	6.7
Documentary	9	15.0
News and News Analysis	10	16.6
Panel Discussions	2	3.3
Political Programs	10	16.6
Speeches	1	1.7
Sports and Sports News	2	3.3
Variety		
Circus Variety	2	3.3
Comedy Variety	3	5.0
Musical Variety	6	10.0
Non-classifiable	1	1.7
Totals	60	100.0%

Non-duplicated competitive CBS-TV specials contested most frequently with NBC-TV specials. Thirty-six such programs on CBS coincided with special NBC programs, while 23 CBS prime time specials competed with ABC specials. In one instance a CBS-TV nighttime special was scheduled opposite specials on both ABC-TV and NBC-TV.

Table 43 is a categorical resumé of CBS-TV's simultaneously duplicated and non-duplicated competitive special programming. The most conspicuous pattern that emerged from Table 43 was the same as that for ABC-TV: most of the competing specials appeared against specials of similar types. This was due to the relatively large proportion of simultaneously duplicated programs which appeared on CBS-TV and other networks. Prominent among the sub-categories heavily cross programmed were political programs, news, and speeches, which, as indicated in Table 41, were the sub-categories most frequently simultaneously duplicated. Aside from the simultaneously duplicated specials, most CBS-TV prime time non-regular programs that competed with specials on other networks were scheduled against documentaries.

When analyzed by gross classifications, 145 of the 170 CBS-TV prime time specials scheduled versus other specials were cross programmed. This accounted for 85.3 per cent of the 170 specials. Twenty-four specials were counter programmed, comprising 14.1 per cent of the total, and one program, 0.6 per cent, could not be identified as to type. By sub-categories, 124 CBS-TV prime time specials were scheduled opposite programs of the same sub-type, comprising 72.9 per cent of the 170 specials. Twenty-six per cent--44 programs--were scheduled against specials of different sub-types, and two programs, 1.1 per cent, could not be identified as to sub-classification. Hence, cross programming was the outstanding characteristic of CBS-TV specials scheduled in competition with specials on other networks.

TABLE 43

CROSS AND COUNTER PROGRAMMING OF CBS-TV PRIME TIME SPECIALS

	Drama	Talks								
Drama	Unknown	Actualities	Awards	Documentary	News	Panel	Political	Religious	Speeches	Sports
Action	-	-	-	1	1	-	-	1	-	-
Comedy	-	-	-	-	1	-	-	-	-	-
Crime	-	-	-	-	1	-	-	-	-	-
Readings	-	-	-	-	-	-	-	-	-	-
Puppets	-	-	-	-	-	-	-	-	-	-
History	-	-	-	-	-	-	-	-	-	-
Movies	-	-	-	-	-	-	-	-	-	-
Musical	-	-	-	-	-	-	-	-	-	-
Prestige	-	-	-	1	-	-	-	-	1	-
Western	-	-	-	-	-	-	-	-	-	-
Unknown	1	-	-	-	-	-	-	-	-	-
Talks										
Actualities	-	1	-	-	-	-	-	-	-	-
Awards	-	-	2	1	-	-	1	-	-	1
Documentary	-	-	-	5	1	-	-	-	1	-
Instructional	-	-	-	-	-	-	-	-	-	-
News	-	-	1	3	17	-	-	-	1	-
Panel	-	-	-	1	-	1	1	-	-	-
Political	-	-	-	1	-	-	60	-	-	-
Religious	-	-	-	-	-	-	-	-	-	-
Speeches	-	-	-	1	-	-	-	-	28	-
Sports	-	-	1	-	1	-	-	-	-	-
Variety										
Circus	-	-	-	1	-	-	-	-	-	-
Comedy	-	-	-	1	-	-	-	-	-	-
Musical	-	-	-	2	1	1	-	-	1	-
Vaudeville	-	-	-	-	-	-	-	-	-	-
Non-classifiable*	-	-	-	-	-	-	-	-	-	-

*Eight non-classifiable programs were simultaneously duplicated and can therefore logically be counted with the cross programmed specials. Whether the other non-classifiable program was cross or counter programmed cannot be determined.

Variety				
Comedy	Musical	Vaudeville	Non-classified	Totals
-	-	-	-	3
-	-	-	-	1
-	-	-	-	1
-	-	-	-	
1	-	-	-	1
-	-	-	-	
-	-	-	-	
-	-	-	-	
1	-	-	-	3
-	-	-	-	
-	1	-	-	2
-	-	-	-	1
-	-	-	-	5
-	3	-	-	10
-	-	-	-	
-	1	2	-	25
-	-	-	-	3
1	-	-	-	62
-	-	-	-	
-	-	-	-	29
-	-	-	-	2
-	1	-	-	2
-	2	-	-	3
1	1	-	-	7
-	-	1	-	1
-	1	-	8	9
				170

NBC-TV

During the period under study, NBC-TV broadcast 1,053 prime time special programs, 108 of which--10.3 per cent--were simultaneously duplicated on other networks. The number of non-duplicated competitive specials broadcast by NBC-TV was 86, or 8.2 per cent of all NBC night-time special programs. Thus, a total of 18.5 per cent of NBC-TV prime time non-regular programs coincided with special programs telecast by other networks. Types of NBC programs simultaneously duplicated on one or more other national networks are listed in Table 44.

TABLE 44

NBC-TV SIMULTANEOUSLY DUPLICATED PRIME TIME SPECIAL PROGRAM CATEGORIES

Category	No. of Programs	Percentage of Total Duplicated
Drama		
Unclassified Drama	1	0.9
Talks		
Actualities	1	0.9
Documentary	1	0.9
Speeches	25	23.2
News and News Analysis	15	13.9
Panel Discussions	1	0.9
Political Programs	54	50.0
Variety		
Musical Variety	1	0.9
Vaudeville Variety	1	0.9
Non-classifiable*	8	7.5
Totals	108	100.0%

*This classification included programs inaugurating the mid-west coaxial cable on January 11, 1949, and the coast-to-coast microwave facilities on September 30, 1951, two experimental programs telecast via communications satellite on July 10th and 11th, 1962, and coverage of events surrounding the Kennedy assassination of November, 1963.

As with the other networks, political programs, speeches, and news specials were the most frequently duplicated program types on NBC-TV. The 108 simultaneously duplicated NBC-TV prime time specials included the 87 programs telecast by all networks, 12 specials which appeared on NBC and CBS simultaneously, four on NBC and ABC, two on NBC, ABC, and DuMont, one on NBC, CBS, and DuMont, one on NBC and DuMont, and one on all networks except DuMont.

The types of prime time special programs which appeared on NBC-TV in competition with specials on other networks aside from simultaneously duplicated programs, are listed in Table 45. These programs followed the pattern typical of all the networks: documentary, news, and political programs were the sub-types most often scheduled against other specials. However, on NBC-TV the variety sub-categories were more frequently scheduled competitively against specials on other networks than was the case with ABC-TV and CBS-TV. NBC-TV's musical variety classification, in particular, competed with other specials as often as political specials. In this respect, NBC-TV's non-duplicated competitive prime time specials differed from that of the other networks.

These programs competed with ABC-TV specials more than those of any other network; 45 NBC-TV specials were shceulded opposite ABC-TV specials. Thirty-eight nighttime NBC specials competed with CBS specials, two with DuMont specials, and one with specials on CBS and ABC. Note that in a few cases the figures on competitive specials did not read both ways. For example, although 46 ABC-TV non-duplicated prime time specials competed with NBC-TV specials, only 45 NBC-TV

TABLE 45

NBC-TV NON-DUPLICATED COMPETITIVE PRIME TIME SPECIAL PROGRAM CATEGORIES

Category	No. of Programs	Percentage of Total Non-duplicated
Drama		
Crime, Mystery Drama	4	4.6
Historical Drama	1	1.2
Prestige Drama	2	2.3
Unclassified Drama	1	1.2
Talks		
Awards and Pageants	3	3.5
Documentary	24	27.9
Instructional Programs	1	1.2
News and News Analysis	15	17.4
Political Programs	11	12.8
Religious Programs	1	1.2
Sports and Sports News	2	2.3
Variety		
Comedy Variety	8	9.3
Musical Variety	11	12.8
Vaudeville Variety	2	2.3
Totals	86	100.0%

specials competed with ABC-TV specials. This occurred because two half-hour ABC-TV specials happened to be scheduled opposite one hour-long NBC-TV special. The same was true of competing specials on NBC and CBS, and NBC and DuMont.

NBC-TV's cross and counter programmed specials are plotted in Table 46. The most common situation on NBC-TV, as on the other networks, was for <u>talks</u> specials to be programmed against other <u>talks</u> specials. This occurred in 140 instances. NBC-TV <u>variety</u> versus

TABLE 46

CROSS AND COUNTER PROGRAMMING OF NBC-TV PRIME TIME SPECIALS

	Drama						Talks					
Drama	Action	Comedy	Crime	Puppets	Prestige	Unknown	Actualities	Awards	Documentary	News	Panel	Political
Action	-	-	-	-	-	-	-	-	-	-	-	-
Comedy	-	-	-	-	-	-	-	-	-	-	-	-
Crime	-	-	-	-	-	-	-	-	3	1	-	-
Readings	-	-	-	-	-	-	-	-	-	-	-	-
Puppets	-	-	-	-	-	-	-	-	-	-	-	-
History	-	-	-	-	-	-	-	-	-	-	-	-
Movies	-	-	-	-	-	-	-	-	-	-	-	-
Musical	-	-	-	-	-	-	-	-	-	-	-	-
Prestige	-	-	-	-	-	-	-	-	1	-	-	-
Western	-	-	-	-	-	-	-	-	-	-	-	-
Unknown	-	-	-	-	-	1	-	-	-	1	-	-
Talks												
Actualities	-	-	-	-	-	-	1	-	-	-	-	-
Awards	-	-	-	-	-	-	-	1	1	-	-	-
Documentary	1	1	-	-	-	-	-	-	8	3	1	2
Instructional	-	-	-	-	-	-	-	-	1	-	-	-
News	-	1	1	-	-	-	-	2	2	16	-	1
Panel	-	-	-	-	-	-	-	-	-	-	1	-
Political	-	-	-	-	-	-	-	1	1	-	1	60
Religious	-	-	-	-	-	-	-	-	-	-	-	-
Speeches	-	-	-	-	-	-	-	-	-	-	-	-
Sports	-	-	-	-	-	-	-	-	1	-	-	1
Variety												
Circus	-	-	-	-	-	-	-	-	-	-	-	-
Comedy	-	1	-	1	1	-	-	-	-	2	-	1
Musical	-	-	-	-	-	-	-	1	5	1	1	-
Vaudeville	-	-	-	-	-	-	-	-	-	2	-	-
Non-classified*		-	-	-	-	-	-	-	-	-	-	-

*The eight non-classifiable programs were simultaneously duplicated and therefore qualify as cross programmed specials.

Speeches	Sports	Variety: Circus	Variety: Comedy	Variety: Musical	Variety: Vaudeville	Non-classified	Totals
-	-	-	-	-	-	-	
-	-	-	-	-	-	-	
-	-	-	-	-	-	-	4
-	-	-	-	-	-	-	
-	-	-	-	-	-	-	
-	-	-	-	1	-	-	1
-	-	-	-	-	-	-	
-	-	-	-	-	-	-	
1	-	-	-	-	-	-	2
-	-	-	-	-	-	-	
-	-	-	-	-	-	-	2
-	-	-	-	-	-	-	1
-	1	-	-	-	-	-	3
1	1	1	4	2	-	-	25
-	-	-	-	-	-	-	1
-	4	-	-	3	-	-	30
-	-	-	-	-	-	-	1
-	2	-	-	-	-	-	65
-	1	-	-	-	-	-	1
25	-	-	-	-	-	-	25
-	-	-	-	-	-	-	2
-	-	-	-	-	-	-	
-	-	-	-	2	-	-	8
-	1	-	1	1	-	1	12
-	-	-	-	-	1	-	3
-	-	-	-	-	-	8	8
							194

talks on other networks was the next most usual circumstance, occurring, however, with far less frequency: only 14 times. In 10 instances NBC-TV talks competed with variety on other networks. By broad classifications, 154 of NBC-TV's 194 competitively scheduled prime time specials were cross programmed. This represented 79.4 per cent of the 194 programs. Thirty-nine programs, 20.1 per cent, were counter programmed, and one special, 0.5 per cent, was of undetermined type.

When broken down by sub-categories, 62.8 per cent, 122 programs, were cross programmed with specials of similar types on other networks. Most of these programs were political specials, speeches, news and news analysis, and documentaries. Seventy NBC-TV specials were counter programmed against other specials, or 36.1 per cent. Two specials could not be categorized by sub-type, or 1.1 per cent. Hence, in the area of specials versus specials, the pattern on NBC-TV paralleled that of the other networks with the great majority of such programs cross programmed rather than counter programmed.

DuMont

From September, 1948 through September 15, 1955, the DuMont Television Network telecast 72 prime time special programs, 39 of which--54.2 per cent--consisted of program material duplicated simultaneously on one or more other networks. Only two of DuMont's 72 nighttime specials were non-duplicated programs which competed with other specials, or 2.8 per cent. Thus, a total of 57.0 per cent of DuMont's prime time special programs were scheduled against specials on other networks.

Table 47 notes the types of DuMont specials carried simultaneously by all other networks, five were carried by DuMont and ABC, two by DuMont, ABC, and NBC, one by DuMont and NBC, and one by DuMont, CBS, and NBC.

TABLE 47

DuMONT SIMULTANEOUSLY DUPLICATED PRIME TIME SPECIAL PROGRAM CATEGORIES

Category	No. of Programs	Percentage of Total Duplicated
Drama		
Unclassified Drama	1	2.6
Talks		
Awards and Pageants	1	2.6
Documentary	1	2.6
News and News Analysis	2	5.1
Panel Discussions	1	2.6
Political Programs	14	35.8
Speeches	16	41.0
Variety		
Musical Variety	1	2.6
Non-classifiable*	2	5.1
Totals	39	100.0%

*This category included the mid-west cable inaugural program of January 11, 1949, and the program inaugurating the coast-to-coast microwave facilities on September 30, 1951.

About three fourths of all DuMont simultaneously duplicated specials consisted of <u>speeches</u> and <u>political</u> programs. This was consistent with the patterns on the other networks.

The two non-duplicated competitive DuMont specials were a sports program that was scheduled against two political half-hours on NBC-TV, and a political program that appeared opposite another political program on ABC-TV.

There are other ways in which competitive specials can be structured for analysis: by their function[3]--entertainment or information--and by sponsorship[4]--commercial or sustaining.

To re-group the sub-categories used in this study by function, they were roughly divided into two classifications, entertainment and information. The entertainment classification consisted of all drama sub-types, all variety sub-types, plus two talks sub-types, awards and pageants, and sports. The information classification consisted of all remaining talks sub-categories.[5] With the sub-categories re-classified in this manner, competitive specials were analyzed to ascertain the incidence of entertainment vs. entertainment, entertainment vs. information, and information vs. information specials. Note that Tables 40, 43, and 46 illustrate these forms of competition also. The simultaneously duplicated programs were not included in this analysis since they consisted almost wholly of information vs. information specials.

The most common form of competition among the non-duplicated specials was information vs. entertainment. Almost half--49.5 per

---

[3]The entertainment and information functions of special programs are dealt with in Chapter VI.

[4]Sponsorship characteristics of specials programs are the subject of Chapter V.

[5]These divisions are discussed more fully in Chapter VI.

cent--of all competitive but non-duplicated specials were involved in this type of competition. The contending programs were both sponsored 51.9 per cent of the time; 30.8 per cent of the time sponsored programs competed with sustaining programs, and invariably the sustaining programs were information specials. In the remaining cases, sponsored or sustaining programs competed with programs for which sponsorship was not ascertained.

In 37.1 per cent of the cases, non-duplicated competitive prime time specials were involved in information vs. information competition. Of these 46.2 per cent involved sponsored specials, 23.1 per cent involved sponsored against sustaining specials, 12.9 per cent involved sustaining programs, while sponsorship for the balance of the contending programs was not ascertained.

For both information vs. entertainment and information vs. information, 10:00 p.m., New York time, was the most common time for the competition to begin. This was not true of the smallest group of non-duplicated competitive specials, entertainment vs. entertainment, which appeared randomly throughout prime time. Entertainment vs. entertainment specials accounted for 13.4 per cent of non-duplicated but competitive specials, virtually all of which were sponsored.

Hence, the networks appeared most reluctant to schedule entertainment specials in conflict, preferring to schedule entertainment against information specials. This would appear to be the safest course since, as Chapter V will confirm, entertainment-type specials invariably out-rate information-type specials.

Comparative Analysis

A substantial proportion of each network's prime time special programs competed against specials on one or more other networks: 28.5 per cent of ABC-TV's nighttime specials, 18.5 per cent of both CBS-TV's and NBC-TV's prime time special offerings, and 57.0 per cent of DuMont's evening special programs. When the total number of competitive prime time special programs was divided into two groups, one composed of programs or program material duplicated simultaneously by two or more networks, and the other composed of non-duplicated specials which competed with diverse specials on other networks, the duplicated specials were found to far outnumber the latter group. The exact figures for each network are compared in Table 48.

TABLE 48

NUMBERS OF PRIME TIME SPECIALS SCHEDULED AGAINST SPECIALS

Network	Simultaneously Duplicated Programs	Non-duplicated Competitive Programs
ABC-TV	108	71
CBS-TV	110	60
NBC-TV	108	86
DuMont	39	2
Totals	365	219

There has been a tendency for simultaneously duplicated programs to appear on all networks together. About 80 per cent of these programs were available on all networks. Program material broadcast in this way obviously received much greater distribution than that telecast by one or two networks. Such total coverage also probably tended to underscore the importance of the event being broadcast.

Most simultaneously duplicated network television prime time non-regular programming has involved only three program types: political programs, speeches, and news. Of the total simultaneously duplicated nighttime specials which have appeared on each network during the years under study, the following percentages were devoted to the above mentioned categories: ABC-TV, 86.1 per cent; CBS-TV, 86.4 per cent; NBC-TV, 87.0 per cent; DuMont, 82.1 per cent.

The non-duplicated but competitive specials scheduled by each network also included only a few program types, most prominent among them being documentary, political, news, and musical variety. Again, most such specials were talks programs. Percentages of each network's total non-duplicated competitive specials composed of the above four sub-categories were ABC-TV, 69.1 per cent; CBS-TV, 58.2 per cent; NBC-TV, 70.9 per cent. DuMont scheduled only two non-duplicated competitive specials. Thus, while the incidence of network television prime time specials programmed against other specials has been rather high, comprising a substantial proportion of each network's total nighttime non-regular programs, only a few categories have been so scheduled to any great extent.

In most cases where non-duplicated specials were competitive, information specials contested with entertainment specials. Information opposing information specials was the next most frequent situation, while occurring least was entertainment against entertainment specials. Hence, with regard to function, non-duplicated competitive prime time special programs were most often counter programmed. The great majority of these specials were sponsored.

Nearly all-over 98 per cent--the simultaneously duplicated specials were <u>information-type</u> programs.

When regarded as a whole, simultaneously duplicated and non-duplicated competitive prime time specials together, the outstanding characteristic in the specials versus specials area was cross programming. On all networks, most cross programming involved <u>talks</u> against <u>talks</u> specials, specifically <u>political</u> vs. <u>political</u>, <u>news</u> vs. <u>news</u>, and <u>speeches</u> vs. <u>speeches</u>. Each of these sub-types contained a large number of simultaneously duplicated specials. Cross programming accounted for 83.8 per cent of ABC-TV's, 85.3 per cent of CBS-TV's, 79.4 per cent of NBC-TV's, and virtually all of DuMont's specials versus specials.

CHAPTER V

SPONSORSHIP AND RATING CHARACTERISTICS OF NETWORK TELEVISION PRIME TIME SPECIAL PROGRAMMING

Broadcast programs can be categorized as commercial or sustaining. Commercial programs are revenue-producing programs paid for (sponsored) by business enterprises whose advertising messages are inserted in the programs. Sustaining programs, or sustainers, are unsponsored and produce no revenue. Not only do networks forego any income from time devoted to sustaining programs, they must also bear production costs of such shows. In the case of pre-emptive sustaining programs, of course, the networks suffer the loss of income ordinarily realized from the pre-empted program. Hence, the presentation of network television sustaining programs is apparently an expensive proposition, particularly when these programs appear in prime time, ordinarily the most remunerative portion of the broadcast day. In view of the expense involved, the networks might be expected to televise few sustaining prime time special programs. However, an examination of non-regularly scheduled prime time network television programs revealed that many specials have been televised as sustainers.

One of this study's stated objectives was to determine as nearly as possible the number and kinds of nighttime network special programs televised on a commercial or sustaining basis during the 18 winter and summer seasons between September, 1948 and September, 1966. For this analysis a commercial program was defined as one which was either wholly or partially sponsored by one or more business concerns. All other programs were considered sustainers. (Networks will sometimes refer to a program not entirely paid for by sponsors as "partially sustaining." This designation was avoided here.)

The focus in this analysis was on sponsored and sustaining programs. No tabulation of the amount of time within programs that was devoted to advertising could be made since the many programs in the study were not actually viewed.

Sponsorship data for 159 of the 2,671 programs analyzed in this study--5.9 per cent--could not be located. This percentage was not large enough to affect findings appreciably. A list of companies sponsoring these programs is included in Appendix B.

Table 49 presents the commercial-sustaining breakdown by categories of network television prime time special programs televised during the period under examination. As this table points out, some program categories were almost always sponsored, others frequently or nearly always sustaining. Generally, sub-categories under the drama and variety headings were most often commercial, while talks programs were frequently sustaining.

Virtually all speeches were sustaining--only one speech on CBS-TV and one on NBC-TV were sponsored. Other sub-types notable for large proportions of sustaining programs were documentary, news, panel discussions, political programs, actuality, and religious specials.

ABC-TV and DuMont scheduled the greatest proportions of sustaining prime time specials. Exactly one-third--33.3 per cent--of

TABLE 49

DISTRIBUTION OF COMMERCIAL AND SUSTAINING PRIME TIME SPECIAL PROGRAMS BY CATEGORIES

	ABC-TV			CBS-TV			NBC-TV			DuMONT		
	Com.	Sus.	NA*	Com.	Sus.	NA	Com.	Sus.	NA	Com.	Sus.	NA
Drama												
Action	4	-	-	12	-	-	1	1	-	-	-	-
Comedy	1	-	1	28	1	-	12	1	-	-	-	-
Crime	4	-	-	6	3	-	19	-	1	-	-	-
Readings	-	-	-	4	2	1	-	-	1	-	-	-
Fairy Tales	2	-	1	6	1	-	19	-	-	-	-	-
Historical	-	-	-	2	5	-	21	-	-	-	-	-
Movies	-	-	-	8	-	-	-	-	-	-	-	-
Musical	4	-	-	14	1	2	13	1	2	-	-	-
Prestige	-	-	-	30	1	-	23	-	-	-	-	-
Western	1	-	-	1	-	-	2	-	-	-	-	-
Unclassified	5	-	1	15	2	-	6	-	-	1	-	-
Talks												
Actuality	-	1	-	-	2	-	1	2	-	-	-	-
Awards	20	1	6	25	10	3	39	2	2	-	1	1
Documentary	77	50	14	79	33	11	174	39	11	1	1	-
Instructional	-	-	-	2	-	-	8	-	-	-	-	-
News	4	36	16	58	39	4	89	60	4	3	3	-
Panel	3	13	5	27	25	7	12	8	-	-	1	-
Political	79	35	2	100	16	12	110	19	-	23	2	-
Religious	-	5	-	-	-	-	-	1	-	-	-	-
Speeches	-	52	-	1	71	-	1	33	-	-	20	-
Sports	52	3	14	25	11	6	23	-	17	4	-	7
Variety												
Circus	2	-	-	10	-	-	4	-	2	-	-	-
Comedy	24	-	1	46	1	5	89	1	2	-	-	-
Musical	57	3	10	92	2	6	135	3	1	1	-	-
Vaudeville	2	1	-	4	4	1	9	3	6	-	1	-
Non-classifiable	5	9	3	14	20	-	9	7	4	1	1	-
Totals	346	209	74	609	250	58	819	181	53	34	30	8

*Indicates sponsorship not ascertained.

ABC-TV's nighttime non-regular programs and 41.6 per cent of DuMont's were unsponsored. Sponsorship for the balance of the programs could not be ascertained. On CBS-TV, 66.4 per cent of the nighttime pre-emptive programs were commercially sponsored, 28.2 per cent were sustaining, while sponsorship for 5.4 per cent was not determined. NBC-TV telecast the largest proportion of sponsored prime time specials: 79.4 per cent sponsored, 17.6 per cent sustaining, and 3 per cent undetermined. No patterns with respect to sponsor-type and program categories appeared.

A total of 685 programs were televised as sustainers in prime time by all networks during the period under study, representing just over one-fourth of total nighttime non-regular programs--25.6 per cent--certainly a substantial share of pre-emptive programming.

There were no doubt several reasons for the presentation of these prime time non-regular programs on a sustaining basis. In some cases, specials were inappropriate for sponsorship. Programs commemorating the deaths of public figures, presidential speeches, coverage of tragedies--such as airplane crashes--with great loss of life, are examples of programs presented sustaining in the interests of good taste. In a very few instances, however, such specials have been sponsored. On NBC-TV, the Gulf Oil Corporation sponsored programs dealing with the death of United Nations Secretary-General Dag Hammarskjold in 1961 ("Death of a Statesman," September 18, 1961, 9:30-10:30 N.Y.T.) and the tragic sinking of the United States nuclear submarine <u>Thresher</u> in 1963 ("The Loss of the Thresher," April 11, 1963, 7:30-8:30 N.Y.T.). To avoid offending good taste in presenting these programs, Gulf Oil

TABLE 50

SPONSORED AND SUSTAINING PRIME TIME SPECIAL PROGRAMS BY CATEGORIES

	ABC-TV	CBS-TV	NBC-TV	DuMONT
Drama				
Per Cent Commercial	87.5%	85.6%	94.3%	100.0%
Per Cent Sustaining	-	11.7	2.4	-
Per Cent Unknown	12.5	2.7	3.3	-
Totals	100.0%	100.0%	100.0%	100.0%
Talks				
Per Cent Commercial	48.6%	55.4%	71.3%	46.3%
Per Cent Sustaining	40.2	38.3	25.8	41.8
Per Cent Unknown	11.2	6.3	2.9	11.9
Totals	100.0%	100.0%	100.0%	100.0%
Variety				
Per Cent Commercial	85.0%	91.8%	95.7%	50.0%
Per Cent Sustaining	4.0	3.5	2.7	50.0
Per Cent Unknown	11.0	4.7	1.6	-
Totals	100.0%	100.0%	100.0%	100.0%
Non-classifiable				
Per Cent Commercial	29.4%	41.2%	45.0%	50.0%
Per Cent Sustaining	52.9	58.8	35.0	50.0
Per Cent Unknown	17.7	-	20.0	-
Totals	100.0%	100.0%	100.0%	100.0%

omitted all commercial messages. Such altruism on the part of sponsors, however, has been the exception, not the rule, since the purpose of sponsorship is obviously to secure product identification in order to influence consumer behavior.

Another possible reason for the presentation of some specials as sustainers rather than commercial programs involves a time factor. In the case of "instant specials" (programs put together sometimes in a matter of hours in response to some important event) there may not be enough time for network salesmen to offer the program to prospective sponsors. Provision was made for just such contingencies by the Gulf Oil Corporation and NBC-TV in 1960 and again for 1968.[1] In both cases, Gulf agreed to sponsor an undetermined number of NBC-TV news specials in response to major news developments as they might occur.

No doubt sponsors simply could not be found for some prime time specials. Programs on controversial or "taboo" subjects cometimes go a-begging for sponsorship. A case in point was the NBC-TV special "Pursuit of Pleasure" televised May 8, 1967. The program's scheduled sponsor cancelled support of the special because its content was considered "unsuitable" and "inappropriate."[2] The program dealt with apparent changes in American morality, especially among the young, and featured a segment devoted to new attitudes toward sex. Although other sponsors were found for this program, the fact remains that some firms

---

[1] Broadcasting, December 26, 1960, p. 41. See also "Behind those Gulf News Specials," Printer's Ink, May 26, 1961, p. 40. "Gulf's $10-Million Buy," Broadcasting, May 1, 1967, p. 23.

[2] "NBC's Hedonistic Show Loses Sponsor," Broadcasting, May 8, 1967, p. 46.

are extremely sensitive to the possibility of offending potential customers by sponsoring certain types of subject matter.

Political programs were occasionally televised as sustainers as a public service (e.g., "The Great Debates," or, as they were actually titled, "Face to Face," a series of four debates between presidential aspirants Nixon and Kennedy in 1960), or to honor valid requests for "equal time" made by political candidates under the provisions of section 315 of the Federal Communications Act. Interestingly, prior to the first network television coverage of national political conventions in 1948, there was some feeling such programs should go unsponsored as a matter of policy. At that time, NBC-TV maintained the official position that political convention coverage should be offered as a public service, not as a commercial enterprise.[3] An NBC-TV office memorandum dated March 15, 1948, stated:

> . . . NBC Management is of the opinion that the importance of this [1948 political conventions] coverage as a service to our listeners makes commercialization inappropriate. However, if any of the other parties to the television broadcasting pool [ABC-TV, CBS-TV, and DuMont] actually sell, then NBC will also undertake sponsorship.[4]

Some specials may have been presented as sustainers to promote a network and its regular programming. Sustaining programs generally include promotional material for other programs on the same network.

Finally, some sustaining programs were probably offered from a network's sense of public responsibility. Coverage of the Kennedy

---

[3]"Convention Bulletin No. 3," NBC, undated (about January, 1948).

[4]NBC Interdepartmental Correspondence, letter from N. Ray Kelly to Raymond R. Kraft, February 26, 1948.

assassination in November, 1963--three-and-one-half days of completely sustaining programming--was certainly a manifestation of the networks' sense of public duty.

Whatever the reasons, a significant proportion of network television prime time special programs have been offered on a sustaining basis.

Another characteristic of broadcast program sponsorship examined in this analysis was single- or multiple-sponsorship. Programs presented by only one sponsor were defined as single-sponsorship programs, those presented by two or more sponsors were termed multiple-sponsorship programs.

The most frequently occurring type of sponsorship observed in the programs analyzed for this study was single-sponsorship. On every network, considerably more prime time special programs were sponsored by one rather than by two or more sponsors. Table 51 indicates the number of programs and the percentage of each network's total programs

TABLE 51

SINGLE- AND MULTIPLE-SPONSORSHIP CHARACTERISTICS OF NETWORK TELEVISION PRIME TIME SPECIAL PROGRAMMING

Type Sponsorship	ABC-TV		CBS-TV		NBC-TV		DuMONT	
	Shows	%*	Shows	%	Shows	%	Shows	%
Single	264	41.9	441	48.1	651	61.8	33	45.8
Multiple	84	13.4	168	18.3	185	17.6	1	1.4
Sustaining	209	33.3	260	28.4	186	17.6	30	41.6
Unknown	72	11.4	48	5.2	31	3.0	8	11.2
Totals	629	100.0%	917	100.0%	1053	100.0%	72	100.0%

*Percentage of each network's total number of prime time special programs.

sponsored by each method. The large proportion of single-sponsorship prime time special programs offered a contrast to the sponsorship characteristics of regular television programs. Regarding regular programs, the trend has been away from single-sponsorship toward multiple-sponsorship due primarily to the high cost of television advertising.[5] However, no such trend has occurred with respect to prime time special programming.

Until the rising cost of sponsoring regular television programs forced advertisers to turn largely to multiple-sponsorship arrangements, single sponsorship was the rule.[6] Advertisers apparently found single-sponsorship an effective means of building product identification. When single-sponsorship became too expensive on a regular basis, some firms evidently turned to single-sponsorship on an occasional or special basis. This unwillingness to abandon single-sponsorship entirely, yet keep advertising budgets within bounds, has no doubt been a factor in the high incidence of single-sponsorship of prime time special programs.

Single-sponsorship of most prime time specials has always been the rule; no trends have been apparent. The most consistent exceptions to the rule have been political and sports specials.

Table 52 shows the single- and multiple-sponsorship characteristics of network television prime time special programming by categories.

---

[5] Robert E. Summers and Harrison B. Summers, Broadcasting and the Public (Belmont, California: Wadsworth Publishing Company, 1966), p.102.

[6] Ibid.

TABLE 52

SPONSORSHIP CHARACTERISTICS OF PRIME TIME SPECIAL PROGRAMMING BY CATEGORIES

Category	ABC-TV S*	ABC-TV M**	CBS-TV S	CBS-TV M	NBC-TV S	NBC-TV M	DuMONT S	DuMONT M
Drama								
Action/Adventure	2	2	9	3	1	-	-	-
Comedy	-	1	26	2	12	-	-	-
Crime, Mystery	2	2	5	1	19	-	-	-
Readings	-	-	1	3	-	-	-	-
Fairy Tales	1	1	5	1	6	13	-	-
Historical	-	-	1	1	21	-	-	-
Motion Picture	-	-	6	2	-	-	-	-
Musical	4	-	9	5	11	2	-	-
Prestige	-	-	24	6	22	1	-	-
Western	1	-	1	-	2	-	-	-
Unclassified	4	1	9	6	5	1	1	-
Talks								
Actualities	-	-	-	-	1	-	-	-
Awards	15	5	15	10	26	13	-	-
Documentary	74	3	52	27	134	40	1	-
Instructional	-	-	2	-	8	-	-	-
News	2	2	46	12	74	15	3	-
Panel	3	-	9	18	8	4	-	-
Political	57	22	80	20	76	34	23	-
Religious	-	-	-	-	-	-	-	-
Speeches	-	-	1	-	1	-	-	-
Sports	12	40	11	14	15	8	3	1
Variety								
Circus	2	-	9	1	4	-	-	-
Comedy	24	-	36	10	61	28	-	-
Musical	50	7	64	28	124	11	1	-
Vaudeville	2	-	4	-	8	1	-	-
Non-classifiable	5	-	14	-	5	4	1	-
Totals	260	86	439	170	644	175	33	1

* Indicates single-sponsorship programs.
**Indicates multiple-sponsorship programs.

Within each broad classification, single-sponsorship far outweighed multiple sponsorship.

In the drama category, sub-types with conspicuously more cases of single-sponsorship than multiple-sponsorship were comedy drama on CBS and NBC, crime drama on NBC, historical and biographical drama on NBC, and prestige drama on CBS and NBC. In most other drama sub-types, single-sponsorship also led multiple-sponsorship, but by smaller margins. In only one drama sub-type was there a notably greater number of multiple-sponsorship programs: fairy tale and puppet/cartoon drama on NBC-TV (this sub-category was comprised mainly of "Shirley Temple's Storybook" specials), where about twice as many multiple- as single-sponsorship programs appeared.

In the talks classification, the sub-types presented largely by the single-sponsorship method were awards and documentary on ABC, CBS, and NBC, news on CBS and NBC, and political programs on all networks. Note that many political specials were sponsored by political organizations rather than business firms. Sports specials were most often sponsored by more than one advertiser on ABC and CBS, with the pattern reversed on NBC and DuMont.

All variety sub-categories were sponsored by single advertisers more often than by two or more; however, this was most notably true of the comedy and musical variety specials.

Some advertisers established certain patterns of single-sponsorship.[7] In some cases an advertiser tended to sponsor certain kinds of

---

[7]For a list of firms which have engaged in single-sponsorship of prime time special programs, see Appendix C.

specials on only one network. For example, the Hallmark Company appeared exclusively on NBC-TV and almost exclusively sponsored drama specials (in one instance, Hallmark sponsored a vaudeville variety program). The Gulf Oil Company also appeared exclusively on NBC-TV and only sponsored talks specials, primarily news, documentary, and panel discussions. Apparently such sponsors selected a specific audience. A brief study which tended to substantiate this premise was made by Marilynn Baxter at the University of Wisconsin.[8] Miss Baxter's examination of Hallmark's television program sponsorship found that the firm's advertising was directed at what Hallmark considered were "important people," those who had a higher level of education, social, and professional attainment, and that the programs Hallmark sponsored tended to collect such an audience.[9]

On the other hand, some advertisers appeared to use what might be termed a "shotgun" technique: attempting to reach a large, heterogeneous audience by sponsoring a wide variety of program types on various networks. Procter and Gamble afforded the outstanding example of this advertising technique.

Since the A. C. Nielsen Market Research Company rates only sponsored programs with few exceptions, to include a consideration of program ratings with the discussion of sponsorship seemed appropriate. Program ratings computed by the A. C. Nielsen Company of Chicago were

---

[8]"Radio-Television-Film Audience Studies," Department of Speech, University of Wisconsin, No. 2, June, 1966.

[9]Ibid., pp. 1 and 4.

obtained for 1,230 of the specials in this study. These ratings, all of which appear in Appendix A, were national average ratings and average share of audience figures. Nielsen national average ratings indicate the percentage of U. S. TV households (homes equipped with television receivers) tuned to a particular program during the average minute the program was on the air; national share of audience figures indicate the percentage of U. S. TV households <u>using</u> television which were tuned to a particular program during the program's average minute.[10] Nielsen projects these figures from a randomly selected national sample of some 1,150[11] TV households which are equipped with a device designed to record when the set was turned on and off and to which channel the set was tuned at any given time it was on.

Ratings are percentages usually expressed as a whole number and a fraction, i.e., 20.4. However, since there is a statistical margin of error in these figures the Nielsen company places at 1.1 percentage points in either direction,[12] the fractional figures were not considered important. The ratings were therefore rounded off to the nearest whole number before being entered on punch cards for machine analysis. The fractional figures resulting from the analysis were retained, however.

---

[10] "Nielsen Television Index, Second Report for July, 1965," Chicago, A. C. Nielsen Company, 1965, p. 7. For a complete set of definitions of rating terms see Standard Definitions of Broadcast Research Terms (New York: National Association of Broadcasters), January, 1967.

[11] Summers and Summers, loc. cit., p. 249.

[12] "The Ratings: A Photo Finish," Broadcasting, October 17, 1966, p. 66.

The A. C. Nielsen company rates only sponsored television programs unless specific requests are made for ratings of sustaining programs.[13] Hence, ratings for very few sustaining programs were obtained for this study. Other programs for which no ratings were available were those which appeared during Nielsen "Black Weeks." "Black Weeks" are four weeks set aside each year during which no program ratings at all are computed. An indeterminate number of specials have been televised during Black Weeks for which no ratings were obtained. Finally, since Nielsen did not begin to officially issue national ratings for television programs until 1950[14] no ratings were available for specials aired prior to that year.

Of the 2,671 programs in this study, 1,816 were commercially sponsored specials appearing after January 1, 1950. The 1,230 ratings found for prime time specials comprised 67.3 per cent of the sponsored programs, making no provision for specials which may have been televised during Black Weeks (pure chance indicates this would have amounted to about 140 specials). Ratings for the other 486 specials were not furnished by the Nielsen company since that would have involved "instituting a comprehensive research project" which the company was apparently unwilling to undertake.[15] The data on ratings is therefore presented with the caution that figures for slightly less

---

[13] Giraud Chester, et. al., Television and Radio, 3rd edition (New York: Appleton-Century-Crofts, 1963), p. 113.

[14] Notation on mimeographed material obtained from the A. C. Nielsen Company.

[15] Letter from Laurence Frerk, promotion director of the A. C. Nielsen Company, to the author, dated August 16, 1966.

than one-third the sponsored specials telecast in prime time between January 1, 1950 and September 14, 1966 are absent.

Rating and share figures for all networks were combined to arrive at average ratings and shares, within the limitations of the data, for each program category. To combine the data for all networks seemed appropriate since the point of interest was how the programs performed, not the networks.

Because ratings for all sponsored prime time special programs were not available to this study, Table 53 was prepared listing the number of sponsored programs in each category, the number of ratings available for each category, and what percentage of sponsored programs the latter figure represented. Table 54, giving average ratings and shares for each program category, can thus be considered in the light of Table 53's qualifying figures.

Table 53 shows the ratings data were most complete for specials in the drama classification. Taken as a whole, ratings for 80.9 per cent of all drama sub-categories were obtained together with ratings for 61.4 per cent of all talks sub-categories, and 72.6 per cent of all variety sub-categories. Average ratings presented in Table 54 can be considered more accurate for those sub-categories for which a high percentage of ratings were obtained.

Table 54 shows that variety programs received the highest ratings. Prime time specials under the variety classification scored an average rating of 22.1 per cent and an average share of 38.2 per cent. The Nielsen study of specials telecast in the 1960-1961 season found the

TABLE 53

PERCENTAGE OF SPONSORED PRIME TIME SPECIAL PROGRAMS FOR WHICH RATINGS DATA WAS AVAILABLE BY CATEGORIES*

Category	1 Sponsored Programs	2 Ratings Available	3 Per Cent of Column One
Drama			
Action/Adventure	18	15	83.3%
Comedy	41	36	87.8
Crime, Mystery, Spy	29	21	72.4
Dramatic Readings	2	3	150.0**
Fairy Tale/Puppet Cartoon	27	23	85.2
Historical/Biographical	23	16	69.6
Motion Picture	8	7	87.5
Musical	32	26	81.3
Prestige	52	46	88.5
Western	4	2	50.0
Unclassified Drama	26	17	65.4
Talks			
Actualities	1	-	-
Awards and Pageants	85	58	68.2
Documentary	322	254	78.9
Instructional	10	7	70.0
News and News Analysis	156	86	55.1
Panel Talks	43	33	76.7
Political	308	132	42.9
Religious	-	-	-
Speeches	2	2	100.0
Sports and Sports News	122	73	59.8
Variety			
Circus	17	14	82.5
Comedy	161	125	77.6
Musical	289	204	70.2
Vaudeville	20	11	55.0
Non-classifiable	29	19	68.9

* Includes only programs televised after January 1, 1950.
**Exceeds 100 per cent because a sustaining program was rated.

TABLE 54

AVERAGE RATING AND SHARE OF AUDIENCE FIGURES FOR SPONSORED NETWORK TELEVISION PRIME TIME SPECIAL PROGRAMS[a]

Category	Highest		Lowest		Range		Average	
Drama	Rt[b]	Sh[c]	Rt	Sh	Rt	Sh	Rt	Sh
Action	27	43	9	18	18	25	17.1	29.1
Comedy	47	62	7	14	40	48	20.6	34.3
Crime	23	36	5	10	18	26	14.3	25.6
Readings	13	21	5	10	8	16	8.0	14.3
Fairy Tale	42	59	14	27	28	32	24.9	40.2
Historical	21	33	9	15	12	18	13.8	24.2
Movie	36	59	31	49	5	10	33.6	53.6
Musical	48	64	9	14	39	50	20.9	34.1
Prestige	25	42	7	12	18	30	14.9	27.1
Western	15	33	14	24	1	11	14.5	28.5
Unclassifiable	29	47	4	6	25	41	14.4	24.4
Talks								
Actuality	-	-	-	-	-	-	-	-
Awards	46	82	5	8	41	74	29.5	54.9
Documentary	32	46	5	9	17	37	12.3	23.2
Instructional	26	38	13	21	13	17	18.7	28.6
News	30	44	5	10	25	34	10.2	20.7
Panel	17	28	3	7	14	21	7.9	16.7
Political	32	43	2	11	30	32	10.2	17.5
Religious	-	-	-	-	-	-	-	-
Speeches	14	20	6	15	8	5	10.0	17.5
Sports	33	56	3	8	30	48	13.6	27.3
Variety								
Circus	48	67	19	33	29	34	27.5	46.2
Comedy	42	59	7	16	35	43	22.2	38.2
Musical	37	55	5	8	32	50	16.9	29.7
Vaudeville	30	47	14	21	16	26	21.8	34.8
Non-classifiable	26	46	7	26	19	20	14.6	33.8
Average all types					21.7	31.1	15.7	28.6

[a]Based on the Nielsen National Television Index.

[b]Rating.

[c]Share of audience.

average rating of all variety prime time specials to be 23.6 per cent,[16] a figure just 1.5 per cent higher than that discovered for all the variety specials in this study.

Drama specials ranked next with an average rating of 17.9 per cent and an average share of 30.5 per cent. This rating figure was also close to the Nielsen average rating for drama specials appearing during the 1960-1961 season: 16.7 per cent.[17]

Talks programs generally received the lowest ratings, averaging a 12.8 per cent rating and 26.1 per cent share. (The 1961 Nielsen study offered no figures comparable to this study's talks classification.) Thus, the largest prime time specials category, talks programs, which comprised 66.5 per cent of all nighttime specials broadcast by all television networks, has received the lowest ratings.

Motion picture drama was the sub-category with the highest average rating and share of audience. These figures were based on seven of eight telecasts of the film "The Wizard of Oz" on CBS-TV, the only motion picture scheduled as a prime time special during the period covered by this study. The highest rating this picture received was a 36 in December, 1959, and again in January, 1966. Consistently high ratings no doubt account for the film's reappearance each holiday season.

Although the talks classification received the lowest overall ratings, one of its sub-categories, awards and pageants, was the second

---

[16]"The TV Special: It's No Gamble," Sponsor, September 11, 1961, p. 37.

[17]Ibid.

highest sub-category in the ratings. Scoring consistently high ratings were three annually recurring specials: the "Miss America Beauty Pageant," the "Motion Picture Academy Award Presentations," and the "Miss Universe Contest." The "Miss America" special won its highest rating of 42 in 1961.

The "Miss America Beauty Pageant" originated the beauty contest television special. First telecast September 11, 1954 on ABC-TV with Bess Meyerson and John Daly (Bert Parks and the song "Miss America" were to come later), the program became an annual September television event. High ratings have made the program a prized property for which the networks bid competitively. "Miss America" has appeared on all networks except DuMont at one time or another.

"Miss America's" success as a television special resulted in a proliferation of beauty contest specials, none of which have equalled the prototype's performance in the ratings. Other beauty contest specials include the "Miss Universe Contest," "Miss Teen Age America," "Hollywood's Deb Star Ball," "Miss U.S.A.," "America's Junior Miss Pageant," and the "International Beauty Show." "Miss Universe" apparently has come closest to "Miss America" in the ratings, earning its highest Nielsen rating of 34 in 1961.

The "Motion Picture Academy Awards" special, which annually recognizes members of the motion picture industry for excellence in various areas, has nearly equalled "Miss America" in the Nielsen ratings. This program, the progenitor of such carbon-copy specials as the "Television Emmy Awards" and, more recently, the "Golden Globe

Awards" for Broadway performers, was originally an ABC radio special.[18] The "Academy Awards" appeared on television for the first time in 1953 as an NBC-TV special. Bob Hope acted as master of ceremonies in Hollywood for this initial telecast, with Conrad Nagel hosting the New York portion of the broadcast. Sixty-one NBC-TV affiliates carried the program which received a national Nielsen rating of 45.7 and a share of 82.5 per cent.

Ranking just behind awards and pageants was the circus variety sub-category. Highest rating in this class went to "Circus Highlights of 1955," which won a 48 per cent rating and a 67 per cent share of audience. Circus variety specials generally featured either the Ringling Brothers, Barnum and Bailey Circus, or Marineland-of-the-Pacific performances.

Fairy tale and puppet/cartoon drama was the fourth-ranked sub-category. A CBS-TV production of "Cinderella" in 1965 apparently was the highest rated program in this classification with a 42 per cent rating and a 59 per cent share of audience. Other programs which figured prominently in this sub-category were several "Shirley Temple's Storybook" specials, several repeats of "Mr. Magoo's Christmas Carol," and some "Charlie Brown" animated cartoons.

Other sub-categories with Nielsen ratings above 20 per cent were comedy variety, 22.2, vaudeville variety, 21.8, musical drama, 20.9, and comedy drama, 20.6.

---

[18] "RCA Victor to Sponsor 'Oscar' Awards Simulcast," Broadcasting, February 16, 1953, p. 38.

Sub-categories with the lowest ratings, in the vicinity of 10 and below, were panel talks, 7.9, dramatic readings, 8.0, speeches, 10, and news and political programs, both 10.2.

The overall average figures for all categories combined were a rating of 15.7 and a share of 28.6 per cent. The rating figure compared with the average audience found for all specials in the 1960-1961 Nielsen study of 17.2,[19] 1.5 per cent higher than found in this study.

There was a great disparity in the ranges between the highest and lowest rated program in each sub-category. The smallest range in rating was a difference of one per cent in the western drama subtype (there were only two ratings available for this little-used special program type), the largest range was a difference of 41 per cent in awards and pageants. As noted in Table 54, the average rating range was 21.7 while the average share of audience range was 31.1 per cent. This indicated that for most program types there was wide variance in audience acceptance for individual programs. Obviously, program type alone was not enough to assure consistently a certain level of audience acceptance. Other variables that probably came into play here were specific program content, featured performers, advance promotion, time of year the program was scheduled, and competition.

There was little variation in the average ratings and shares of prime time special programs when, taken as a whole, they were distributed by starting times. The averaged ratings and shares for all

---

[19] Ibid.

programs and networks by time periods follow: 7:30, 14.0 and 24.8; 8:00, 17.0 and 27.9; 8:30, 15.6 and 25.3; 9:00, 16.6 and 26.8; 9:30, 15.5 and 28.5; 10:00, 13.9 and 29.3; 10:30, 14.8 and 31.4; other times (generally starting earlier than 7:30), 16.3 and 30.7.

Ratings for the non-classifiable category were not meaningful since they represented programs of indeterminate types. However, included among them were ratings pertaining to network coverage of events surrounding President John F. Kennedy's assassination. These ratings are of special interest since they involved network television's most outstanding effort in the area of pre-emptive programming. They are presented separately in Table 55, which was reproduced from a table prepared by the ABC-TV program research department.

TABLE 55

PRESIDENT KENNEDY MEMORIAL PROGRAMMING
RATINGS BY INDIVIDUAL DAY
SIGN ON TO SIGN OFF*

	ABC-TV		CBS-TV		NBC-TV	
	Rtg	Share	Rtg	Share	Rtg	Share
Fri., 11-22-63	9.6	19.5	26.6	45.7	18.7	35.6
Sat., 11-23-63	8.1	19.6	12.6	29.2	19.1	48.8
Sun., 11-24-63	8.5	18.5	15.2	31.4	16.8	50.2
Mon., 11-25-63	9.3	16.8	21.8	37.7	22.5	43.6
Average	8.8	18.4	18.2	35.7	19.1	44.9

*According to the A. C. Nielsen National Television Index. Note that these figures are not confined to prime time hours.

To summarize briefly, over the years covered by this study, the national networks televised some 2,671 prime time special programs, 68.5 per cent of which were known to be sponsored, and 25.6 per cent sustainin while sponsorship data for 5.9 per cent of the programs was not ascertained. Thus, about one-fourth of all special programs broadcast in prime time by the networks produced no revenue, but in fact represented expenses since the networks bore production costs.

Talks programs were more likely to be sustaining than were programs of any other type; 89 per cent of all sustaining prime time specials were talks programs of various types, 8.1 per cent were variety specials, and 2.9 per cent were drama programs. Hence, entertainment-type programs were nearly always sponsored, information-type programs were frequently sustaining.

The distribution of sponsored programs by categories indicated 57.5 per cent were talks, 28.2 per cent were variety specials, and 14.3 were dramas.

The outstanding commercial characteristic of prime time network specials was single-sponsorship. Over three-fourths (76.1 per cent) of the 1,872 sponsored nighttime pre-emptive programs were sponsored by this method, while 23.9 per cent were sponsored by the multiple-sponsorship method. This stood in contrast to regular television programs which have become increasingly inclined toward multiple-sponsorship. The suggested reason for this was that although single-sponsorship is an effective form of advertising it is prohibitively expensive on a regular basis, but becomes financially practicable on an occasional or special basis.

An analysis of the ratings of sponsored prime time network special programs showed variety programs to have the highest average rating and share of audience, based on A. C. Nielsen National Television Index figures. Variety programs also comprised the largest group of entertainment-type programs. Drama specials ranked next to variety shows in the ratings, while the talks classification received the lowest average rating and audience share. Thus, the largest specials classification, talks, received the lowest ratings.

When the program sub-categories were analyzed separately, motion picture, drama, awards and pageants, circus variety, and fairy tales, all entertainment-type specials, were found to have received the highest ratings, while the lowest ratings went to information-type sub-categories, panel discussions, dramatic readings, speeches, news and news analysis, and political programs.

CHAPTER VI

THE ENTERTAINMENT-INFORMATION FUNCTIONS OF NETWORK TELEVISION PRIME TIME SPECIAL PROGRAMMING

Television programming is generally considered to consist of two basic kinds of programs: those designed to entertain and those designed to inform the audience. As Burns W. Roper stated in a recent study of audience attitudes toward the mass media, "The two basic components of television are information (news, public affairs, and documentaries) on the one hand, and entertainment on the other."[1] From the standpoint of the audience, then, the primary functions television programming performs are to entertain or to inform (other functions could be identified from the standpoint of the networks or the sponsor.)

Based on this dichotomous concept of television programming, this study's final objective was to determine whether network prime time special programming consisted primarily of information or entertainment programs.

A somewhat similar analysis of regular television programming was carried out in the series of studies sponsored by the National

---

[1]Burns W. Roper, _Emerging Profiles of Television and Other Mass Media: Public Attitudes 1959-1967_ (New York: Television Information Office, 1967).

Association of Educational Broadcasters between 1951 and 1954.[2] However, the NAEB studies attempted to define three rather than two functions of television programming: entertainment, information, and orientation. These classifications were defined as follows:

> In our presentation we have grouped these categories into three kinds of program classes: entertainment-type, where the predominant manifest intent was to entertain; information-type, where the imparting of information was the prime purpose; and orientation-type, where effecting attitudes and values was the predominant manifest intent. These groupings are rough, for obviously program classes placed in any one of the three groups may also partake of the characteristics of the other two groups.[3]

---

[2]There were seven studies in this series: Dallas W. Smythe and Donald Horton, "Analysis of Television Programs in New York City, January 4-10, 1951," Newsletter of the National Association of Educational Broadcasters, January-February, 1951.

Dallas W. Smythe and Angus Campbell, Los Angeles Television, May 23-29, 1951 (Urbana: NAEB, 1951).

Donald Horton, Hans O. Mauksch, and Kurt Lang, Chicago Summer Television, July 30-August 5, 1951 (Chicago: National Opinion Research Center and the University of Chicago, 1951).

_______, Chicago Television, January 4-10, 1952 (Chicago: National Opinion Research Center and the University of Chicago, 1952).

Dallas W. Smythe, New Haven Television, May 15-21, 1952 (Urbana: NAEB, 1952).

_______, Three Years of New York Television, 1951-1953 (Urbana: NAEB, 1953).

H. H. Remmers, Four Years of New York Television, 1951-1954 (Urbana: NAEB, 1954).

[3]Dallas W. Smythe, "The Content and Effects of Broadcasting" in Henry B. Nelson, ed., Mass Media and Education, the Fifty-Third Yearbook of the National Society of Education, Part II (Chicago: University of Chicago Press, 1954), p. 195.

However, a distinction between information and orientation programs is probably impossible to make. Certainly when dealing with programs that have not been actually observed and relying on sometimes sketchy program information in the categorization process, this distinction becomes impossible. The programs in this study, therefore, were distributed into just two types in this regard: information and entertainment. This classification system was used in the full realization that entertainment programs can also be informative, and that informative programs can certainly be entertaining. In this respect, there is no absolute mutual exclusivity in the system; as Smythe indicated, the groupings are rough.

To accomplish the functional analysis, this study's program sub-categories were distributed into three classes: entertainment, information, and non-classifiable. The entertainment class consisted of all drama and variety sub-types plus two sub-categories in the talks group: action and adventure drama, comedy drama, crime drama, dramatic readings, fairy tales and puppet/cartoon drama, historical and biographical drama, western drama, unclassified drama, awards and pageants, sports and sports news, circus variety, comedy variety, musical variety, and vaudeville variety.

The information class was composed of actualities, documentary, instructional programs, news, panel discussions, political programs, religious programs, and speeches. The non-classifiable category remained unchanged.

Taking network television special programming as a whole (all networks, all seasons), 2,606 prime time hours have been pre-empted in favor of non-regular programs within the period covered by this study. The entertainment/information breakdown of this figure is indicated in Table 56.

TABLE 56

NETWORK TELEVISION SPECIAL PRIME TIME HOURS DISTRIBUTED BY FUNCTION

Class	Hours	Percentage of Total
Entertainment	1132:05	43.1%
Information	1381:40	53.0
Non-classifiable	92:15	3.9
Total	2606:00	100.0%

As shown above, slightly more than half of all prime time special hours carried by the networks consisted of content that could be described as information. Put another way, there were about 10 per cent more hours devoted to information than entertainment specials during prime time between September 15, 1948 and September 14, 1966.

The results of this analysis are not directly comparable with those of the NAEB monitoring studies since they dealt with both local and network programming while this study was confined to network programming only. However, it is interesting to note an apparent contrast in this area between general television programming and special programming. About three-fourths of all television programs analyzed in the 1954 NAEB study consisted of entertainment-type programs.[4] During what the NAEB studies termed the "adult viewing hours," 7:00 to 11:00 p.m.,

[4] Remmers, loc. cit., p. 3.

Eastern Standard Time (nearly identical to this study's "prime time" hours of 7:30 to 11:00 p.m. New York City Time), entertainment-type programs were even more prevalent, comprising 83 per cent of television time on New York stations between 1951 and 1954.[5] So, while there has been a strong entertainment bias in regular television programming, prime time special programming has inclined toward information.

Table 57 distributed time devoted to entertainment and information specials by networks to determine individual network patterns in scheduling these types. In the case of each network, more time was given over to information specials than entertainment specials; however, the difference between the two classes on CBS-TV was negligible. ABC-TV and the DuMont Television Network displayed greater concentration on non-entertainment pre-emptive programs than CBS-TV and NBC-TV, scheduling larger proportions of their total special hours as information specials.

TABLE 57

PERCENTAGE OF SPECIAL PRIME TIME DEVOTED TO INFORMATION AND ENTERTAINMENT SPECIALS BY EACH NETWORK

Class	ABC-TV	CBS-TV	NBC-TV	DuMONT
Entertainment	34.4	47.7	45.5	32.8
Information	62.0	47.9	51.7	63.8
Non-classifiable	3.6	4.4	2.8	3.4
Total	100.0%	100.0%	100.0%	100.0%

A further analysis of the entertainment/information functions of prime time special programming was accomplished by breaking down

[5] Ibid., p. 14.

the data into winter and summer seasons. Table 58 presents the results of this distribution.

Most information special program time occurred during summer seasons. In winter seasons, all networks except ABC spent more pre-emptive time on entertainment shows than information programs. ABC-TV scheduled more information specials than entertainment specials in both winter and summer seasons.

The preponderance of information prime time special hours during summer seasons was due primarily to the large amounts of time each network spent on political convention coverage in 1952, 1956, 1960, and 1964. The networks also probably saved their attractive and expensive entertainment specials for winter seasons when larger audiences were available.

Seasonal trends in the amount of time pre-empted for entertainment and information prime time specials by each network are illustrated in the following graphs. Note that non-classifiable programs are not represented. Winter and summer seasons were treated separately to point out characteristic patterns in each.

ABC-TV's special programming over the entire period was dominated by information specials. The 1954-1955 season was the first in which entertainment specials outranked information specials on ABC-TV. (1954-1955 was the season in which NBC-TV began to exploit the concept of "spectacular" programming with lavishly produced entertainment programs offered on a regular, usually monthly, basis.[6]) Again in

---

[6]Giraud Chester, et. al., Television and Radio, 3rd edition (New York: Appleton-Century-Crofts, 1963), p. 58.

TABLE 58

SPECIAL PRIME TIME DEVOTED TO ENTERTAINMENT AND INFORMATION SHOWS BY SEASONS

	ABC-TV		CBS-TV		NBC-TV		DuMONT	
	Hours	%	Hours	%	Hours	%	Hours	%
Winter Seasons								
Entertainment	142:30	24.2%	356:05	40.5%	435:45	40.7%	22:00	29.5%
Information-Orientation	208:50	35.8	236:00	26.9	342:45	32.1	19:35	26.2
Non-classifiable	17:30	3.0	35:30	4.0	25:50	2.4	2:30	3.4
Summer Seasons								
Entertainment	59:00	10.2	63:00	7.2	51:30	4.8	2:15	3.3
Information-Orientation	152:05	26.2	184:35	21.0	209:50	19.6	28:00	37.6
Non-classifiable	3:30	0.6	2:45	0.4	4:40	0.4	-	-
TOTALS	583:25	100.0%	877:55	100.0%	1070:20	100.0%	74:20	100.0%

1959-1960, <u>entertainment</u> specials were programmed slightly more on ABC than <u>information</u> shows. The greatest edge ABC-TV ever gave to <u>entertainment</u> specials in the prime time hours occurred in 1961-1962. Finally, in 1963-1964, slightly more time went to <u>entertainment</u> specials; in all other winter seasons, <u>information</u> specials predominated on ABC-TV.

The pattern which emerged from distributing ABC-TV's summer season prime time special programming into <u>entertainment</u> and <u>information</u> classes was typical in its major respects with that of the other networks. The outstanding feature of this programming, illustrated in Figure 20, was the great stress each presidential election year on <u>information-type</u> specials. In other summers, special programming of either type on ABC-TV during prime time rarely exceeded five hours.

CBS-TV winter season special programming in prime time hours offered a contrast to ABC-TV's in its distribution between <u>entertainment</u> and <u>information</u> programs. With the exception of the first season, 1948-1949, CBS-TV pre-empted more nighttime hours for <u>information</u> specials than <u>entertainment</u> specials during the early years of television networking. In 1953-1954, CBS-TV <u>entertainment</u> pre-emptions moved slightly ahead of the others. The difference became more pronounced the following season, coinciding with the development of "spectacular" programs on NBC-TV. 1956-1957, an election year, saw CBS non-entertainment programs predominate by a narrow margin; however, in 1957-1958, CBS-TV scheduled considerably more <u>entertainment</u> than <u>information</u> specials. Between 1957-1958 and 1965-1966, CBS-TV nighttime non-regular programs were largely <u>entertainment</u> offerings, with 1959-1960 the peak season for this type of special. The only

FIGURE 20

WINTER SEASON TRENDS IN ABC-TV'S ENTERTAINMENT AND INFORMATION PRIME TIME SPECIAL PROGRAMMING

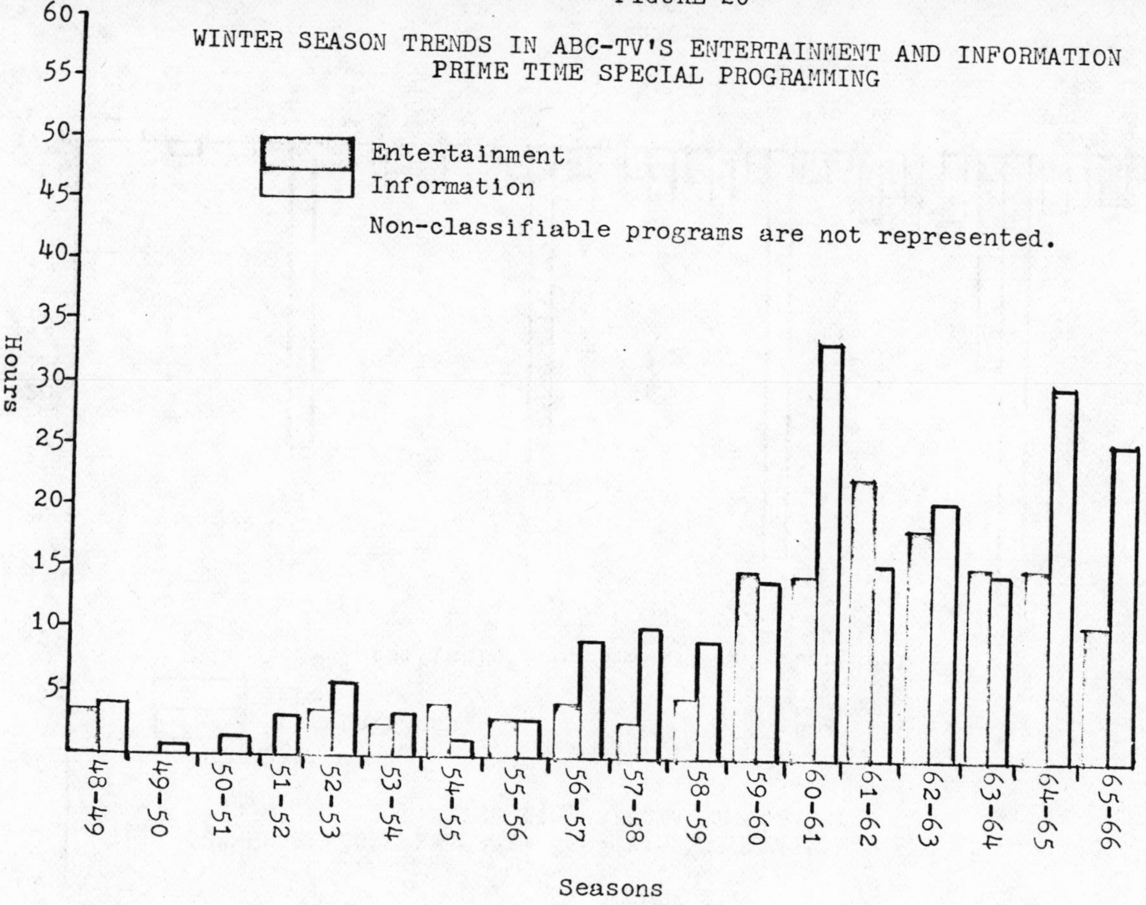

FIGURE 21

SUMMER SEASON TRENDS IN ABC-TV'S ENTERTAINMENT AND INFORMATION PRIME TIME SPECIAL PROGRAMMING

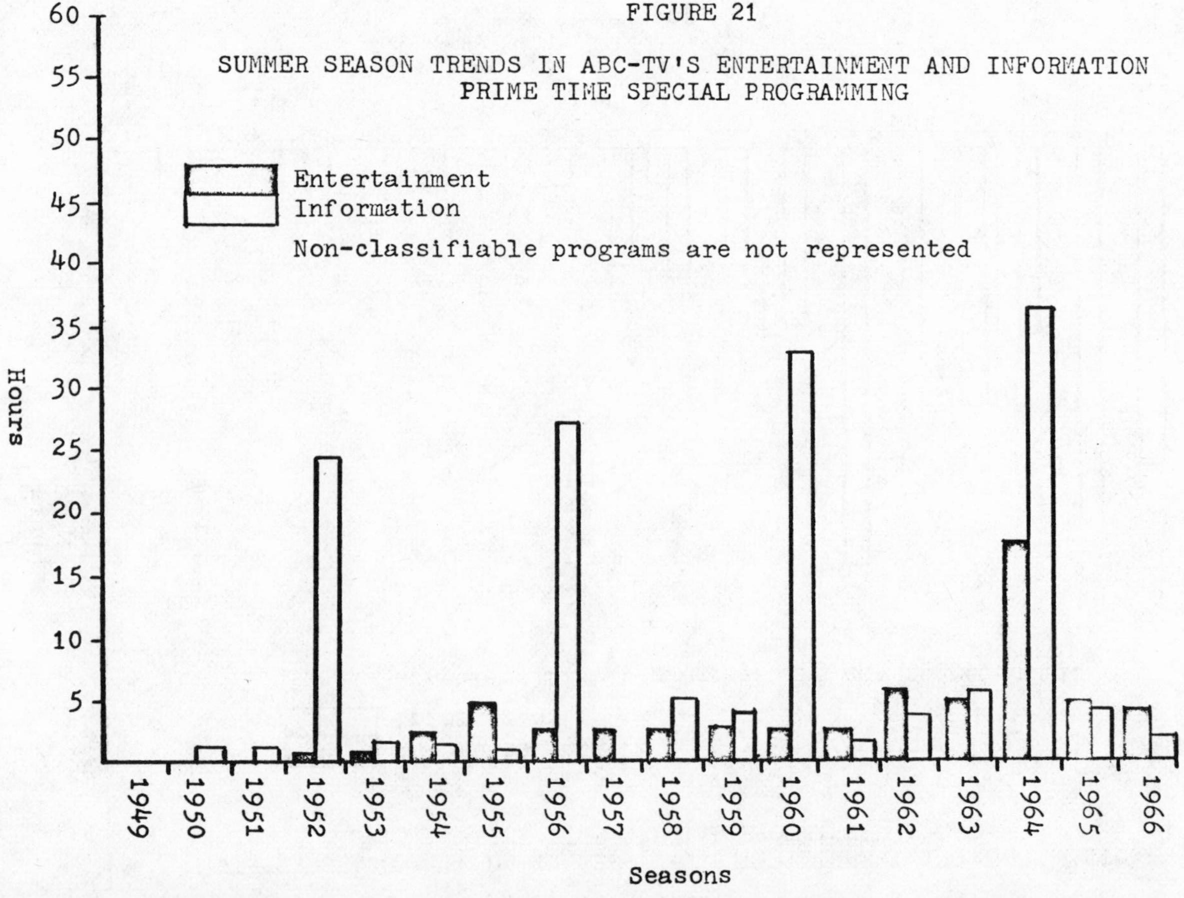

FIGURE 22

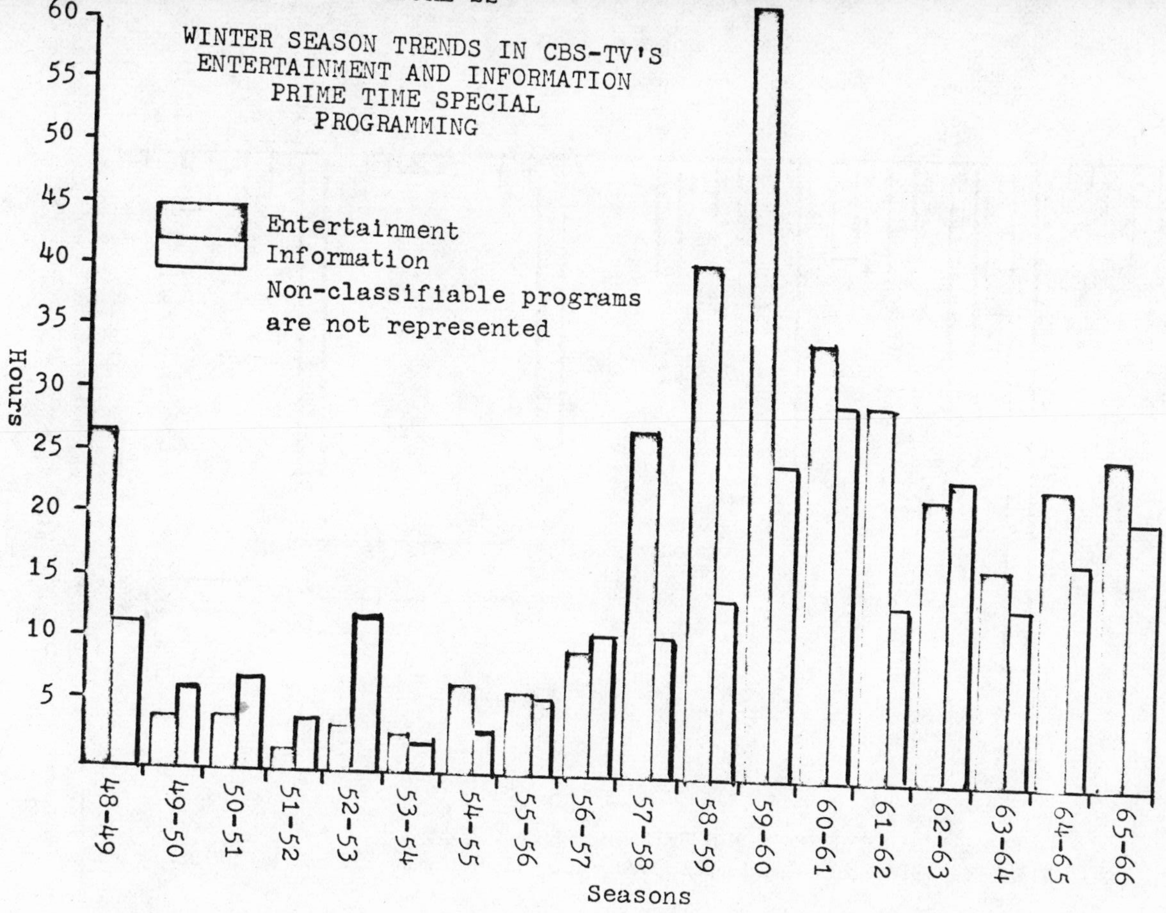
WINTER SEASON TRENDS IN CBS-TV'S
ENTERTAINMENT AND INFORMATION
PRIME TIME SPECIAL
PROGRAMMING
Entertainment
Information
Non-classifiable programs
are not represented
Hours
60
55
50
45
40
35
30
25
20
15
10
5
48-49
49-50
50-51
51-52
52-53
53-54
54-55
55-56
56-57
57-58
58-59
59-60
60-61
61-62
62-63
63-64
64-65
65-66
Seasons

FIGURE 23

SUMMER SEASON TRENDS IN CBS-TV'S ENTERTAINMENT AND INFORMATION PRIME TIME SPECIAL PROGRAMMING

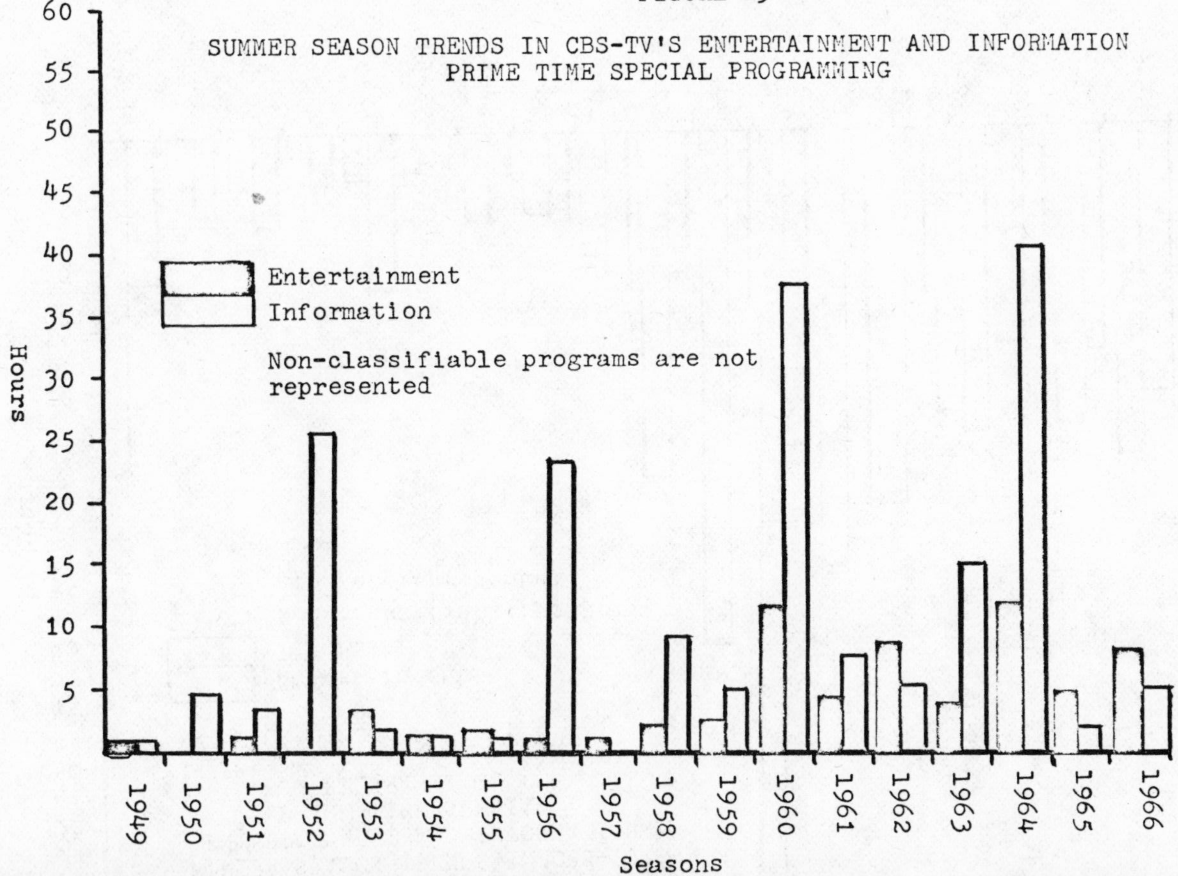

season subsequent to 1957-1958 in which CBS-TV pre-empted more time for information specials than entertainment specials was 1962-1963.

CBS-TV summer season nighttime special programming displayed a characteristic concentration on information programs each election year. During the other summers, the balance between entertainment and non-entertainment specials apparently varied randomly.

Figure 24 depicts NBC-TV's nighttime non-regular programming during winter seasons. In the early years, entertainment programs generally predominated NBC-TV's prime time special offerings. The 1952 presidential election boosted information specials over entertainment programs, a situation which occurred again to a lesser degree in 1956. In all other winter seasons from 1954-1955 through 1959-1960, information specials ran far behind entertainment specials on NBC-TV in prime time hours. A sudden change occurred in 1960-1961 when information specials accounted for more pre-empted time than did entertainment shows. During this period of the early 1960's, broadcasters were under pressure from the newly appointed Federal Communications Commission Chairman, Newton Minow, to improve programming in the "vast wasteland." The predominance of non-entertainment specials on NBC-TV continued for five seasons, from 1960-1961 through 1964-1965. In 1965-1966, entertainment pre-emptions regained their prominence. Thus, entertainment was the primary function of NBC-TV's prime time special programming during the late 1950's, information during the early 1960's, while 1965-1966 represented a shift back to the entertainment function.

FIGURE 24

WINTER SEASON TRENDS IN NBC-TV'S ENTERTAINMENT AND INFORMATION
PRIME TIME SPECIAL PROGRAMMING

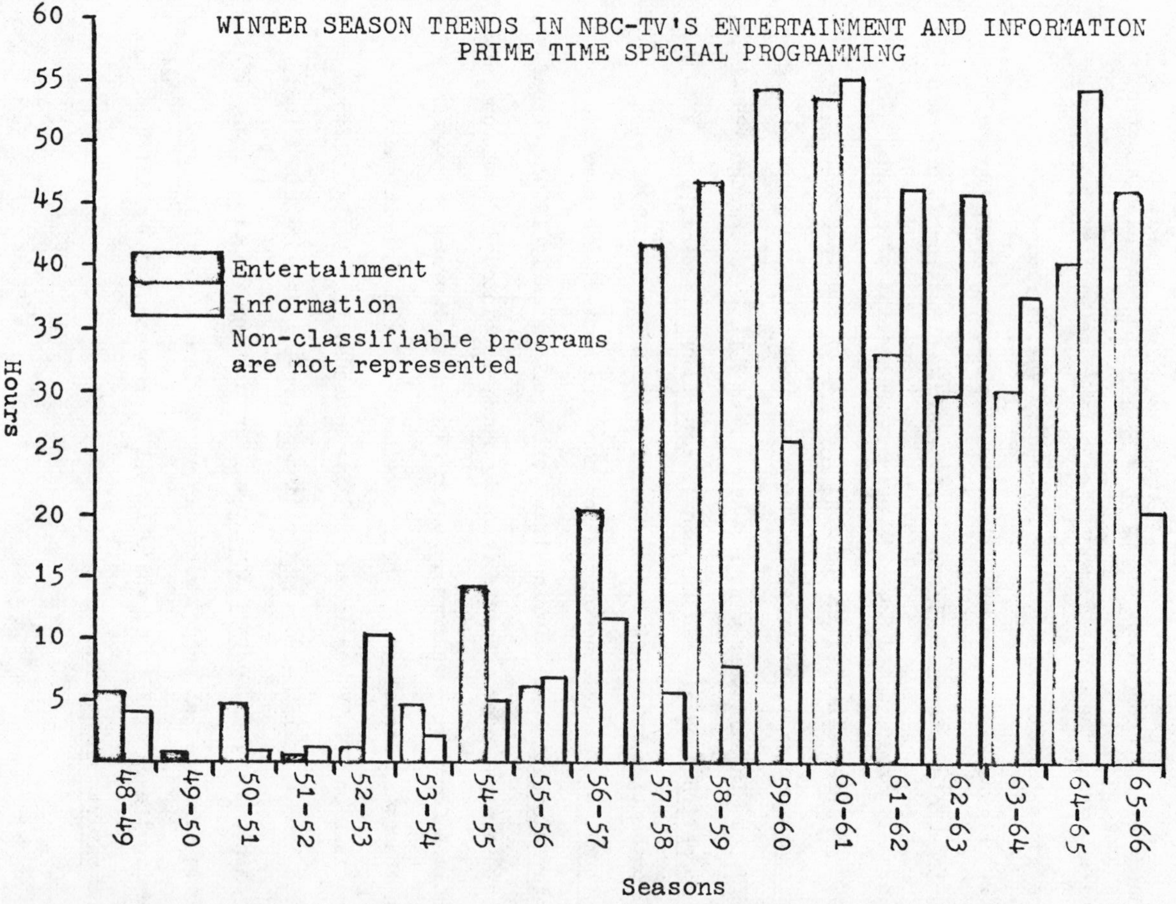

FIGURE 25

SUMMER SEASON TRENDS IN NBC-TV'S ENTERTAINMENT AND INFORMATION PRIME TIME SPECIAL PROGRAMMING

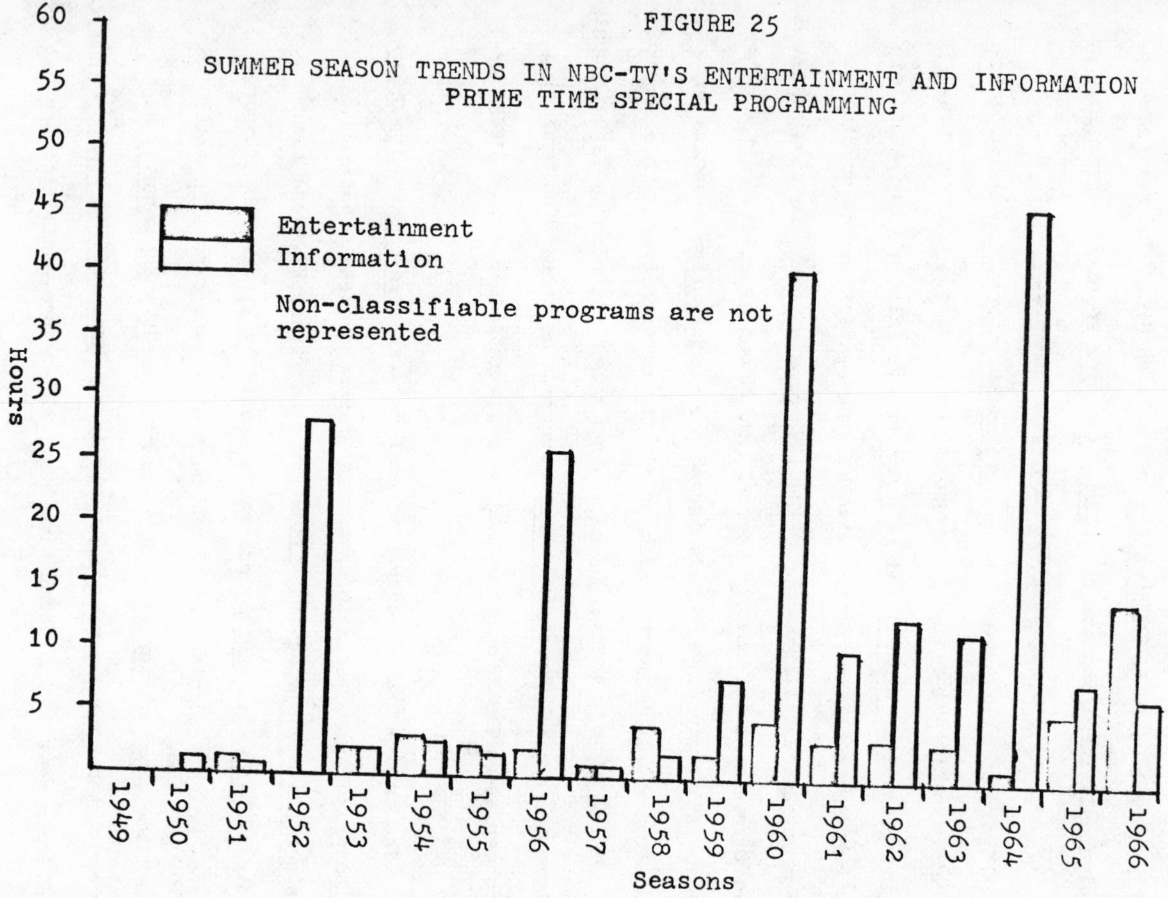

The entertainment-information pattern in NBC-TV's summer season nighttime non-regular programming, Figure 25, generally conformed to that of the other networks. Summers from 1959 through the early 1960's were largely devoted to information specials on NBC. The summers with conspicuously large amounts of information-type special programming were, of course, presidential election year summers.

Figure 26 illustrates the entertainment-information characteristics of DuMont's prime time non-regular programming. DuMont's pre-emptions for entertainment and information specials followed a pattern recognizable in all the other networks. Non-entertainment specials were prominent until 1954-1955. The 1952 presidential election resulted in an increase in information specials on DuMont as it did on the other chains. Entertainment specials surged past information programs on DuMont in 1954-1955, as they did on all the other networks that season.

The summer of 1952 stood out as one which contained a large amount of time pre-empted for information programs. No other distinguishing characteristics in DuMont's summer season nighttime specials programming was apparent.

The categorical structure of each network's entertainment/information prime time special programming presented certain patterns. ABC-TV's entertainment specials, illustrated in Figure 27, were composed mostly of talks and variety programs, specifically the sub-categories sports, which accounted for 12 per cent of ABC-TV's total special prime time, musical variety, 10 per cent, awards and pageants, 4.3 per cent, and comedy variety, 2.6 per cent. Unclassified drama made up 1.3 per cent of the prime time hours ABC-TV pre-empted for special

FIGURE 26

WINTER AND SUMMER SEASON TRENDS IN DuMONT'S ENTERTAINMENT AND INFORMATION PRIME TIME SPECIAL PROGRAMMING

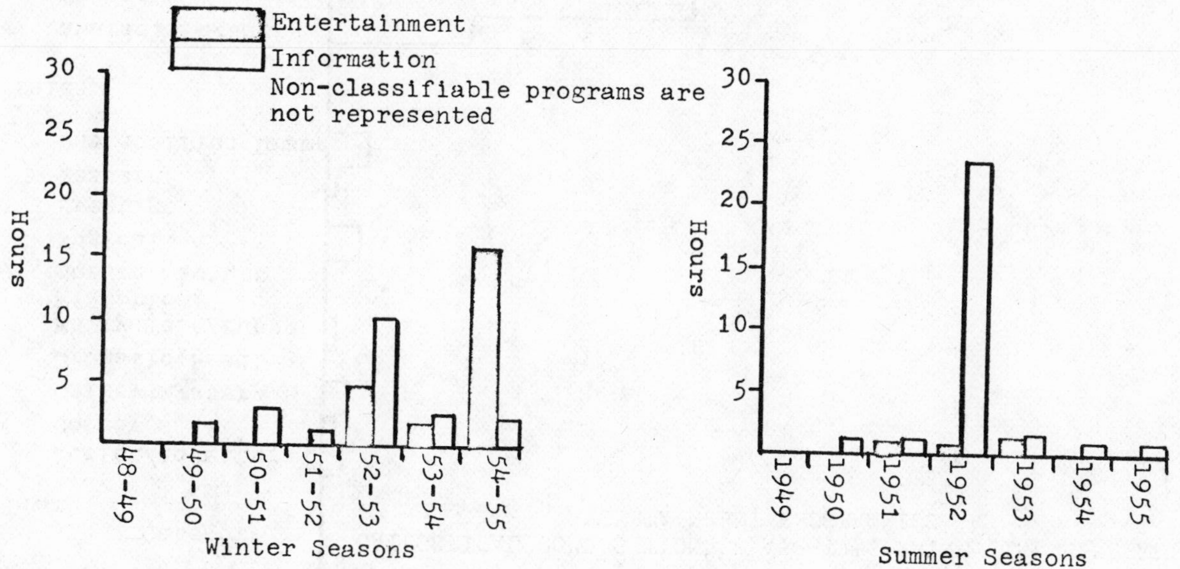

FIGURE 27

CATEGORICAL COMPOSITION OF ABC-TV'S PRIME TIME SPECIAL ENTERTAINMENT PROGRAMMING

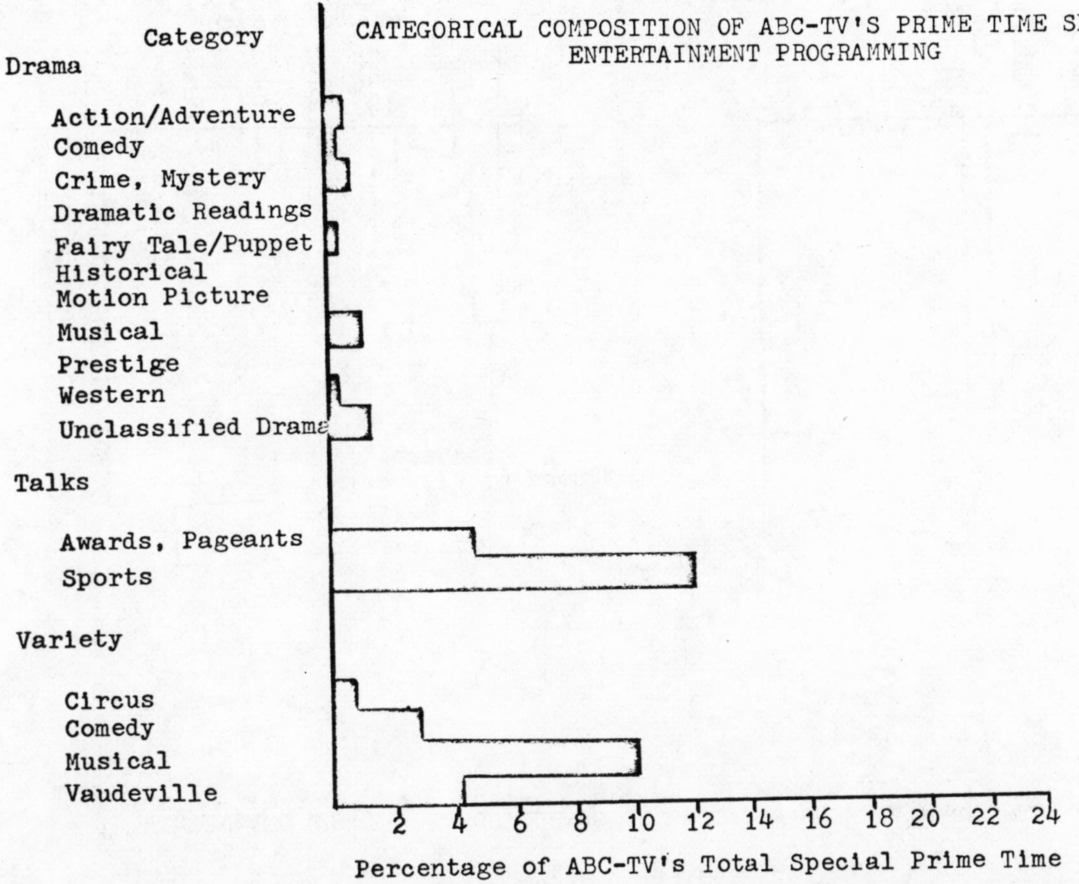

programs; the remaining sub-categories each comprised one per cent or less. All drama categories combined made up only 4.5 per cent of ABC-TV's total nighttime non-regular hours, or about the same amount as the awards sub-category alone.

In ABC-TV's information-type special programming, Figure 28, political programs, comprising 28.5 per cent of all ABC-TV's pre-empted prime time hours, and documentary, 20.5 per cent, were the prime elements. Together, these two sub-categories accounted for nearly half--49 per cent--of ABC's prime time special hours. Other sub-types of less importance were news, 5.7 per cent, speeches, 4.4 per cent, and panel discussions, 2.1 per cent. The remaining sub-categories in ABC-TV's information-type special programming accounted for less than one per cent each of that network's total pre-empted prime time hours.

CBS-TV's entertainment specials were more inclined to be drama programs than were those of any other network. More than 19 per cent of all prime time hours CBS-TV pre-empted for non-regular programming were devoted to various kinds of drama, more special drama than offered by any of the other chains. Within this general category, the sub-type prestige drama was the largest, accounting for 4.5 per cent of CBS-TV's total special time. Comedy drama ranked next at 3.7 per cent, followed by musical drama, 2.4 per cent, unclassified drama, 2.3 per cent, action and adventure drama, 2.1 per cent, and crime drama, 1.3 per cent. All other drama sub-categories comprised less than one per cent of CBS-TV's total special prime time each.

Both talks sub-categories in the entertainment group, awards and sports, figured in CBS-TV's special programming, although not to

FIGURE 28

CATEGORICAL COMPOSITION OF ABC-TV'S PRIME TIME SPECIAL INFORMATION PROGRAMMING

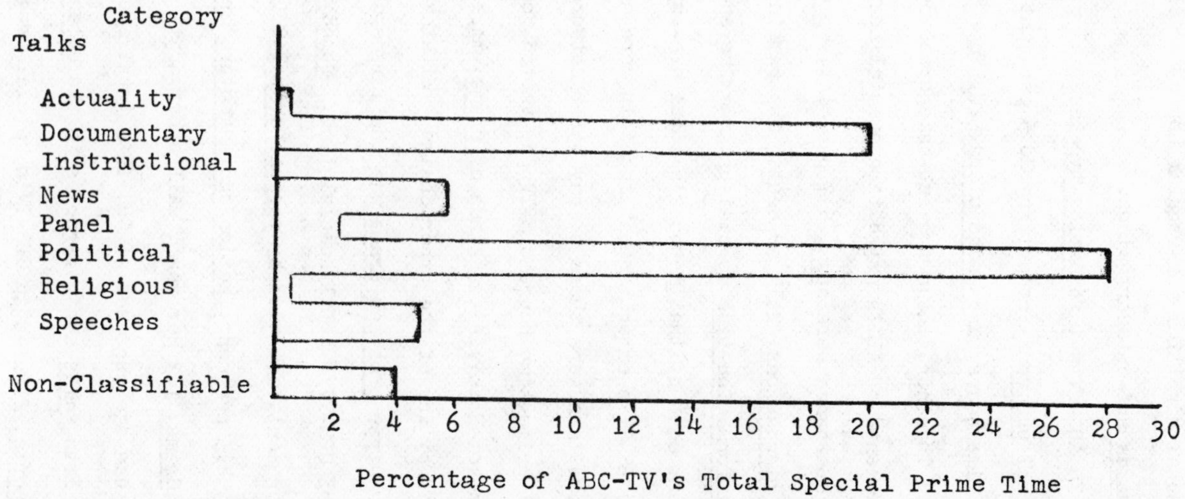

FIGURE 29

CATEGORICAL COMPOSITION OF CBS-TV'S PRIME TIME SPECIAL ENTERTAINMENT PROGRAMMING

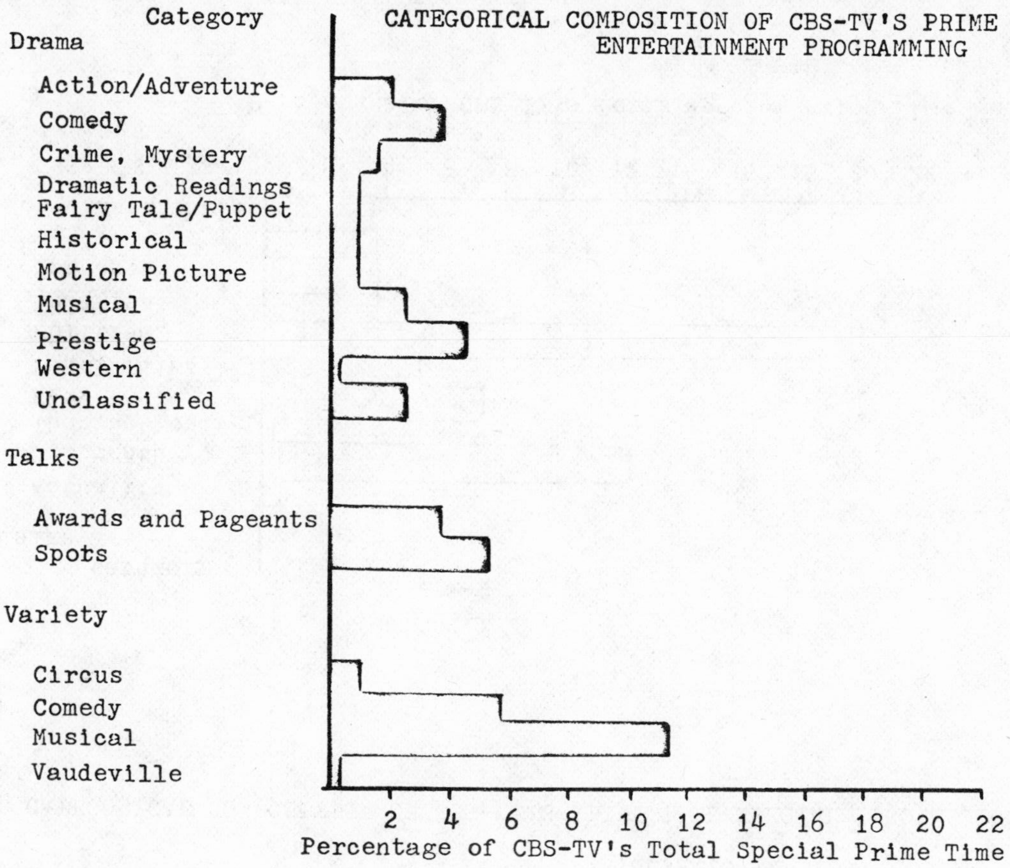

FIGURE 30

CATEGORICAL COMPOSITION OF CBS-TV'S PRIME TIME SPECIAL INFORMATION PROGRAMMING

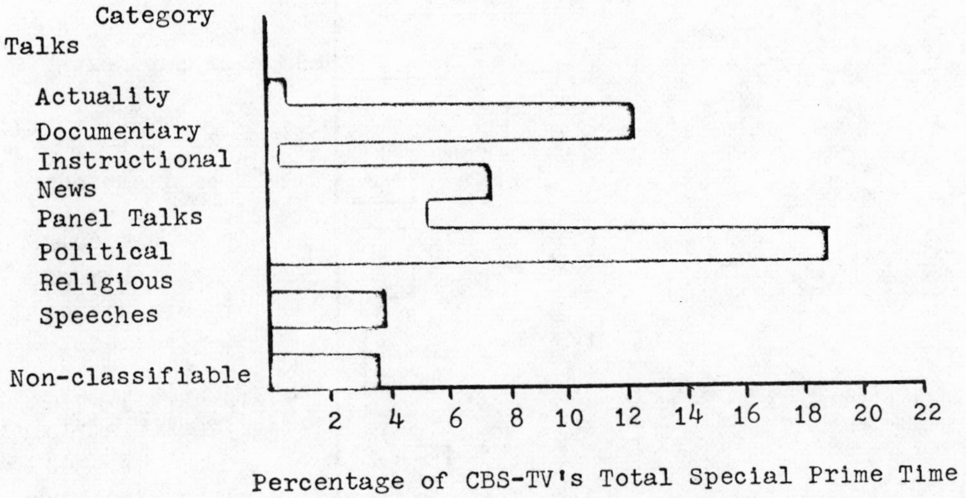

the extent they did on ABC-TV. CBS pre-empted 5.3 per cent of its total special prime time for sports shows, 3.7 per cent for awards and pageants.

Musical variety constituted the largest single sub-category in CBS-TV's entertainment-type pre-emptive programming, 11.4 per cent. Comedy variety made up 5.6 per cent, and circus and vaudeville variety each comprised less than one per cent.

The categorical organization of CBS-TV's prime time information-type special programming was similar to that of ABC-TV's, but on a slightly smaller scale. Political and documentary specials constituted the largest non-entertainment categories, accounting for 18.7 and 12.2 per cent of CBS-TV's total nighttime special hours. Whereas on ABC-TV these two sub-types made up nearly half all pre-empted prime time hours, on CBS-TV they accounted for less than one-third. Following in rank order on CBS were news, 7.2 per cent, panel discussions, 5.1 per cent, and speeches, 3.9 per cent. Other sub-categories each made up less than one per cent of total CBS-TV special prime time.

NBC-TV depended more on variety programs in its entertainment-type prime time special programming than did the other networks. Musical variety in particular was prominent, making up 12.9 per cent of NBC's total special prime time hours. NBC-TV also scheduled more comedy variety than ABC-TV, and CBS-TV, but less vaudeville variety than ABC-TV. Comedy variety and vaudeville variety accounted for 8.5 and 2.3 per cent of NBC-TV's total prime time pre-emptive hours.

NBC scheduled fewer hours of talks specials than the other networks, but in the same general proportions, i.e., more sports specials, 4.4 per cent, than awards, 3.5 per cent.

FIGURE 31

CATEGORICAL COMPOSITION OF NBC-TV'S PRIME TIME SPECIAL ENTERTAINMENT PROGRAMMING

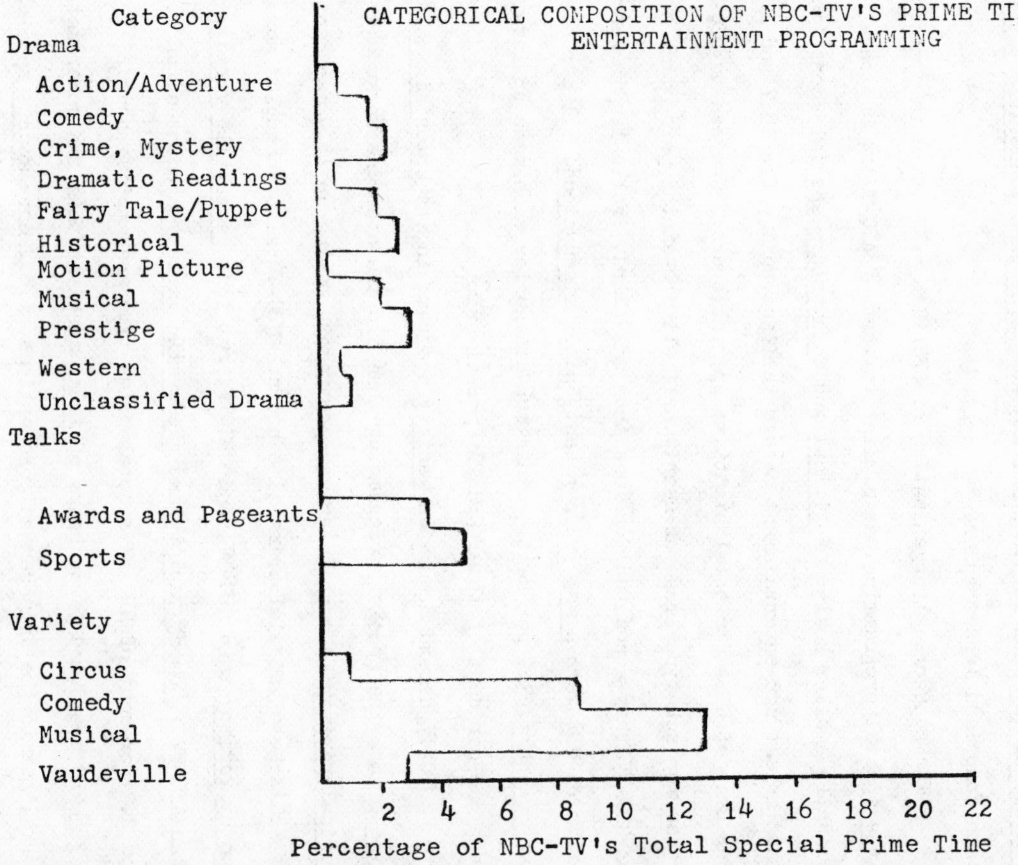

FIGURE 32

CATEGORICAL COMPOSITION OF NBC-TV'S PRIME TIME SPECIAL INFORMATION PROGRAMMING

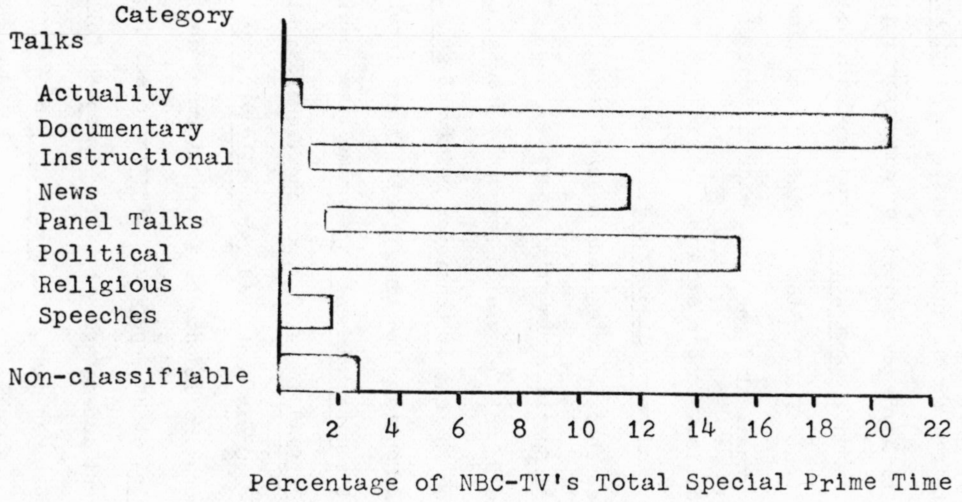

As on CBS-TV, prestige drama was the largest drama sub-category on NBC-TV, accounting for 2.7 per cent of that network's total prime time. Other drama types making up more than one per cent of all NBC special nighttime hours were historical and biographical drama, 2.2 per cent, crime drama, 2.0 per cent, fairy tale drama, 1.9 per cent, and musical drama, also 1.9 per cent.

NBC-TV's information-type specials set up a pattern somewhat different from the other networks. Where political specials comprised the bulk of hours pre-empted for non-entertainment specials on ABC, CBS, and DuMont, documentary shows predominated on NBC. Documentaries, 20.5 per cent of NBC's total special prime time, politicals, 15.2 per cent, and news, 11.7 per cent, made up most of NBC-TV's information-type specials. Lesser amounts of time were devoted to speeches, 1.6 per cent, and panel discussions, 1.3 per cent. The remaining information-type sub-categories each made up less than one per cent of NBC-TV's total special prime time hours.

The DuMont Television Network's special entertainment schedule was unique in that it consisted mainly of sports programs; 24.5 per cent of DuMont's prime time special hours involved sports. The balance of DuMont's entertainment-type prime time special programming consisted of unclassified drama, 2.7 per cent, awards, also 2.7 per cent, musical variety, 2.0 per cent, and vaudeville variety, 0.7 per cent.

Among the DuMont specials performing an information function, politicals, at 43.0 per cent of total special prime time, constituted the largest sub-category by far. Speeches followed at 12.1 per cent, news at 5.4 per cent, and documentary at 2.7 per cent. Panel discussions accounted for less than one per cent of DuMont's special prime time.

FIGURE 33

CATEGORICAL COMPOSITION OF DuMONT'S PRIME TIME SPECIAL ENTERTAINMENT PROGRAMMING

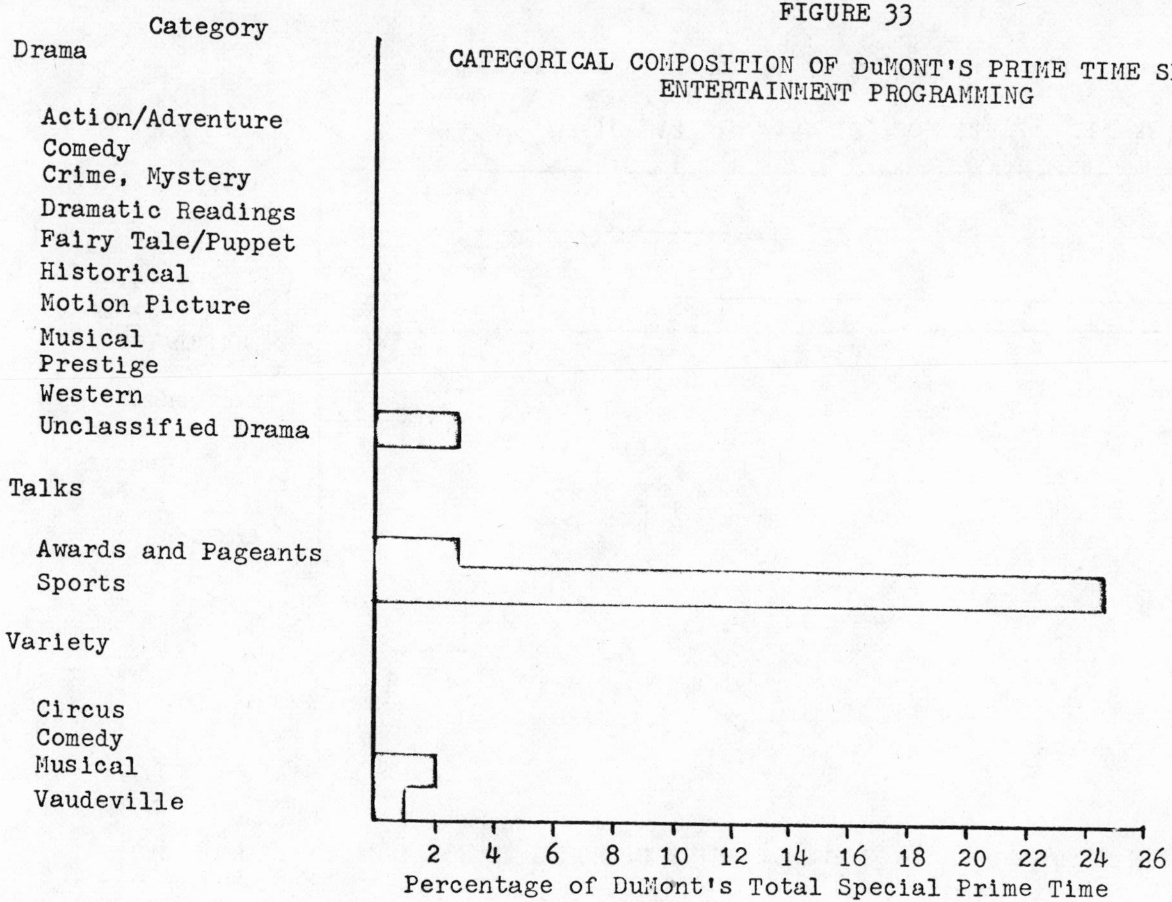

FIGURE 34

CATEGORICAL COMPOSITION OF DuMONT'S PRIME TIME SPECIAL INFORMATION PROGRAMMING

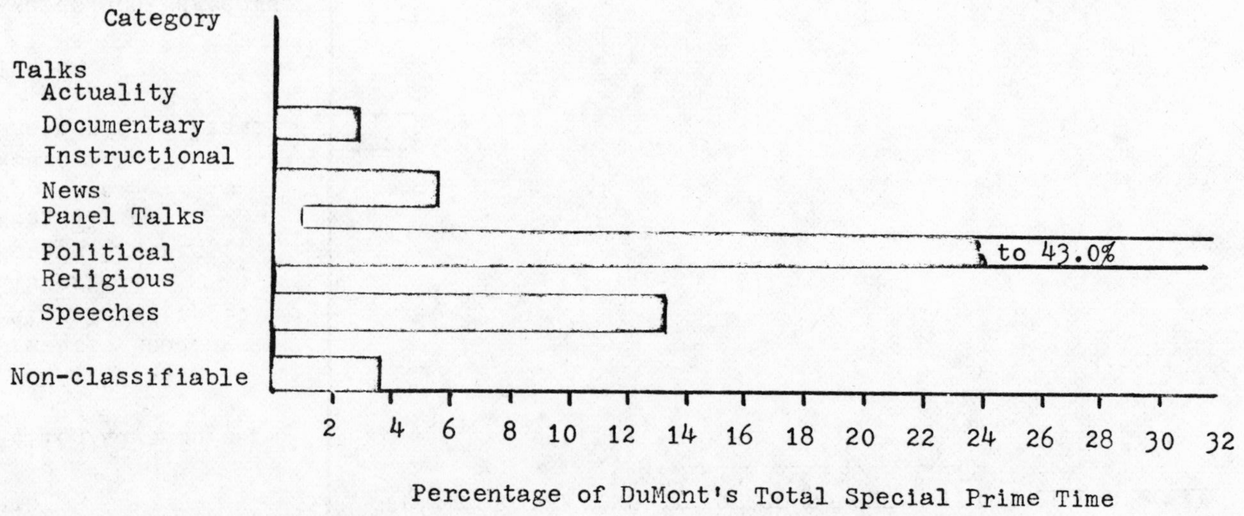

Combining the nighttime non-regular programming of all networks, a composite picture of the categorical structure of entertainment- and information-type programming was constructed in Figures 35 and 36. In this overall picture, total prime time special programming performing the entertainment function consisted primarily of variety programs. In Chapter V, variety specials were noted as having earned the highest ratings.[7] This may explain in part why the variety category predominated the entertainment-type pre-emptions. Within the variety classification, musical variety was scheduled the most frequently, although Table 54 showed musical variety received lower ratings than any other variety sub-type. Musical variety accounted for 11.4 per cent of pre-empted prime time hours on all networks combined, followed by comedy variety, 5.9 per cent, vaudeville variety, 1.4 per cent, and circus variety, 0.6 per cent.

Drama programs constituted the next largest classification in the entertainment group. This category also followed variety in average ratings.[8] Prestige drama, one of the lower rated drama sub-types,[9] predominated in this group, making up 2.6 per cent of total pre-empted prime time hours. Other types of drama comprising more than one per cent of total special hours were comedy drama, 1.9 per cent, musical drama, 1.8 per cent, crime drama, 1.4 per cent, historical and biographical drama, 1.2 per cent, and fairy tale drama, 1.1 per cent.

---

[7] *Supra*, p. 175.

[8] *Supra*, p. 178.

[9] *Supra*, p. 177.

FIGURE 35

COMPOSITE CATEGORICAL COMPOSITION OF PRIME TIME SPECIAL ENTERTAINMENT PROGRAMMING, ALL NETWORKS

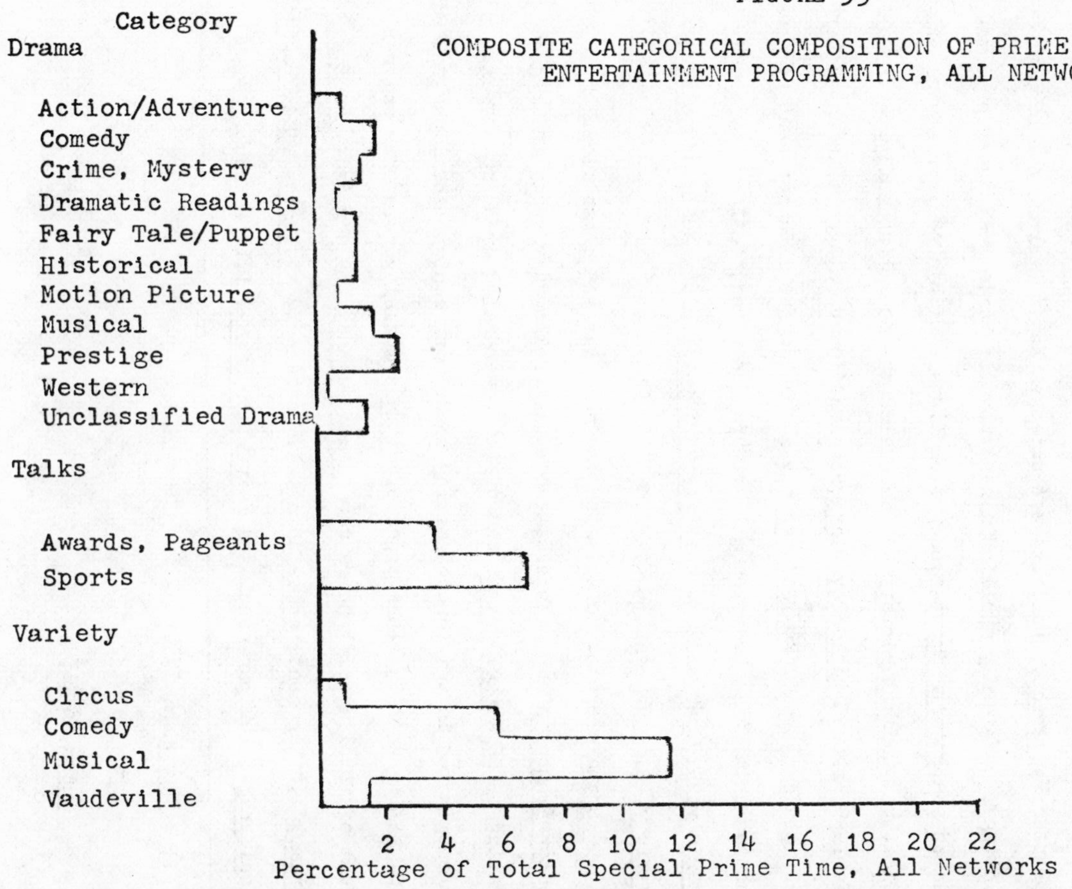

FIGURE 36

COMPOSITE CATEGORICAL COMPOSITION OF PRIME TIME SPECIAL INFORMATION PROGRAMMING, ALL NETWORKS

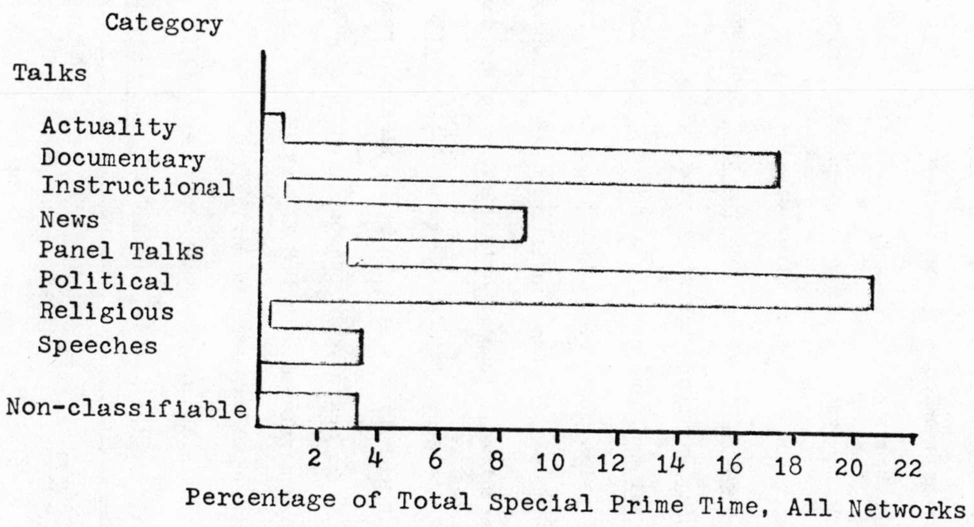

The composite picture of prime time specials performing primarily an information function, Figure 36, put political specials at the forefront with 20.6 per cent of the pre-empted hours falling into this subtype. Political programs were among the lowest rated talks specials.[10] Documentary followed politicals closely, accounting for 17.2 per cent of all pre-empted prime time hours, after which came news, 8.7 per cent, speeches, 3.3 per cent, and panel discussions, 2.7 per cent. Other talks sub-categories each amounted to less than one per cent of total prime time hours on all networks combined.

This analysis has shown that network television prime time special programming has struck a better balance than regular programming between entertainment-type and information-type programs. Regular television programming was characterized by the NAEB studies as consisting largely of entertainment programs. This study found that slightly more than half all prime time pre-emptive programs consisted of information programs. The pattern was consistent. All networks have programmed more non-entertainment than entertainment specials during prime time.

Specials performing an essentially entertainment function began to play a significant role in prime time non-regular programming with the 1954-1955 season, the season in which NBC-TV's "spectacular" programs were developed. On CBS-TV and NBC-TV, entertainment specials predominated winter seasons during the latter 1950's. Non-entertainment specials became more prevalent, especially on NBC, during the first half of the 1960's. On ABC-TV, information-type specials have

---

[10] *Supra*, p. 177.

nearly always equalled or surpassed the amount of time given to _entertainment_ specials during prime time.

Summer season prime time special programming exhibited a highly uniform pattern of its own on all networks, its most outstanding characteristic being the large number of _information-type_ programs scheduled during each presidential election year summer.

The categorical structure of _entertainment_ specials programming during prime time ran largely to _variety_ and _drama_ programs on CBS and NBC, _variety_ and _talks_ programs on ABC and DuMont. On CBS and NBC, the largest single _entertainment_ sub-category was _musical variety_, while on ABC and DuMont it was _sports_.

In _information-type_ special programming during nighttime hours, _political programs_ dominated on all networks except NBC-TV where _documentary_ was the most prominent sub-category. The _documentary_ type was secondary on CBS-TV and ABC-TV, while _politicals_ were secondary on NBC-TV.

In sum, network television prime time special programming has been quite evenly divided between performing an _entertainment_ and an _information_ function.

CHAPTER VII

CONCLUSION

This study set out to describe the extent and certain characteristics of special programming during prime time hours on the national, interconnected television networks, the American Broadcasting Company, the Columbia Broadcasting System, the National Broadcasting Company, and the defunct DuMont Television Network. No attempt was made to evaluate this programming or assess effects thereof; the study was designed to be strictly quantitative.

Fundamental assumptions underlying the study were that a substantial amount of prime time special television programming had been done, that an accurate record of it could be compiled and categorized for analysis, and that the analysis would reveal trends, patterns, and characteristics relative to scheduling, sponsorship, ratings, and functions. Results of the study appeared to validate the assumptions.

Certainly, a substantial amount of prime time was pre-empted in favor of special programs by each network. Enough prime time hours were devoted to special programs between September 15, 1948 and September 14, 1966 by all the networks, 2,606 hours, to completely program one network's prime time schedule for two winter and two summer seasons with hours to spare. During winter seasons in recent years, weeks containing no pre-emptions of regular programs have been the exception rather than the rule. Commenting on the proliferation of pre-emptive programs, Variety, a major trade publication, stated, "In short, the unusual on tv has become the usual."[1] Special programming has become an important part of American network television.

This study has shown that the national television networks have engaged in pre-emptive programming from the earliest days of regular broadcasting; however, prime time special programming did not begin in earnest until the 1956-1957 season on CBS-TV and NBC-TV, and 1959-1960 on ABC-TV. Strong trends toward more prime time pre-emptions followed these seasons culminating in the 1959-1960 season on CBS-TV and the 1960-1961 season on NBC-TV and ABC-TV. Again in 1964-1965, ABC-TV equalled its pre-emptions of the 1960-1961 season; however, the other networks have thus far not scheduled as many prime time specials in any one year as they did during their peak seasons.

As special programming gained importance in the networks' prime time schedules, its character changed. From primarily sustaining information-type programs, which comprised much of the early-day specials programming, pre-emptive programming became more commercial and entertainment-oriented; however, these trends did not overwhelm special programming. Sustaining programs continued to play an important part in specials schedules, making up about one-fourth the total, while entertainment and information-type specials struck a near even balance.

Contrasting patterns between winter and summer season prime time special programming appeared in the analysis. While regular season

---

[1]"Bull Market for TV Specs," Variety, April 26, 1967, p. 167.

special programming exhibited some relatively long range trends, summer season specials fell into a regular cyclical display, attaining highs each presidential election year, then falling back to relatively low levels. Political specials were the prime causal factor in this pattern, representing extensive coverage of the national political conventions, election night returns, and miscellaneous specials devoted to campaign coverage and talks by political candidates and their supporters.

Regarding the categorical organization of prime time specials, the largest classification was talks programs, the smallest was drama, with variety specials in between. The makeup of specials programming has remained consistent in this pattern throughout the years under study, and reflects the important roles political and documentary specials have played. These two special sub-types dominated each network's schedule of special programs offered in prime time during the entire period.

In the variety category, musical variety was the predominant subtype, followed by comedy drama. This pattern held true for each network. No such consistent pattern appeared for prime time special drama, however. CBS-TV interrupted its regular nighttime schedule to present special drama more often than the other networks, most frequently offering prestige and comedy drama. On NBC-TV, prestige drama was the prominent drama type, but only by a slight margin over historical and biographical drama. ABC-TV scheduled very little special drama in prime time.

While CBS offered the most special drama, the greatest number of both talks and variety specials were broadcast by NBC-TV, the overall leader in prime time special programming.

The general picture of network television prime time special programming was shown to be heavily influenced by the amount of time all networks have given to covering national political events. The total pattern showed the most pre-empted hours occurred during summer months, due to political convention coverage. Other months showing heavy pre-emptions were months in which political campaign activity was carried out. However, when political programs were disregarded, specials pre-emptions settled into a greatly changed pattern, with most hours occurring in fall and winter months, fewest in summer and spring months. The similarity in this pattern and the general pattern of audience television usage throughout the year was apparent. The indication was the networks saved their specials for months in which the television audience tended to be largest, i.e., the fall and winter. This pattern was also probably influenced by the tradition of summer vacations; talent and other production personnel off on vacation were not available to produce summer season specials.

A further analysis regarding the scheduling of specials discovered they were most likely to conclude the prime time segment, beginning at 10:00 or 10:30 p.m., New York Time, with 10:00 p.m. the most frequently pre-empted hour on all networks save DuMont. This is the hour during which the sets-in-use figure begins to decline for the evening[2] and represents the final hour of prime time network feeds to

---

[2]Summers and Summers, loc. cit., p. 258.

local stations; hence, 10:00 to 11:00 p.m. is a safe hour in which to insert specials, particularly those for which a high rating is not anticipated. Scheduled at 10:00 or 10:30 p.m., a weak special will not lower the rating of any following network program, since none exist. Further, a special achieving a low rating in a declining sets-in-use period is not so disastrous as one getting a low rating during a peak viewing hour.

The most prominent sub-category to appear in the 10:00 to 11:00 p.m. time period was documentary, one of the lowest rated special program types (average rating 12.3, share 23.2). Thus, apparently each network attempted to protect the ratings of its regular shows by scheduling many of its documentary specials between 10:00 and 11:00, rather than earlier in the evening. However, the 10:00 to 11:00 p.m. hour was not always a "throw-away" time period. Many awards and pageants also appeared during this hour, earning unusually high ratings (average rating 29.5, share 54.9).

The next most frequently pre-empted hour was 7:30, the beginning of the prime time period. The specials beginning at 10:00 or 10:30 and those beginning at 7:30 set up an early-or-late scheduling pattern into which about half all prime time specials fell. Sets-in-use at 7:30, as at 10:00 p.m. and later, are fewer in number than during the heart of prime time.[3] However, this time slot is not as safe as the 10:00 p.m. period, since regular programs following a 7:30 presentation may be affected by a low rating achieved by the preceeding program (or may benefit from the earlier program's high rating if one is achieved). Nevertheless, the networks also scheduled their generally

[3]Ibid.

low-rated sub-categories in this early time period: documentary, news, and political programs. Conspicuously fewer numbers of the low-rated program types appeared during the middle hours of prime time when viewing is at a peak, than during the early and late hours.

Of all prime time special programming on all networks, 21.8 per cent competed with other specials. Simultaneously duplicated specials (special programs consisting of identical subject matter scheduled on two or more networks at the same time) were found to comprise 13.6 per cent of all prime time specials in the study, while 8.2 per cent competed with other specials on other networks. The most frequently duplicated special program types were political programs, speeches, and news, events the networks tended to cover in concert. This represented cross programming in an ultimate degree: identical program content.

Cross programming was the outstanding characteristic of specials scheduled against other specials when both duplicated and non-duplicated competitive programs were taken as a whole. However, when non-duplicated competitive programs were considered separately, counter programming appeared most frequently for this group. Only infrequently were highly rated program types scheduled in competition. The most common competitive situation involved information-type specials programmed against entertainment-type specials. In such cases the entertainment-type programs were almost invariably rated higher than their competition. Information versus information specials was the next most frequently occurring circumstance. Entertainment versus entertainment specials was the least likely competitive situation, occurring far less frequently than the others described. This pattern was another indication that specials were most often scheduled in a safe manner. An _entertainment_ special thrown against an _information_ special was assured of rating success, while an _entertainment_ special scheduled opposite another _entertainment_ special was a riskier proposition. _Information-type_ specials were not programmed for their prowess in the ratings, since they represented the lowest-rated program type; hence, programming an _information-type_ special against a similar type could also be considered a safe tactic.

When the data were examined for sponsorship characteristics, just over one-fourth all prime time specials telecast by all networks were identified as sustaining (unsponsored) programs. Most sustainers fell in the _speeches_, _documentary_, _news_, _panel discussions_, _political_, _actuality_, and _religious_ sub-categories. Two elements these sub-types held in common were that they were all _talks_ specials and low-rated classifications. Most _speeches_, some _documentary_ and _news_, some _actuality_, and all _religious_ specials could be considered inappropriate for sponsorship. Sponsored specials made up 68.5 per cent of all the programs analyzed, while sponsorship data for 5.9 per cent was not ascertained.

Of the sponsored specials, over three-fourths--76.1 per cent--were presented by single advertisers (the single-sponsorship method) while the balance were sponsored by more than one advertiser (the multiple-sponsorship method). The predominance of single-sponsorship over multiple-sponsorship in prime time specials programming was consistent over all the years of the study. This characteristic differed markedly from that obtaining in the area of regular programming. The trend in regular programming has been from single-sponsorship to multiple-sponsorship. While single sponsorship of television programs on a regular basis has become prohibitively expensive in recent years, advertisers convinced of the value of program identification through single-sponsorship have apparently gone into this type of advertising on an occasional or special basis. This probably accounts for the prevalence of single-sponsorship prime time specials.

National Nielsen ratings for 1,230 prime time specials, 67.2 per cent of all sponsored prime time specials televised between January 1, 1950 and September 14, 1966, were analyzed by categories and subcategories to determine, within the limitations of the data, average ratings and share of audience for special program types. Variety programs received the highest ratings, followed by drama specials, while talks shows received the lowest ratings as a class. These findings were consistent with the results of a Nielsen study conducted on special programs which appeared in the 1960-1961 season.[4]

Entertainment specials fared best in the ratings, although there were more information specials offered by each network. Since the networks consistently programmed more of the lowly-rated than highly-rated program types, apparently much special programming was done with a disregard for acquiring high ratings. Other considerations evidently motivated the bulk of special programming. Much of this programming could be considered "public affairs" programming, i.e., documentaries, panel discussions, and news specials on current problems and events,

---

[4]"The TV Special: It's No Gamble," loc. cit.

political programs covering campaigns and elections, in short, the type of programming the Federal Communications Commission tends to consider is in the public interest. The networks apparently used this type of special programming as a means of discharging what might be termed a responsibility to inform as well as entertain the audience.

This type of special programming was also the type most likely to be presented on a sustaining basis, further indicating its public service nature.

The average rating and share for all special program types taken together was 15.7 and 28.6 per cent.

An analysis according to function performed on the data revealed 43.1 per cent of the prime time special programs under examination performed basically an entertainment function, while 53 per cent performed an information function (3.9 per cent were unclassified as to function). This contrasted with the final NAEB-sponsored study of general television programming which found 83 per cent of nighttime television offerings on New York City stations between 1951 and 1954 to be entertainment-type programs. Thus, apparently prime time special programming has been more evenly divided between the entertainment and information functions than has regular television programming.

Television broadcasting on the national networks has been characterized as being "so similar most of the time that it amounts to a single service."[5] That observation certainly applies to prime time special programming. A sometimes remarkable similarity among the

---

[5]Fred W. Friendly, "World Without Distance," NAEB Journal, 26:1, January-February, 1967, p. 9.

networks in various aspects of special programming was observed in this study. Growth trends in special programming have in many respects been highly similar; employment of similar program types in similar proportions has been striking; a substantial amount of simultaneously duplicated programs has added increased uniformity to the special program service offered by the networks; sponsorship and scheduling characteristics bore obvious similarities. The major difference appears to have been the amounts of time each network spent on prime time pre-emptive programming. In most other respects, that programming was highly similar.

Special programming will undoubtedly continue to be a major component in network television prime time schedules. There are several indicators which suggest this conclusion. There appears to be no change in the networks' plans for handling political coverage, which accounts for more pre-empted time than any other single category. Each network has indicated plans to offer "gavel-to-gavel" coverage of the 1968 national political conventions.[6] Hence, there will be no reduction in the amount of time expended on <u>political</u> specials in the near future. In fact, in 1968, viewers will probably have available more programs dealing with national political activity than in any previous year, since the National Educational Television network (NET) also plans to cover convention and campaign events.[7]

---

[6]"Network Views Vary on Convention Coverage," <u>Broadcasting</u>, April 17, 1967, p. 92.

[7]"Ford Foundation to Cover 1968 Political Events for NET," <u>Variety</u>, April 19, 1967, p. 68.

Sponsor demand for television special programs is another important factor which influences their number, and sponsor demand for programs is influenced by viewer acceptance. Viewer acceptance can be judged by the ratings programs receive. During the 1967-1968 season, certain specials, notably the entertainment-types, were reported to have earned higher ratings in most cases than the regular programs they pre-empted.[8] Thus, sponsor demand for specials will most likely remain high. Moreover, so long as advertisers find specials effective and financially feasible programs for single-sponsorship, there will continue to be a demand for them by advertisers who desire the prestige and program identification single-sponsorship offers, but cannot afford it on a regular basis, or who, for other reasons, require only occasional television exposure.

As network television regular schedules have come under increasingly severe criticism, pre-emptive programming has been pointed to as the bright spot in television programming.[9] This should encourage the networks' special efforts.

Specials also give the networks opportunities to try out new program ideas, to send up "trial balloons," to experiment in the area of programming. Such experimentation might lead to different forms of regular programming.

Specials are a practical form of programming for other reasons also. Each network's news department maintains a staff charged with

---

[8]"Specs-Happy Webs Could Program Fourth Network With '67-'68 Rosters," Variety, February 22, 1967, p. 31.

[9]"RX for Ailing Video: Specs," Variety, May 17, 1967, p. 27.

the responsibility of producing information-type specials. As a practical measure, these staffs must be kept busy and the results of their efforts placed in the program schedules. There is an increasing number of former regular television featured performers who appear unwilling to continue in regular series, but prefer to appear on special programs. Thus the networks have an availability of name performers on which to draw for entertainment-type specials. Finally, the networks appear to be committed to competition in the area of pre-emptive programming.

Commenting on the increasing number of television specials planned for the 1967-1968 season, which advance publicity bills as the biggest season yet for pre-emptive programming, *Variety* observed, "At this rate, it may evolve that regular programming will be the exception rather than the rule."[10] Specials have undoubtedly become integral parts of network television programming, and for the reasons indicated above will probably increase rather than decrease in years to come.

---

[10] "ABC's $75-Mil Specs Splurge," *Variety*, March 29, 1967, p. 33.

APPENDIX A

Following is the schedule of network television prime time special programs which comprised the corpus of data for this study. This program inventory includes virtually all non-regular programs telecast in prime time by the national networks between September 15, 1948 and September 14, 1966.

The programs are grouped by categories for each winter and summer television season. As defined in Chapter I, winter seasons were considered to begin on September 15th each year and end on June 14th. Summer seasons were considered to begin each June 15th and end on September 14th.

The program schedule was printed from punch cards prepared to permit machine processing of the data, and thus some information appears in the form of a number code. The number immediately preceeding each program title identifies the network on which the special was telecast: the number one refers to ABC-TV, two to CBS-TV, three to NBC-TV, and four to DuMont. The date on which the program appeared follows the title. The single-digit number printed after the date indicates the weekday on which the program appeared: the number one refers to Sunday, two to Monday, three to Tuesday, four to Wednesday, five to Thursday, six to Friday, and seven to Saturday. The next two- or three-digit figure gives the number of prime time minutes devoted to the program. In most cases this also represents the program's entire length; however, in some instances, programs began prior to or ran later than prime time. Only those portions of specials appearing after 7:30 and before 11:00 p.m. New York City Time, were included in the program length figure. Next, the starting time of each special, expressed in New York City Time, appears. In all cases except three the starting times were p.m.; the three exceptions were programs covering events subsequent to President Kennedy's assassination on November 23, 24, and 25, 1963, which began in the early morning and continued until sign-off. After the program starting time, figures representing the average audience rating and share of audience are listed. The first one- or two-digit number indicates the program's rating, and next two digits indicate share, based on the Nielsen National Television Index. These figures were rounded off to the nearest whole number before being entered on punch cards. The next number, which may consist of one, two, or three digits, is a code number for the program's sponsor. This number may be interpreted in Appendix B which lists program sponsors by name and number. Space did not permit listing more than one sponsor per program. No sponsor code appears for programs which were sustaining or for which sponsorship could not be ascertained. In some cases, a plus sign (+) appears between the share of audience figure and sponsor code number. This indicates the program was a repeat telecast.

1948 - 1949

FAIRY TALE/CARTOON DRAMA

2	ENCHANTED FOREST	12/25/48	7	25	6-00			

MUSICAL DRAMA

3	OPERA--THE MEDIUM	9/26/48	1	60	9-00			
1	OTHELLO	11/30/48	2	180	8-00			255

SPEECHES

2	SECRETARY OF STATE SPEECH	3/18/49	6	30	10-30			
2	WINSTON CHURCHILL ADDRESS	3/31/49	5	60	9-00			

PANEL TALKS

3	ARMY VS HARVARD DEBATE	10/16/48	7	30	8-00			
2	HERALD TRIBUNE FORUM	10/18/48	2	150	8-30			
2	HERALD TRIBUNE FORUM	10/19/48	3	60	8-00			
2	HERALD TRIBUNE FORUM	10/19/48	3	60	10-00			

POLITICAL PROGRAMS

2	STRAWS IN THE WIND	9/21/48	3	30	9-30			
2	STRAWS IN THE WIND	10/05/48	3	30	9-30			
2	PRESIDENT TRUMAN RALLY	10/28/48	5	40	10-25			
2	REPUBLICAN RALLY	10/30/48	7	30	9-30			
1	ELECTION RETURNS	11/02/48	3	210	7-00	11	21	133
2	ELECTION RETURNS	11/02/48	3	210	6-00	14	26	295
3	ELECTION RETURNS	11/02/48	3	180	8-00	16	29	146

SPORTS AND SPORTS NEWS

2	SPORTSMAN SHOW	2/22/49	3	30	9-30			
2	RODEO	10/14/48	5	145	8-30			279
2	PROFESSIONAL FOOTBALL	10/15/48	6	150	8-30			
2	CHAMPIONSHIP BOXING	10/21/48	5	60	9-45			34
2	RODEO	10/23/48	7	95	9-15			279
2	NATIONAL HORSE SHOW	11/04/48	5	150	8-30			
2	NATIONAL HORSE SHOW	11/06/48	7	150	8-30			
2	ROLLER SKATING DERBY	11/29/48	2	135	8-45			
2	ROLLER SKATING DERBY	12/03/48	6	150	8-30			
2	ROLLER SKATING DERBY	12/10/48	6	150	8-30			
2	ROLLER SKATING DERBY	12/13/48	2	85	9-35			
2	BOXING MATCHES	12/29/48	4	105	9-00			

MUSICAL VARIETY

2	AUTO SHOW	1/21/49	6	30	8-00			197
2	TRANSPORTATION UNLIMITED	1/24/49	2	30	9-00			103
2	WELCOME BACK BASEBALL	4/17/49	1	60	10-00			
3	NBC CONCERT HALL	12/25/48	7	60	8-00			

VAUDEVILLE VARIETY

3	MILTON BERLE TELETHON	4/09/49	7	210	12-00	

NON-CLASSIFIABLE

1	COAXIAL CABLE INAUGURAL	1/11/49	3	90	9-30	
2	MIDWEST CABLE INAUGURAL	1/11/49	3	90	9-30	
3	MIDWEST CABLE INAUGURAL	1/11/49	3	90	9-30	
4	MIDWEST CABLE INAUGURAL	1/11/49	3	90	9-30	
2	ART DIRECTORS' CLUB	3/16/49	4	30	10-00	
3	SPECIAL AIR FORCE SHOW	9/18/48	7	60	8-00	
3	SALUTE TO THE UN	10/23/48	7	60	7-30	
3	MUSEUM OF SCIENCE PROGRAM	12/06/48	2	50	8-50	
3	CHRISTMAS PROGRAM	12/15/48	4	30	8-30	
2	SURPRISE FROM SANTA	12/24/48	6	60	7-00	63
2	CBS CHRISTMAS PARTY	12/25/48	7	45	8-00	

SUMMER 1949

SPEECHES

2	PRESIDENT TRUMAN ADDRESS	7/13/49	4	30	10-30

NON-CLASSIFIABLE

2	GIANT IN A HURRY	7/02/49	5	30	9-00

1949 - 1950

AWARDS AND PAGENTS

2	ROSE BOWL PARADE	1/03/50	3	30	10-00
2	COACH OF THE YEAR DINNER	1/12/50	5	30	8-30
2	FLOWER SHOW	3/23/50	5	30	10-30
2	FOUR FREEDOMS AWARD	5/11/50	5	30	10-30
2	FREEDOM HOUSE AWARD	10/13/49	5	50	10-00
3	VEILED PROPHETS BALL	10/13/49	5	30	9-00

DOCUMENTARY

1	OUR COMMON DESTINY	1/04/50	4	30	8-30	196
2	PREFACE TO A LIFE	5/20/50	7	30	10-00	
4	THE DUMONT STORY	9/26/49	2	90	7-30	293

SPEECHES

2	UNIV. OF PENN. FOUNDERS	1/12/50	5	30	9-30
2	JEFFERSON-JACKSON DAY	2/16/50	5	45	10-15
2	SECRETARY OF DEFENSE TALK	3/03/50	6	30	10-30
2	SECRETARY OF DEFENSE TALK	3/30/50	6	30	10-30

2	REPORT ON CHEMISTRY	9/20/49	3	30	10-15	
2	SECRETARY OF DEFENSE TALK	9/21/49	4	30	9-30	
2	CARDINAL SPELLMAN ADDRESS	10/20/49	5	30	9-30	
2	SECRETARY OF DEFENSE TALK	12/21/49	4	30	9-30	
	NEWS AND NEWS ANALYSIS					
2	THE WORLD AT MID-CENTURY	1/01/50	1	45	10-00	
	POLITICAL PROGRAMS					
2	BRITISH ELECTIONS	2/23/50	5	60	10-00	
	SPORTS AND SPORTS NEWS					
2	MILROSE GAMES TRACK MEET	1/28/50	7	60	10-00	
2	KENTUCKY DERBY	5/07/50	1	15	10-30	107
2	THE PREAKNESS RACE	5/20/50	7	15	10-30	28
	VAUDEVILLE VARIETY					
2	GREATER NEW YORK FUND	5/06/50	7	60	8-00	
2	NEW YEAR'S EVE PARTY	12/31/49	7	30	10-30	
	NON-CLASSIFIABLE					
2	KEN MURRAY PREVIEW	1/07/50	7	30	7-30	
2	AUTO SHOW	1/18/50	4	30	9-30	103
2	A DATE AT THE WALDORF	1/19/50	5	30	9-30	103
2	COMMAND POST	2/14/50	3	60	8-00	
2	BRITISH AUTO SHOW	4/20/50	5	30	10-30	
2	RED FEATHER U.S.A.	10/29/49	7	30	8-30	

SUMMER 1950

	DOCUMENTARY				
2	THAT THEY MAY HELP SELVES	6/28/50	4	45	10-00
	SPEECHES				
2	PRESIDENT TRUMAN ADDRESS	6/25/50	1	15	9-15
2	PRESIDENT TRUMAN ADDRESS	7/19/50	4	25	10-30
1	TRUMAN ADDRESS	9/01/50	6	30	10-00
2	PRESIDENT TRUMAN ADDRESS	9/01/50	6	30	10-00
3	PRESIDENT TRUMAN ADDRESS	9/01/50	6	30	10-00
4	PRESIDENT TRUMAN ADDRESS	9/01/50	6	30	10-00
1	TRUMAN ADDRESS	9/09/50	7	30	10-30
2	PRESIDENT TRUMAN ADDRESS	9/09/50	7	25	10-30
3	PRESIDENT TRUMAN ADDRESS	9/09/50	7	30	10-30
4	PRESIDENT TRUMAN ADDRESS	9/09/50	7	30	10-30

NEWS AND NEWS ANALYSIS

2 HURRICANE REPORT 8/18/50 6 30 10-00

PANEL TALKS

2 LOOK TO THE EAST 7/16/50 1 30 9-00
2 LOOK TO THE EAST 7/23/50 1 30 9-30
2 LOOK TO THE EAST 7/30/50 1 30 9-30

1950 - 1951

MUSICAL DRAMA

2 OPERA MINIATURES--CARMEN 6/08/51 6 30 9-30

AWARDS AND PAGENTS

2 VEILED PROPHETS' BALL 10/03/50 3 30 10-30

DOCUMENTARY

2 CRISIS IN KOREA 3/22/51 5 30 10-30
2 CRISIS IN KOREA 3/29/51 5 30 10-30
2 CRISIS IN KOREA 4/05/51 5 30 10-30
2 WE HOLD THESE TRUTHS 4/10/51 3 30 8-30
2 CRISIS IN KOREA 4/12/51 5 30 10-30
2 ROAD TO REASON 4/13/51 6 30 10-30
2 STRATEGIC AIR POWER 5/10/51 5 30 10-30
2 FACTS WE FACE 9/24/50 1 45 10-15

SPEECHES

1 EISENHOWER ADDRESS 2/02/51 6 15 10-45
2 GEN. EISENHOWER ADDRESS 2/02/51 6 15 10-45
3 GEN. EISENHOWER ADDRESS 2/02/51 6 15 10-45
4 GEN. EISENHOWER ADDRESS 2/02/51 6 15 10-45
2 PRESIDENT TRUMAN ADDRESS 4/11/51 4 30 10-30
1 TRUMAN ADDRESS 6/14/51 5 30 10-00
2 PRESIDENT TRUMAN ADDRESS 6/14/51 5 30 10-30
3 PRESIDENT TRUMAN ADDRESS 6/14/51 5 30 10-00
4 PRESIDENT TRUMAN ADDRESS 6/14/51 5 30 10-00
1 TRUMAN ADDRESS 12/15/50 6 30 10-30
2 PRESIDENT TRUMAN ADDRESS 12/15/50 6 25 10-30
3 PRESIDENT TRUMAN ADDRESS 12/15/50 6 30 10-30
4 PRESIDENT TRUMAN ADDRESS 12/15/50 6 30 10-30

NEWS AND NEWS ANALYSIS

2 CRIME HEARINGS HIGHLIGHTS 3/23/51 6 30 10-30
4 MACARTHUR IN NEW YORK 4/19/51 5 50 9-00 27 36 291
4 REPORT ON MACARTHUR 4/19/51 5 30 10-00 14 21 292

POLITICAL PROGRAMS

2	PRESIDENT TRUMAN ADDRESS	11/04/50	7	30	10-00	
2	ELECTION RETURNS	11/07/50	3	30	10-30	150
	SPORTS AND SPORTS NEWS					
2	KENTUCKY DERBY	5/05/51	7	15	9-45	107
2	FIGHT PREVIEW	9/26/50	3	15	10-45	
	COMEDY VARIETY					
2	THE JACK BENNY SHOW	1/28/51	1	30	7-30	22
2	THE JACK BENNY SHOW	4/01/51	1	30	7-30	22
2	WELCOME WAGON	9/30/50	7	60	8-00	
2	THE JACK BENNY SHOW	10/28/50	7	45	8-00	22
	MUSICAL VARIETY					
3	SALUTE TO RICHARD RODGERS	3/04/51	1	60	9-00	208
	VAUDEVILLE VARIETY					
3	MILTON BERLE TELETHON	6/09/51	7	210	12-00	
	NON-CLASSIFIABLE					
2	RED CROSS PROGRAM	2/27/51	3	30	10-30	
2	WHAT IN THE WORLD	4/10/51	3	30	8-00	
2	SUPERSTITION	4/13/51	6	30	9-00	52
2	NATIONAL SPELLING BEE	5/25/51	6	30	9-30	

SUMMER 1951

	MUSICAL DRAMA					
2	OPERA MINIATURES	6/22/51	6	30	10-00	
2	OPERA MINIATURES--FIGARO	6/29/51	6	30	10-00	
	DOCUMENTARY					
2	A YEAR OF WAR	6/22/51	6	30	9-30	
2	FLOOD CONTROL	7/24/51	3	30	8-30	
2	YOUR STAKE IN JAPAN	9/07/51	6	60	10-00	296
	SPEECHES					
1	TRUMAN ADDRESS	7/04/51	4	30	9-30	
2	PRESIDENT TRUMAN ADDRESS	7/04/51	4	15	10-45	
4	PRESIDENT TRUMAN ADDRESS	7/04/51	4	30	9-30	
1	TRUMAN ADDRESS	9/04/51	3	30	10-30	
2	PRESIDENT TRUMAN ADDRESS	9/04/51	3	30	10-30	
3	PRESIDENT TRUMAN ADDRESS	9/04/51	3	30	10-30	
4	PRESIDENT TRUMAN ADDRESS	9/04/51	3	30	10-30	

PANEL TALKS

2	ROUND TABLE DISCUSSION	7/24/51	3	30	8-00	

SPORTS AND SPORTS NEWS

4	CHARLES-WALCOTT FIGHT	7/18/51	4	45	10-00	3

MUSICAL VARIETY

3	IRVING BERLIN SALUTE	9/12/51	4	60	8-00	208

1951 - 1952

DOCUMENTARY

2	YEARS OF CHANGE	4/18/52	6	30	10-30	
2	IT CAN'T HAPPEN HERE	4/29/52	3	30	8-30	

SPEECHES

1	TRUMAN ADDRESS	3/06/52	5	30	10-30	
2	PRESIDENT TRUMAN ADDRESS	3/06/52	5	30	10-30	
3	PRESIDENT TRUMAN ADDRESS	3/06/52	5	30	10-30	
4	PRESIDENT TRUMAN ADDRESS	3/06/52	5	30	10-30	
2	PRESIDENT TRUMAN ADDRESS	4/08/52	3	30	10-30	
1	TRUMAN ADDRESS	11/07/51	4	30	10-30	
2	PRESIDENT TRUMAN ADDRESS	11/07/51	4	30	10-30	
3	PRESIDENT TRUMAN ADDRESS	11/07/51	4	30	10-30	
4	PRESIDENT TRUMAN ADDRESS	11/07/51	4	30	10-30	
1	FRANK MCKINNEY ADDRESS	11/26/51	2	30	10-00	

NEWS AND NEWS ANALYSIS

2	FUNERAL OF KING GEORGE	2/16/52	7	15	9-30	
2	EISENHOWER PRESS CONF	6/03/52	3	60	10-00	

PANEL TALKS

1	AIR FORCE WATCH DOG	5/12/52	2	30	8-30	

POLITICAL PROGRAMS

1	LEAGUE OF WOMEN VOTERS	5/01/52	5	60	8-00	193
2	CANDIDATE CLOSEUP	6/06/52	6	30	10-30	

SPORTS AND SPORTS NEWS

3	WALCOTT-EZZARD FIGHT	6/05/52	5	30	10-00	107

COMEDY VARIETY

2	THE JACK BENNY SHOW	1/27/52	1	30	7-30	22
2	THE JACK BENNY SHOW	4/20/52	1	30	7-30	22

2	THE JACK BENNY SHOW	12/09/51	1	30	7-30	22

NON-CLASSIFIABLE

2	JACKSON DAY DINNER	3/29/52	7	30	10-30	
3	TODAY	3/31/52	2	30	9-00	
2	AUTO SHOW PREVIEW	4/01/52	3	30	9-30	103
1	MICROWAVE INAUGURAL	9/30/51	1	60	9-00	39
2	COAST-TO-COAST MICROWAVE	9/30/51	1	60	9-00	39
3	COAST-TO-COAST MICROWAVE	9/30/51	1	60	9-00	39
4	COAST-TO-COAST MICROWAVE	9/30/51	1	60	9-00	39
2	PUBLIC SERVICE PROGRAM	11/27/51	3	30	10-30	
2	PUBLIC SERVICE PROGRAM	12/04/51	3	30	10-30	

SUMMER 1952

AWARDS AND PAGENTS

1	AUTO GUILD AWARD DINNER	8/19/52	3	30	9-30	
4	AUTO GUILD AWARD DINNER	8/19/52	3	30	9-30	

POLITICAL PROGRAMS

3	PRE-CONVENTION PROGRAM	7/02/52	4	60	8-00	
3	PRE-CONVENTION PROGRAM	7/02/52	4	30	10-00	
3	PRE-CONVENTION PROGRAM	7/03/52	5	30	8-30	
2	CANDIDATE CLOSEUP	7/04/52	6	30	10-30	
2	TAFT ARRIVAL IN CHICAGO	7/05/52	7	60	8-00	
3	PRE-CONVENTION PROGRAM	7/05/52	7	30	10-00	
1	REP NATIONAL CONVENTION	7/07/52	2	90	9-30	3
2	REP NATIONAL CONVENTION	7/07/52	2	90	9-30	277
3	REP NATIONAL CONVENTION	7/07/52	2	90	9-30	188
4	REP. NATIONAL CONVENTION	7/07/52	2	90	9-30	277
1	REP NATIONAL CONVENTION	7/08/52	3	90	9-30	3
2	REP NATIONAL CONVENTION	7/08/52	3	90	9-30	277
3	REP NATIONAL CONVENTION	7/08/52	3	90	9-30	188
4	KEEP POSTED	7/08/52	3	30	7-30	
4	REP. NATIONAL CONVENTION	7/08/52	3	90	9-30	277
1	REP NATIONAL CONVENTION	7/09/52	4	120	9-00	3
2	REP NATIONAL CONVENTION	7/09/52	4	180	8-00	277
3	CONVENTION CALL	7/09/52	4	60	8-00	188
3	REP NATIONAL CONVENTION	7/09/52	4	120	9-00	188
4	REP. NATIONAL CONVENTION	7/09/52	4	90	9-30	277
1	REP NATIONAL CONVENTION	7/10/52	5	150	8-30	3
2	REP NATIONAL CONVENTION	7/10/52	5	90	9-30	277
3	CONVENTION CALL	7/10/52	5	30	8-30	188
3	REP NATIONAL CONVENTION	7/10/52	5	90	9-30	188
4	THE WORKING PRESS	7/10/52	5	30	8-00	
4	REP. NATIONAL CONVENTION	7/10/52	5	90	9-30	277
1	REP NATIONAL CONVENTION	7/11/52	6	210	6-30	3
2	REP NATIONAL CONVENTION	7/11/52	6	120	8-30	277
2	CANDIDATE CLOSEUP	7/11/52	6	30	10-30	
3	REP NATIONAL CONVENTION	7/11/52	6	210	7-30	188

4	REP. NATIONAL CONVENTION	7/11/52	6	210	7-00	277
2	CANDIDATE CLOSEUP	7/18/52	6	30	10-30	
1	DEM NATIONAL CONVENTION	7/21/52	2	120	9-00	3
2	DEM NATIONAL CONVENTION	7/21/52	2	120	9-00	277
3	DEM NATIONAL CONVENTION	7/21/52	2	120	9-00	188
4	DEM. NATIONAL CONVENTION	7/21/52	2	120	9-00	277
1	DEM NATIONAL CONVENTION	7/22/52	3	120	9-00	3
2	DEM NATIONAL CONVENTION	7/22/52	3	120	9-00	277
3	DEM NATIONAL CONVENTION	7/22/52	3	120	9-00	188
4	DEM. NATIONAL CONVENTION	7/22/52	3	120	9-00	277
1	DEM NATIONAL CONVENTION	7/23/52	4	120	9-00	3
2	DEM NATIONAL CONVENTION	7/23/52	4	120	9-00	277
3	DEM NATIONAL CONVENTION	7/23/52	4	120	9-00	188
4	DEM. NATIONAL CONVENTION	7/23/52	4	120	9-00	277
4	DEM. NATIONAL CONVENTION	7/23/52	5	210	6-00	277
1	DEM NATIONAL CONVENTION	7/24/52	5	210	6-00	3
2	DEM NATIONAL CONVENTION	7/24/52	5	210	6-00	277
3	DEM NATIONAL CONVENTION	7/24/52	5	210	6-00	188
4	DEM. NATIONAL CONVENTION	7/24/52	6	210	6-00	277
1	DEM NATIONAL CONVENTION	7/25/52	6	210	6-00	3
2	DEM NATIONAL CONVENTION	7/25/52	6	180	6-00	277
2	CANDIDATE CLOSEUP	7/25/52	6	30	10-30	
3	DEM NATIONAL CONVENTION	7/25/52	6	210	6-00	188
3	GEN EISENHOWER ADDRESS	9/04/52	5	30	9-30	196
1	ADLAI STEVENSON ADDRESS	9/05/52	6	30	9-00	196
3	PROGRESSIVE PARTY TALK	9/06/52	7	30	9-30	
2	ADLAI STEVENSON ADDRESS	9/09/52	3	30	10-30	196

1952 - 1953

AWARDS AND PAGENTS

2	MARDI GRAS PARADE	2/17/53	3	60	8-00			
3	MOVIE ACADEMY AWARDS	3/19/53	5	30	10-30	46	82	206
4	CORONATION PREVIEW	5/31/53	1	90	7-30			
1	CORONATION FILMS	6/02/53	3	150	8-00			115
2	EYE ON LONDON	6/02/53	3	30	10-30			280
3	QUEEN'S CORONATION FILMS	6/02/53	3	30	10-30			103
1	MOVIE PREMIERE	12/22/52	2	30	8-30			263
1	MOVIE PREMIERE	12/24/52	4	30	8-30			263

SPEECHES

1	TRUMAN FAREWELL ADDRESS	1/15/53	5	30	10-30
2	TRUMAN FAREWELL ADDRESS	1/15/53	5	30	10-30
3	PRES TRUMAN FAREWELL TALK	1/15/53	5	30	10-30
4	TRUMAN FAREWELL ADDRESS	1/15/53	5	30	10-30
2	JOHN FOSTER DULLES TALK	1/27/53	3	30	10-30
2	ADLAI STEVENSON ADDRESS	2/14/53	7	30	9-30
1	EMANUEL CELLAR ADDRESS	2/15/53	1	15	10-15
4	JOHN FOSTER DULLES TALK	6/01/53	2	30	9-00

NEWS AND NEWS ANALYSIS

1 INAUGURAL HIGHLIGHTS	1/20/53	3	60	9-30	
4 INAUGURAL HIGHLIGHTS	1/20/53	3	60	10-00	294
2 OPERATION DOORSTEP	3/17/53	3	60	8-00	

PANEL TALKS

2 PHILADELPHIA FORUM	3/10/53	3	60	8-00	
1 EISENHOWER CABINET TALK	6/03/53	4	30	9-30	
2 EISENHOWER CABINET FORUM	6/03/53	4	30	9-30	
3 EISENHOWER CABINET TALK	6/03/53	4	30	9-30	
4 EISENHOWER CABINET FORUM	6/03/53	4	30	9-30	
3 MARCH OF MEDICINE	6/04/53	5	30	8-30	239

POLITICAL PROGRAMS

3 DEMOCRATIC PAID POLITICAL	9/15/52	2	30	10-30	196
3 SEN TAFT ADDRESS	9/17/52	4	30	10-00	196
3 GEN EISENHOWER ADDRESS	9/19/52	6	15	10-45	196
2 ADLAI STEVENSON ADDRESS	9/23/52	3	30	10-00	196
3 RICHARD NIXON ADDRESS	9/23/52	3	30	9-30	196
4 GEN. EISENHOWER ADDRESS	9/24/52	4	30	9-30	196
2 DEM PAID POLITICAL	10/07/52	3	30	10-30	196
2 GEN EISENHOWER ADDRESS	10/09/52	5	30	10-00	196
4 ADLAI STEVENSON ADDRESS	10/09/52	5	30	10-30	196
2 RICHARD NIXON ADDRESS	10/13/52	2	30	8-00	196
4 ADLAI STEVENSON ADDRESS	10/14/52	3	30	10-30	196
4 ADLAI STEVENSON ADDRESS	10/16/52	5	30	10-30	196
2 PHILLIP MURRAY ADDRESS	10/21/52	3	15	10-30	196
3 ADLAI STEVENSON ADDRESS	10/21/52	3	30	9-30	196
2 PRESIDENT TRUMAN ADDRESS	10/22/52	4	30	8-30	196
3 ADLAI STEVENSON ADDRESS	10/23/52	5	30	9-00	196
4 VICE PRES BARKLEY ADDRESS	10/23/52	5	30	10-30	196
3 GEN EISENHOWER ADDRESS	10/24/52	6	30	9-00	196
4 ADLAI STEVENSON ADDRESS	10/25/52	7	30	10-30	196
1 JOSEPH MCCARTHY ADDRESS	10/27/52	2	30	10-00	196
2 DEM PAID POLITICAL	10/28/52	3	30	9-30	196
3 GEN EISENHOWER ADDRESS	10/28/52	3	30	9-00	196
3 ADLAI STEVENSON RALLY	10/28/52	3	30	10-30	196
4 ADLAI STEVENSON TV RALLY	10/28/52	3	60	10-00	196
1 ADLAI STEVENSON ADDRESS	10/29/52	4	15	10-15	196
2 RICHARD NIXON ADDRESS	10/29/52	4	30	8-30	196
2 GEN EISENHOWER ADDRESS	10/29/52	4	45	10-00	196
3 GEN EISENHOWER ADDRESS	10/30/52	5	30	10-00	196
4 PRESIDENT TRUMAN ADDRESS	10/30/52	5	30	10-30	196
3 ADLAI STEVENSON ADDRESS	10/31/52	6	30	9-30	196
3 GEN EISENHOWER ADDRESS	11/01/52	7	30	10-00	196
4 ADLAI STEVENSON ADDRESS	11/01/52	7	30	10-30	196
1 REP ELECTION EVE TV RALLY	11/03/52	2	30	10-00	196
1 ADLAI STEVENSON ADDRESS	11/03/52	2	30	10-30	196
2 PICK THE WINNER	11/03/52	2	30	10-00	
2 ADLAI STEVENSON ADDRESS	11/03/52	2	30	10-30	196
3 REP ELECTION EVE TV RALLY	11/03/52	2	30	10-00	196
3 ADLAI STEVENSON ADDRESS	11/03/52	2	30	10-30	196
4 ADLAI STEVENSON ADDRESS	11/03/52	2	30	10-30	196

1	ELECTION RETURNS	11/04/52	3	180	8-00	3
2	ELECTION RETURNS	11/04/52	3	180	8-00	277
3	ELECTION RETURNS	11/04/52	3	120	9-00	188
4	ELECTION RETURNS	11/04/52	3	120	9-00	277

SPORTS AND SPORTS NEWS

4	GOLDEN GLOVES BOXING	3/06/53	6	90	9-30	3
4	GOLDEN GLOVES BOXING	3/26/53	5	90	9-30	3

COMEDY VARIETY

2	THE JACK BENNY SHOW	10/05/52	1	30	7-30	22
2	THE JACK BENNY SHOW	11/02/52	1	30	7-30	22

VAUDEVILLE VARIETY

2	DEDICATION OF CBS TV CITY	11/15/52	7	60	9-00	

NON-CLASSIFIABLE

2	MOTORAMA	1/16/53	6	60	9-00	103
2	AUTO SHOW	4/07/53	3	30	9-30	31

SUMMER 1953

DOCUMENTARY

3	ASSIGNMENT TOMORROW	8/23/53	1	30	7-00	

SPEECHES

1	THE CONGRESS-AN APPRAISAL	8/10/53	2	30	9-00	
4	CONGRESS--AN APPRAISAL	8/11/53	3	30	10-00	

NEWS AND NEWS ANALYSIS

1	KOREAN ARMISTICE SIGNING	7/26/53	1	60	10-00	
2	KOREAN ARMISTICE SIGNING	7/26/53	1	60	10-00	
3	THE OUTBREAK OF PEACE	7/26/53	1	30	9-30	
3	KOREAN ARMISTICE SIGNING	7/26/53	1	60	10-00	
4	KOREAN ARMISTICE SIGNING	7/26/53	1	60	10-00	

PANEL TALKS

2	DULLES-ROBERTSON TALK	7/17/53	6	30	10-30	

SPORTS AND SPORTS NEWS

4	GOLDEN GLOVES BOXING	6/16/53	3	30	10-30	3

COMEDY VARIETY

2	THE JACK BENNY SHOW	9/13/53	1	30	7-30		22

VAUDEVILLE VARIETY

2	FORD GOLDEN ANNIVERSARY	6/15/53	2	120	9-00		96
3	FORD GOLDEN ANNIVERSARY	6/15/53	2	120	9-00		96
1	GIVE THEM THIS DAY	7/28/53	3	30	8-00		
2	GIVE THEM THIS DAY	7/28/53	3	30	8-30		
4	GIVE THEM THIS DAY	7/28/53	3	30	9-30		

NON-CLASSIFIABLE

2	BOY SCOUT JAMBOREE	7/18/53	7	60	9-00		

1953 - 1954

COMEDY DRAMA

3	BACKBONE OF AMERICA	12/29/53	3	60	8-00		165

AWARDS AND PAGENTS

3	NEW ORLEANS MARDI GRAS	3/02/54	3	30	9-30		96
3	MOVIE ACADEMY AWARDS	3/25/54	5	30	10-30	44 80	180
1	DINNER WITH THE PRESIDENT	11/23/53	2	30	7-00		
2	DINNER WITH THE PRESIDENT	11/23/53	2	30	7-00		

DOCUMENTARY

1	OPERATION IVY	4/01/54	5	30	8-00		
4	OPERATION IVY	4/01/54	5	30	8-00		
3	MARCH OF MEDICINE	4/29/54	5	30	8-00		239

SPEECHES

1	EISENHOWER ADDRESS	1/04/54	2	30	9-30		
2	PRES. EISENHOWER ADDRESS	1/04/54	2	30	9-30		
3	PRES EISENHOWER ADDRESS	1/04/54	2	30	9-30		
4	PRES. EISENHOWER ADDRESS	1/04/54	2	30	9-30		
2	ADLAI STEVENSON ADDRESS	3/06/54	7	30	10-30		
2	RICHARD NIXON ADDRESS	3/13/54	7	30	10-30		
1	EISENHOWER ADDRESS	3/15/54	2	15	9-00		
2	PRES. EISENHOWER ADDRESS	3/15/54	2	15	9-00		
3	PRES EISENHOWER ADDRESS	3/15/54	2	15	9-00		
4	PRES. EISENHOWER ADDRESS	3/15/54	2	15	9-00		
4	REPLY TO EISENHOWER TALK	3/16/54	3	15	9-00		
1	EISENHOWER ADDRESS	4/06/54	3	30	8-30		
2	PRES. EISENHOWER ADDRESS	4/06/54	3	30	10-30		
3	PRES EISENHOWER ADDRESS	4/06/54	3	30	8-30		
4	PRES. EISENHOWER ADDRESS	4/06/54	3	30	8-30		
2	HERBERT BROWNELL ADDRESS	4/09/54	7	30	9-00		
1	EISENHOWER ADDRESS	4/22/54	5	30	9-00		
3	PRES EISENHOWER ADDRESS	4/22/54	5	30	10-30		

4	PRES. EISENHOWER ADDRESS	4/22/54	5	30	9-00			
1	EISENHOWER ADDRESS	5/31/54	2	30	8-30			
1	EISENHOWER ADDRESS	10/15/53	5	30	9-00			

SPORTS AND SPORTS NEWS

1	INDIANAPOLIS THRILLS	5/31/54	2	30	7-30			

MUSICAL VARIETY

2	THE BING CROSBY SHOW	1/03/54	1	30	9-00			100
1	GENERAL FOODS ANNIVERSARY	3/28/54	1	90	8-00	5	8	101
2	GEN FOODS ANNIVERSARY PGM	3/28/54	1	90	8-00	33	46	101
3	GEN FOODS ANNIVERSARY PGM	3/28/54	1	90	8-00	33	46	101
4	GEN. FOODS ANNIVERSARY	3/28/54	1	90	8-00			101
2	THE BING CROSBY SHOW	4/25/54	1	30	9-00			100
3	CHRISTMAS WITH THE STARS	12/25/53	6	60	10-00			107

NON-CLASSIFIABLE

2	MOTORAMA	1/20/54	4	45	10-00			103
2	PARADE OF STARS AUTO SHOW	4/06/54	3	30	9-30			31
3	MARCH OF MEDICINE	10/08/53	5	30	10-00			19

SUMMER 1954

HISTORICAL DRAMA

2	A PRECIOUS HERITAGE	9/05/54	1	30	10-00			
2	A PRECIOUS HERITAGE	9/12/54	1	30	10-00			

AWARDS AND PAGENTS

3	MODEL CAR AWARDS	7/20/54	3	30	8-30			
1	MISS AMERICA PAGEANT	9/11/54	7	30	10-30			188

DOCUMENTARY

3	MARCH OF MEDICINE	6/24/54	5	30	9-00			239
3	THREE, TWO, ONE, ZERO	9/13/54	2	60	8-00			

SPEECHES

3	VICE PRES NIXON ADDRESS	6/24/54	5	30	9-30			
1	SYNGMAN RHEE ADDRESS	8/02/54	2	30	8-00			
1	EISENHOWER ADDRESS	8/23/54	2	30	9-00			
2	PRES. EISENHOWER ADDRESS	8/23/54	2	30	9-00			
3	PRES EISENHOWER ADDRESS	8/23/54	2	30	9-00			
4	PRES. EISENHOWER ADDRESS	8/23/54	2	30	9-00			
2	FRANK STANTON ADDRESS	8/26/54	5	15	8-00			
2	JUDGE HAROLD MEDINA TALK	9/02/54	5	15	8-00			

SPORTS AND SPORTS NEWS

3	ALL STAR FOOTBALL GAME	8/13/54	6	150	8-30			
1	WORLD CHAMPIONSHIP GOLF	8/15/54	1	60	8-00			95
1	FOOTBALL RALLY	9/11/54	7	30	8-00			

1954 - 1955

PRESTIGE DRAMA

2	BARRETS OF WIMPOLE STREET	6/08/55	4	60	9-00			

HISTORICAL DRAMA

2	A PRECIOUS HERITAGE	9/19/54	1	30	10-00			
2	A PRECIOUS HERITAGE	9/26/54	1	30	10-00			

UNCLASSIFIED DRAMA

1	LIGHTS DIAMOND JUBILEE	10/24/54	1	120	9-00			86
2	LIGHT'S DIAMOND JUBILEE	10/24/54	1	120	9-00			86
3	LIGHT'S DIAMOND JUBILEE	10/24/54	1	120	9-00			86
4	LIGHT'S DIAMOND JUBILEE	10/24/54	1	120	9-00			86

AWARDS AND PAGENTS

3	ACADEMY AWARD NOMINATIONS	2/12/55	7	90	9-00	33	49	180
3	MOVIE ACADEMY AWARDS	3/30/55	4	30	10-30	44	74	180
1	CORONATION FILMS	5/29/55	1	60	8-00			
3	LOOK MAGAZINE TV AWARDS	12/18/54	7	30	8-30			151

DOCUMENTARY

3	MARCH OF MEDICINE	3/29/55	3	30	9-30			239
1	IMPRINT OF A MAN	4/04/55	2	30	9-00			
3	MARCH OF MEDICINE	5/15/55	1	30	9-00			239
3	MARCH OF MEDICINE	6/07/55	3	30	8-30			239

SPEECHES

1	STEPHEN MITCHELL ADDRESS	9/14/54	3	30	7-30			
4	PRES. EISENHOWER ADDRESS	10/21/54	5	30	10-30			
3	PRES EISENHOWER ADDRESS	10/25/54	2	30	10-00			

NEWS AND NEWS ANALYSIS

4	EISENHOWER PRESS CONF.	1/20/55	5	30	10-00			

POLITICAL PROGRAMS

2	EISENHOWER-NIXON ADDRESS	10/08/54	6	30	9-30			196
4	PRES. EISENHOWER ADDRESS	10/15/54	6	30	9-00			196
2	EISENHOWER-NIXON ADDRESS	10/28/54	5	30	9-30			196
3	PRES EISENHOWER ADDRESS	10/28/54	5	30	9-30			196
4	PRES. EISENHOWER ADDRESS	10/28/54	5	30	9-30			196

3	REP SUSTAINING POLITICAL	10/30/54	7	30	8-00			
3	DEM SUSTAINING POLITICAL	10/30/54	7	30	8-30			
2	EISENHOWER-NIXON ADDRESS	11/01/54	2	30	9-00			196
2	ELECTION RETURNS	11/02/54	3	120	9-00			216
3	ELECTION COVERAGE	11/02/54	3	90	9-30			216
	SPORTS AND SPORTS NEWS							
4	PROFESSIONAL FOOTBALL	10/02/54	7	120	8-00			
4	PROFESSIONAL FOOTBALL	10/09/54	7	120	8-00			
4	PROFESSIONAL FOOTBALL	10/23/54	7	120	8-00			
4	PROFESSIONAL FOOTBALL	10/30/54	7	120	8-00			
4	PROFESSIONAL FOOTBALL	11/06/54	7	120	8-00			
4	PROFESSIONAL FOOTBALL	11/13/54	7	120	8-00			
4	PROFESSIONAL FOOTBALL	11/20/54	7	120	8-00			
3	SPORTS HIGHLIGHTS	12/24/54	6	30	10-00			107
	CIRCUS VARIETY							
3	CIRCUS HIGHLIGHTS	3/29/55	3	60	8-00	48	67	
	COMEDY VARIETY							
3	THE VICTOR BORGE SHOW	1/01/55	7	30	7-30			
3	THE BOB HOPE SHOW	2/01/55	3	60	8-00	42	59	101
3	THE BOB HOPE SHOW	3/01/55	3	60	8-00	35	51	101
3	THE BOB HOPE SHOW	10/12/54	3	60	8-00			101
3	THE STEVE ALLEN SHOW	11/09/54	3	60	8-00			101
3	THE BOB HOPE SHOW	12/07/54	3	60	8-00	32	48	101
	MUSICAL VARIETY							
2	STAGE SHOW	1/01/55	7	60	8-00			
3	SMALL TOWN BOY	1/04/55	3	60	8-00	31	45	
2	STAGE SHOW	1/08/55	7	60	8-00			
2	STAGE SHOW	3/12/55	7	60	8-00	34	50	
3	GRAND OLE OPRY	6/11/55	7	30	8-00			215
	VAUDEVILLE VARIETY							
3	OPERATION ENTERTAINMENT	9/20/54	2	60	8-00			
	NON-CLASSIFIABLE							
3	MOTORAMA PREVIEW	1/19/55	4	60	10-00			103

SUMMER 1955

	MUSICAL DRAMA							
2	THREE FOR TONIGHT	6/22/55	4	60	10-00	13	35	101

AWARDS AND PAGENTS

1	MISS AMERICA PAGEANT	9/10/55	7	90	9-30			188

SPEECHES

1	EISENHOWER ADDRESS	7/15/55	6	15	8-15			
2	PRES. EISENHOWER ADDRESS	7/15/55	6	15	8-15			
3	PRES EISENHOWER ADDRESS	7/15/55	6	15	8-15			
4	PRES. EISENHOWER ADDRESS	7/15/55	6	15	8-15			
2	PRES. EISENHOWER ADDRESS	7/25/55	2	15	10-30			

NEWS AND NEWS ANALYSIS

1	REPORT ON GENEVA	7/15/55	6	15	8-00			
4	GENEVA CONFERENCE	7/15/55	6	15	8-00			
3	MEETING AT THE SUMMIT	7/17/55	7	60	8-00			

PANEL TALKS

3	FIRST STEP INTO SPACE	8/06/55	7	30	8-00			

SPORTS AND SPORTS NEWS

3	NATIONAL OPEN GOLF	6/18/55	7	30	7-00			
3	ROY ROGERS RODEO	6/21/55	3	60	8-00			101
1	ALL STAR FOOTBALL GAME	8/12/55	6	120	7-30			

COMEDY VARIETY

3	REMEMBER 1938	6/19/55	1	30	6-30	15	36	

VAUDEVILLE VARIETY

1	CONVENTION IN MIAMI BEACH	6/28/55	3	60	8-00			188
2	FLOOD RELIEF SHOW	8/30/55	3	30	10-30			

NON-CLASSIFIABLE

1	DATELINE DISNEYLAND	7/17/55	1	30	6-30	20	51	20

1955 - 1956

MUSICAL DRAMA

3	AMAHL AND THE NIGHT VISIT	12/25/55	1	60	9-00			

WESTERN DRAMA

1	THE LONE RANGER LEGEND	2/18/56	7	60	7-30			101
3	STAGE TO YUMA	12/07/55	4	30	8-30			228

AWARDS AND PAGENTS

3	ACADEMY AWARD NOMINATIONS	2/18/56	7	90	9-00	30	45	180

3	MOVIE ACADEMY AWARDS	3/21/56	4	30	10-30	36	68	180
1	HOMEMAKER AWARD	4/12/56	5	60	8-00			

DOCUMENTARY

3	PROJECT XX--RED NIGHTMARE	1/24/56	3	60	9-30			
3	PROJECT XX--TWISTED CROSS	3/14/56	4	60	9-00			175
3	MARCH OF MEDICINE	4/01/56	1	30	10-30			239
2	REPORT FROM AFRICA PT ONE	4/23/56	2	60	10-00			235
2	REPORT FROM AFRICA PT TWO	5/17/56	5	60	10-00			235
3	PROJECT XX--TWISTED CROSS	6/12/56	3	60	8-00			
3	MARCH OF MEDICINE	9/20/55	3	30	9-30			239
3	SHOW BIZ--A HISTORY	10/09/55	1	30	6-30	26	43	
2	MAN'S FIGHT TO FLY	10/22/55	7	60	10-00			150
3	MARCH OF MEDICINE	12/04/55	1	30	10-30			239
3	PROJECT XX--RED NIGHTMARE	12/27/55	3	60	9-30			27

SPEECHES

2	EZRA TAFT BENSON ADDRESS	2/23/56	5	30	10-30
2	SEN. CLINTON ANDERSON	3/01/56	5	30	10-30
1	EISENHOWER ADDRESS	4/16/56	2	30	10-00
2	PRES. EISENHOWER ADDRESS	4/16/56	2	30	10-00
3	PRES EISENHOWER ADDRESS	4/16/56	2	30	10-00
2	PRES. EISENHOWER ADDRESS	4/21/56	7	30	10-00
1	LYNDON B JOHNSON ADDRESS	4/23/56	2	30	10-00

NEWS AND NEWS ANALYSIS

2	SPECIAL NEWS REPORT	2/29/56	4	42	10-18

PANEL TALKS

1	SHROUD OF TURIN	3/30/56	6	30	10-30

POLITICAL PROGRAMS

1	EISENHOWER ADDRESS	2/29/56	4	30	10-00
2	PRES. EISENHOWER ADDRESS	2/29/56	4	18	10-00
3	PRES EISENHOWER ADDRESS	2/29/56	4	30	10-00
1	STEVENSON-KEFAUVER DEBATE	5/21/56	2	60	10-00

SPORTS AND SPORTS NEWS

3	BASKETBALL TOURNAMENT	12/30/55	6	45	10-00
3	EAST-WEST FOOTBALL GAME	12/31/55	7	30	5-00

CIRCUS VARIETY

2	GREATEST SHOW ON EARTH	4/03/56	3	60	7-30	32	49	101
2	GREATEST SHOW ON EARTH	12/16/55	6	60	8-00	27	43	101

COMEDY VARIETY

3	THE BOB HOPE SHOW	2/07/56	3	60	8-00			63
2	THE PETER LIND HAYES SHOW	3/28/56	4	60	8-00			58
2	THE PAUL WINCHELL SHOW	5/16/56	4	60	8-00			190
2	THE VICTOR BORGE SHOW	6/14/56	5	60	10-00	11	22	235

MUSICAL VARIETY

1	VOICE OF FIRESTONE	3/19/56	2	60	8-30	11	15	94
2	SPRING HOLIDAY	3/21/56	4	60	8-00			190
2	THE JUDY GARLAND SHOW	4/08/56	1	30	9-00			100
3	PATTI PAGE PREMIERE PARTY	11/02/55	4	30	10-30			103

NON-CLASSIFIABLE

2	G. M. MOTORAMA	1/24/56	3	30	10-30			103

SUMMER 1956

HISTORICAL DRAMA

3	THE MAGIC BOX	9/09/56	1	60	8-00	11	20	139

AWARDS AND PAGENTS

1	MISS AMERICA PAGEANT	9/08/56	7	30	10-30	22	42	188

SPEECHES

2	ADMIRAL MORRELL ADDRESS	6/28/56	5	15	10-30			246

NEWS AND NEWS ANALYSIS

2	ANDREA DORIA SINKING	7/26/56	5	30	10-30			

POLITICAL PROGRAMS

1	DEM NATIONAL CONVENTION	8/13/56	2	150	8-30			188
2	DEM NATIONAL CONVENTION	8/13/56	2	90	9-30			277
3	DEM NATIONAL CONVENTION	8/13/56	2	150	8-30			207
1	DEM NATIONAL CONVENTION	8/14/56	3	150	8-30			188
2	DEM NATIONAL CONVENTION	8/14/56	3	120	9-00			277
3	DEM NATIONAL CONVENTION	8/14/56	3	150	8-30			207
1	DEM NATIONAL CONVENTION	8/15/56	4	150	8-30			188
2	DEM NATIONAL CONVENTION	8/15/56	4	120	9-00			277
3	DEM NATIONAL CONVENTION	8/15/56	4	120	9-00			207
1	DEM NATIONAL CONVENTION	8/16/56	5	150	8-30			188
2	DEM NATIONAL CONVENTION	8/16/56	5	90	9-30			277
3	DEM NATIONAL CONVENTION	8/16/56	5	120	9-00			207
1	DEM NATIONAL CONVENTION	8/17/56	6	150	8-30			188
2	DEM NATIONAL CONVENTION	8/17/56	6	90	9-30			277
3	DEM NATIONAL CONVENTION	8/17/56	6	150	8-30			207
1	CONVENTION CITY	8/18/56	7	30	9-00			188
1	REP NATIONAL CONVENTION	8/20/56	2	210	6-00			188

2	REP NATIONAL CONVENTION	8/20/56	2	210	7-00			277
3	REP NATIONAL CONVENTION	8/20/56	2	210	6-00			207
1	REP NATIONAL CONVENTION	8/21/56	3	210	5-30			188
2	REP NATIONAL CONVENTION	8/21/56	3	210	6-00			277
3	REP NATIONAL CONVENTION	8/21/56	3	210	5-30			207
1	REP NATIONAL CONVENTION	8/22/56	4	210	5-30			188
2	REP NATIONAL CONVENTION	8/22/56	4	210	6-00			277
3	REP NATIONAL CONVENTION	8/22/56	4	210	5-30			207
1	REP NATIONAL CONVENTION	8/23/56	5	210	5-30			188
2	REP NATIONAL CONVENTION	8/23/56	5	180	7-00			277
3	REP NATIONAL CONVENTION	8/23/56	5	210	5-30			207
1	ADLAI STEVENSON ADDRESS	9/13/56	5	30	9-30			196
2	ADLAI STEVENSON ADDRESS	9/13/56	5	30	9-30			196
3	ADLAI STEVENSON ADDRESS	9/13/56	5	30	9-30			196

SPORTS AND SPORTS NEWS

2	MAKING OF CHAMPIONS	6/16/56	7	30	9-30			
1	ALL STAR FOOTBALL GAME	8/10/56	6	120	8-30			

MUSICAL VARIETY

3	FRED WARING	7/24/56	3	60	8-00			63

1956 - 1957

PRESTIGE DRAMA

3	HALLMARK HALL OF FAME	3/17/57	1	90	7-30			114
3	HALLMARK HALL OF FAME	10/28/56	1	90	7-30			114
3	HALLMARK HALL OF FAME	11/25/56	1	90	9-00			114
3	HALLMARK HALL OF FAME	12/16/56	1	90	7-30			114

COMEDY DRAMA

3	RUGGLES OF RED GAP	2/03/57	1	90	7-30	21	31	252

CRIME, SPY DRAMA

3	HALLMARK HALL OF FAME	2/10/57	1	90	9-00			114

HISTORICAL DRAMA

3	MR. BROADWAY	5/11/57	7	90	9-00			252

MOTION PICTURE DRAMA

2	THE WIZARD OF OZ	11/03/56	7	120	9-00			96

MUSICAL DRAMA

2	CINDERELLA	3/31/57	1	90	8-00	48	64	185

UNCLASSIFIED DRAMA

3	HALLMARK HALL OF FAME	4/10/57	4	90	8-30			114

AWARDS AND PAGENTS

3	ACADEMY AWARD NOMINATIONS	2/16/57	7	90	9-00			180
3	MOVIE ACADEMY AWARDS	3/27/57	4	30	10-30	36	67	180
1	MRS AMERICA PAGEANT	5/11/57	7	60	10-30			289

DOCUMENTARY

3	PROJECT XX--FREEDOM CALL	1/07/57	2	90	8-00			206
3	MARCH OF MEDICINE	3/05/57	3	60	9-30			239
3	MAURICE CHAVALIER'S PARIS	3/06/57	4	60	8-00	13	19	45
3	PROJECT XX--THE GREAT WAR	10/16/56	3	60	8-00			175
3	MARCH OF MEDICINE	11/27/56	3	60	9-30			239
3	PROJECT XX--THE JAZZ AGE	12/06/56	5	60	10-00	27	47	175

INSTRUCTIONAL PROGRAMS

2	BELL SCIENCE SERIES	3/20/57	4	60	9-00	26	38	39
2	BELL SCIENCE SERIES	11/19/56	2	60	10-00			39

SPEECHES

2	PRES. EISENHOWER ADDRESS	2/20/57	4	30	9-00			
3	VICE PRES NIXON ADDRESS	4/09/57	3	15	7-30			
2	PRES. EISENHOWER ADDRESS	5/21/57	3	30	8-30			

PANEL TALKS

2	GRANDMA MOSES INTERVIEW	12/01/56	7	30	10-30			

POLITICAL PROGRAMS

1	HASS AND COZZINI ADDRESS	9/18/56	3	30	10-00			
2	PRES. EISENHOWER ADDRESS	9/19/56	4	25	9-30			196
1	DOBBS AND WEISS ADDRESS	9/20/56	5	30	10-00			
1	HOOPS AND FREEDMAN TALK	9/25/56	3	30	10-00			
2	PRES. EISENHOWER ADDRESS	9/25/56	3	30	9-30			196
2	DEM PAID POLITICAL	9/28/56	6	30	8-30			196
1	EISENHOWER ADDRESS	10/01/56	2	30	8-30			196
2	REP PAID POLITICAL	10/01/56	2	30	8-00			196
1	RICHARD NIXON ADDRESS	10/04/56	5	30	7-30			196
3	REPUBLICAN PAID POLITICAL	10/04/56	5	30	8-30			104
3	PRES EISENHOWER ADDRESS	10/09/56	3	30	9-00	16	23	196
1	ADLAI STEVENSON ADDRESS	10/11/56	5	30	8-00			196
3	ADLAI STEVENSON ADDRESS	10/11/56	3	30	9-00	11	17	196
3	PRES EISENHOWER ADDRESS	10/12/56	6	30	9-00	13	21	196
2	PRESIDENT'S BIRTHDAY	10/13/56	7	30	10-00	23	37	196
1	ADLAI STEVENSON ADDRESS	10/15/56	2	30	10-30	4	7	196
1	THOMAS DEWEY ADDRESS	10/16/56	3	30	8-30			196
1	ESTES KEFAUVER ADDRESS	10/16/56	3	30	9-00	6	9	196
2	RICHARD NIXON ADDRESS	10/17/56	4	30	9-00			196

3	VICE PRES NIXON ADDRESS	10/17/56	4	30	10-30	16	24	196
2	JAMES P. MITCHELL ADDRESS	10/22/56	2	30	9-30			196
1	PROHIBITION PARTY ADDRESS	10/23/56	3	30	9-00			
2	ADLAI STEVENSON ADDRESS	10/23/56	3	30	9-00			196
1	EISENHOWER ADDRESS	10/25/56	5	30	8-00			196
1	ADLAI STEVENSON ADDRESS	10/29/56	2	30	8-30			196
3	PRES EISENHOWER ADDRESS	11/01/56	5	30	9-30			196
2	REP PAID POLITICAL	11/02/56	6	30	9-30			196
2	ADLAI STEVENSON ADDRESS	11/05/56	2	45	10-00			196
1	ELECTION COVERAGE	11/06/56	3	150	8-30			49
2	ELECTION RETURNS	11/06/56	3	150	8-30			277
3	ELECTION COVERAGE	11/06/56	3	120	9-00			180

RELIGIOUS PROGRAMS

1	MISSION TO THE WORLD	9/30/56	1	30	9-00			

SPORTS AND SPORTS NEWS

3	ROY RODERS RODEO	2/22/57	6	60	9-00	30	45	101

COMEDY VARIETY

2	THE PETER LIND HAYES SHOW	2/27/57	4	60	8-00			47
2	THE VICTOR BORGE SHOW	12/11/56	3	60	9-00	23	36	235

MUSICAL VARIETY

2	THE GUY MITCHELL SHOW	3/06/57	4	60	8-00			15
2	THE JO STAFFORD SHOW	3/13/57	4	60	8-00			47
2	THE TERESA BREWER SHOW	3/20/57	4	60	8-00			15
2	THE VIC DAMONE SHOW	3/27/57	4	60	8-00			47
1	AMER SALUTES KATE SMITH	4/28/57	1	60	9-00	14	23	285
1	ROCK AND ROLL	5/04/57	7	30	7-30			
3	WASHINGTON SQUARE	5/09/57	5	60	9-00			217
1	ROCK AND ROLL	5/11/57	7	30	7-30			
3	WASHINGTON SQUARE	5/20/57	2	60	9-30			217
3	FIVE STARS IN SPRINGTIME	6/01/57	7	60	9-00	21	36	50
3	WASHINGTON SQUARE	6/04/57	3	60	8-00			217
3	WASHINGTON SQUARE	6/13/57	5	60	8-00			217
3	KICKOFF 1956	9/16/56	1	30	7-30			104
1	ROCKET REVIEW	11/08/56	5	30	8-30			180
1	WELCOME TO THE NEW YEAR	12/31/56	2	30	10-30			64

NON-CLASSIFIABLE

1	AUTO SHOW	1/27/57	1	30	8-30			103
1	HIDDEN TREASURE	4/09/57	3	60	9-00			76
1	INTRO THE UNITED KINGDOM	6/01/57	7	30	7-30			

SUMMER 1957

AWARDS AND PAGENTS

2 MISS AMERICA PAGEANT	9/07/57	7	30	10-30	29	52	188

DOCUMENTARY

3 PROJECT XX--THE JAZZ AGE	9/11/57	4	60	7-30			

SPORTS AND SPORTS NEWS

3 CHAMPIONSHIP BOXING	7/29/57	2	60	10-00			49
1 ALL STAR FOOTBALL GAME	8/09/57	6	90	9-30			182
1 GOLD CUP RACE	8/11/57	1	60	9-00			

1957 - 1958

ACTION/ADVENTURE DRAMA

2 DUPONT SHOW OF THE MONTH	1/21/58	3	90	9-30	27	43	85
2 DUPONT SHOW OF THE MONTH	9/29/57	1	90	9-00	27	43	85
2 DUPONT SHOW OF THE MONTH	11/25/57	2	90	9-30	24	38	85

PRESTIGE DRAMA

3 HALLMARK HALL OF FAME	3/24/58	2	90	9-30	18	30	114
2 DUPONT SHOW OF THE MONTH	3/27/58	5	90	9-30	21	37	85
2 DUPONT SHOW OF THE MONTH	5/09/58	6	90	9-30	22	39	85
3 HALLMARK HALL OF FAME	10/17/57	5	60	10-00	18	28	114
2 DUPONT SHOW OF THE MONTH	10/28/57	2	90	9-30	23	38	85
3 HALLMARK HALL OF FAME	12/15/57	1	30	6-30	7	12	114

COMEDY DRAMA

2 THE LUCY-DESI SHOW	1/03/58	6	60	9-00	43	61	96
2 THE LUCY-DESI SHOW	2/03/58	2	60	8-00	41	55	96
2 THE LUCY-DESI SHOW	4/14/58	2	60	8-30	37	51	96
2 DUPONT SHOW OF THE MONTH	4/19/58	7	90	7-30	16	28	85
2 DUPONT SHOW OF THE MONTH	6/12/58	5	90	9-30	17	34	85
2 THE LUCY-DESI SHOW	11/06/57	4	75	9-00	47	62	96
2 THE LUCY-DESI SHOW	12/03/57	3	60	9-00	39	54	96
2 DUPONT SHOW OF THE MONTH	12/20/57	6	90	7-30	24	41	85

CRIME, SPY DRAMA

3 HALLMARK HALL OF FAME	4/25/58	6	90	9-30			114

FAIRY TALE/CARTOON DRAMA

3 SHIRLEY TEMPLE STORYBOOK	1/12/58	1	60	8-00	30	42	172
3 SHIRLEY TEMPLE STORYBOOK	2/19/58	4	60	7-30	27	36	172
3 SHIRLEY TEMPLE STORYBOOK	3/05/58	4	60	7-30	26	37	172
3 SHIRLEY TEMPLE STORYBOOK	4/18/58	6	60	7-30	17	35	172
3 SHIRLEY TEMPLE STORYBOOK	5/08/58	5	60	7-30	22	42	172
3 SHIRLEY TEMPLE STORYBOOK	6/08/58	1	60	8-00	22	40	172

MUSICAL DRAMA

3	HALLMARK HALL OF FAME	2/09/58	1	30	6-30	27	38	114
2	DUPONT SHOW OF THE MONTH	2/21/58	6	90	7-30	29	44	85
3	PIED PIPER OF HAMLIN	11/26/57	3	90	7-30	23	32	288
3	ANNIE GET YOUR GUN	11/27/57	4	120	8-30	38	53	197

AWARDS AND PAGENTS

3	MOVIE ACADEMY AWARDS	3/26/58	4	30	10-30	45	76	2
3	TELEVISION EMMY AWARDS	4/15/58	3	60	10-00	33	65	197
2	MIKE TODD PARTY	10/17/57	5	90	8-30	31	47	

DOCUMENTARY

2	HIGH ADVENTURE	1/22/58	4	60	8-00	21	28	266
3	MARCH OF MEDICINE	1/23/58	5	60	10-00	16	28	239
2	HIGH ADVENTURE	2/25/58	3	60	8-00	22	30	266
2	HIGH ADVENTURE	3/24/58	2	60	8-00	25	35	266
1	JUST BY CHANCE	4/04/58	6	30	10-00			
2	HIGH ADVENTURE	4/19/58	7	60	9-00	29	45	266
1	EXPLORER LAUNCHINGS	4/26/58	7	30	10-00			
1	REPORT CARD	5/05/58	2	60	7-30			
2	HIGH ADVENTURE	5/28/58	4	60	10-00	19	34	266
3	ELEVEN AGAINST THE ICE	9/23/57	2	60	9-30	17	27	258
2	HIGH ADVENTURE	11/12/57	3	60	8-00	27	39	266
1	MEN AND MISSILES	12/22/57	1	30	9-30			
2	HIGH ADVENTURE	12/23/57	2	60	10-00			266
2	LADY FROM PHILADELPHIA	12/30/57	2	60	10-00	16	27	126

INSTRUCTIONAL PROGRAMS

3	BELL SCIENCE SERIES	2/12/58	4	60	9-00	24	33	39
3	BELL SCIENCE SERIES	10/25/57	6	60	9-00			39

SPEECHES

3	PRES EISENHOWER ADDRESS	1/20/58	2	30	9-30	14	20	196
1	ADLAI STEVENSON ADDRESS	1/31/58	6	30	10-30			
2	HARRY S. TRUMAN ADDRESS	2/22/58	7	30	10-30			
1	EISENHOWER ADDRESS	3/27/58	5	30	9-30			
2	PRES. EISENHOWER ADDRESS	5/06/58	3	30	10-30			
1	RICHARD ARENS ADDRESS	5/19/58	2	30	7-30			
1	EISENHOWER ADDRESS	5/20/58	3	30	10-30			
2	PRES. EISENHOWER ADDRESS	5/20/58	3	30	10-30			
3	PRES EISENHOWER ADDRESS	5/20/58	3	30	9-30			
1	EISENHOWER ADDRESS	9/24/57	3	30	9-00			
2	PRES. EISENHOWER ADDRESS	9/24/57	3	15	9-00			
3	PRES EISENHOWER ADDRESS	9/24/57	3	30	9-00			
1	QUEEN ELIZABETH ADDRESS	10/13/57	1	30	8-00			
2	PRES. EISENHOWER ADDRESS	11/07/57	5	30	8-00			
3	PRES EISENHOWER ADDRESS	11/14/57	5	30	10-30			
2	PRES. EISENHOWER ADDRESS	12/23/57	2	30	8-30			

NEWS AND NEWS ANALYSIS

1	LAUNCHING OF JUPITER C	2/01/58	7	25	8-30			
2	LITTLE ROCK REPORT	9/24/57	3	30	10-30			
1	PROLOG	12/29/57	1	60	9-00			
	PANEL TALKS							
1	DEDICATION TO JUSTICE	1/05/58	1	30	9-30			
	POLITICAL PROGRAMS							
1	CAMPAIGN ROUNDUP	5/12/58	2	30	8-00			
1	CAMPAIGN ROUNDUP	5/19/58	2	30	8-00			
1	CAMPAIGN ROUNDUP	5/26/58	2	30	8-00			
1	CAMPAIGN ROUNDUP	6/02/58	2	30	8-00			
1	CAMPAIGN ROUNDUP	6/09/58	2	30	8-00			
	RELIGIOUS PROGRAMS							
1	MISSION TO THE WORLD	9/29/57	1	30	9-30			
1	THE TROPHY	12/15/57	1	30	9-30			
	SPORTS AND SPORTS NEWS							
1	ALL STAR BOWLING FINALS	1/19/58	1	60	9-00	12	17	18
1	GOLDEN GLOVES BOXING	3/05/58	4	60	10-00			
2	WORLD CHAMPIONSHIP RODEO	9/14/57	7	60	8-00	21	42	102
1	WORLD SERIES SPECIAL	10/01/57	3	30	10-00			171
3	BOWLING CHAMPIONSHIPS	12/13/57	6	60	9-00			
	COMEDY VARIETY							
3	THE BOB HOPE SHOW	1/17/58	6	60	8-00	30	42	192
3	THE BOB HOPE SHOW	2/06/58	5	60	8-30	27	36	192
3	THE JERRY LEWIS SHOW	2/18/58	3	60	8-00	32	42	180
2	THE VICTOR BORGE SHOW	2/19/58	4	60	9-00	26	36	103
3	THE BOB HOPE SHOW	3/02/58	1	60	9-00	32	48	130
3	THE BOB HOPE SHOW	4/05/58	7	60	9-00	23	34	130
3	THE JERRY LEWIS SHOW	4/15/58	3	60	9-00	28	42	180
2	PHIL SILVERS ON BROADWAY	5/13/58	3	60	10-00	23	43	197
3	THE JERRY LEWIS SHOW	5/16/58	6	60	10-00	22	45	180
3	TEXACO COMMAND APPEARANCE	9/19/57	5	60	10-00	19	36	255
3	THE JERRY LEWIS SHOW	10/05/57	7	60	9-00	27	39	180
3	THE BOB HOPE SHOW	10/06/57	1	60	9-00	31	47	257
3	THE JERRY LEWIS SHOW	11/05/57	3	60	9-00	26	38	180
3	THE BOB HOPE SHOW	11/24/57	1	30	7-00	23	34	192
3	THE JERRY LEWIS SHOW	12/27/57	6	60	8-00			180
	MUSICAL VARIETY							
3	OMNIBUS--SUBURBAN REVIEW	1/14/58	3	60	8-00	13	18	9
3	THE DEAN MARTIN SHOW	2/01/58	7	60	9-00	19	26	288
3	SWING INTO SPRING	4/09/58	4	60	9-00	18	27	255
2	ALL STAR JAZZ	4/30/58	4	60	10-00	18	32	257
3	THE DEAN MARTIN SHOW	10/05/57	7	60	10-00	17	29	171

2	THE EDSEL SHOW	10/13/57	1	60	8-00	37	55	84
3	STANDARD OIL ANNIVERSARY	10/13/57	1	90	9-00	30	46	244
3	THE TONY MARTIN SHOW	11/10/57	1	60	9-00			
3	HOLIDAY IN LAS VEGAS	11/16/57	7	60	8-00	30	44	90
3	TEXACO COMMAND APPEARANCE	11/23/57	7	60	10-00	17	28	255
2	CHRISTMAS CARD	12/11/57	4	60	10-00			235
3	ARTHUR MURRAY PARTY	12/28/57	7	60	9-00			
3	TIMEX ALL STAR JAZZ SHOW	12/30/57	2	60	10-00	17	30	257

VAUDEVILLE VARIETY

3	GM GOLDEN ANNIVERSARY	11/17/57	1	120	9-00	30	47	103

NON-CLASSIFIABLE

1	THE UNKNOWN SOLDIERS	5/30/58	6	30	8-00
3	XMAS WITH DAVE GARROWAY	12/24/57	3	30	10-00

SUMMER 1958

CRIME, SPY DRAMA

3	MR. KANE	9/09/58	3	60	8-00

FAIRY TALE/CARTOON DRAMA

3	SHIRLEY TEMPLE STORYBOOK	7/15/58	3	60	8-00	18	39	172
3	SHIRLEY TEMPLE STORYBOOK	8/19/58	3	60	8-00	15	31	172
3	SHIRLEY TEMPLE STORYBOOK	9/12/58	6	60	8-30	16	30	172

ACTUALITIES

2	UN SESSION ON MIDDLE EAST	7/17/58	5	105	8-45

AWARDS AND PAGENTS

2	MISS AMERICA PAGEANT	9/06/58	7	60	10-00	38	66	188

DOCUMENTARY

1	REPORT CARD	6/16/58	2	60	9-30
2	HUNGARY--RETURN OF TERROR	6/20/58	6	30	7-30
2	THE FORTY-NINTH STATE	7/02/58	4	30	8-00
1	RIVAL WORLD	7/04/58	6	30	9-00
2	LOUIS PASTEUR	7/17/58	5	30	10-30
1	INTERNATIONAL ALBUM	8/29/58	6	30	9-00
3	THE PAPER SAINTS	8/29/58	6	30	8-30
3	THE FIFTH FRENCH REPUBLIC	9/05/58	6	30	8-30
1	DEW LINE PART ONE	9/09/58	3	30	9-30

SPEECHES

1	EISENHOWER ADDRESS	7/09/58	4	30	9-30

1	EISENHOWER ADDRESS	8/11/58	2	30	10-00				
3	PRINCESS MARGARET ADDRESS	8/11/58	2	30	7-30				

NEWS AND NEWS ANALYSIS

1	UNITED NATIONS SPECIAL	7/15/58	3	30	10-00				
2	MIDDLE EAST CRISIS REPORT	7/15/58	3	30	10-30				
1	UNITED NATIONS SPECIAL	7/17/58	5	50	9-10				
2	KUWAIT--MIDEAST OIL PRIZE	7/23/58	4	30	7-30				
2	PROLOGUE TO THE SUMMIT	7/30/58	4	30	7-30				
2	UNITED NATIONS SUMMARY	8/13/58	4	30	7-30				
2	UNITED NATIONS SUMMARY	8/15/58	6	30	7-30				
2	KEY TO THE MIDDLE EAST	8/27/58	4	30	7-30				

PANEL TALKS

3	RUSSIAN EDUCATION	7/18/58	6	30	7-30				
2	THE RUBLE WAR	7/21/58	2	60	10-00				
2	THE CONGRESS--APPRAISAL	8/22/58	6	30	7-30				

SPORTS AND SPORTS NEWS

1	GOLD CUP RACE	8/10/58	1	60	9-30				
1	ALL STAR FOOTBALL GAME	8/15/58	6	90	9-30				

MUSICAL VARIETY

2	MUSIC U.S.A.	9/08/58	2	60	10-00	9	19		277

1958 - 1959

ACTION/ADVENTURE DRAMA

2	DUPONT SHOW OF THE MONTH	10/28/58	3	90	7-30	15	25		85

PRESTIGE DRAMA

3	HALLMARK HALL OF FAME	2/05/59	5	90	9-30	15	27		114
2	DUPONT SHOW OF THE MONTH	2/24/59	3	90	9-30	15	26		85
3	HALLMARK HALL OF FAME	3/23/59	2	90	9-30	25	42	+	114
2	DUPONT SHOW OF THE MONTH	3/28/59	7	90	9-30	20	32		85
3	HALLMARK HALL OF FAME	4/28/59	3	90	9-30	16	28		114
2	DUPONT SHOW OF THE MONTH	5/25/59	2	90	9-30	17	33		85
3	HALLMARK HALL OF FAME	10/13/58	2	90	9-30	23	42		114
2	DUPONT SHOW OF THE MONTH	12/18/58	5	90	9-30	22	37		85

COMEDY DRAMA

2	DUPONT SHOW OF THE MONTH	1/28/59	4	90	9-30	18	30		85
2	THE LUCY-DESI SHOW	2/09/59	2	60	10-00	35	58		277
2	THE LUCY-DESI SHOW	3/09/59	2	60	10-00	24	43		277
2	THE LUCY-DESI SHOW	4/13/59	2	60	10-00	28	53		277
2	THE LUCI-DESI SHOW	6/08/59	2	60	10-00	25	54		277

2	DUPONT SHOW OF THE MONTH	9/22/58	2	90	9-30	31	55		85
2	THE LUCY-DESI SHOW	10/06/58	2	60	10-00	30	55		277
2	DUPONT SHOW OF THE MONTH	11/13/58	5	90	9-30	17	30		85
2	THE LUCY-DESI SHOW	12/01/58	2	60	10-00	30	51		277

CRIME, SPY DRAMA

3	TEN LITTLE INDIANS	1/18/59	1	30	7-00	18	28		214
2	THE DEFENDER PART ONE	9/24/58	4	60	8-00				
2	THE DEFENDER PART TWO	10/01/58	4	60	8-00				
2	DEAD OF NOON	10/15/58	4	60	8-00				

FAIRY TALE/CARTOON DRAMA

3	SHIRLEY TEMPLE STORYBOOK	10/05/58	1	60	8-00	23	35		172
3	SHIRLEY TEMPLE STORYBOOK	10/27/58	2	60	8-00	29	43		172
3	SHIRLEY TEMPLE STORYBOOK	11/12/58	4	60	7-30	30	44		172
3	SHIRLEY TEMPLE STORYBOOK	11/25/58	3	60	8-00	20	28		172
3	SHIRLEY TEMPLE STORYBOOK	12/21/58	1	60	8-00				172

MUSICAL DRAMA

2	PONTIAC STAR PARADE	1/23/59	6	60	9-00	24	36		197
2	MEET ME IN ST. LOUIS	4/26/59	1	120	9-00	33	53		276
3	THE PIED PIPER OF HAMLIN	9/16/58	3	90	7-30	14	24	+	288
3	BOB HOPE SHOW--ROBERTA	9/19/58	6	90	7-30	22	41		49
2	LITTLE WOMEN	10/16/58	5	60	8-30	21	33		232
3	HALLMARK HALL OF FAME	11/20/58	5	90	9-00	18	28		114
2	WONDERFUL TOWN	11/30/58	1	120	9-00	25	39		276
2	GIFT OF THE MAGI	12/09/58	3	60	9-00	23	33		232

UNCLASSIFIED DRAMA

2	DUPONT SHOW OF THE MONTH	4/23/59	5	90	8-00	14	23		85

AWARDS AND PAGENTS

3	MOVIE ACADEMY AWARDS	4/06/59	2	30	10-30	46	80		2
2	ROYAL WEDDING IN JAPAN	4/14/59	3	30	8-00				
3	TELEVISION EMMY AWARDS	5/06/59	4	60	10-00	33	63		40

DOCUMENTARY

1	YOUTH ANONYMOUS	1/19/59	2	60	7-30				
2	HIGH ADVENTURE	1/19/59	2	60	10-00	26	45		266
2	LOST CLASS OF FIFTY-NINE	1/21/59	4	60	8-00				
2	FIDEL CASTRO--A REPORT	1/28/59	4	30	8-00				
1	YOUTH ANONYMOUS	2/01/59	1	60	9-30				
3	PROJECT XX--MEET LINCOLN	2/11/59	4	30	8-30	24	35		149
2	HIGH ADVENTURE	3/27/59	6	60	8-00	21	33		266
3	PROJECT XX--THE JAZZ AGE	3/29/59	1	30	7-00	8	15	+	248
1	INVESTIGATORS AND THE LAW	4/20/59	2	60	9-30				
2	MONTY SPEAKS HIS MIND	4/28/59	3	60	7-30				
3	I TAKE THEE	6/04/59	5	60	7-30				

2	CHINA--WAR OR PEACE	9/14/58	1	30	10-00			
1	DEW LINE PART TWO	9/16/58	3	30	9-30			
2	INTEGRATION--COURT BATTLE	9/17/58	4	30	7-30			
1	CROWDED OUT	9/20/58	7	30	8-00			
2	HIGH ADVENTURE	10/08/58	4	60	8-00	14	22	266
1	MEMORIAL TO POPE PIUS XII	10/09/58	5	30	10-00			
2	HIGH ADVENTURE	12/06/58	7	60	7-30	26	37	266
2	BERLIN--BELEAGURED ISLAND	12/09/58	3	30	8-00			
2	WHERE WE STAND	12/16/58	3	60	7-30			

INSTRUCTIONAL PROGRAMS

3	BELL SCIENCE SERIES	1/26/59	2	60	7-30	19	28	39
3	BELL SCIENCE SERIES	10/23/58	5	60	8-00			39

SPEECHES

1	EISENHOWER ADDRESS	1/14/59	4	30	9-30
1	EISENHOWER ADDRESS	3/16/59	2	30	9-30
2	PRES. EISENHOWER ADDRESS	3/16/59	2	30	9-30
1	CHRISTIAN HERTER ADDRESS	5/07/59	5	30	10-00
2	CHRISTIAN HERTER ADDRESS	5/07/59	5	30	9-00
1	EISENHOWER ADDRESS	10/12/58	1	30	10-30

NEWS AND NEWS ANALYSIS

2	THE MACMILLAN MISSION	3/24/59	3	30	8-00			
3	PRIMER ON GENEVA	5/03/59	1	60	7-30			
3	WHY BERLIN	5/08/59	6	60	8-00			38
1	PROLOGUE	12/28/58	1	60	9-30			
2	YEARS OF CRISIS	12/28/58	1	60	10-00	12	25	134

POLITICAL PROGRAMS

1	ELECTION COVERAGE	11/04/58	3	60	10-00	
2	ELECTION RETURNS	11/04/58	3	120	9-00	15
3	ELECTION COVERAGE	11/04/58	3	120	9-00	35
2	ELECTION RECAP	11/05/58	4	30	7-30	

RELIGIOUS PROGRAMS

1	CHRISTMAS BY BISHOP SHEEN	12/24/58	4	30	10-00
1	CHRISTMAS LUTHERN SERVICE	12/24/58	4	30	10-30

SPORTS AND SPORTS NEWS

1	ALL STAR BOWLING TOURNEY	1/18/59	1	60	9-30			18
3	ALL STAR BASKETBALL GAME	1/23/59	6	60	10-00	14	30	107
3	WORLD SERIES SPECIAL	9/30/58	3	30	10-30			171
3	ROY ROGERS RODEO	11/09/58	1	60	9-00	31	46	101
3	BOWLING CHAMPIONSHIP	12/12/58	6	60	10-00			

CIRCUS VARIETY

1	GREATEST SHOW ON EARTH	3/09/59	2	60	7-30	21	31		148

COMEDY VARIETY

3	THE BOB HOPE SHOW	1/16/59	6	60	9-00	27	40		49
3	THE BOB HOPE SHOW	2/10/59	3	60	9-30	22	34		49
3	THE BOB HOPE SHOW	3/13/59	6	60	8-00	22	33		49
2	THE JACK BENNY SPECIAL	3/18/59	4	60	10-00	23	40		111
3	THE BOB HOPE SHOW	4/15/59	4	60	9-00	27	41		103
3	AT THE MOVIES	5/03/59	1	60	10-00	22	45		214
3	THE BOB HOPE SHOW	5/15/59	6	60	10-00	23	42		49
3	KOVACS ON MUSIC	5/22/59	6	60	8-00	8	18		210
2	THE JACK BENNY SPECIAL	5/23/59	7	60	8-30	24	41		111
3	THE BOB HOPE SHOW	10/14/58	3	60	9-00	24	36		49
3	THE JERRY LEWIS SHOW	10/18/58	7	60	9-00	23	36		257
3	THE BOB HOPE SHOW	11/21/58	6	60	8-00	24	37		49
2	THE VICTOR BORGE SHOW	11/29/58	7	60	9-00	24	34		103
3	THE JERRY LEWIS SHOW	12/10/58	4	60	9-00	26	38		257

MUSICAL VARIETY

2	THE GOLDEN AGE OF JAZZ	1/07/59	4	60	8-00	10	14		257
3	BELL TELEPHONE HOUR	1/12/59	2	60	8-30	17	24		39
3	THE PHIL HARRIS SHOW	2/06/59	6	60	8-00	19	29		257
3	BELL TELEPHONE HOUR	2/10/59	3	60	8-00	14	20		39
3	EVENING WITH FRED ASTAIRE	2/11/59	4	60	10-00	19	34	+	64
3	ACCENT ON LOVE	2/28/59	7	60	9-00	18	26		197
1	THE BING CROSBY SHOW	3/02/59	2	60	9-30	22	33		180
3	BELL TELEPHONE HOUR	3/04/59	4	60	9-00	14	20		39
3	THE DEAN MARTIN SHOW	3/19/59	5	60	8-00	17	26		257
3	MUSIC WITH MARY MARTIN	3/29/59	1	60	8-00	15	24		257
3	BELL TELEPHONE HOUR	4/09/59	5	60	8-00	14	20		39
2	SWING INTO SPRING	4/10/59	6	60	9-00	15	24		255
2	PONTIAC STAR PARADE	4/24/59	6	60	9-30				197
3	THE DEAN MARTIN SHOW	5/03/59	1	60	8-30	15	28		257
3	SUMMER ON ICE	6/01/59	2	60	10-00	30	59		270
2	HOLLIDAY USA	6/03/59	4	60	9-00	20	36		255
1	THE BING CROSBY SHOW	10/01/58	4	60	9-30	20	32		180
2	PONTIAC STAR PARADE	10/15/58	4	60	10-00	17	33		197
3	EVENING WITH FRED ASTAIRE	10/17/58	6	60	10-00	18	31		64
2	ALL STAR JAZZ	11/10/58	2	60	10-00	14	27		257
3	THE DEAN MARTIN SHOW	11/22/58	7	60	9-00	21	31		257

VAUDEVILLE VARIETY

3	SOME OF MANIE'S FRIENDS	3/03/59	3	90	7-30	28	40	288
3	FRANCES LANGFORD PRESENTS	3/15/59	1	60	10-00	22	40	214
3	PERRY COMO ON BROADWAY	3/24/59	3	60	8-00	23	33	197
2	AMERICA PAUSES FOR SPRING	3/30/59	2	60	7-30	21	34	67
2	THE MERRY MONTH OF MAY	5/18/59	2	60	8-00	19	34	67
3	HALLMARK HALL OF FAME	12/14/58	1	30	7-00	14	21	114

SUMMER 1959

COMEDY DRAMA

3	THE RANSOM OF RED CHIEF	8/16/59	1	60	10-00	18	40	214

AWARDS AND PAGENTS

2	PASSPORT TO GLAMOUR	7/18/59	7	30	10-30			
2	MISS AMERICA PARADE	9/08/59	3	30	8-00	20	40	157
2	MISS AMERICA PAGEANT	9/12/59	7	60	10-00	38	69	188

DOCUMENTARY

2	HOFFA AND THE TEAMSTERS	6/24/59	4	60	10-00			
1	YOUR NEIGHBOR THE WORLD	6/25/59	5	30	10-00			
1	INVESTIGATOR AND THE LAW	8/14/59	6	60	8-00			
3	BACK TO SCHOOL	8/25/59	3	60	8-00	5	12	
3	EMERGING AFRICA	9/13/59	1	60	8-00			

SPEECHES

1	CHRISTIAN HERTER ADDRESS	6/23/59	3	30	10-30			
2	CHRISTIAN HERTER ADDRESS	6/23/59	3	15	9-00			
1	EISENHOWER ADDRESS	8/06/59	5	30	7-30			
2	PRES. EISENHOWER REPORT	8/06/59	5	15	7-30			
2	VICE PRES. NIXON REPORTS	8/09/59	1	30	7-30			
1	ROOSEVELT-THOMPSON TALK	8/10/59	2	15	7-30			
2	EISENHOWER SPEAKS IN ENG.	9/01/59	3	30	8-00			
1	EISENHOWER ADDRESS	9/10/59	5	30	7-30			
2	PRES. EISENHOWER ADDRESS	9/10/59	5	15	7-30			
3	PRES EISENHOWER ADDRESS	9/10/59	5	30	7-30			

NEWS AND NEWS ANALYSIS

2	GENEVA NEWS CONFERENCE	6/23/59	3	15	9-15			
3	ST. LAWRENCE SEAWAY	6/26/59	6	60	8-00			29
1	QUEENS VISIT TO THE U.S.	7/06/59	2	30	10-30			
2	SPECIAL REPORT	8/02/59	1	30	7-30			
1	KHRUSHCHEV TO VISIT U.S.	8/03/59	2	30	10-30			
2	CBS SPECIAL NEWS	8/06/59	5	15	7-45			
2	HOUSE LABOR DEBATE	8/11/59	3	30	7-30			
3	JOURNEY TO UNDERSTANDING	8/27/59	5	30	8-30			
3	JOURNEY TO UNDERSTANDING	8/29/59	7	60	9-30			
3	JOURNEY TO UNDERSTANDING	9/01/59	3	30	9-30			
3	JOURNEY TO UNDERSTANDING	9/03/59	5	30	7-30			
3	JOURNEY TO UNDERSTANDING	9/04/59	6	60	8-00			
2	EYEWITNESS TO HISTORY	9/06/59	1	30	7-30			94
2	REPORT ON LAOS	9/10/59	5	15	7-45			
3	THE LAST QUARTER	9/11/59	6	60	8-30			

SPORTS AND SPORTS NEWS

3	ALL STAR FOOTBALL GAME	8/03/59	2	150	6-45	25	56	
1	ALL STAR FOOTBALL GAME	8/14/59	6	90	9-30	15	42	55

MUSICAL VARIETY

1	DICK CLARKS RECORD YEARS	6/28/59	1	60	9-30.			18

NON-CLASSIFIABLE

1	KODAK PRESENTS DISNEYLAND	6/15/59	2	90	7-30	17	36	83

1959 - 1960

ACTION/ADVENTURE DRAMA

2	PLAYHOUSE NINETY	2/09/60	3	90	9-30	21	37	8
2	DUPONT SHOW OF THE MONTH	2/18/60	5	90	9-30	19	30	85
2	SPECIAL TONIGHT	3/20/60	1	90	9-30	22	41	102
2	PLAYHOUSE NINETY	3/22/60	3	90	8-00	17	26	8
2	BUICK ELECTRA PLAYHOUSE	3/25/60	6	90	8-30	17	28	49
2	DUPONT SHOW OF THE MONTH	9/28/59	2	90	8-30	19	33	85

PRESTIGE DRAMA

2	SPECIAL TONIGHT	1/07/60	5	90	9-30	17	29	102
2	DUPONT SHOW OF THE MONTH	1/17/60	1	90	9-30	22	40	85
3	HALLMARK HALL OF FAME	2/03/60	4	90	7-30	18	28	114
2	DUPONT SHOW OF THE MONTH	3/05/60	7	90	7-30	20	31	85
3	HALLMARK HALL OF FAME	5/02/60	2	90	9-30	11	22	114
3	HALLMARK HALL OF FAME	10/26/59	2	90	9-30	18	34	114
3	HALLMARK HALL OF FAME	11/15/59	1	90	7-30	13	20	114
2	DUPONT SHOW OF THE MONTH	12/04/59	6	90	7-30	16	26	85
3	SPECIAL TONIGHT	12/07/59	2	90	9-30	18	34	102

COMEDY DRAMA

2	PLAYHOUSE NINETY	4/03/60	1	90	8-00	29	43	8
1	NINOTCHKA	4/20/60	4	90	8-30			102
2	SLOWEST GUN IN THE WEST	5/07/60	7	60	9-00	30	48	55
3	STRAWBERRY BLONDE	10/18/59	1	60	10-00	15	27	214
2	DUPONT SHOW OF THE MONTH	11/09/59	2	90	9-30	13	25	85

CRIME, SPY DRAMA

2	BUICK ELECTRA PLAYHOUSE	1/29/60	6	90	8-30	14	22	49
2	IF I SHOULD DIE	3/11/60	6	60	9-00	14	21	198
3	DOW HOUR OF GREAT MYSTERY	3/31/60	5	60	9-00	23	36	79
3	DOW HOUR OF GREAT MYSTERY	4/24/60	1	60	10-00			79
2	BUICK ELECTRA PLAYHOUSE	5/19/60	5	90	9-30	18	27	49
3	DOW HOUR OF GREAT MYSTERY	5/23/60	2	60	10-00	16	33	79
3	SACCO-VANZETTI STORY, I	6/03/60	6	60	8-30	10	20	201
3	SACCO-VANZETTI STORY, II	6/10/60	6	60	8-30	9	19	201
2	BUICK ELECTRA PLAYHOUSE	11/19/59	5	90	9-30	20	35	49

HISTORICAL DRAMA

2	DUPONT SHOW OF THF MONTH	4/21/60	5	90	8-00				85
2	PLAYHOUSF NINFTY	5/02/60	2	90	8-00	14	25		8
3	BRFCK GOLDEN SHOWCASF	6/13/60	2	60	10-00	12	25	+	129

MOTION PICTURF DRAMA

2	THF WIZARD OF OZ	12/13/59	1	30	6-00	36	58	+	40

MUSICAL DRAMA

3	BELL TELFPHONE HOUR	4/29/60	6	60	8-30	16	28		39
2	PHIL SILVERS SPECIAL	10/17/59	7	60	9-00	20	31		55
3	ONCE UPON CHRISTMAS TIME	12/09/59	4	60	7-30	27	44		150
3	PONTIAC STAR PARADE	12/24/59	5	60	8-00				197

UNCLASSIFIED DRAMA

3	CALL ME RACK	1/16/60	7	60	9-30	13	20		201
1	THE CITADFL	2/19/60	6	90	8-30	15	24		102
2	PLAYHOUSF NINETY	2/24/60	4	90	8-00	16	22		8
2	PLAYHOUSF NINETY	3/07/60	2	90	9-30	26	45		8
2	THE AMERICAN THEATFR	4/08/60	6	60	9-00				
3	HALLMARK HALL OF FAME	4/10/60	1	30	6-30	16	30	+	114
3	SPECIAL LORETTA YOUNG PGM	4/10/60	1	60	10-00	19	36	+	259
2	PLAYHOUSF NINETY	4/22/60	6	90	9-00				8
2	PLAYHOUSF NINETY	5/18/60	4	90	8-30	16	27		8
3	SPECIAL LORETTA YOUNG PGM	9/20/59	1	60	10-00	19	39		259
2	I'M A LAWYFR	9/25/59	6	30	8-30				
1	HOW LONG THE NIGHT	9/30/59	4	30	10-00				
2	DUPONT SHOW OF THE MONTH	10/14/59	4	90	8-30	20	30		85
2	THE BELLS OF ST. MARY'S	10/27/59	3	90	8-30	24	37		102

AWARDS AND PAGENTS

3	PARIS A LA MODE	2/29/60	2	60	10-00	13	25		62
3	OSCAR NIGHT IN HOLLYWOOD	4/04/60	2	30	10-00	32	51		198
3	MOVIE ACADEMY AWARDS	4/04/60	2	30	10-30	45	81		2
3	THE ROYAL WEDDING	5/06/60	6	60	7-30	20	38		97
1	SALUTE TO DR. DOOLEY	11/10/59	3	30	10-00				170
3	GRAMMY AWARDS	11/29/59	1	60	8-00	14	20		275

DOCUMFNTARY

2	CBS RFPORTS--SPACE LAG	1/06/60	4	60	10-00				38
2	CBS REPORTS--POPULATION	1/14/60	5	90	9-30				38
2	THE AMERICAN COWBOY	2/10/60	4	60	10-00	23	42		272
3	PROJECT XX--MEET LINCOLN	2/11/60	5	30	9-00				149
2	DILLINGER--A YEAR TO KILL	2/12/60	6	60	9-00	21	33		198
2	CBS REPORTS	2/15/60	2	60	7-30				38
2	CBS REPORTS--TRUJILLO	3/17/60	5	60	10-00				38
1	KOREA--NO PARALLEL	3/29/60	3	60	10-00				
3	OVERTURE TO ROYAL WEDDING	4/24/60	1	60	8-00				97
1	THE DARK AND THE LIGHT	4/27/60	4	60	7-30				
3	ADOLF HITLER	4/30/60	7	60	9-30				

1	NOT BY BREAD ALONE	5/11/60	4	30	8-00			
2	CBS REPORTS	5/27/60	6	60	10-00	15	28	38
3	MARCH OF MEDICINE	5/27/60	6	60	8-30	9	17	239
3	HOW TALL IS A GIANT	6/14/60	3	90	8-30	16	29	198
1	SPLENDID AMERICAN	9/27/59	1	60	9-30			
2	BIOGRAPHY OF A MISSILE	10/27/59	3	60	10-00			43
2	THE POPULATION EXPLOSION	11/11/59	4	60	10-00			43
2	IRAN--BRITTLE ALLY	12/18/59	6	60	10-00			43

SPEECHES

1	EISENHOWER ADDRESS	5/02/60	2	30	10-30
1	EISENHOWER ADDRESS	5/25/60	4	30	8-00
2	PRES. EISENHOWER ADDRESS	5/25/60	4	30	8-00
3	PRES EISENHOWER ADDRESS	5/25/60	4	30	10-00

NEWS AND NEWS ANALYSIS

2	EYEWITNESS TO HISTORY	1/01/60	6	60	9-00			94
2	EYEWITNESS TO HISTORY	2/24/60	4	30	7-30			94
2	EYEWITNESS TO HISTORY	2/26/60	6	30	10-30			94
3	JOURNEY TO UNDERSTANDING	2/27/60	7	60	9-30			20
3	JOURNEY TO UNDERSTANDING	3/03/60	5	30	7-30			20
2	EYEWITNESS TO HISTORY	3/05/60	7	30	10-30			94
3	JOURNEY TO UNDERSTANDING	3/05/60	7	60	9-30			20
2	EYEWITNESS TO HISTORY	3/25/60	6	30	10-30			94
3	JOURNEY TO UNDERSTANDING	4/02/60	7	60	9-30			20
3	JOURNEY TO UNDERSTANDING	4/22/60	6	30	7-30			175
3	JOURNEY TO UNDERSTANDING	4/28/60	5	30	7-30	8	17	20
2	EYEWITNESS TO HISTORY	4/29/60	6	30	10-30	10	23	94
3	JOURNEY TO UNDERSTANDING	5/14/60	7	30	8-30	10	20	175
2	EYEWITNESS TO HISTORY	5/16/60	2	30	8-00	13	27	94
3	THE SUMMIT CRISIS	5/16/60	2	60	7-30			
1	PRESIDENTIAL MISSION	5/17/60	3	30	10-30			
2	EYEWITNESS TO HISTORY	5/17/60	3	30	8-00	13	27	94
3	JOURNEY TO UNDERSTANDING	5/17/60	3	30	10-30	8	20	20
1	PRESIDENTIAL MISSION	5/18/60	4	30	8-00			
2	EYEWITNESS TO HISTORY	5/18/60	4	30	7-30			
3	KHRUSHCHEV NEWS MEETING	5/18/60	4	30	10-30			
3	JOURNEY TO UNDERSTANDING	5/19/60	5	30	10-30	11	24	175
3	JOURNEY TO UNDERSTANDING	5/21/60	7	60	9-30	6	11	175
3	UN SECURITY COUNCIL	5/23/60	2	60	7-30			175
1	HIGHLIGHTS OF UN SESSION	5/24/60	3	30	10-30			
3	UN SECURITY COUNCIL	5/24/60	3	30	10-00			
1	SETTING THE SCENE	5/25/60	4	30	7-30			
1	HIGHLIGHTS OF UN SESSION	5/26/60	5	30	7-30			
3	UN SECURITY COUNCIL	5/26/60	5	30	7-30			
3	JOURNEY TO UNDERSTANDING	6/10/60	6	30	7-30			20
2	EYEWITNESS TO HISTORY	6/14/60	3	30	8-00			
1	KHRUSHCHEV ARRIVAL	9/15/59	3	30	10-30			
2	KHRUSHCHEV IN THE U.S.	9/15/59	3	30	7-30			94
3	JOURNEY TO UNDERSTANDING	9/15/59	3	30	9-00			
1	KHRUSHCHEV ABROAD	9/16/59	4	30	9-30			
2	KHRUSHCHEV IN THE U.S.	9/16/59	4	30	7-30			94

1	KHRUSHCHEV ABROAD	9/17/59	5	30	10-00			
2	KHRUSHCHEV IN THE U.S.	9/17/59	5	30	7-30			94
3	JOURNEY TO UNDERSTANDING	9/17/59	5	30	7-30			
1	KHRUSHCHEV ABROAD	9/18/59	6	30	8-30			
3	JOURNEY TO UNDERSTANDING	9/19/59	7	60	9-30			
1	KHRUSHCHEV ABROAD	9/20/59	1	30	10-00			
2	KHRUSHCHEV IN THE U.S.	9/21/59	2	30	10-00			94
3	JOURNEY TO UNDERSTANDING	9/21/59	2	30	7-30			
2	KHRUSHCHEV IN THE U.S.	9/22/59	3	30	7-30			94
1	KHRUSHCHEV ABROAD	9/23/59	4	30	9-30			
2	KHRUSHCHEV IN THE U.S.	9/23/59	4	30	8-00			94
3	JOURNEY TO UNDERSTANDING	9/23/59	4	30	10-30			
1	KHRUSHCHEV ABROAD	9/24/59	5	30	7-30			
2	KHRUSHCHEV IN THE U.S.	9/24/59	5	30	7-30			94
3	JOURNEY TO UNDERSTANDING	9/24/59	5	30	7-30			
1	KHRUSHCHEV ABROAD	9/25/59	6	30	10-30			
2	KHRUSHCHEV GOES HOME	9/27/59	1	30	10-00			
3	JOURNEY TO UNDERSTANDING	9/27/59	1	30	10-30			
1	EISENHOWER NEWS CONF	9/28/59	2	30	9-00			
2	EYEWITNESS TO HISTORY	12/07/59	2	30	7-30			94
3	JOURNEY TO UNDERSTANDING	12/07/59	2	30	8-00			48
3	JOURNEY TO UNDERSTANDING	12/10/59	5	30	10-30			48
1	PRESIDENTIAL MISSION	12/12/59	7	30	10-30			
2	EYEWITNESS TO HISTORY	12/12/59	7	30	10-30			94
3	JOURNEY TO UNDERSTANDING	12/12/59	7	60	9-30			48
3	JOURNEY TO UNDERSTANDING	12/18/59	6	30	8-00			48
2	EYEWITNESS TO HISTORY	12/20/59	1	30	10-30			94
3	JOURNEY TO UNDERSTANDING	12/20/59	1	60	8-00			48
3	JOURNEY TO UNDERSTANDING	12/22/59	3	30	10-30			48
1	PRESIDENTIAL MISSION	12/23/59	4	30	7-30			
2	EYEWITNESS TO HISTORY	12/23/59	4	60	7-30			94
1	PROLOGUE	12/27/59	1	60	9-30			26
3	PROJECTION 'SIXTY	12/27/59	1	60	8-00			
	PANEL TALKS							
3	STEEL WORKERS' STRIKE	1/04/60	2	30	7-30			246
2	CBS REPORTS	4/21/60	5	60	10-00			38
2	EYEWITNESS TO HISTORY	5/20/60	6	60	9-00	13	23	94
1	THE PROPHECIES OF WILSON	9/20/59	1	30	9-30			
1	DR DOOLEY TELLS HIS STORY	12/08/59	3	30	10-30			170
	SPORTS AND SPORTS NEWS							
2	NATIONAL FINALS RODEO	1/15/60	6	60	9-00	21	31	57
3	ALL STAR BOWLING	1/15/60	6	60	10-00			
2	WINTER OLYMPICS	2/18/60	5	30	7-30	24	37	210
2	WINTER OLYMPICS	2/23/60	3	60	7-30	28	42	210
2	WINTER OLYMPICS	2/26/60	6	60	9-00	24	35	210
1	GOLDEN GLOVES BOXING	3/09/60	4	60	10-00			
3	WORLD SERIES SPECIAL	9/29/59	3	60	9-30			264
3	BOWLING CHAMPIONSHIP	12/11/59	6	60	10-00			
3	SPORTS HIGHLIGHTS	12/25/59	6	30	10-00			107

CIRCUS VARIETY

1	ALL STAR CIRCUS	3/31/60	5	60	7-30	23	39		257
2	THRILLS OF THE CIRCUS	5/27/60	6	60	9-00	19	33		260
2	CHRISTMAS AT THE CIRCUS	12/10/59	5	60	7-30	29	48		209

COMEDY VARIETY

3	THE BOB HOPE SHOW	1/13/60	4	60	9-00	33	47		49
3	THE JERRY LEWIS SHOW	1/16/60	7	60	8-30	27	38		257
3	PONTIAC STAR PARADE	1/22/60	6	60	8-30	17	25		197
2	THE FABULOUS FIFTIES	1/31/60	1	120	7-30	29	42		100
3	THE BOB HOPE SHOW	2/22/60	2	60	8-30	28	38		49
2	WAY BACK IN NINTEEN-SIXTY	3/10/60	5	60	8-30				
2	JACK BENNY SPECIAL	3/19/60	7	60	10-00	30	51		40
2	NIGHT CLUBS--NEW YORK	4/07/60	5	60	10-00				
3	THE BOB HOPE SHOW	4/20/60	4	60	9-00				49
3	JACK PARR PRESENTS	4/26/60	3	60	10-00	16	31		87
2	TIPTOE THROUGH TV	5/05/60	5	60	10-00	12	22		
2	JACK BENNY SPECIAL	5/18/60	4	60	10-00	19	34		40
2	THE WORLD OF SHOW BIZ	6/02/60	5	60	10-00				
3	THE GEORGE BURNS SHOW	6/07/60	3	60	8-30	14	26		274
3	THE BOB HOPE SHOW	10/08/59	5	60	8-00	28	44		49
2	RED SKELTON SPECIAL	10/09/59	6	60	9-00	29	48		103
3	PONTIAC STAR PARADE	10/16/59	6	60	10-00	19	36		197
2	HOLIDAY ON WHEELS	10/21/59	4	60	10-00				272
2	JACK BENNY SPECIAL	11/07/59	7	60	7-30	30	48		111
3	THE BOB HOPE SHOW	11/09/59	2	60	8-30	26	39		49
2	SID CAESAR SPECIAL	12/02/59	4	60	10-00	18	33		272
3	THE BOB HOPE SHOW	12/11/59	6	60	8-30	24	39		49

MUSICAL VARIETY

3	LINCOLN-MERCURY STAR TIME	1/12/60	3	60	9-30				148
1	THE FRANK SINATRA SHOW	2/15/60	2	60	9-30	16	26		257
3	PONTIAC STAR PARADE	2/24/60	4	60	10-00	16	30		197
1	THE BING CROSBY SHOW	2/29/60	2	60	8-30	30	42		180
3	PONTIAC STAR PARADE	3/18/60	6	60	8-30	19	31		197
3	PONTIAC STAR PARADE	4/16/60	7	60	8-30	13	22		197
3	EASTER EVENING HOUR	4/17/60	1	60	8-00				
1	INVITATION TO PARIS	4/27/60	4	60	10-00	10	20		210
2	ARTHUR GODFREY SPECIAL	5/06/60	6	60	9-00	16	27		137
3	EVENING WITH FRED ASTAIRE	5/09/60	2	60	10-00	14	28	+	64
1	THE FRANK SINATRA SHOW	5/12/60	5	60	9-30	33	54		257
3	PONTIAC STAR PARADE	5/13/60	6	60	10-00	14	28	+	197
3	SUMMER ON ICE	6/02/60	5	60	9-30	29	51		270
2	ARTHUR GODFREY SPECIAL	9/16/59	4	60	10-00	25	49		122
3	A TOAST TO JEROME KERN	9/22/59	3	90	9-00	16	30		270
1	THE BING CROSBY SHOW	9/29/59	3	60	9-30	23	41		180
1	THE PAT BOONE SHOW	10/01/59	5	60	9-00	12	21		63
1	THE FRANK SINATRA SHOW	10/19/59	2	60	9-30				257
3	EVENING WITH FRED ASTAIRE	11/04/59	4	60	9-00	24	37		64
3	TIMEX SHOW--LOUIS JOURDAN	11/11/59	4	60	10-00	23	45		257
3	MUSIC FROM SHUBERT ALLEY	11/13/59	6	60	10-00	15	27		236
3	PONTIAC STAR PARADE	11/21/59	7	60	8-30	19	30		197

1	GOLDEN CIRCLE	11/25/59	4	60	10-00	16	30	132
2	AN EVENING WITH BELAFONTE	12/10/59	5	60	8-30	19	29	212
1	THE FRANK SINATRA SHOW	12/13/59	1	60	8-30	17	25	257
3	CHRISTMAS, TEMPLE SQUARE	12/25/59	6	30	10-30			
2	NEW YEAR'S EVE PARTY	12/31/59	5	90	9-30			
	VAUDEVILLE VARIETY							
3	THE NIGHT OF CHRISTMAS	12/25/59	6	60	8-30			

SUMMER 1960

	AWARDS AND PAGEANTS							
3	TELEVISION EMMY AWARDS	6/20/60	2	90	10-00			198
2	MISS UNIVERSE PAGEANT	7/09/60	7	30	10-30	25	61	198
2	MISS AMERICA PARADE	9/06/60	3	30	8-00	16	33	188
2	MISS AMERICA PAGEANT	9/10/60	7	60	10-00	38	72	180
	DOCUMENTARY							
1	LISTENING POST EAST	6/15/60	4	60	7-30			
2	CBS REPORTS--BERLIN	6/17/60	6	60	9-00	10	20	43
2	DILLINGER--A YEAR TO KILL	6/24/60	6	60	9-00			198
1	JAPAN--ANCHOR IN THE EAST	6/29/60	4	60	7-30			
1	INSIDE ARGONNE	8/06/60	7	60	10-00			
3	PROJECT ECHO	8/12/60	6	30	9-30	9	18	21
3	PROJECT XX--RED NIGHTMARE	9/03/60	7	60	9-30			
	SPEECHES							
2	PRES. EISENHOWER ADDRESS	6/27/60	2	30	7-30			
3	PRES. EISENHOWER ADDRESS	6/27/60	2	30	7-30			
	NEWS AND NEWS ANALYSIS							
3	JOURNEY TO UNDERSTANDING	6/15/60	4	30	10-30			
3	JOURNEY TO UNDERSTANDING	6/16/60	5	30	7-30			
2	EYEWITNESS TO HISTORY	6/17/60	6	30	10-30	11	25	94
3	JOURNEY TO UNDERSTANDING	6/17/60	6	60	8-30			
2	EYEWITNESS TO HISTORY	6/21/60	3	30	8-00			94
3	THE PRESIDENT'S JOURNEY	6/21/60	3	60	8-30			
2	EYEWITNESS TO HISTORY	6/24/60	6	30	10-30			
3	THE PRESIDENT'S JOURNEY	6/25/60	7	60	9-30			
2	WHAT CAN WE DO ABOUT CUBA	8/18/60	5	30	8-00			
3	THE CONGO CRISIS	8/21/60	1	30	10-30			
3	REPORT FROM THE CONGO	9/09/60	6	30	9-00			
3	NBC NEWS SPECIAL REPORT	9/10/60	7	60	9-30			
	PANEL TALKS							
2	CBS REPORTS--LIPPMAN	7/07/60	5	60	7-30			
2	CBS REPORTS--LIPPMAN	8/11/60	5	60	7-30			+
	POLITICAL PROGRAMS							
2	PRE-CONVENTION HIGHLIGHTS	7/05/60	3	30	8-00			
2	PRE-CONVENTION HIGHLIGHTS	7/07/60	5	30	10-00			
3	CONVENTION PREVIEW	7/07/60	5	30	7-30			

3	CONVENTION PREVIEW	7/08/60	6	30	9-00			
1	CONVENTION CITY	7/09/60	7	30	10-30			
3	CONVENTIONS 1960	7/09/60	7	30	9-30	7	14	43
3	CONVENTION PREVIEW	7/10/60	1	30	7-30			
1	DEM NATIONAL CONVENTION	7/11/60	2	180	8-00	4	12	170
2	DEM NATIONAL CONVENTION	7/11/60	2	210	7-30	11	33	277
3	DEM NATIONAL CONVENTION	7/11/60	2	210	7-30	12	37	43
1	DEM NATIONAL CONVENTION	7/12/60	3	210	7-00	3	11	170
2	DEM NATIONAL CONVENTION	7/12/60	3	210	6-00	8	30	277
3	DEM NATIONAL CONVENTION	7/12/60	3	210	6-00	11	41	43
1	DEM NATIONAL CONVENTION	7/13/60	4	210	6-00	4	10	170
2	DEM NATIONAL CONVENTION	7/13/60	4	210	6-00	11	30	277
3	DEM NATIONAL CONVENTION	7/13/60	4	210	6-00	17	49	43
1	DEM NATIONAL CONVENTION	7/14/60	5	180	8-00	4	10	170
2	DEM NATIONAL CONVENTION	7/14/60	5	180	8-00	11	31	277
3	DEM NATIONAL CONVENTION	7/14/60	5	180	8-00	17	44	43
1	DEM NATIONAL CONVENTION	7/15/60	6	120	9-00	6	16	170
2	DEM NATIONAL CONVENTION	7/15/60	6	120	9-00	12	29	277
3	DEM NATIONAL CONVENTION	7/15/60	6	120	9-00	15	36	43
3	CONVENTION PREVIEW	7/21/60	5	30	7-30	8	27	
2	PRE-CONVENTION HIGHLIGHTS	7/21/60	5	30	10-00			
3	CONVENTION PREVIEW	7/22/60	6	30	9-00			
3	CONVENTION PREVIEW	7/23/60	7	30	9-30	6	13	
1	CONVENTION CITY	7/23/60	7	30	10-30			
1	REP NATIONAL CONVENTION	7/25/60	2	210	7-30			170
2	REP NATIONAL CONVENTION	7/25/60	2	210	7-30			277
3	REP NATIONAL CONVENTION	7/25/60	2	210	7-30			43
1	REP NATIONAL CONVENTION	7/26/60	3	210	7-30			170
2	REP NATIONAL CONVENTION	7/26/60	3	210	7-30			277
3	REP NATIONAL CONVENTION	7/26/60	3	210	7-30			43
1	REP NATIONAL CONVENTION	7/27/60	4	210	7-30			170
2	REP NATIONAL CONVENTION	7/27/60	4	210	7-30			277
3	REP NATIONAL CONVENTION	7/27/60	4	210	7-30			43
1	REP NATIONAL CONVENTION	7/28/60	5	210	7-30			170
2	REP NATIONAL CONVENTION	7/28/60	5	210	7-30			277
3	REP NATIONAL CONVENTION	7/28/60	5	210	7-30			43
	SPORTS AND SPORTS NEWS							
3	NATIONAL OPEN GOLF	6/18/60	7	60	9-30	5	9	166
1	BIOGRAPHY OF THE FIGHT	6/19/60	1	30	10-30	12	27	
2	CALIFORNIA ALL STAR RODEO	8/05/60	6	60	8-30			57
1	ALL STAR FOOTBALL GAME	8/12/60	6	60	10-00	15	44	244
2	SUMMER OLYMPICS	8/26/60	6	60	9-00	18	36	30
2	SUMMER OLYMPICS	8/30/60	3	30	8-00	12	27	30
2	SUMMER OLYMPICS	9/01/60	5	30	7-30	11	32	30
2	SUMMER OLYMPICS	9/02/60	6	30	8-30	17	38	102
2	SUMMER OLYMPICS	9/03/60	7	30	8-30	16	36	30

2	SUMMER OLYMPICS	9/06/60	3	30	9-00	18	35	30
2	SUMMER OLYMPICS	9/07/60	4	60	7-30	11	25	30
2	SUMMER OLYMPICS	9/08/60	5	30	8-00	15	33	30
2	SUMMER OLYMPICS	9/09/60	6	30	9-00	15	30	102
2	SUMMER OLYMPICS	9/10/60	7	30	9-00	19	35	30
2	SUMMER OLYMPICS	9/12/60	2	30	7-30	13	27	15
	COMEDY VARIETY							
2	SUMMER IN NEW YORK	6/30/60	5	60	10-00	11	23	55
3	ESTER WILLIAMS SHOW	8/08/60	2	60	10-00	29	59	270
	MUSICAL VARIETY							
2	SECRET WORLD OF E. HODGES	6/23/60	5	60	10-00			14
1	THE PAT BOONE SHOW	6/27/60	2	60	9-30	22	45	67
3	BRECK GOLDEN SHOWCASE	8/01/60	2	60	10-00	9	20	+ 129

1960 - 1961

	ACTION/ADVENTURE DRAMA							
2	DUPONT SHOW OF THE MONTH	1/18/61	4	90	8-30	17	25	85
2	DUPONT SHOW OF THE MONTH	3/21/61	3	90	9-30	22	39	85
3	HALLMARK HALL OF FAME	10/24/60	2	90	9-30	13	25	114
1	SPIRIT OF THE ALAMO	11/14/60	2	60	9-30	19	31	197
3	O'CONNOR'S OCEAN	12/13/60	3	60	10-00			
	PRESTIGE DRAMA							
2	FAMILY CLASSICS	1/12/61	5	60	7-30	15	24	129
2	FAMILY CLASSICS	1/13/61	6	60	7-30	16	27	129
3	STORY OF LOVE	2/07/61	3	60	10-00	15	29	247
2	FAMILY CLASSICS	2/13/61	2	60	8-00	17	25	129
2	FAMILY CLASSICS	3/16/61	5	60	8-00	10	16	129
3	HALLMARK HALL OF FAME	3/26/61	1	30	6-30	14	28	114
2	FAMILY CLASSICS	4/27/61	5	60	9-00	16	26	129
2	FAMILY CLASSICS	10/28/60	6	60	7-30	14	25	129
2	FAMILY CLASSICS	10/29/60	7	60	7-30	13	22	129
2	DUPONT SHOW OF THE MONTH	11/16/60	4	90	9-30	14	26	85
3	HALLMARK HALL OF FAME	11/20/60	1	30	6-00	14	23	114
2	FAMILY CLASSICS	11/30/60	4	60	7-30	12	18	129
2	FAMILY CLASSICS	12/01/60	5	60	7-30	12	20	129
	COMEDY DRAMA							
3	HALLMARK HALL OF FAME	2/07/61	3	90	7-30	16	24	114
3	AFTER HOURS	3/07/61	3	60	10-00			
2	DUPONT SHOW OF THE MONTH	12/13/60	3	90	8-30	21	32	85
	CRIME, SPY DRAMA							
2	DUPONT SHOW OF THE MONTH	2/18/61	7	90	9-30	30	49	85

3	CRY VENGEANCE	4/18/61	3	60	10-00				201
3	DOW HOUR OF GREAT MYSTERY	9/20/60	3	60	10-00	11	25		79
3	DOW HOUR OF GREAT MYSTERY	9/27/60	3	60	10-00	13	28		79
3	DOW HOUR OF GREAT MYSTERY	10/18/60	3	60	10-00				79
3	DOW HOUR OF GREAT MYSTERY	11/15/60	3	60	10-00	13	26		79

FAIRY TALE/CARTOON DRAMA

1	THE PIED PIPER OF HAMLIN	4/13/61	5	30	7-00				
3	PETER PAN	12/08/60	5	120	7-30	33	50		212

HISTORICAL DRAMA

3	OUR AMERICAN HERITAGE	1/13/61	6	60	9-00	14	23		89
3	OUR AMERICAN HERITAGE	3/11/61	7	30	9-30	9	15		89
3	OUR AMERICAN HERITAGE	4/01/61	7	30	9-30	11	16		89
3	OUR AMERICAN HERITAGE	4/22/61	7	30	9-30				89
3	OUR AMERICAN HERITAGE	5/13/61	7	30	9-30	9	16		89
3	RIVAK THE BARBARIAN	10/04/60	3	60	10-00				289
3	OUR AMERICAN HERITAGE	10/21/60	6	60	7-30				89
3	PUREX SPECIAL--JOHN BROWN	10/25/60	3	60	10-00	10	21		201
3	OUR AMERICAN HERITAGE	12/02/60	6	60	9-00	12	20		89

MOTION PICTURE DRAMA

2	THE WIZARD OF OZ	12/11/60	1	30	6-00	33	52	+	40

MUSICAL DRAMA

3	HALLMARK HALL OF FAME	12/16/60	6	90	8-30	9	14		114

WESTERN DRAMA

3	HALLMARK HALL OF FAME	5/05/61	6	90	8-30	14	24		114

UNCLASSIFIED DRAMA

2	A DAY IN A WOMAN'S LIFE	3/20/61	2	90	9-00	29	47		212
2	DUPONT SHOW THE THE MONTH	9/30/60	6	90	8-30	18	32		85

ACTUALITIES

3	KHRUSHCHEV ARRIVAL IN NY	9/19/60	2	90	9-00				

AWARDS AND PAGENTS

3	BOB HOPE SPORTS AWARDS	2/15/61	4	60	10-00	22	38		49
1	ACADEMY AWARDS	4/17/61	2	30	10-30				137
3	TELEVISION EMMY AWARDS	5/16/61	3	60	10-00	33	64		198
3	TV GUIDE AWARDS	6/13/61	3	60	10-00	18	38		143

DOCUMENTARY

1	THE WILL TO VICTORY	1/01/61	1	60	9-30	11	19		159

3	PROJECT XX--TWISTED CROSS	1/03/61	3	60	10-00				
1	MEDICINE--BLUE BABY	1/10/61	3	60	9-00				
3	TRIBUTE TO A PATRIOT	1/10/61	3	60	10-00				
1	CLOSE-UP	1/22/61	1	60	9-30	9	15		38
3	PROJECT XX	1/24/61	3	30	10-30				
2	REPORT ON HONG KONG	2/02/61	5	60	9-00	10	14		15
1	CLOSE-UP	2/06/61	2	30	10-30	13	27		38
3	NBC WHITE PAPER--PANAMA	2/14/61	3	60	10-00	13	25		257
1	CLOSE-UP	2/16/61	5	30	10-30	11	22		38
2	CBS REPORTS	2/16/61	5	60	10-00				
1	MEDICINE--ARTERY SURGERY	2/19/61	1	60	9-30				
3	JFK--REPORT NO. ONE	2/28/61	3	60	10-00	14	26		201
3	TWENTY-FIVE YEARS OF LIFE	3/02/61	5	90	9-30	27	44		146
3	NBC WHITE PAPER	3/14/61	3	60	10-00	7	14		257
1	MEDICINE--ANESTHESIA	3/15/61	4	60	10-00				
3	DANGER ON OUR DOORSTEP	3/18/61	7	60	9-30				
3	OUR MAN IN HONG KONG	3/21/61	3	60	10-00				
3	HOW TALL IS A GIANT	3/23/61	5	60	7-30	19	31	+	198
1	CLOSE-UP	3/28/61	3	60	10-00	7	13		38
3	PROJECT XX--WILL ROGERS	3/28/61	3	60	9-00	28	41		201
3	WAY OF THE CROSS	3/28/61	3	60	10-00				
3	PROJECT XX--THE REAL WEST	3/29/61	4	60	7-30	27	45		223
3	PROJECT XX-INNOCENT YEARS	4/04/61	3	60	10-00				
3	JFK--REPORT NO. TWO	4/11/61	3	60	10-00	11	21		198
2	FIRST MAN IN SPACE	4/12/61	4	60	7-30				57
1	CLOSE-UP	4/14/61	6	30	10-30	11	22		38
3	NBC WHITE PAPER	4/16/61	1	60	10-00	10	20		257
1	CLOSE-UP	4/18/61	3	30	10-00				38
2	PROJECT XX--THE REAL WEST	4/18/61	3	30	7-00				
1	CLOSE-UP	4/27/61	5	30	10-30	7	19		38
2	CBS REPORTS	4/27/61	5	60	10-00	9	20		
1	ROAD TO THE STARS	4/28/61	6	30	7-30				
3	MAYDAY IN MOSCOW	5/01/61	2	30	9-00				
1	CLOSE-UP	5/09/61	3	30	10-00	9	17		38
1	CLOSE-UP	5/16/61	3	30	8-30	9	17		38
1	MEDICINE-THE FIRST BREATH	5/17/61	4	60	9-00				
3	NBC WHITE PAPER-RAILROADS	5/23/61	3	60	10-00	9	20		257
1	CLOSE-UP	5/30/61	3	30	10-00	8	16		38
3	PROJECT XX--NOT LONG AGO	5/30/61	3	60	10-00	11	24	+	201
1	CLOSE-UP	6/13/61	3	30	10-00	7	14		38
2	CBS REPORTS--TRUJILLO	9/15/60	5	60	7-30				
2	THE UN ASSEMBLY	9/20/60	3	30	9-00				
1	CLOSE-UP	9/27/60	3	60	9-00	10	16		38
2	CBS REPORTS--THE POLARIS	10/11/60	3	60	8-00	13	21		189
1	CLOSE-UP	10/13/60	5	30	10-30	7	17		38
2	THE THINKING MACHINE	10/26/60	4	60	10-00	11	25		18
2	CBS REPORTS	10/27/60	5	60	8-30	9	14		189
1	CLOSE-UP	11/03/60	5	30	10-30	7	17		38
2	INFLUENTIAL AMERICANS	11/13/60	1	60	9-00	14	22		100
3	STORY OF A FAMILY	11/14/60	2	60	7-30	12	19		178
2	TOMORROW--BIG CITY	11/21/60	2	60	9-30	18	32		18
3	PROJECT XX--RAGTIME YEARS	11/22/60	3	60	10-00	12	24		201
1	CLOSE-UP	11/25/60	6	30	8-00	9	16		38
2	CBS REPORTS	11/25/60	6	60	9-30	14	26		189

3	WHITE PAPER--U-2 AFFAIR	11/29/60	3	60	10-00	17	31	257
1	MEDICINE--BRAIN SURGERY	12/07/60	4	60	9-00			
1	CLOSE-UP	12/07/60	4	60	10-00	11	23	38
1	CLOSE-UP	12/09/60	6	30	10-30	11	25	38
2	CBS REPORTS	12/10/60	7	60	8-30	17	26	189
3	NBC WHITE PAPER--SIT IN	12/20/60	3	60	10-00			257
3	PROJECT XX	12/21/60	4	30	8-30			272
2	CBS REPORTS	12/26/60	2	60	8-00	18	33	189
3	WHERE IS ABEL	12/27/60	3	60	10-00			
3	PROJECT XX-VICTORY AT SEA	12/29/60	5	90	9-30	22	39	198

INSTRUCTIONAL PROGRAMS

3	BELL SCIENCE SERIES	12/09/60	6	60	9-00	13	21	39

SPEECHES

1	EISENHOWER FAREWELL TALK	1/17/61	3	30	8-30
2	PRES. EISENHOWER FAREWELL	1/17/61	3	30	8-30
3	PRES EISENHOWER FAREWELL	1/17/61	3	30	8-30
2	VICE PRES. JOHNSON TALK	5/04/61	5	30	10-00

NEWS AND NEWS ANALYSIS

3	CRISIS IN LAOS	1/02/61	2	30	9-00	14	21	113
3	PIRACY IN THE CARIBBEAN	1/24/61	3	30	10-00	11	19	113
1	STEP TOWARD SPACE	1/31/61	3	15	10-30			
3	THE BLIZZARD OF SIXTY-ONE	2/04/61	7	15	9-30	9	13	113
3	LUMUMBA--AFRICAN MARTYR	2/13/61	2	30	9-00	14	21	113
3	AFRICA--5 MINUTES TO 12	2/21/61	3	60	10-00	10	19	113
3	LAOS--TIME FOR DECISION	3/27/61	2	30	9-00	12	18	113
3	FIRST MAN INTO SPACE	4/12/61	4	60	7-30	16	29	113
3	MAN INTO SPACE	4/12/61	4	30	10-30	6	12	113
3	CUBA--ISLAND IN REVOLT	4/17/61	2	30	9-30			113
3	THE TROUBLE SPOTS	4/22/61	7	30	10-00			113
1	PROJECT MERCURY	5/05/61	6	30	7-30			
3	FREEDOM SEVEN	5/05/61	6	30	8-00			113
3	THE MAN OF FREEDOM SEVEN	5/08/61	2	30	9-00	15	24	113
3	TRIAL OF ADOLF EICHMANN	5/09/61	3	60	10-00			
3	ALABAMA, USA	5/22/61	2	30	10-30			
2	THE KENNEDY MISSION	6/01/61	5	30	10-00	6	11	92
3	JFK--REPORT NO. FOUR	6/01/61	5	30	10-30			
1	PRESIDENTIAL MISSION	6/02/61	6	30	7-30	4	10	107
3	JFK--REPORT NO. FIVE	6/02/61	6	30	8-00			
2	THE KENNEDY MISSION	6/03/61	7	30	10-30			
3	JFK--REPORT NO. SIX	6/03/61	7	30	9-30			
2	THE KENNEDY MISSION	6/05/61	2	30	8-00			109
3	JFK--REPORT NO. EIGHT	6/05/61	2	30	10-30	8	20	113
1	HIGHLIGHTS OF UN SESSION	9/20/60	3	30	10-30			
3	THE UN GENERAL ASSEMBLY	9/20/60	3	30	8-30			
1	HIGHLIGHTS OF UN SESSION	9/21/60	4	30	8-00			
1	HIGHLIGHTS OF UN SESSION	9/22/60	5	30	7-30			
2	BIG DAY AT THE UN	9/22/60	5	30	8-00			
3	THE UN GENERAL ASSEMBLY	9/22/60	5	30	8-30			

3	THE UN GENERAL ASSEMBLY	9/23/60	6	30	9-30			
1	HIGHLIGHTS OF UN SESSION	9/29/60	5	30	10-30			
1	HIGHLIGHTS OF UN SESSION	10/01/60	7	30	8-00			
3	THE UN GENERAL ASSEMBLY	10/05/60	4	30	10-00			289
3	MID-AIR PLANE CRASH NEWS	12/16/60	6	30	8-00			
2	CONSTELLATION FIRE	12/19/60	2	30	10-30			
2	THE YEARS OF CRISIS	12/29/60	5	60	10-00			
3	PROJECTION 'SIXTY-ONE	12/30/60	6	60	9-00	9	15	113
	PANEL TALKS							
3	THE ASTRONAUTS	4/30/61	1	30	7-00	11	23	113
1	MAN AND THE MANDATE	11/20/60	1	30	10-30			
3	OPEN END--COMIC RELIEF	12/06/60	3	60	10-00	15	29	141
	POLITICAL PROGRAMS							
1	CAMPAIGN ROUNDUP	9/17/60	7	30	7-30			
1	JOHN F KENNEDY ADDRESS	9/20/60	3	30	8-30			196
1	CAMPAIGN ROUNDUP	9/24/60	7	30	7-30			
1	FACE TO FACE	9/26/60	2	60	9-30			
2	FACE TO FACE	9/26/60	2	60	9-30			
3	FACE TO FACE	9/26/60	2	60	9-30			
1	CAMPAIGN ROUNDUP	10/01/60	7	30	7-30			
1	FARRELL DOBBS ADDRESS	10/01/60	7	15	10-30			196
1	ERIC HASS ADDRESS	10/01/60	7	15	10-45			196
2	HENRY CABOT LODGE ADDRESS	10/03/60	2	30	8-30	12	18	196
1	FACE TO FACE	10/07/60	6	60	7-30			
2	FACE TO FACE	10/07/60	6	60	7-30			
3	FACE TO FACE	10/07/60	6	60	7-30			
1	CAMPAIGN ROUNDUP	10/08/60	7	30	8-00			
3	REPUBLICAN PAID POLITICAL	10/10/60	2	30	8-30	15	23	196
1	FACE TO FACE	10/13/60	5	60	7-30			
2	FACE TO FACE	10/13/60	5	60	7-30			
3	FACE TO FACE	10/13/60	5	60	7-30			196
1	CAMPAIGN ROUNDUP	10/20/60	5	30	10-00			
1	HENRY CABOT LODGE ADDRESS	10/20/60	5	30	10-30			196
1	FACE TO FACE	10/21/60	6	60	10-00			
2	FACE TO FACE	10/21/60	6	60	10-00			
3	FACE TO FACE	10/21/60	6	60	10-00			196
1	CAMPAIGN ROUNDUP	10/22/60	7	30	7-30			
2	RICHARD NIXON ADDRESS	10/25/60	3	30	9-00			196
1	EISENHOWER ADDRESS	10/28/60	6	30	10-00			196
3	JOHN F. KENNEDY ADDRESS	10/31/60	2	30	8-30			196
2	PRES. EISENHOWER ADDRESS	11/01/60	3	30	8-00			196
3	VICE PRES NIXON ADDRESS	11/02/60	4	30	8-30			196
2	PRESIDENTIAL COUNTDOWN	11/04/60	6	30	9-30			
3	PRES EISENHOWER ADDRESS	11/04/60	6	30	9-00			196
3	JOHN F. KENNEDY ADDRESS	11/04/60	6	30	9-30			196
2	JOHN F. KENNEDY ADDRESS	11/05/60	7	30	9-30			196
2	RICHARD NIXON ADDRESS	11/05/60	7	30	10-00			196
2	RICHARD NIXON ADDRESS	11/06/60	1	30	9-00			196
3	JOHN F. KENNEDY ADDRESS	11/06/60	1	30	10-30			196
2	NIXON-LODGE ADDRESS	11/07/60	2	30	10-30			196

1	ELECTION COVERAGE	11/08/60	3	150	8-30	8	10		70
2	ELECTION RETURNS	11/08/60	3	210	7-30	26	35		277
3	ELECTION COVERAGE	11/08/60	3	210	7-30	32	43		48
1	ELECTION AFTERMATH	11/13/60	1	30	10-30				

RELIGIOUS PROGRAMS

3	CHRISTMAS EVE SERVICES	12/24/60	7	90	9-30				

SPORTS AND SPORTS NEWS

1	ALL STAR BOWLING TOURNEY	1/21/61	7	60	10-00	12	19		164
1	FOOTBALL KICKOFF	9/14/60	4	60	7-30				
1	WORLD SERIES PREVIEW	10/04/60	3	30	7-30	7	14		264
1	WORLD SERIES PREVIEW	10/14/60	6	60	7-30				264
1	SPORT HIGHLIGHTS	12/24/60	7	30	10-00				164
1	COLLEGE BASKETBALL	12/31/60	7	60	10-00	8	16		164

CIRCUS VARIETY

3	TIMEX ALL STAR CIRCUS	3/25/61	7	60	7-30	26	40		257
2	MARINELAND CIRCUS	4/02/61	1	60	8-00	27	44		101
2	CIRCUS HIGHLIGHTS	4/20/61	5	60	8-00				260
3	TIMEX ALL STAR CIRCUS	10/21/60	6	60	9-00				257
3	THANKSGIVING DAY CIRCUS	11/24/60	5	60	10-00				

COMEDY VARIETY

3	THE BOB HOPE SHOW	1/11/61	4	60	9-00	30	45		49
3	EVERYBODY'S DOIN' IT	1/17/61	3	60	10-00	14	27		137
3	SQUARE WORLD OF JACK PARR	1/31/61	3	60	10-00	17	32		198
2	US STEEL HOUR-PRIVATE EYE	3/08/61	4	60	10-00				272
3	THE BOB HOPE SHOW	4/12/61	4	60	9-00	26	42		49
1	THE ERNIE KOVACS SHOW	4/20/61	5	30	10-30				69
2	MILLION DOLLAR INCIDENT	4/21/61	6	90	8-30				257
3	SQUARE WORLD OF JACK PARR	5/02/61	3	60	10-00	10	21	+	198
3	THE BOB HOPE SHOW	5/13/61	7	60	8-30	21	38		49
1	THE ERNIE KOVACS SHOW	5/18/61	5	30	10-30				69
2	HOORAY FOR LOVE	10/02/60	1	60	9-00	21	34		100
3	THE BOB HOPE SHOW	10/03/60	2	60	8-30	30	46		49
2	THE BIG SELL	10/09/60	1	60	9-00	23	37		242
2	U.S. STEEL HOUR	10/19/60	4	60	10-00				272
2	THE RIGHT MAN	10/24/60	2	60	8-30	19	30		261
1	A DATE WITH DEBBIE	10/27/60	5	60	9-30	28	49		212
2	AN HOUR WITH DANNY KAYE	10/30/60	1	60	8-00	26	39		103
3	THE BOB HOPE SHOW	11/16/60	4	60	9-00	31	48		49
2	RED SKELTON SPECIAL	11/30/60	4	60	8-30	29	40		257
3	THE BOB HOPE SHOW	12/12/60	2	60	9-30	23	36		49

MUSICAL VARIETY

1	MUSIC FOR NEW YEARS NIGHT	1/01/61	1	30	10-30				
2	THE GERSHWIN YEARS	1/15/61	1	90	8-00	24	35		100
3	BOBBY DARIN AND FRIENDS	1/31/61	3	60	9-00	22	34		212

3	REMEMBER HOW GREAT	2/09/61	5	60	8-30	24	35		22
3	ASTAIRE TIME	2/20/61	2	60	8-30	18	26	+	64
1	THE BING CROSBY SHOW	3/20/61	2	60	9-30	18	30		180
1	THE PAT BOONE SHOW	4/20/61	5	60	8-30				50
3	THE DEAN MARTIN SHOW	4/25/61	3	60	10-00	14	28		198
3	YOUNG AT HEART	4/28/61	6	60	10-00	14	29		185
2	ARTHUR GODFREY ON THE GO	5/19/61	6	60	9-30	20	36		50
3	SUMMER ON ICE	6/06/61	3	60	10-00	18	37		270
3	ASTAIRE TIME	9/28/60	4	60	10-00	19	41		64
3	COUNTRY FAIR, USA	10/02/60	1	60	9-00				63
1	THE BING CROSBY SHOW	10/05/60	4	60	10-00	22	45		180
1	THE VICTOR BORGE SHOW	10/06/60	5	60	9-30	17	30		197
2	JUST POLLY AND ME	10/08/60	7	60	8-30	20	33		55
3	THE DONALD O'CONNOR SHOW	10/11/60	3	60	10-00	13	26		270
3	THE BOB HOPE SHOW	10/22/60	7	60	8-30				49
3	THE DEAN MARTIN SHOW	11/01/60	3	60	10-00	16	33		242
3	WONDERLAND ON ICE	11/17/60	5	60	7-30	22	35		260
3	DAVE'S PLACE	11/18/60	6	60	9-00	9	15		87
2	NEW YORK NINETEEN	11/20/60	1	60	10-00	21	40		212
1	MUSIC FOR A WINTER NIGHT	12/18/60	1	30	10-30				
1	CHRISTMAS CAROLS	12/24/60	7	15	10-45				
1	MUSIC FOR CHRISTMAS NIGHT	12/25/60	1	30	10-30				

VAUDEVILLE VARIETY

3	ROOSEVELT DIAMOND JUBILEE	10/07/60	6	60	9-00	18	30		298
3	SOMETHING SPECIAL	12/04/60	1	60	10-00	17	30		13

NON-CLASSIFIABLE

1	THE PROVIDERS	10/01/60	7	30	10-00				

SUMMER 1961

PRESTIGE DRAMA

2	FAMILY CLASSICS	8/06/61	1	60	10-00	16	37	+	129

COMEDY DRAMA

3	FAMILY CLASSICS	6/18/61	1	60	9-00	14	29	+	129
2	THE PLAYHOUSE	7/25/61	3	30	9-30				227

CRIME, SPY DRAMA

3	THE ACCOMPLICE	6/19/61	2	60	10-00				201

AWARDS AND PAGENTS

2	MISS UNIVERSE CONTEST	7/15/61	7	60	10-00	34	68		198
2	MISS AMERICA PAGEANT	9/09/61	7	90	9-30	42	75		185

DOCUMENTARY

1	CLOSE-UP	6/22/61	5	30	10-30				38
3	DOCTOR B	6/27/61	3	60	10-00	8	16		153
3	PROJECT XX--THE GREAT WAR	7/04/61	3	60	10-00	11	29	+	256
3	RETURN OF GEN. MACARTHUR	7/10/61	2	60	7-30				
2	SECRET LIFE OF DANNY KAYE	7/13/61	5	60	10-00	10	23	+	103
2	MANSHOOT II	7/21/61	6	30	9-30	14	31		109
1	CLOSE-UP	8/04/61	6	30	8-00				38
3	THE SAVAGE, MY KINSMAN	8/11/61	6	30	8-30				
2	BERLIN--ACT OF WAR	8/18/61	6	60	8-30	10	23		195
3	TRIAL OF ADOLF EICHMANN	8/18/61	6	60	7-30				
	SPEECHES								
1	PRESIDENT KENNEDY ADDRESS	7/25/61	3	30	10-00				
2	PRES. KENNEDY ADDRESS	7/25/61	3	30	10-00	6	15		
3	PRES KENNEDY ADDRESS	7/25/61	3	30	10-00				
	NEWS AND NEWS ANALYSIS								
3	FLIGHT OF LIBERTY BELL	7/21/61	6	60	7-30	11	31		113
3	GUS GRISSOM PRESS CONF.	7/22/61	7	30	9-30	8	17		113
3	BERLIN WHERE WEST BEGINS	7/23/61	1	30	7-00				
2	CBS NEWS SPECIAL REPORT	7/25/61	3	30	10-30				193
3	COMMENT ON KENNEDY'S TALK	7/25/61	3	30	10-30				
3	THE GREAT PLANE ROBBERY	8/03/61	5	30	8-30				113
2	THE FOREIGN AID ISSUE	8/04/61	6	30	9-30				
2	MEN IN ORBIT	8/07/61	2	30	10-30				
3	RUSSIAN PANDORA	8/31/61	5	30	10-00				113
3	ATLANTA, 1961	9/01/61	6	30	8-00				
3	REPORT ON HURRICANE CARLA	9/10/61	1	30	10-30	12	27		113
	PANEL TALKS								
3	JFK SPECIAL REPORT	6/20/61	3	60	10-00				143
2	AT THE SOURCE	7/27/61	5	30	10-00				
2	JOINT APPEARANCE	8/10/61	5	60	10-00				
2	AT THE SOURCE	8/24/61	5	30	10-00				
2	JOINT APPEARANCE	9/07/61	5	60	10-00				
	SPORTS AND SPORTS NEWS								
1	ALL STAR FOOTBALL GAME	8/04/61	6	60	10-00				55
	COMEDY VARIETY								
1	THE ERNIE KOVACS SHOW	6/15/61	5	30	10-30				69
3	THE JIMMY DURANTE SHOW	8/09/61	4	60	10-00	25	51		270
	MUSICAL VARIETY								
1	CONNIE FRANCIS SPECIAL	9/13/61	4	60	9-00	16	29		36

1961 - 1962

	PRESTIGE DRAMA						
2	WESTINGHOUSE PRESENTS	2/03/62	7	60	10-00	17 29	277
2	BRECK GOLDEN SHOWCASE	2/25/62	1	60	10-00	20 38	129
3	HALLMARK HALL OF FAME	10/20/61	6	120	8-30		114
2	POWER AND GLORY	10/29/61	1	120	9-00	18 32	129
3	THEATRE SIXTY-TWO	11/19/61	1	60	10-00	8 15	14
2	BRECK GOLDEN SHOWCASE	12/06/61	4	60	8-30	14 23	129
2	WESTINGHOUSE PRESENTS	12/08/61	6	60	10-00	22 43	277
	COMEDY DRAMA						
2	BRECK GOLDEN SHOWCASE	1/13/62	7	60	8-30	19 30	129
3	THEATER SIXTY-TWO	1/14/62	1	60	10-00	13 24	14
2	BRECK GOLDEN SHOWCASE	3/24/62	7	60	8-30	20 31	129
3	THEATRE SIXTY-TWO	4/08/62	1	60	10-00	7 14	14
2	WESTINGHOUSE PRESENTS	4/17/62	3	60	10-00		277
2	THE ALAN KING SHOW	9/18/61	2	30	10-00	17 34	101
2	CBS TELEVISION WORKSHOP	9/21/61	5	60	9-00		
	CRIME, SPY DRAMA						
3	HALLMARK HALL OF FAME	2/05/62	2	90	9-30	11 19	114
3	THEATER SIXTY-TWO	2/11/62	1	60	10-00	12 21	14
3	THEATRE SIXTY-TWO	3/11/62	1	60	10-00	9 16	14
1	PLOT AT TEHERAN PART ONE	9/23/61	7	60	7-30	6 12	26
1	PLOT AT TEHERAN PART TWO	9/30/61	7	60	7-30	5 10	26
3	THEATER SIXTY-TWO	10/04/61	4	60	10-00	12 26	14
3	THEATRE SIXTY-TWO	12/10/61	1	60	10-00	13 24	14
	FAIRY TALE/CARTOON DRAMA						
2	BRECK GOLDEN SHOWCASE	4/30/62	2	60	8-00	14 27	129
	HISTORICAL DRAMA						
2	CBS TELEVISION WORKSHOP	9/28/61	5	60	9-00		
3	HALLMARK HALL OF FAME	11/30/61	5	90	9-30	18 33	114
	MOTION PICTURE DRAMA						
2	THE WIZARD OF OZ	12/10/61	1	30	6-00	32 53	198
	MUSICAL DRAMA						
2	BRECK GOLDEN SHOWCASE	6/14/62	5	60	9-00	9 16	129
1	FEATHERTOP	10/19/61	5	60	8-30		155
1	WESTINGHOUSE PRESENTS	12/23/61	7	60	7-30		277
	WESTERN DRAMA						
2	WESTINGHOUSE PRESENTS	10/24/61	3	60	10-00	15 33	277

AWARDS AND PAGENTS

1	ACADEMY AWARDS	4/09/62	2	30	10-30	37	75	198
3	TELEVISION EMMY AWARDS	5/22/62	3	60	10-00	28	61	198
1	KING ORANGE PARADE	12/30/61	7	60	7-30	10	16	256

DOCUMENTARY

1	PROFILE OF AN ASTRONAUT	1/03/62	4	30	7-30			
3	BEYOND THE THRESHOLD	1/05/62	6	60	8-30	11	17	39
3	LEE, THE VIRGINIAN	1/15/62	2	30	8-00	11	17	265
1	STARS--PATHWAY TO SPACE	1/17/62	4	30	7-30			
3	WORLD OF JIMMY DOOLITTLE	1/18/62	5	60	8-30	20	30	201
1	MISSION--MAN IN ORBIT	1/23/62	3	30	10-30			
3	WESTINGHOUSE PRESENTS	1/24/62	4	60	10-00	14	29	277
3	NBC WHITE PAPER	1/28/62	1	60	10-00	15	25	47
1	ADOULA OF THE CONGO	2/07/62	4	30	7-30			
3	DEBUTANTE SIXTY-TWO	2/09/62	6	60	9-30	10	18	66
2	A TOUR OF THE WHITE HOUSE	2/14/62	4	60	10-00			
3	WHITE HOUSE TOUR	2/14/62	4	60	10-00			
1	SO PROUDLY WE HAIL	2/23/62	6	30	7-30			
3	NBC WHITE PAPER-RED CHINA	2/25/62	1	60	10-00	16	29	47
3	WORLD OF SOPHIA LOREN	2/27/62	3	60	7-30	18	27	201
3	THRESHOLDS FOR TOMORROW	3/10/62	7	60	7-30	10	16	39
3	WESTINGHOUSE PRESENTS	3/13/62	3	60	10-00	12	23	277
3	PROJECT XX--THE REAL WEST	3/25/62	1	60	9-00	19	31 +	201
3	NBC WHITE PAPER	3/25/62	1	60	10-00	5	10	112
3	U.S. NO. ONE--AM. PROFILE	3/29/62	5	60	7-30	17	28	223
3	THE VANISHING 400	4/06/62	6	60	9-30	13	24	66
3	FLIGHT OF FRIENDSHIP 7	4/09/62	2	60	7-30	13	39	113
1	THE GENERAL	4/15/62	1	60	7-30			
3	PROJECT XX--HE IS RISEN	4/15/62	1	30	8-30	17	24	272
3	BREAKTHROUGH--SURGERY	4/23/62	2	60	10-00	10	18	201
1	SIXTY HOURS TO THE MOON	4/29/62	1	60	7-30	8	16	181
1	TITOV AND GLENN	5/04/62	6	30	7-30			
1	SAC--THE BIG STICK	5/08/62	3	60	10-00			
3	VIETNAM--LAST CHANCE	5/08/62	3	60	10-00	9	19	47
1	HELEN KELLER--WORLD I SEE	5/11/62	6	60	10-00			
3	NBC WHITE PAPER-RED CHINA	5/18/62	6	60	9-30	8	18 +	85
3	ROBERT RUARK'S AFRICA	5/25/62	6	60	9-30	10	20	201
2	UPS AND DOWNS OF WALL ST.	5/30/62	4	30	7-30	5	15	15
1	THE CROWDED IDOL	6/03/62	1	60	7-30			
3	BREAKTHROUGH--CANCER	6/08/62	6	60	9-30			
3	NBC WHITE PAPER--ANGOLA	9/19/61	3	60	9-00			
1	MEDICINE--NEW EAR DRUMS	9/20/61	4	55	9-00			
2	PROJECT HOPE	9/20/61	4	30	8-30			
3	THE WORLD OF BOB HOPE	10/29/61	1	60	7-30	22	36	201
3	WESTINGHOUSE PRESENTS	11/14/61	3	60	10-00	13	26	277
1	MEDICINE--NEW JOINTS	11/15/61	4	60	10-00			
2	MR. SAM--A BIOGRAPHY	11/16/61	5	30	10-30			
1	MR SAM STORY OF AN AMER	11/17/61	6	30	7-30			
3	SELF PORTRAIT--VAN GOGH	11/17/61	6	60	9-30	10	18	148
1	CLOSE-UP	11/23/61	5	30	9-30	10	16	38
3	GRANT--AN IMPROBABLE HERO	11/24/61	6	30	8-30	13	21	265
3	CROSSING THE THRESHOLD	11/24/61	6	90	9-00	12	21	39

3 NOW, IN OUR TIME	11/28/61	3	60	7-30	18	29	87
3 HOLLYWOOD--GOLDEN YEARS	11/29/61	4	60	7-30	27	44	198
3 THE WORLD OF BILLY GRAHAM	11/29/61	4	60	10-00	14	28	201
3 JAPAN--EAST IS WEST	12/04/61	2	60	8-00	15	24	148
3 NOW, IN OUR TIME	12/07/61	5	60	7-30	14	24	87
1 CLOSE-UP	12/10/61	1	60	10-00	6	11	38
1 CLOSE-UP	12/13/61	4	30	8-30	8	13	38
3 NOW, IN OUR TIME	12/15/61	6	60	9-30	10	19	87
3 PROJECT XX	12/20/61	4	30	8-30			272
3 BERLIN--CHRISTMAS 1961	12/25/61	2	30	7-30			
3 NBC WHITE PAPER	12/26/61	3	60	10-00	11	22	159

INSTRUCTIONAL PROGRAMS

3 BELL SCIENCE SERIES	2/05/62	2	60	8-30	14	21	39

NEWS AND NEWS ANALYSIS

2 ACCENT ON THE OLD YEAR	1/04/62	5	60	9-00	9	14	101
3 PROJECTION 'SIXTY-TWO	1/05/62	6	60	9-30	8	14	113
1 CONGRESS--VITAL ISSUES	1/10/62	4	30	7-30			
3 JFK REPORT	1/12/62	6	60	9-30	8	14	148
1 KENNEDY NEWS CONFERENCE	1/31/62	4	30	7-30			
3 TELEVISION AND THE FCC	2/04/62	1	60	10-00			
2 THE FLIGHT OF JOHN GLENN	2/20/62	3	30	9-30	30	44	273
3 AMERICAN IN ORBIT	2/20/62	3	60	10-00	24	42	113
3 CHALLENGE IN LAOS	5/14/62	2	30	8-00	8	17	83
2 FLIGHT OF AURORA SEVEN	5/24/62	5	30	9-00	10	18	241
3 QUESTION OF WAR OR PEACE	9/17/61	1	30	7-00			
3 DEATH OF A STATESMAN	9/18/61	2	60	9-30	18	32	113
3 JFK REPORT	9/28/61	5	60	7-30	13	25	148
2 KENNEDY'S TRIP TO SO. AM.	12/18/61	2	30	8-00			15
3 MISSION FOR ALLIANCE	12/18/61	2	30	8-00			113
1 WORLD PROSPECTS	12/26/61	3	60	10-00			
2 YEARS OF CRISIS	12/28/61	5	60	10-00	7	12	15
3 NEWS CAVALCADE OF 1961	12/30/61	7	60	8-00			

PANEL TALKS

3 MEET THE PRESS SPECIAL	1/05/62	6	30	10-30			289
2 AT THE SOURCE	1/11/62	5	30	10-00	4	7	159
1 TOWER-HUMPHREY DEBATE	1/24/62	4	30	7-30			
2 THE GREAT CHALLENGE	2/01/62	5	60	10-00	5	9	48
2 THE GREAT CHALLENGE	3/01/62	5	60	10-00	4	8	48
2 THE GREAT CHALLENGE	4/05/62	5	60	10-00	4	9	61
2 AT THE SOURCE	5/03/62	5	30	10-00	4	9	
3 YOUR DOCTOR REPORTS	5/21/62	2	30	8-00	9	20	19
1 REPORT FROM CONGRESS ONE	6/12/62	3	30	10-30			
2 AT THE SOURCE	9/21/61	5	30	10-00			
2 AMERICAN MUSICAL THEATRE	9/27/61	4	30	8-30			
2 AT THE SOURCE	10/26/61	5	30	10-00	4	8	
2 AT THE SOURCE	11/16/61	5	30	10-00			
3 WE, THE PEOPLE--1961	11/29/61	4	60	9-00	17	28	140
2 THE GREAT CHALLENGE	12/07/61	5	60	10-00	4	9	195

POLITICAL PROGRAMS

2	FIFTY FACES OF SIXTY-TWO	5/30/62	4	60	10-00	6	15	85

SPORTS AND SPORTS NEWS

1	ALL STAR BOWLING	1/13/62	7	60	10-00	10	17	107
1	SALUTE TO FOOTBALL	9/15/61	6	30	7-00			
1	WORLD SERIES SPECIAL	10/03/61	3	30	10-30	3	8	264
1	BASKETBALL TOURNAMENT	12/30/61	7	45	10-00	8	13	107

CIRCUS VARIETY

2	MARINELAND CIRCUS	4/22/62	1	30	7-00			67

COMEDY VARIETY

1	THE ERNIE KOVACS SHOW	1/23/62	3	30	10-00	12	21	69
3	BOB HOPE CHRISTMAS SHOW	1/24/62	4	60	9-00	35	53	64
2	FONDA AND THE FAMILY	2/06/62	3	60	8-30	26	29	198
3	THE BOB HOPE SHOW	2/27/62	3	60	9-00	29	43	229
3	THE BOB HOPE SHOW	3/22/62	5	60	8-30	27	40	37
1	ALL STAR COMEDY SHOW	4/06/62	6	60	10-00	18	36	257
3	THE BOB HOPE SHOW	4/25/62	4	60	9-00	28	48	37
1	WESTINGHOUSE PRESENTS	5/29/62	3	60	10-00	21	40	277
1	THE ERNIE KOVACS SHOW	9/21/61	5	30	10-30	8	20	69
1	THE UNSWITCHABLES	9/24/61	1	30	9-00			
1	THE ERNIE KOVACS SHOW	9/26/61	3	30	10-30			69
2	VICTOR BORGE	9/27/61	4	60	9-00	20	36	197
1	THE ERNIE KOVACS SHOW	10/28/61	7	30	8-30	12	21	69
2	AN HOUR WITH DANNY KAYE	11/06/61	2	60	9-00	23	36	103
1	THE ERNIE KOVACS SHOW	11/24/61	6	30	8-30	15	24	69
1	THE ERNIE KOVACS SHOW	12/12/61	3	30	10-30	4	9	69
3	THE BOB HOPE SHOW	12/13/61	4	60	9-00	33	57	212

MUSICAL VARIETY

1	MUSIC FOR THE YOUNG	1/05/62	6	30	7-30			
1	MUSIC FOR THE YOUNG	1/12/62	6	30	7-30			
2	WESTINGHOUSE PRESENTS	1/12/62	6	90	8-30	24	38	
2	YOUNG PEOPLE'S CONCERT	1/18/62	5	60	7-30	8	12	233
1	MUSIC FOR THE YOUNG	1/19/62	6	30	7-30			
3	BELL TELEPHONE HOUR	1/19/62	6	60	9-30			39
2	YOUNG PEOPLE'S CONCERT	1/21/62	1	60	7-30	9	15	233
3	BELL TELEPHONE HOUR	2/02/62	6	60	9-30			39
2	LEONARD BERNSTEIN	2/06/62	3	60	7-30	10	17	96
3	B'WAY OF LERNER AND LOEWE	2/11/62	1	60	7-30	16	24	64
1	WESTINGHOUSE PRESENTS	2/23/62	6	60	10-00	17	30	277
2	THE JUDY GARLAND SHOW	2/25/62	1	60	9-00	26	37	61
3	THE KRAFT MUSIC HALL	2/28/62	4	60	9-00	21	34	140
3	THE MILTON BERLE SHOW	3/09/62	6	60	9-30	24	40	64
3	HOLLYWOOD MELODY	3/19/62	2	60	9-00	22	32	64
2	YOUNG PEOPLE'S CONCERT	3/26/62	2	60	7-30	9	17	233

1	HERE'S EDIE	4/09/62	2	30	10-00	21	35	69
3	KRAFT MUSIC HALL	4/11/62	4	60	9-00	18	31	140
2	YOUNG PEOPLE'S CONCERT	4/13/62	6	60	7-30	9	16	233
3	RAINBOW OF STARS	4/17/62	3	60	9-00			64
3	HIGHWAYS OF MELODY	4/22/62	1	60	10-00			65
3	BELL TELEPHONE HOUR	4/27/62	6	60	9-30			39
3	THE ANDY WILLIAMS SHOW	5/04/62	6	60	9-30	16	32	64
3	YVES MONTAND ON BROADWAY	5/11/62	6	60	8-30	9	18	+ 257
1	THE BING CROSBY SHOW	5/14/62	2	60	10-00	27	54	5
2	JULIE AND CAROL	6/11/62	2	60	10-00	26	47	256
2	JACK BENNY AT CARNEGIE H.	9/27/61	4	60	10-00	18	37	137
3	WESTINGHOUSE PRESENTS	10/09/61	2	60	10-00	14	28	277
1	SEASONS OF YOUTH	10/25/61	4	60	10-00	11	24	277
1	WESTINGHOUSE PRESENTS	11/21/61	3	60	10-00	6	13	277
1	YVES MONTAND ON BROADWAY	11/30/61	5	60	10-00	13	26	257
2	YOUNG PEOPLE'S CONCERT	12/01/61	6	60	7-30	7	13	233
3	HIGHWAYS OF MELODY	12/03/61	1	60	10-00	8	16	65
1	BING IN LONDON	12/11/61	2	60	9-00	20	31	169
2	LEONARD BERNSTEIN	12/14/61	5	60	7-30	10	16	96
3	HIGHWAYS OF MELODY	12/31/61	1	60	10-00	8	16	65

VAUDEVILLE VARIETY

1	AT THIS VERY MOMENT	4/01/62	1	60	9-00	15	22	11

NON-CLASSIFIABLE

2	CHEVVY GOLDEN ANNIVERSARY	11/03/61	6	60	8-30	16	26	63

SUMMER 1962

DRAMATIC READINGS

2	JOHN BROWN'S BODY	6/21/62	5	60	8-30			
2	PORTRAIT IN VERSES	8/16/62	5	60	10-00			

UNCLASSIFIED DRAMA

2	WESTINGHOUSE PRESENTS	6/20/62	4	60	10-00			277

AWARDS AND PAGENTS

3	TV GUIDE AWARDS	6/24/62	1	60	9-00			83
2	MISS UNIVERSE PAGEANT	7/14/62	7	60	10-00	33	61	198
2	MISS AMERICA PAGEANT	9/08/62	7	90	9-30	38	66	185

DOCUMENTARY

3	GERMANY--FATHERS AND SONS	6/15/62	6	60	9-30	9	19	201
3	BREAKTHROUGH--MENTAL ILLS	6/22/62	6	60	9-30			19
3	ALGERIA--DAYS OF DECISION	7/02/62	2	30	8-00	6	16	54
1	THE MAN FROM OLIVER ST.	7/10/62	3	60	10-00			
3	THE TELSTAR STORY	7/11/62	4	30	10-30	9	21	21

3	PEACE CORPS IN TANGANYIKA	7/16/62	2	60	10-00	7	14	+	44
3	THE GENTLE PERSUADERS	7/30/62	2	60	10-00	8	19		108
1	THE OVERSEAS CHINESE	8/03/62	6	30	7-30				
3	SELF PORTRAIT--VAN GOGH	8/06/62	2	60	10-00				22
3	JAPAN--EAST IS WEST	8/13/62	2	60	10-00	6	14	+	108
1	TRIO	8/15/62	4	60	10-00				
3	THRESHOLD FOR TOMORROW	8/20/62	2	60	10-00				22
3	RIDDLE OF THE LUSITANIA	8/27/62	2	60	10-00	13	28		22
3	SENTRY ABROAD	9/03/62	2	60	10-00	7	15	+	22
3	GERMANY--FATHERS AND SONS	9/10/62	2	60	10-00	9	19	+	22

NEWS AND NEWS ANALYSIS

1	PRESIDENTIAL MISSION.	6/30/62	7	30	7-30				
3	GOONHILLY DOWNS	7/23/62	2	60	10-00	8	19		108
3	PRESIDENTIAL SPACE SURVEY	9/12/62	4	30	10-30				

PANEL TALKS

1	REPORT FROM CONGRESS TWO	6/19/62	3	30	10-30				
3	CHAMPIONSHIP DEBATE	7/03/62	3	60	7-30				
2	NIGHTTIME CALENDAR	7/12/62	5	60	10-00	9	19		159
2	MACLEISH-VAN DOREN DIALOG	8/02/62	5	60	10-00	4	9		195
2	MONEY TALKS, PART ONE	8/20/62	2	30	10-30				
3	15 MONTHS IN A RED PRISON	8/20/62	2	30	8-00				
2	MONEY TALKS, PART TWO	8/21/62	3	30	9-30				
2	MONEY TALKS, PART THREE	8/22/62	4	30	7-30				
2	MONEY TALKS, PART FOUR	8/23/62	5	30	10-00				
2	MONEY TALKS, PART FIVE	8/24/62	6	30	10-00				288
2	OUR NEXT MAN IN SPACE	9/13/62	5	30	10-00	9	21		284

POLITICAL PROGRAMS

3	CAMPAIGN AND CANDIDATES	9/08/62	7	30	8-30	8	15		223

SPORTS AND SPORTS NEWS

3	ALL AMERICA FOOTBALL GAME	6/29/62	6	90	9-30	10	24		
3	BUICK OPEN GOLF	7/08/62	1	30	5-30	4	17		49
1	U.S.-RUSSIAN TRACK MEET	7/21/62	7	60	7-30	6	18		47
1	U.S.-RUSSIAN TRACK MEET	7/22/62	1	30	10-00				224
1	ALL STAR FOOTBALL GAME	8/03/62	6	60	10-00	17	47		
2	KICKOFF SIXTY-TWO	9/13/62	5	60	8-30	6	12		47

COMEDY VARIETY

1	SHELLEY BERMAN	8/14/62	3	60	10-00	11	26		187

MUSICAL VARIETY

2	JACK BENNY AT CARNEGIE H.	7/31/62	3	60	9-00	11	23	+	256
1	INVITATION TO PARIS	8/11/62	7	60	10-00	9	19		
1	THE BING CROSBY SHOW	8/12/62	1	60	10-00	12	26		187
2	ARIAS AND ARABESQUES	8/30/62	5	60	10-00	6	14		239

NON-CLASSIFIABLE

1	SPACE TV--TEST NO. ONE	7/10/62	3	30	7-30				
2	TELEVISION BY SATELLITE	7/10/62	3	30	7-30	11	34		156
3	TELSTAR COMMUNICATIONS	7/10/62	3	30	7-30	7	26		113
1	SPACE TV--TEST NO. TWO	7/11/62	4	30	7-30				
2	TELEVISION BY SATELLITE	7/11/62	4	15	7-30				
3	TELSTAR COMMUNICATIONS	7/11/62	4	15	7-30	8	32		113
1	SPACE TV--TWO CONTINENTS	7/23/62	2	30	8-30				198
2	TRANSATLANTIC TELEVISION	7/23/62	2	30	8-00	11	27		56

1962 - 1963

ACTION/ADVENTURE DRAMA

1	THE EXPENDABLES	9/27/62	5	60	10-00	9	18		198

PRESTIGE DRAMA

2	RUSSIANS--SELF IMPRESSION	1/16/63	4	60	7-30	8	13		138
3	HALLMARK HALL OF FAME	12/06/62	5	90	9-30	12	24		114

COMEDY DRAMA

3	HALLMARK HALL OF FAME	2/06/63	4	90	7-30	21	32		114
3	HALLMARK HALL OF FAME	10/26/62	6	90	8-30				114

CRIME, SPY DRAMA

1	BOSTON TERRIER	6/11/63	3	30	10-30	8	17		5

DRAMATIC READINGS

2	FIRST LADY	1/02/63	4	30	7-30	13	21		66

FAIRY TALE/CARTOON DRAMA

3	MAGOO'S CHRISTMAS CAROL	12/18/62	3	60	7-30	23	39		257

HISTORICAL DRAMA

3	HALLMARK HALL OF FAME	4/04/63	5	90	8-30	13	21		114

MOTION PICTURE DRAMA

2	THE WIZARD OF OZ	12/09/62	1	30	6-00	33	55	+	198

MUSICAL DRAMA

3	PETER PAN	2/09/63	7	90	7-00	27	42	+	256

UNCLASSIFIED DRAMA

2	DICKENS CHRONICLE	2/13/63	4	60	7-30	8	13	138
	AWARDS AND PAGENTS							
2	DINNER WITH JFK	1/31/63	5	60	10-00			
1	CHINESE NEW YEAR PARADE	2/19/63	3	30	10-30			
1	ACADEMY AWARDS	4/08/63	2	60	10-00	37	71	137
3	WHITE HOUSE RECEPTION	5/02/63	3	60	7-30			
3	TELEVISION EMMY AWARDS	5/26/63	1	60	10-00	30	63	198
2	MISS TEENAGE AMERICA	10/26/62	6	25	10-35			73
1	KING ORANGE PARADE	12/31/62	2	60	9-00	13	22	26
	DOCUMENTARY							
1	HOLLYWOOD--FABULOUS ERA	1/23/63	4	60	7-30	22	33	198
3	WORLD OF BENNY GOODMAN	1/24/63	5	60	8-30	17	24	201
3	WHITE PAPER--STALIN DEATH	1/27/63	1	60	10-00	19	32	228
3	DAVID BRINKLEY'S JOURNAL	1/28/63	2	60	9-30			78
3	WHITE PAPER--KHRUSHCHEV	2/03/63	1	60	10-00	17	31	228
1	CROWN AND CRISIS	2/12/63	3	60	8-30			
2	A LOOK AT MONACO	2/17/63	1	60	8-00	32	46	61
3	WORLD--MAURICE CHEVALIER	2/22/63	6	60	8-30	17	26	201
3	THE PROBLEM WITH WATER	2/24/63	1	60	10-00	11	20	125
3	A PRIMER ON COMMUNISIM	3/01/63	6	60	7-30	11	18	228
3	A COUNTRY CALLED EUROPE	3/03/63	1	60	10-00			
1	CLOSE-UP	3/07/63	5	60	10-00	10	20	38
1	HOLLYWOOD--GREAT STARS	3/13/63	4	60	10-00	19	37	198
3	CALIFORNIA--THE MOST	3/14/63	5	60	7-30	14	24	148
2	A WALL AROUND CUBA	3/22/63	6	30	10-30	8	16	162
1	THE LAST BANZAI	3/23/63	7	60	10-00			
1	MARILYN MONROE	3/24/63	1	30	9-30	20	31	278
3	PROJECT XX--GARY COOPER	3/26/63	3	60	7-30	26	42	223
3	NBC WHITE PAPER	3/31/63	1	60	10-00			
3	DAVID BRINKLEY'S JOURNAL	4/01/63	2	60	10-00			284
3	WORLD OF DARRYL F ZANUCK	4/02/63	3	60	8-30	11	17	201
2	IN THE MOUTH OF THE WOLF	4/10/63	4	60	7-30	7	14	46
3	PROFILE OF COMMUNISM	4/10/63	4	60	7-30	10	19	269
3	THE LOSS OF THE THRESHER	4/11/63	5	60	7-30	14	26	113
3	AMERICAN LANDMARK	4/21/63	1	30	8-30	16	25	125
1	KING COAL	4/22/63	2	60	9-00			
3	NBC WHITE PAPER--GAMBLING	4/28/63	1	60	10-00			201
2	ISRAEL--IT'S NO FABLE	5/08/63	4	60	7-30	6	15	20
3	THE KREMLIN	5/21/63	3	60	9-30	12	23	284
3	QUIET REVOLUTION	5/24/63	6	60	10-00	9	19	201
1	POPE JOHN XXIII	6/03/63	2	60	7-30			
3	POPE JOHN XXIII MEMORIAL	6/03/63	2	30	9-30			
3	THE KREMLIN	6/04/63	3	60	7-30	9	22	+ 284
3	POPE JOHN XXIII	6/04/63	3	60	8-30			
3	HOLLYWOOD--GOLDEN YEARS	9/18/62	3	60	10-00	13	28	+ 198
2	PRO FOOTBALL EXPLOSION	9/20/62	5	60	8-30	7	11	47
2	ROAD TO BUTTON BAY	9/24/62	2	60	9-00	19	32	101
3	ORDEAL OF WOODROW WILSON	9/25/62	3	30	10-30	8	20	265
1	CLOSE-UP	9/28/62	6	60	7-30	9	17	38
3	DAVID BRINKLEY'S JOURNAL	10/01/62	2	60	10-00			191

3	THE RIVER NILE	10/28/62	1	60	10-00			47
3	ROME--THE VATICAN COUNCIL	10/30/62	3	30	10-30			
2	CLOWNS AND HEROS	11/14/62	4	30	7-30	9	17	239
1	CLOSE-UP	11/17/62	7	60	10-00	6	10	38
1	VOICE OF CHANGE	11/18/62	1	60	10-00			
3	THE CHOSEN CHILD	11/25/62	1	60	10-00	12	23	47
3	SOUL OF AN AGE	11/30/62	6	60	7-30	10	17	148
3	WORLD OF JACKIE KENNEDY	11/30/62	6	60	10-00	19	35	201
2	PEARL HARBOR--UNFORGOTTEN	12/05/62	4	30	7-30	12	22	15
1	THE PRICE OF PEACE	12/06/62	5	60	10-00			
3	THE TUNNEL	12/10/62	2	90	8-30	21	31	113
3	POLARIS SUBMARINE	12/19/62	4	60	10-00	12	24	277

SPEECHES

1	PRESIDENT KENNEDY ADDRESS	6/11/63	3	15	8-00			
2	PRES. KENNEDY ADDRESS	6/11/63	3	30	8-00			
1	PRESIDENT KENNEDY ADDRESS	9/30/62	1	15	10-00			

NEWS AND NEWS ANALYSIS

1	NEW YEAR AND THE NATION	1/01/63	3	30	10-30			
3	PROJECTION 'SIXTY-THREE	1/06/63	1	60	10-00	9	17	113
2	WHERE WE STAND	3/06/63	4	60	7-30	9	15	162
3	PRESIDENTIAL MISSION	3/19/63	3	30	10-30	9	19	113
2	DEATH OF THE THRESHER	4/11/63	5	30	7-30	13	25	162
3	THE FLIGHT OF FAITH SEVEN	5/13/63	2	30	10-30	5	11	113
2	A DAY AND A HALF IN SPACE	5/15/63	4	30	10-30	8	39	162
1	COOPER SPACE MISSION	5/16/63	5	60	6-45			
2	A DAY AND A HALF IN SPACE	5/16/63	5	60	7-00	21	37	162
2	A DAY AND A HALF IN SPACE	5/16/63	5	30	9-30	14	23	162
3	THE FLIGHT OF FAITH SEVEN	5/16/63	5	60	6-55	25	44	113
3	THE FLIGHT OF FAITH SEVEN	5/16/63	5	60	10-00	19	40	113
1	COOPER MISSION HIGHLIGHTS	5/19/63	1	30	10-30			
2	DEATH OF POPE JOHN XXIII	6/03/63	2	30	10-30			
2	THE US VS. GOV. WALLACE	6/11/63	3	30	7-30			
3	INTEGRATION--ALA. STORY	6/11/63	3	60	7-30			
2	KENNEDY AND MISSISSIPPI	9/30/62	1	30	10-00			
2	ORDEAL AT OXFORD	10/01/62	2	30	10-30			
3	REPORT ON MISSISSIPPI	10/01/62	2	60	7-30			
2	QUARANTINE OF CUBA	10/22/62	2	30	10-30			162
3	CLEAR AND PRESENT DANGER	10/31/62	4	90	7-30	16	30	47
1	WHATS NEW IN SHOW BIZ	11/11/62	1	15	9-45			
1	YEAR OF CONFRONTATION	12/23/62	1	30	9-30			
2	BACK FROM THE BAY OF PIGS	12/23/62	1	30	9-30	20	33	162
2	YEARS OF CRISIS	12/26/62	4	90	7-30			162

PANEL TALKS

1	HOW SAFE IS FLYING	1/22/63	3	30	10-30			
1	BIG BOMBER BATTLE	1/29/63	3	30	10-30			
2	FROST--AN AMERICAN POET	1/30/63	4	30	7-30			
3	EISENHOWER ON LINCOLN	2/11/63	2	30	9-30	11	17	265
2	SELF PORTRAIT	2/27/63	4	30	7-30	9	15	239

1	A CONVERSATION WITH L.B.J	3/26/63	3	30	10-30			
2	PORTRAIT--ROCKEFELLER	3/27/63	4	30	7-30	8	15	239
2	PORTRAIT--EILEEN FARRELL	4/24/63	4	30	7-30			20
1	CASTRO INTERVIEW	5/10/63	6	60	7-30			
1	THEATER OF TOMORROW	5/19/63	1	30	7-00			
2	PORTRAIT--F. WM. HENRY	6/05/63	4	30	7-30	4	12	20
2	WHERE WE STAND	10/10/62	4	60	7-30	8	15	20
3	AFTER TWO YEARS	12/17/62	2	60	8-30			
	POLITICAL PROGRAMS							
3	CANADIAN ELECTIONS	4/08/63	2	30	10-00	3	6	191
3	CAMPAIGN AND CANDIDATES	9/14/62	6	30	10-30	7	19	223
3	CAMPAIGN AND CANDIDATES	9/26/62	4	30	10-30	5	11	223
2	CAMPAIGN SIXTY-TWO REPORT	10/17/62	4	30	7-30	9	16	53
3	NBC ELECTION DEBATE	10/29/62	2	60	8-30			
3	CAMPAIGN AND CANDIDATES	11/05/62	2	30	10-30	5	11	223
1	ELECTION COVERAGE	11/06/62	3	210	7-30	5	9	
2	ELECTION COVERAGE	11/06/62	3	210	7-00	16	30	125
3	ELECTION COVERAGE	11/06/62	3	210	7-00	22	41	201
2	WHAT THE ELECTION MEANS	11/07/62	4	60	7-30	10	17	125
	SPORTS AND SPORTS NEWS							
3	ROSE BOWL FOOTBALL GAME	1/01/63	3	60	4-45	33	56	
1	BOWLING TOURNAMENT	1/26/63	7	60	10-00	9	14	99
3	NCAA BASKETBALL	3/23/63	7	90	9-30			
3	BASEBALL '63	4/05/63	6	30	9-30	13	23	116
1	INDIANAPOLIS RACE	5/30/63	5	60	10-00			
3	AMERICAS CUP RACE	9/17/62	2	60	10-00	8	18	193
1	COLLEGE BASKETBALL	12/29/62	7	60	10-00			107
	COMEDY VARIETY							
1	AS CAESAR SEES IT	1/15/63	3	30	10-30	8	16	69
3	BOB HOPE CHRISTMAS SHOW	1/16/63	4	60	9-00	30	43	257
1	AS CAESAR SEES IT	2/12/63	3	30	10-30	8	17	69
2	CAROL AND COMPANY	2/24/63	1	60	10-00	39	68	256
1	VICTOR BORGE	2/25/63	2	60	9-00	16	23	197
3	THE BOB HOPE SHOW	3/13/63	4	60	9-00	29	42	257
1	AS CAESAR SEES IT	3/21/63	5	30	9-00	14	21	69
3	THE BOB HOPE SHOW	4/14/63	1	60	9-00	28	46	143
1	AS CAESAR SEES IT	4/16/63	3	30	10-30	8	19	69
1	AS CAESAR SEES IT	5/14/63	3	30	10-30	6	17	69
3	THE BOB HOPE SHOW	5/15/63	4	60	9-00	21	33	143
1	AS CAESAR SEES IT	6/10/63	2	30	8-30	7	16	69
2	OPENING NIGHT	9/24/62	2	60	8-00	28	45	101
1	THE SID CAESAR SHOW	10/16/62	3	30	10-30	9	21	69
3	THE BOB HOPE SHOW	10/24/62	4	60	9-00			61
3	THE DANNY KAYE SHOW	11/11/62	1	60	9-00	28	42	103
1	AS CAESAR SEES IT	11/25/62	1	30	9-30	12	19	69
3	THE BOB HOPE SHOW	11/29/62	5	60	8-30	24	37	137
1	AS CAESAR SEES IT	12/15/62	7	30	8-30	11	19	69

MUSICAL VARIETY

2	LEONARD BERNSTEIN	1/05/63	7	60	7-30	9	15	+	96
2	YOUNG PEOPLE'S CONCERT	1/15/63	3	60	7-30	12	19		233
3	BELL TELEPHONE HOUR	1/18/63	6	60	10-00	13	24		39
1	HERE'S EDIE	1/20/63	1	30	9-30	8	11		69
2	THE SOUNDS OF NEW YORK	2/01/63	6	60	8-30	18	28		15
3	BELL TELEPHONE HOUR	2/04/63	2	60	9-30	7	12		39
2	LEONARD BERNSTEIN	2/21/63	5	60	8-00	8	12	+	96
1	HERE'S EDIE	2/26/63	3	30	10-30	13	29		69
2	YOUNG PEOPLE'S CONCERT	3/08/63	6	60	7-30	7	13		233
3	BELL TELEPHONE HOUR	3/13/63	4	60	10-00	14	27		39
1	HERE'S EDIE	3/17/63	1	30	9-30	9	15		69
2	GODFREY LOVES ANIMALS	3/18/63	2	60	8-30	27	38		47
2	THE JUDY GARLAND SHOW	3/19/63	3	60	8-30	24	37		61
1	OPERA AUDITION WINNERS	4/02/63	3	30	10-30				
3	BELL TELEPHONE HOUR	4/11/63	5	60	10-00	12	24		39
1	HERE'S EDIE	4/19/63	6	30	9-00	12	19		69
1	HERE'S EDIE	5/28/63	3	30	10-30	7	18		69
2	JULIE AND CAROL	6/12/63	4	60	9-00	21	39	+	143
2	VARIETY GARDENS	9/18/62	3	60	10-00	16	36		215
2	THE JUDY GARLAND SHOW	9/19/62	4	60	10-00	14	32	+	61
2	LINCOLN CENTER OPENING	9/23/62	1	120	9-00	9	16		72
3	BELL TELEPHONE HOUR	9/24/62	2	60	10-00	8	16		39
3	BELL TELEPHONE HOUR	10/22/62	2	60	10-00				39
1	HERE'S EDIE	10/23/62	3	30	10-30				69
2	GODFREY IN HOLLYWOOD	11/10/62	7	60	8-30	24	39		27
2	YOUNG PEOPLE'S CONCERT	11/21/62	4	60	7-30	8	14		233
3	BELL TELEPHONE HOUR	11/22/62	5	60	7-30	11	21		39
2	LEONARD BERNSTEIN	12/03/62	2	60	7-30	11	19		96
1	HERE'S EDIE	12/13/62	5	30	9-30	10	17		69
2	YOUNG PEOPLE'S CONCERT	12/21/62	6	60	7-30	9	15		233
3	BELL TELEPHONE HOUR	12/23/62	1	60	10-00	14	25		39
1	THE BING CROSBY SHOW	12/24/62	2	60	10-00				198
1	GIFT OF TALENT	12/25/62	3	30	10-30				47
1	GIFT OF TALENT	12/30/62	1	30	10-30				47

NON-CLASSIFIABLE

1	THIS IS DISCOVERY	3/12/63	3	30	10-30				

SUMMER 1963

UNCLASSIFIED DRAMA

2	THE PLAYHOUSE	9/10/63	3	30	8-00				198

AWARDS AND PAGENTS

2	MISS UNIVERSE PAGEANT	7/20/63	7	60	10-00	31	62		198
3	INTERNATIONAL BEAUTY SHOW	8/16/63	6	60	10-00	23	48		187
2	MISS AMERICA PAGEANT	9/07/63	7	60	10-00	40	72		180

DOCUMENTARY

1	THE VATICAN	6/19/63	4	60	7-30			
1	MARILYN MONROE	6/23/63	1	30	10-00	9	18	+ 5
3	CORONATION OF POPE PAUL	7/04/63	5	60	7-30	4	15	113
2	HOLLYWOOD--FABULOUS ERA	8/07/63	4	60	10-00	21	51	198
3	AMERICAN REVOLUTION OF 63	9/02/63	2	180	7-30			
1	THAT EVER LIVING BABE	9/03/63	3	60	8-30			
2	TEST BAN TREATY	9/03/63	3	60	7-30	6	14	48
2	HOLLYWOOD--THE GREAT STAR	9/03/63	3	60	10-00	19	43	198
2	CLOWNS AND HEROS	9/04/63	4	30	7-30			44
1	WHAT HAPPENED TO ROYALTY	9/09/63	2	60	9-00	9	18	188
2	EDUCATION IN LATIN AM.	9/11/63	4	60	7-30			44
2	ROOTS OF FREEDOM	9/11/63	4	60	10-00			
2	GOLDWATER--A PORTRAIT	9/13/63	6	30	10-30	6	14	22

NEWS AND NEWS ANALYSIS

3	SCHOOL PRAYER DECISION	6/17/63	2	30	10-00			
3	BRITISH GOVERNMENT CRISIS	6/18/63	3	30	10-30			
3	CONCLAVE OF THE CARDINALS	6/20/63	5	60	7-30			
3	POPE PAUL VI	6/22/63	7	30	8-30			
1	PRESIDENTIAL MISSION	6/23/63	1	30	10-30			
2	THE PRESIDENT'S TRIP	6/23/63	1	30	7-30	11	30	162
3	PRESIDENT'S JOURNEY	6/24/63	2	30	10-00			48
1	PRESIDENTIAL MISSION	6/25/63	3	30	10-30			
2	THE PRESIDENT'S TRIP	6/25/63	3	30	7-30			162
3	PRESIDENT'S JOURNEY	6/25/63	3	30	10-30			48
2	THE PRESIDENT'S TRIP	6/26/63	4	60	7-30			162
2	THE PRESIDENT'S TRIP	6/27/63	5	30	7-30			162
3	PRESIDENT'S JOURNEY	6/29/63	7	30	10-30			48
1	PRESIDENTIAL MISSION	6/30/63	1	30	10-30			
3	PRESIDENT'S JOURNEY	7/01/63	2	30	10-00	5	10	48
1	PRESIDENTIAL MISSION	7/02/63	3	30	10-30			
2	THE PRESIDENT'S TRIP	7/02/63	3	30	10-30			
3	PRESIDENT'S JOURNEY	7/02/63	3	30	10-30	8	21	48
3	PRESIDENT'S JOURNEY	7/05/63	6	60	7-30	5	16	48
3	REPORT FROM TOKYO	7/09/63	3	30	10-30	7	18	
3	REPORT FROM PARIS	7/16/63	3	30	10-30	7	18	
3	REPORT FROM LONDON	7/23/63	3	30	10-30	5	13	
2	MINE RESCUE IN HAZELTON	8/27/63	3	30	10-00			161
2	THE GREAT MARCH	8/28/63	4	60	7-30			44
3	JFK REPORT	9/09/63	2	30	10-00	6	12	1

PANEL TALKS

2	TAX CUT	7/03/63	4	60	7-30	5	17	142
2	TOWN MEETING OF THE WORLD	7/10/63	4	60	7-30	7	20	159
2	PORTRAIT--RICHARD RUSSELL	7/17/63	4	30	7-30	6	21	159
2	NEVINS-STEELE DIALOGUES	7/31/63	4	60	7-30			159
2	PRESS AND THE RACE ISSUE	8/21/63	4	60	7-30	7	19	44

SPORTS AND SPORTS NEWS

1	ALL AMERICA FOOTBALL GAME	6/29/63	7	60	10-00			47
1	U.S.-RUSSIAN TRACK MEET	7/23/63	3	90	9-30			22

```
1 U.S.-RUSSIAN TRACK MEET        8/02/63 6  60  7-30              289
1 ALL STAR FOOTBALL GAME         8/02/63 6  60 10-00 16 43        215


    COMEDY VARIETY
3 THE MILTON BERLE SHOW          8/12/63 2  60  9-30 14 29 +  187


    MUSICAL VARIETY
1 HERE'S EDIE                    6/18/63 3  30 10-30  6 17         69
3 THE BING CROSBY SHOW           8/14/63 4  60 10-00 21 51 +  187
2 THE JO STAFFORD SHOW           8/18/63 1  60  9-00 16 31        198


                      1963 - 1964


    PRESTIGE DRAMA
2 HEDDA GABLER                   9/20/63 6  90  9-30                1


    COMEDY DRAMA
3 HALLMARK HALL OF FAME          3/18/64 4  90  7-30 16 26        114
2 THE LUCY COMEDY HOUR           4/19/64 1  60  8-00 36 56        143


    FAIRY TALE/CARTOON DRAMA
3 MAGOO'S CHRISTMAS CAROL       12/13/63 6  60  7-30 27 46 +  257


    HISTORICAL DRAMA
3 HALLMARK HALL OF FAME          2/05/64 4  90  7-30 21 33        114
3 HALLMARK HALL OF FAME         11/15/63 6  90  9-30 13 24        114


    MOTION PICTURE DRAMA
2 THE WIZARD OF OZ               1/26/64 1  30  6-00 36 59 +  198


    MUSICAL DRAMA
2 ONCE UPON A MATTRESS           6/03/64 4  90  9-30 32 59        256
2 CALAMITY JANE                 11/12/63 3  90  9-30 29 50        143
3 AMAHL AND NIGHT VISITORS      12/25/63 4  60  9-00


    UNCLASSIFIED DRAMA
2 THE PLAYHOUSE                  9/17/63 3  30  8-00              198


    ACTUALITIES
3 WORLD'S FAIR OPENING           4/22/64 4  90  7-30              272


    AWARDS AND PAGENTS
```

1	ACADEMY AWARDS	4/13/64	2	120	10-00	37	71		198
3	TELEVISION EMMY AWARDS	5/25/64	2	60	10-00	32	65		257
3	APRIL IN PARIS BALL	10/27/63	1	60	10-00	13	27		66
2	MISS TEENAGE AMERICA	11/01/63	6	60	10-00	30	53		81
1	HOLLYWOOD DEB STAR BALL	12/28/63	7	60	9-30				66
1	KING ORANGE PARADE	12/31/63	3	60	10-00				

DOCUMENTARY

3	ESSO REPORT-ORIENT EXPRES	1/07/64	3	60	10-00	9	18		123
3	DAVID BRINKLEY'S JOURNAL	1/12/64	7	60	10-00				
3	THE KREMLIN	1/26/64	1	60	10-00	11	19	+	284
3	WHITE PAPER--BAY OF PIGS	2/04/64	3	60	10-00				
3	WHITE PAPER--CUBAN CRISIS	2/09/64	1	60	10-00	16	28		284
1	SAGA OF WESTERN MAN	2/29/64	7	60	7-30	10	16		269
3	DAVID BRINKLEY'S JOURNAL	3/03/64	3	60	10-00	9	17		284
3	WHITE PAPER--ADAM POWELL	3/12/64	5	60	7-30				
3	AMERICAN SPECTACLE	3/20/64	6	60	7-30	18	31		223
3	INSIDE THE MOVIE KINGDOM	3/20/64	6	90	9-30	17	30		71
1	SAGA OF WESTERN MAN	3/29/64	1	60	7-30	5	9		269
3	BREAKTHROUGH--MEDICINE	3/29/64	1	60	10-00	9	18		213
3	ESSO REPORT--AUSTRALIA	3/31/64	3	60	10-00	8	16		123
2	VIETNAM--DEADLY DECISION	4/01/64	4	60	7-30				
1	SALUTE TO GEN. MACARTHUR	4/05/64	1	30	10-00				
3	DAVID BRINKLEY'S JOURNAL	4/28/64	3	60	10-00	10	21		284
3	JAWAN--DEFENSE OF INDIA	5/26/64	3	60	10-00				
2	ROOTS OF FREEDOM	6/03/64	4	60	7-30	6	14		271
2	D-DAY PLUS TWENTY YEARS	6/05/64	6	90	8-30	15	30		
3	PROJECT XX	6/09/64	3	60	9-00	11	23		223
3	ESSO REPORT--FRENCH ARMY	6/09/64	3	60	10-00	6	14		123
1	MAKING OF THE PRESIDENT	6/11/64	5	90	9-30	10	21	+	284
3	A CHANCE TO ACHIEVE	9/17/63	3	30	10-30	7	16		1
3	EXPERIMENT IN EXCELLENCE	9/19/63	5	60	10-00	7	17		113
3	THE NEGRO IN WASHINGTON	9/26/63	5	60	10-00	11	23		284
3	APPOLO--JOURNEY TO MOON	10/01/63	3	60	10-00				
2	ELIZABETH TAYLOR'S LONDON	10/06/63	1	60	10-00	23	46		61
3	A MAN NAMED MAYS	10/06/63	1	60	10-00	16	33		233
1	SAGA OF WESTERN MAN	10/16/63	4	60	10-00	8	19		269
1	PRESIDENTIAL COMMITMENT	10/21/63	2	60	7-30	7	11		284
1	THE WORLD'S GIRLS	10/25/63	6	60	10-00	11	22		188
1	THE YANKS ARE COMING	11/11/63	2	60	10-00				
3	GREECE--THE GOLDEN AGE	11/19/63	3	60	9-00	10	17		213
1	FESTIVAL FRENZY	11/20/63	4	60	10-00	9	18		188
3	PROJECT XX--WAR IN KOREA	11/20/63	4	90	7-30	22	35		284
3	WORLD'S GREATEST SHOWMAN	12/01/63	1	90	8-30	30	45		83
3	PROJECT XX-VICTORY AT SEA	12/07/63	7	90	7-30	18	29	+	198
1	SOVIET WOMAN	12/10/63	3	60	10-00	14	27		188
3	THE MAKING OF A PRO	12/15/63	1	60	10-00	14	25		113
3	CONFORMITY	12/26/63	5	60	7-30				
1	MAKING OF THE PRESIDENT	12/29/63	1	90	8-30				284

INSTRUCTIONAL PROGRAMS

3	BELL SCIENCE SERIES	1/24/64	6	60	7-30	20	34		39

NEWS AND NEWS ANALYSIS

2	YEARS OF CRISIS	1/01/64	4	60	7-30	10	15	239
2	THE PILGRIMAGE OF PAUL	1/06/64	2	60	10-00	12	24	8
3	THE POPE'S PILGRIMAGE	1/08/64	4	60	9-00			
3	SMOKING AND HEALTH	1/11/64	7	60	7-30	12	18	164
2	THE COURT AND THE SCHOOLS	5/13/64	4	60	7-30	7	15	271
3	THE COSA NOSTRA	10/03/63	5	60	7-30	8	14	113
2	DEATH OF A REGIME	11/03/63	1	30	10-30	19	42	162
1	THE FISCHER QUINTUPLETS	11/17/63	1	30	10-30	9	19	37
1	TRANSITION AND TRAGEDY	12/29/63	1	60	10-00			
3	PROJECTION SIXTY-FOUR	12/29/63	1	60	10-00			113

PANEL TALKS

3	PROBLEMS OF PRESIDENCY	1/05/64	1	60	10-00	8	16	99
2	DEAR CBS	5/20/64	4	30	7-30	6	16	195
1	BIG BROTHER IS LISTENING	5/21/64	5	30	10-30	5	13	284
1	CIVIL RIGHTS AND THE BILL	5/22/64	6	60	7-30			
2	TOWN MEETING OF THE WORLD	5/27/64	4	60	7-30			
3	THE LOYAL OPPOSITION	9/16/63	2	30	10-00	5	11	1
1	ISSUES AND ANSWERS	10/06/63	1	30	10-00			
2	TOWN MEETING OF THE WORLD	10/16/63	4	60	7-30	7	14	138

POLITICAL PROGRAMS

2	NEW HAMPSHIRE PRIMARY	3/10/64	3	30	9-30	21	34	136
3	CAMPAIGN AND CANDIDATES	3/10/64	3	30	8-30	9	14	284
3	CAMPAIGN AND CANDIDATES	5/12/64	3	30	8-30			289
2	BARRY GOLDWATER ADDRESS	5/13/64	4	30	8-30	9	16	196
2	OREGON PRIMARY	5/15/64	6	60	8-00			
2	CAMPAIGN SIXTY-FOUR	5/19/64	3	30	7-30			
2	CAMPAIGN SIXTY-FOUR	6/02/64	3	60	10-00	12	25	5
3	THE CALIFORNIA PRIMARY	6/02/64	3	60	10-00	10	20	40

SPORTS AND SPORTS NEWS

1	WINTER OLYMPICS	1/29/64	4	60	10-00	12	24	94
1	WINTER OLYMPICS	1/30/64	5	60	10-00	16	30	145
1	WINTER OLYMPICS	1/31/64	6	60	10-00	12	21	24
1	WINTER OLYMPICS	2/03/64	2	60	10-00	15	28	94
1	WINTER OLYMPICS	2/04/64	3	60	9-00	17	27	145
1	WINTER OLYMPICS	2/05/64	4	60	10-00	12	28	94
1	WINTER OLYMPICS	2/06/64	5	60	9-00	17	25	145
1	WINTER OLYMPICS	2/07/64	6	60	8-30	17	29	94
1	WINTER OLYMPICS	2/09/64	1	60	10-00	11	19	145
3	ESSO REPORT	5/28/64	5	60	7-30	8	16	123

CIRCUS VARIETY

2	MARINELAND CARNIVAL	3/29/64	1	30	7-00	34	64	120

COMEDY VARIETY

3	BOB HOPE CHRISTMAS SHOW	1/17/64	6	90	8-30	29	47		64
3	THE JONATHAN WINTERS SHOW	2/20/64	5	60	7-30	21	32		87
2	CAROL AND COMPANY	2/28/64	6	60	10-00	20	36	+	256
1	SID CAESAR-EDIE ADAMS	9/19/63	5	60	10-00				69
2	OPENING NIGHT	9/23/63	2	60	9-00	25	38		101
3	THAT WAS TH WEEK THAT WAS	11/10/63	1	60	10-00	16	29		66

MUSICAL VARIETY

1	VICTOR BORGE SHOW	1/02/64	5	60	9-00	11	17	197
3	THE ANDY WILLIAMS SHOW	1/21/64	3	60	10-00			220
3	PERRY COMO'S MUSIC HALL	1/23/64	5	60	10-00	20	37	140
3	PERRY COMO'S MUSIC HALL	2/13/64	5	60	10-00			140
2	THE BING CROSBY SHOW	2/15/64	7	60	8-30	30	44	143
3	THE ANDY WILLIAMS SHOW	2/18/64	3	60	10-00			220
3	PERRY COMO'S MUSIC HALL	3/05/64	5	60	10-00	19	36	140
2	YOUNG PEOPLE'S CONCERT	3/11/64	4	60	7-30	5	9	233
3	THE ANDY WILLIAMS SHOW	3/17/64	3	60	10-00			220
3	PERRY COMO'S MUSIC HALL	4/09/64	5	60	10-00	14	28	140
3	THE ERNIE FORD SHOW	4/10/64	6	60	8-30	26	42	68
3	THE ANDY WILLIAMS SHOW	4/14/64	3	60	10-00			220
3	THE ANDY WILLIAMS SHOW	5/12/64	3	60	10-00			220
3	PERRY COMO'S MUSIC HALL	5/21/64	5	60	10-00	16	35	140
2	TEXACO STAR PARADE	6/04/64	5	60	10-00	14	31	255
2	LINCOLN CENTER DAY	9/22/63	1	60	8-00	10	17	15
3	PERRY COMO'S MUSIC HALL	10/03/63	5	60	10-00			140
1	AN EVENING WITH NAT COLE	10/13/63	7	30	10-00	9	16	69
2	THE BING CROSBY SHOW	11/07/63	5	60	9-00			143
3	PERRY COMO'S MUSIC HALL	11/21/63	5	60	10-00			140
3	THE ARTHUR GODFREY SHOW	11/28/63	5	60	10-00	19	39	168
2	YOUNG PEOPLE'S CONCERT	11/29/63	6	60	7-30	8	13	233
3	THE BEST ON RECORD	12/08/63	1	60	10-00	19	36	257
3	THE STORY OF CHRISTMAS	12/22/63	1	60	10-00	27	44	102
2	YOUNG PEOPLE'S CONCERT	12/23/63	2	60	7-30			233
3	THE ANDY WILLIAMS SHOW	12/31/63	3	60	10-00			220

NON-CLASSIFIABLE

1	KENNEDY ASSASSINATION	11/22/63	6	210	1-42	10	19
2	DEATH OF THE PRESIDENT	11/22/63	6	210	2-00	26	46
3	KENNEDY ASSASSINATION	11/22/63	6	210	1-53	19	36
1	KENNEDY ASSASSINATION	11/23/63	7	210	7-00	8	20
2	DEATH OF THE PRESIDENT	11/23/63	7	210	8-00	13	29
3	KENNEDY ASSASSINATION	11/23/63	7	210	7-00	19	49
1	KENNEDY ASSASSINATION	11/24/63	1	210	7-00	8	18
2	DEATH OF THE PRESIDENT	11/24/63	1	210	9-00	15	31
3	KENNEDY ASSASSINATION	11/24/63	1	210	8-00	17	50
1	KENNEDY ASSASSINATION	11/25/63	2	210	7-00	9	17
2	DEATH OF THE PRESIDENT	11/25/63	2	210	8-00	22	38
3	KENNEDY ASSASSINATION	11/25/63	2	210	7-00	22	44

SUMMER 1964

AWARDS AND PAGENTS

2	MISS UNIVERSE PAGEANT	8/01/64	7	60	10-00	27	57		198
3	INTERNATIONAL BEAUTY SHOW	8/14/64	6	60	8-30				66
2	MISS AMERICA PAGEANT	9/12/64	7	60	10-00	40	68		259

DOCUMENTARY

3	ESSO REPORT--YANKEE QUEEN	6/17/64	4	60	9-00	6	11		123
3	DAVID BRINKLEY'S JOURNAL	6/18/64	5	60	7-30	5	13		1
2	SEARCH IN MISSISSIPPI	6/25/64	5	60	8-00				
3	ESSO REPORT--US NO. ONE	7/02/64	5	60	7-30	4	11	+	123
2	ONE-SEVENTEENTH ST., N.Y.	7/29/64	4	60	7-30				
3	ESSO REPORT--WORLD'S FAIR	7/30/64	5	60	10-00	12	26		123
2	HOLLYWOOD--FABULOUS ERA	8/04/64	3	60	10-00	16	37	+	36
2	COUNTERATTACK IN VIETNAM	8/05/64	4	60	7-30	9	23		161
1	FESTIVAL FRENZY	8/07/64	6	60	7-30				
3	ESSO REPORT--COMMUNISM	8/14/64	6	60	10-00				123
2	THE ONE-FIFTY LIRE ESCAPE	9/02/64	4	60	7-30	6	13		47
2	HOLLYWOOD--GREAT STARS	9/08/64	3	60	10-00	16	35	+	36
3	ESSO REPORT--REAL WEST	9/09/64	4	60	9-00	6	10	+	123
1	LETTERS FROM VIETNAM	9/10/64	5	60	9-30	9	17		201

NEWS AND NEWS ANALYSIS

3	CHANEY GOODMAN SCHWERNER	6/27/64	7	60	7-30				
2	THE SUMMER AHEAD	7/01/64	4	60	7-30				
3	THE CIVIL RIGHTS BILL	7/03/64	6	60	7-30				
3	RANGER SEVEN MOON SHOT	7/31/64	6	30	9-30	9	20		113
3	TONKIN GULF INCIDENT	8/04/64	3	30	8-30	9	19		113
3	THE BATTLE FOR VIETNAM	8/05/64	4	60	9-00	8	15		113
2	CYPRUS AT THE BRINK	8/09/64	1	30	9-30				

PANEL TALKS

2	DEAR CBS	6/17/64	4	30	7-30	6	16		277
2	THE FIRST LADY AT HOME	8/12/64	4	30	7-30				47
2	HOME WITH MRS. GOLDWATER	9/09/64	4	30	7-30	9	20		277

POLITICAL PROGRAMS

2	GOV. WM. SCRANTON ADDRESS	6/28/64	1	30	9-30				196
3	GOV. SCRANTON ADDRESS	7/07/64	3	30	8-30	5	13		196
2	GREAT CONVENTIONS--REP.	7/08/64	4	60	7-30	6	15		174
3	THE REPUBLICAN STRUGGLE	7/08/64	4	60	9-00	5	9		1
1	CONVENTION CITY	7/09/64	5	30	10-30	4	10		
2	GOLDWATER PRESS CONF.	7/09/64	5	30	7-30				
3	THE REPUBLICAN STRUGGLE	7/09/64	5	60	7-30				
1	POLITICS SIXTY-FOUR	7/10/64	6	15	10-45				
1	WOMAN'S TOUCH IN POLITICS	7/11/64	7	30	7-30	3	11		201
1	POLITICS SIXTY-FOUR	7/11/64	7	30	8-00	3	9		66
1	POLITICS SIXTY-FOUR	7/12/64	1	60	7-30	4	10		284
1	REP NATIONAL CONVENTION	7/13/64	2	210	7-30	4	11		284
2	REP NATIONAL CONVENTION	7/13/64	2	210	7-30	9	27		15
3	REP NATIONAL CONVENTION	7/13/64	2	210	7-00	12	36		113

1	REP NATIONAL CONVENTION	7/14/64	3	210	7-00	2	11	284
2	REP NATIONAL CONVENTION	7/14/64	3	210	7-00	5	24	15
3	REP NATIONAL CONVENTION	7/14/64	3	210	7-00	9	40	113
1	REP NATIONAL CONVENTION	7/15/64	4	210	4-30	3	10	284
2	REP NATIONAL CONVENTION	7/15/64	4	210	5-00	7	25	15
3	REP NATIONAL CONVENTION	7/15/64	4	210	5-30	12	45	113
1	REP NATIONAL CONVENTION	7/16/64	5	210	7-00	3	10	284
2	REP NATIONAL CONVENTION	7/16/64	5	210	6-30	7	24	15
3	REP NATIONAL CONVENTION	7/16/64	5	210	7-00	12	40	113
3	GOLDWATER--HOW HE DID IT	7/17/64	6	60	8-30	6	15	113
3	CAMPAIGN AND CANDIDATES	7/30/64	5	60	7-30	4	12	1
3	CAMPAIGN AND CANDIDATES	8/17/64	2	30	9-30	4	8	99
3	CAMPAIGN AND CANDIDATES	8/18/64	3	30	8-30	4	7	99
2	GREAT CONVENTIONS--DEM.	8/19/64	4	60	7-30	6	14	8
3	CAMPAIGN AND CANDIDATES	8/19/64	4	60	9-00	5	9	1
1	GEORGE GOBEL, A MAN WHO..	8/20/64	5	30	10-30	8	18	284
3	CAMPAIGN AND CANDIDATES	8/20/64	5	60	7-30	4	9	161
1	POLITICS SIXTY-FOUR	8/21/64	6	15	10-45	4	9	66
1	WOMAN'S TOUCH IN POLITICS	8/22/64	7	30	7-30	6	13	201
1	TALK WITH THE FIRST LADY	8/22/64	7	30	8-00			
1	POLITICS SIXTY-FOUR	8/23/64	1	60	7-30	4	9	284
2	CONVENTION EVE	8/23/64	1	30	9-30	9	16	22
1	DEM NATIONAL CONVENTION	8/24/64	2	210	7-00	4	11	143
2	DEM NATIONAL CONVENTION	8/24/64	2	210	7-00	10	28	15
3	DEM NATIONAL CONVENTION	8/24/64	2	210	7-00	12	35	113
1	DEM NATIONAL CONVENTION	8/25/64	3	210	7-00	4	11	143
2	DEM NATIONAL CONVENTION	8/25/64	3	210	7-00	10	27	15
3	DEM NATIONAL CONVENTION	8/25/64	3	210	7-00	13	35	113
1	DEM NATIONAL CONVENTION	8/26/64	4	210	7-00	4	12	143
2	DEM NATIONAL CONVENTION	8/26/64	4	210	7-00	9	26	15
3	DEM NATIONAL CONVENTION	8/26/64	4	210	7-00	15	42	113
1	DEM NATIONAL CONVENTION	8/27/64	5	210	7-00	4	12	143
2	DEM NATIONAL CONVENTION	8/27/64	5	210	7-15	10	29	15
3	DEM NATIONAL CONVENTION	8/27/64	5	210	7-00	15	41	113
1	POLITICS SIXTY-FOUR	9/03/64	5	30	10-30			
1	TALK WITH MRS. GOLDWATER	9/10/64	5	30	10-30			
3	CAMPAIGN AND CANDIDATES	9/12/64	7	60	7-30	5	11	1

SPORTS AND SPORTS NEWS

1	ALL AMERICA FOOTBALL GAME	6/27/64	7	120	9-30			105
1	OLYMPIC TRIALS	7/03/64	6	60	7-30	7	21	193
1	OLYMPIC TRIALS	7/04/64	7	90	9-30	7	18	193
1	U.S.-RUSSIAN TRACK MEET	7/25/64	7	60	9-30	7	17	283
1	U.S.-RUSSIAN TRACK MEET	7/26/64	1	60	7-30	6	18	283
1	U.S.-RUSSIAN TRACK MEET	7/26/64	1	60	10-00	7	16	283
1	ALL STAR FOOTBALL GAME	8/07/64	6	60	10-00	15	39	182
2	GOLF PREVIEW	8/28/64	6	30	9-30	8	17	43
1	OLYMPIC TRIALS	8/29/64	7	60	7-30	6	14	193
1	OLYMPIC TRIALS	9/03/64	5	90	9-00	10	20	193
1	OLYNPIC TRIALS	9/04/64	6	60	7-30	8	22	193
1	OLYMPIC TRIALS	9/06/64	1	60	10-00	5	11	193
1	OLYMPIC TRIALS	9/12/64	7	60	9-30	9	15	193
1	OLYMPIC TRIALS	9/13/64	1	60	7-30	6	10	193

1 OLYMPIC TRIALS	9/13/64	1	30	10-00	5	10		193
COMEDY VARIETY								
2 FONDA AND THE FAMILY	6/23/64	3	60	10-00				36
2 THE NUTHOUSE	9/01/64	3	60	10-00	21	46		36
MUSICAL VARIETY								
2 TEXACO STAR PARADE	6/30/64	3	60	10-00	18	40		255
2 THE DONALD O'CONNOR SHOW	7/07/64	3	60	10-00	14	34	+	36
2 THE ESTER WILLIAMS SHOW	7/21/64	3	60	10-00	13	32	+	36
2 TEXACO STAR PARADE	7/28/64	3	60	10-00	14	35		255
2 JUST POLLY AND ME	8/11/64	3	60	10-00				36
2 VARIETY GARDENS	8/18/64	3	60	10-00	12	27	+	36
1 THE KING FAMILY	8/29/64	7	60	9-30	11	22		68
2 TEXACO STAR PARADE	8/31/64	2	60	10-00	14	32	+	255
1 WORLD OF ENTERTAINMENT	9/13/64	1	60	9-00	14	22		61

1964 - 1965

CRIME, SPY DRAMA								
2 MAN WHO BOUGHT PARADISE	1/17/65	1	60	9-00				189
DRAMATIC READINGS								
2 THE HOLLOW CROWN, PART I	2/16/65	3	60	10-00	6	12		25
FAIRY TALE/CARTOON DRAMA								
2 CINDERELLA	2/22/65	2	90	8-30	42	59		198
3 MAGOO'S CHRISTMAS CAROL	12/18/64	6	60	7-30	19	32	+	257
HISTORICAL DRAMA								
3 HALLMARK HALL OF FAME	1/28/65	5	90	9-30	16	27		114
3 HALLMARK HALL OF FAME	4/07/65	4	90	7-30	18	30		114
MOTION PICTURE DRAMA								
2 THE WIZARD OF OZ	1/17/65	1	90	7-00	35	49	+	198
MUSICAL DRAMA								
3 HALLMARK HALL OF FAME	10/18/64	1	60	10-00	10	19		114
2 ONCE UPON A MATTRESS	11/14/64	7	90	8-30	18	28	+	256
2 THE ROYAL BALLET	12/27/64	1	60	9-00				164
UNCLASSIFIED DRAMA								
1 WHO HAS SEEN THE WIND	2/19/65	6	90	9-30	17	29		284
2 LINCOLN CENTER DAY	9/20/64	1	60	9-00	4	6		215

1	CAROL FOR ANOTHER XMAS	12/28/64	2	90	9-30	14	26	284

AWARDS AND PAGENTS

1	HOLLYWOOD DEB STARS	1/02/65	7	60	9-30	16	26	66
3	JUNIOR MISS PAGEANT	3/20/65	7	60	10-00	21	36	228
1	ACADEMY AWARDS	4/05/65	2	60	10-00	37	69	198
3	PATRIOTIC BALL	5/29/65	7	60	8-00	7	14	225
2	MISS USA PAGEANT	6/04/65	6	60	10-00			198
2	MISS TEENAGE AMERICA	11/13/64	6	60	10-00	25	47	198
1	NOBEL PRIZE AWARDS	12/12/64	7	60	7-30	5	8	287

DOCUMENTARY

3	NBC WHITE PAPER	1/05/65	3	90	8-30			
3	CHRONICLE OF FREEDOM	1/12/65	3	60	10-00	6	11	223
1	SIR WINSTON CHURCHILL	1/24/65	1	60	7-30			
2	WINSTON CHURCHILL	1/24/65	1	60	9-00			
3	STATELY GHOSTS OF ENGLAND	1/25/65	2	60	10-00	13	26	125
3	OF MEN AND FREEDOM	1/26/65	3	60	10-00	7	12	108
1	ALCOA PREVIEW	2/04/65	5	60	10-00	10	18	6
3	NBC WHITE PAPER--OSWALD	2/09/65	3	60	10-00	11	20	108
1	THE WAY-OUT MEN	2/13/65	7	60	8-30	11	17	166
2	AN ESSAY ON BRIDGES	2/15/65	2	30	10-00			
1	SAGA OF WESTERN MAN	2/23/65	3	60	10-00	13	24	43
3	JOURNALS OF LEWIS, CLARK	2/23/65	3	60	10-00	16	30	125
1	INGER STEVENS IN SWEDEN	2/26/65	6	60	8-00	17	27	66
3	THE POPE AND THE VATICAN	3/09/65	3	60	10-00	7	13	108
1	THE BOLD MEN	3/13/65	7	60	7-30	11	17	166
1	ALCOA PREVIEW	3/14/65	1	60	7-30	6	9	6
1	MAN INVADES THE SEA	3/18/65	5	60	10-00	13	26	43
3	INTER-AMERICAN HIGHWAY	3/23/65	3	60	10-00	11	20	125
1	THE GENERAL	4/04/65	1	60	7-30	8	13	166
3	NBC WHITE PAPER--TERROR	4/06/65	3	60	10-00	10	19	193
1	SAGA OF WESTERN MAN	4/09/65	2	60	7-30	12	22	43
1	MISSION TO MALAYA	4/10/65	7	60	9-30	10	18	201
3	OUR MAN IN WASHINGTON	4/20/65	3	60	10-00			125
2	LET'S GO TO THE FAIR	4/21/65	4	60	7-30			10
2	AN HOUR WITH ED MURROW	4/30/65	6	60	8-30			
1	MELINA MERCOURI'S GREECE	5/03/65	2	60	9-00	9	15	205
3	THE AMERICAN WEST	5/03/65	2	60	9-00	25	43	202
3	THE SCIENCE OF SPYING	5/04/65	3	60	10-00			
2	VICTORY IN EUROPE	5/08/65	7	60	9-00	9	16	25
1	SAGA OF WESTERN MAN	5/10/65	2	60	7-30	9	19	125
3	A NEW LOOK AT OLD ENGLAND	5/17/65	2	30	7-30			102
3	THE MIDDLE AGES	5/18/65	3	60	10-00	9	19	193
3	SANTO DOMINGO	5/28/65	6	60	7-30			
3	JOSEPH WOOD KRUTCH	6/01/65	3	60	10-00	12	24	125
3	THE LOUVRE--GOLDEN PRISON	6/08/65	3	60	8-30	7	14	+ 284
3	WHO CAN VOTE	6/08/65	3	60	10-00			
1	ASSAULT ON LEMANS	6/13/65	1	60	7-30	7	15	48
3	SMALL TOWN, U.S.A.	9/18/64	6	60	10-00	11	21	223
2	THE PRESIDENCY	9/23/64	4	60	7-30	7	13	20
2	KHRUSHCHEV--END OF AN ERA	10/15/64	5	30	9-30	15	23	189

1	DEATH OF HERBERT HOOVER	10/20/64	3	30	9-00				
2	DEATH OF HERBERT HOOVER	10/20/64	3	30	8-30				
3	HERBERT HOOVER MEMORIAL	10/20/64	3	30	9-30				
1	SOPHIA LOREN IN ROME	11/12/64	5	60	10-00	16	32		61
3	THE LOUVRE--GOLDEN PRISON	11/17/64	3	60	10-00	10	19		284
2	BURDEN AND GLORY OF JFK	11/18/64	4	60	7-30	17	26		44
3	WORLD'S GREATEST SHOWMAN	11/29/64	1	90	8-30	22	33	+	83
3	HALLMARK HALL OF FAME	11/30/64	2	60	10-00	12	22		114
3	VIETNAM--IT'S A MAD WAR	12/01/64	3	60	10-00	10	18		47
2	FIVE FACES OF TOKYO	12/02/64	4	60	7-30	10	16		60
2	CASALS AT EIGHTY-EIGHT	12/14/64	2	60	10-00				
2	NATO IN DANGER	12/15/64	3	30	8-00	8	14		44
3	BATTLE OF THE BULGE	12/15/64	3	60	10-00	12	23		15
3	PROJECT XX	12/21/64	2	30	8-30				265

INSTRUCTIONAL PROGRAMS

3	BELL SCIENCE SERIES	2/26/65	6	60	7-30	15	25	+	39

SPEECHES

1	STATE OF THE UNION SPEECH	1/04/65	2	60	9-00
2	STATE OF THE UNION TALK	1/04/65	2	60	9-00
3	STATE OF THE UNION REPORT	1/04/65	2	60	9-00
1	PRESIDENT JOHNSON ADDRESS	3/15/65	2	60	9-00
2	PRES. JOHNSON ADDRESS	3/15/65	2	60	9-00
3	PRES JOHNSON ADDRESS	3/15/65	2	60	9-00
1	PRESIDENT JOHNSON ADDRESS	4/07/65	4	30	9-00
2	PRES. JOHNSON ADDRESS	4/07/65	4	30	9-00
3	PRES JOHNSON ADDRESS	4/07/65	4	30	9-00
2	PRES. JOHNSON ADDRESS	5/02/65	1	30	10-00
1	PRESIDENT JOHNSON ADDRESS	10/18/64	1	30	8-30
2	PRES. JOHNSON ADDRESS	10/18/64	1	30	8-30
3	PRES JOHNSON ADDRESS	10/18/64	1	30	8-30

NEWS AND NEWS ANALYSIS

3	INAUGURAL REVIEW	1/20/65	4	60	7-30	18	27	82
3	REPORT ON THE PRESIDENT	1/23/65	7	30	8-00	11	15	113
3	WINSTON CHURCHILL FUNERAL	1/30/65	7	30	8-30	10	14	113
3	PICTURES FROM THE MOON	2/20/65	7	60	8-00	9	13	113
3	THE FLIGHT OF GEMINI 3	3/22/65	2	30	7-30			
3	THE FLIGHT OF GEMINI 3	3/23/65	3	30	9-30	15	22	113
3	GEMINI FOUR PREVIEW	6/01/65	3	60	9-00	7	12	227
2	GEMINI FLIGHT PREVIEW	6/02/65	4	30	8-00			223
3	GEMINI FOUR PREVIEW	6/02/65	4	15	10-45			
3	THE FLIGHT OF GEMINI FOUR	6/07/65	2	60	8-00	11	22	113
3	MAN WALKS IN SPACE	6/08/65	3	30	9-30	8	15	68
3	KREMLIN SHAKEUP	10/15/64	5	60	7-30	16	26	113
2	THE COMMUNIST EXPLOSION	10/16/64	6	55	8-30	11	18	47
3	RED CHINA AND THE BOMB	10/16/64	6	60	7-30	10	18	113
2	DRAMA AT THE VATICAN	11/25/64	4	30	7-30	8	15	175
1	YEAR-END REVIEW	12/27/64	1	45	10-15			173
3	PROJECTION 'SIXTY-FIVE	12/29/64	3	60	10-00	6	11	113

PANEL TALKS

3	THE MAN WHO SPACE-WALKED	5/14/65	6	60	8-30	10	21	284
3	PUBLIC DEBATE ON VIETNAM	5/15/65	7	30	8-30			

POLITICAL PROGRAMS

1	POLITICS SIXTY-FOUR	9/16/64	4	30	10-30			
2	FACE THE NATION	9/16/64	4	30	7-30	8	16	
2	POLITICS--A FUNNY BUSINES	9/16/64	4	30	8-00	7	13	233
3	CAMPAIGN AND CANDIDATES	9/17/64	5	60	7-30	5	10	1
2	BARRY GOLDWATER ADDRESS	9/18/64	6	30	9-30	10	18	196
3	CONVERSATION AT GETTYSBRG	9/22/64	3	30	9-30	9	13	196
3	CAMPAIGN AND CANDIDATES	9/22/64	3	60	10-00	5	10	1
1	POLITICS SIXTY-FOUR	9/23/64	4	30	10-30	4	8	284
3	CAMPAIGN AND CANDIDATES	9/29/64	3	60	10-00	5	9	1
1	POLITICS SIXTY-FOUR	9/30/64	4	30	10-30			
2	FACE THE NATION	9/30/64	4	30	7-30			
3	AMERICA ASKS GOLDWATER	10/06/64	3	30	9-30	8	14	196
1	POLITICS SIXTY-FOUR	10/07/64	4	30	10-30	5	10	284
2	PRES. JOHNSON ADDRESS	10/07/64	4	30	9-30	13	22	196
1	THE JOB OF THE PRESIDENCY	10/09/64	6	30	9-30	6	11	196
1	POLITICS SIXTY-FOUR	10/09/64	6	30	10-00			
3	BANNERS FOR BARRY	10/13/64	3	30	9-30	8	13	196
3	CAMPAIGN AND CANDIDATES	10/13/64	3	60	10-00	6	11	1
1	POLITICS SIXTY-FOUR	10/14/64	4	30	10-30			
2	ELECTION EVE IN BRITAIN	10/14/64	4	30	7-30	8	14	22
2	PRES. JOHNSON ADDRESS	10/15/64	5	25	9-00	13	20	196
3	DEAN BURCH ADDRESS	10/19/64	2	30	8-30			
2	BARRY GOLDWATER ADDRESS	10/20/64	3	30	9-30	13	21	196
1	REPUBLICAN POLITICAL TALK	10/21/64	4	30	10-30	6	12	196
1	THE FREE SOCIETY	10/22/64	5	30	10-00	9	18	196
1	POLITICS SIXTY-FOUR	10/22/64	5	30	10-30	5	11	284
3	PRES JOHNSON INTERVIEW	10/24/64	7	30	8-30	8	13	196
3	A TIME FOR CHOOSING	10/27/64	3	30	9-30	8	13	196
3	CAMPAIGN AND CANDIDATES	10/27/64	3	60	10-00	6	12	1
1	POLITICS SIXTY-FOUR	10/28/64	4	30	10-30			
2	CAMPAIGN SIXTY-FOUR	10/28/64	4	60	7-30	9	15	125
2	PRES. JOHNSON INTERVIEW	10/28/64	4	30	8-30	10	16	196
2	BARRY GOLDWATER ADDRESS	10/29/64	5	30	9-30	11	19	196
3	A TIME FOR CHOOSING	10/31/64	7	30	8-00	8	14	+ 196
3	A TIME FOR COURAGE	10/31/64	7	30	8-30	8	14	196
1	POLITICS SIXTY-FOUR	11/01/64	1	30	10-30	5	12	48
2	PRES. JOHNSON ADDRESS	11/01/64	1	30	10-30	12	29	196
1	PRESIDENT JOHNSON ADDRESS	11/02/64	2	30	9-30	10	18	196
1	REAGAN FOR GOLDWATER	11/02/64	2	30	10-00	9	17	196
1	POLITICS SIXTY-FOUR	11/02/64	2	30	10-30			
2	PRES. JOHNSON ADDRESS	11/02/64	2	30	8-00	13	20	196
2	BARRY GOLDWATER ADDRESS	11/02/64	2	30	9-30	15	26	196
3	PRES JOHNSON ADDRESS	11/02/64	2	30	10-00	12	25	196
3	REPUBLICAN POLITICAL TALK	11/02/64	2	30	10-30	9	21	196
1	ELECTION RETURNS	11/03/64	3	210	7-00	8	14	284
2	ELECTION RETURNS	11/03/64	3	210	7-00	20	35	22

3	ELECTION COVERAGE	11/03/64	3	210	7-00	29	51	113
1	POLITICS SIXTY-FOUR	11/04/64	4	30	10-30	4	9	284
2	WHAT HAPPENED LAST NIGHT	11/04/64	4	60	7-30	14	22	22

SPORTS AND SPORTS NEWS

3	ORANGE BOWL FOOTBALL GAME	1/01/65	6	180	7-45			
3	SPORTS ROUNDUP OF 1964	1/01/65	6	15	10-45			
1	SKATING CHAMPIONSHIPS	3/07/65	1	60	7-30			124
1	GRAND AWARD OF SPORTS	3/10/65	4	90	9-30			31
3	OLYMPIC PREVIEW	9/28/64	2	60	10-00	6	14	193
3	SUMMER OLYMPICS	10/07/64	4	30	10-30			113
3	SUMMER OLYMPICS	10/13/64	3	60	7-30	13	21	31
3	SUMMER OLYMPICS	10/15/64	5	60	10-00	16	30	193
3	SUMMER OLYMPICS	10/20/64	3	60	10-00	10	19	193
3	SUMMER OLYMPICS	10/23/64	6	60	7-30	11	20	193

CIRCUS VARIETY

2	MARINELAND CARNIVAL	4/18/65	1	30	7-00	23	50	67

COMEDY VARIETY

3	BOB HOPE CHRISTMAS SHOW	1/15/65	6	90	8-30	36	51	64
3	ALLAN SHERMAN'S FUNNYLAND	1/18/65	2	60	9-00	21	33	257
3	THE JONATHAN WINTERS SHOW	2/01/65	2	60	9-00			108
3	THE DANNY THOMAS SHOW	2/14/65	1	60	7-30	26	39	69
3	THE JONATHAN WINTERS SHOW	2/22/65	2	60	9-00			3
3	THE DANNY THOMAS SHOW	3/14/65	1	60	9-00	39	59	69
3	THE JONATHAN WINTERS SHOW	3/29/65	2	60	9-00			3
3	THE DANNY THOMAS SHOW	4/23/65	6	60	8-30			69
3	THE JONATHAN WINTERS SHOW	5/10/65	2	60	9-00			3
3	THE JONATHAN WINTERS SHOW	11/09/64	2	60	9-00	21	33	165
3	THE DANNY THOMAS SHOW	11/13/64	6	60	8-30	21	34	69
3	THE DANNY THOMAS SHOW	12/10/64	5	60	8-30	20	30	69
3	THE JONATHAN WINTERS SHOW	12/14/64	2	60	9-00	17	28	215
2	THE NUTHOUSE	12/31/64	5	60	9-00			

MUSICAL VARIETY

2	EVENING WITH FRED ASTAIRE	1/03/65	1	60	9-00			5
3	PERRY COMO'S MUSIC HALL	1/07/65	5	60	10-00			140
2	ASTAIRE TIME	1/10/65	1	60	9-00			5
2	YOUNG PEOPLE'S CONCERT	1/28/65	5	60	8-00	10	14	39
3	PERRY COMO'S MUSIC HALL	2/04/65	5	60	10-00			140
1	AQUA VARIETIES	2/07/65	1	60	7-30	14	21	86
1	DINAH SHORE	2/15/65	2	60	10-00	15	29	201
2	YOUNG PEOPLE'S CONCERT	2/19/65	6	60	7-30	8	13	39
3	PERRY COMO'S MUSIC HALL	3/04/65	5	60	10-00			140
1	DINAH SHORE	3/17/65	4	60	8-30	11	16	201
3	PERRY COMO'S MUSIC HALL	4/08/65	5	60	10-00			140
2	MY NAME IS BARBARA	4/28/65	4	60	9-00			61
1	WORLD'S FAIR SPECTACULAR	4/29/65	5	60	10-00			86
3	THE BEST ON RECORD	5/18/65	3	60	8-30			257

3	PERRY COMO'S MUSIC HALL	5/27/65	5	60	10-00				140
2	JAZZ ON A SUMMER'S DAY	6/10/65	5	60	10-00	9	19		25
2	THE FRANCES LANGFORD SHOW	9/15/64	3	60	10-00	10	19	+	36
2	SEVEN WONDERFUL NIGHTS	9/16/64	4	30	8-30				
1	DINAH SHORE	10/17/64	7	60	9-30	15	26		201
3	PERRY COMO'S MUSIC HALL	10/29/64	5	60	10-00	17	34		140
2	YOUNG PEOPLE'S CONCERT	11/06/64	6	60	7-30	6	11		39
1	AROUND THE BEATLES	11/15/64	1	60	7-30	19	28		68
1	DINAH SHORE	11/18/64	4	30	9-30	12	20		201
2	HOUR WITH ROBERT GOULET	11/19/64	5	60	10-00	14	26		223
3	ALL TIME FAVORITE SONGS	11/26/64	5	60	7-30	18	32		168
3	NBC FOLLIES OF 1965	11/27/64	6	60	10-00	22	40		257
2	YOUNG PEOPLE'S CONCERT	11/30/64	2	60	7-30	10	16		39
3	PERRY COMO'S MUSIC HALL	12/17/64	5	60	10-00	23	40		140
2	EVENING WITH FRED ASTAIRE	12/20/64	1	60	9-00	12	18	+	5
3	THE STORY OF CHRISTMAS	12/21/64	2	60	7-30				102
1	WINTERLAND ON ICE	12/27/64	1	60	7-30				86

NON-CLASSIFIABLE

3	PANORAMA	5/03/65	2	30	7-30				128

SUMMER 1965

ACTION/ADVENTURE DRAMA

1	HERCULES	9/12/65	1	30	7-00				176

DRAMATIC READINGS

2	THE HOLLOW CROWN, PART II	6/20/65	1	60	9-00	5	10		164

UNCLASSIFIED DRAMA

1	ONCE UPON A TRACTOR	9/09/65	5	60	8-00				284

AWARDS AND PAGENTS

2	MISS UNIVERSE PAGEANT	7/24/65	7	60	10-00	27	60		198
3	INTERNATIONAL BEAUTY SHOW	8/13/65	6	60	10-00				68
2	MISS AMERICA PAGEANT	9/11/65	7	60	10-00				
3	TELEVISION EMMY AWARDS	9/12/65	1	60	10-00				68

DOCUMENTARY

1	EVERYBODY'S GOT A SYSTEM	6/18/65	6	60	8-30	8	18		43
1	TRIBUTE TO A. STEVENSON	7/15/65	5	30	7-30				
3	PROJECT XX--GARY COOPER	8/15/65	1	60	7-30				43
1	THE AGONY OF VIETNAM	8/25/65	4	60	8-30				107
3	AMERICAN WHITE PAPER	9/07/65	3	210	7-30				82
2	AMERICANS ON EVEREST	9/10/65	6	60	7-30				4

NEWS AND NEWS ANALYSIS

3	MARS--IS THERE LIFE	7/13/65	3	30	8-30	6	15	176
3	REPORT FROM MARS	7/17/65	7	30	8-30	7	18	109
3	THE GHETTOS ERUPT	8/14/65	7	30	8-30			
2	GEMINI FIVE PREVIEW	8/18/65	4	30	7-30			68
3	THE FLIGHT OF GEMINI FIVE	8/18/65	4	15	10-45			
3	THE FLIGHT OF GEMINI FIVE	8/20/65	6	30	8-00			179
1	EIGHT DAYS IN ORBIT	8/21/65	7	30	10-30			
3	THE FLIGHT OF GEMINI FIVE	8/21/65	7	30	8-30			113
3	THE FLIGHT OF GEMINI FIVE	8/29/65	1	60	10-00			113

PANEL TALKS

1	HEALTH CARE CROSSROADS	6/17/65	5	30	7-30	3	7	19
1	MEDICARE THE AMERICAN WAY	6/18/65	6	30	9-30			

SPORTS AND SPORTS NEWS

1	ALL AMERICAN FOOTBALL	6/26/65	7	90	9-30			226
1	COLLEGE FOOTBALL KICKOFF	8/06/65	6	30	9-30			
1	ALL STAR FOOTBALL GAME	8/06/65	6	60	10-00			8

COMEDY VARIETY

3	THE JONATHAN WINTERS SHOW	6/28/65	2	60	9-00			68
3	THE JONATHAN WINTERS SHOW	7/26/65	2	60	9-00			43
3	THE JONATHAN WINTERS SHOW	8/23/65	2	60	9-00			43
3	SECRET AGENT'S DILEMMA	9/06/65	2	30	7-30			

MUSICAL VARIETY

2	IT'S WHAT'S HAPPENING	6/28/65	2	90	9-30	21	41	

1965 - 1966

ACTION/ADVENTURE DRAMA

1	ASSAULT--THE LEGEND	4/19/66	3	60	7-30			22

PRESTIGE DRAMA

2	DEATH OF A SALESMAN	5/08/66	1	120	9-00			284
3	HALLMARK HALL OF FAME	11/18/65	5	90	9-30	14	24	114

COMEDY DRAMA

2	WHERE'S EVERETT	4/18/66	2	30	9-30			198
3	THE DANNY THOMAS SHOW	4/20/66	4	60	9-00			69
1	MAN IN THE SQUARE SUIT	4/22/66	6	30	9-00			

CRIME, SPY DRAMA

1	A POPPY IS ALSO A FLOWER	4/22/66	6	90	7-30			284

DRAMATIC READINGS

2	THE AGES OF MAN, PART ONE	6/03/66	6	60	10-00				
2	THE AGES OF MAN, PART TWO	6/10/66	6	60	10-00				

FAIRY TALE/CARTOON DRAMA

2	CINDERELLA	2/23/66	4	90	7-30	31	45	+	198
1	ALICE IN WONDERLAND	3/30/66	4	60	8-00	29	43		214
2	CHARLIE BROWN'S ALL-STARS	6/08/66	4	30	8-30				67
2	A CHARLIE BROWN CHRISTMAS	12/09/65	5	30	7-30	29	47		67
3	MAGOO'S CHRISTMAS CAROL	12/17/65	6	60	7-30	17	32	+	257
2	THE NUTCRACKER	12/21/65	3	60	7-30				56

HISTORICAL DRAMA

3	HALLMARK HALL OF FAME	2/03/66	5	90	8-30				114
3	HALLMARK HALL OF FAME	4/27/66	4	90	7-30				114
3	HALLMARK HALL OF FAME	10/20/65	4	90	7-30	12	20		114

MOTION PICTURE DRAMA

2	THE WIZARD OF OZ	1/09/66	1	90	7-00	31	49	+	198

MUSICAL DRAMA

3	PETER PAN	1/21/66	6	120	7-30	21	35	+	14
1	RED RIDINGHOOD'S XMAS	11/28/65	1	30	7-00	15	24		100

ACTUALITIES

1	THE PAPAL VISIT	10/04/65	2	90	8-30				
2	PAPAL VISIT TO THE UN	10/04/65	2	150	8-30				
3	POPE PAUL'S VISIT	10/04/65	2	210	7-30				

AWARDS AND PAGENTS

1	HOLLYWOOD DEB STARS	1/07/66	6	60	10-00	18	31		
3	JUNIOR MISS PAGEANT	3/26/66	7	60	8-00	21	35		228
1	MISS TEEN INTERNATIONAL	4/06/66	4	60	10-00	19	37		66
1	ACADEMY AWARDS	4/18/66	2	60	10-00				83
3	THE BEST ON RECORD	5/16/66	2	60	9-00				257
2	MISS USA PAGEANT	5/21/66	7	60	10-00				198
2	TELEVISION EMMY AWARDS	5/22/66	1	60	10-00				20
3	FALL PREVIEW OF FASHIONS	9/20/65	2	30	7-30				
2	MISS TEENAGE AMERICA	10/29/65	6	60	10-00	23	44		81
3	ORANGE BOWL PARADE	12/31/65	6	60	8-30				171

DOCUMENTARY

1	THIS PROUD LAND	1/26/66	4	60	9-00				85
3	HELLO DOLLY FAR EAST TOUR	2/07/66	2	60	9-00	20	30		284
2	NATIONAL GEOGRAPHIC SHOW	2/11/66	6	60	7-30	20	35		4
1	THE MUSIC EXPLOSION	2/15/66	3	60	10-00				43
1	THIS PROUD LAND	2/20/66	1	60	8-00				85

3	MICHELANGELO--LAST GIANT	2/23/66	4	60	9-00			14
2	SIXTEEN IN WEBSTER GROVES	2/25/66	6	60	10-00			297
1	THIN BLUE LINE	3/07/66	2	60	10-00			166
1	OPERATION SEA WAR VIETNAM	3/10/66	5	60	10-00			43
1	SAGA OF WESTERN MAN	3/23/66	4	60	10-00			43
1	THIS PROUD LAND	3/31/66	5	60	9-00			85
3	VIETNAM--THE HOME FRONT	4/01/66	6	60	7-30			
1	REVOLUTION IN THE THREE R	4/07/66	5	60	10-00	6	12	166
2	WEBSTER GROVES REVISITED	4/08/66	6	60	10-00	7	14	23
1	THE BIG GUY	4/15/66	6	60	9-00			43
1	THIS PROUD LAND	4/25/66	2	60	9-00			85
1	CHINA--YEAR OF THE GUN	4/27/66	4	60	10-00			166
2	NATIONAL GEOGRAPHIC SHOW	4/28/66	5	60	7-30			4
2	NATO--THE CRACKED SHIELD	4/29/66	6	60	10-00			
2	THE MAGIC OF BROADCASTING	5/01/66	1	60	10-00			223
1	SAGA OF WESTERN MAN	5/08/66	1	60	8-00			43
3	LYNDON JOHNSON'S TEXAS	5/09/66	2	60	10-00			
2	SEARCH FOR A SAFER CAR	5/13/66	6	60	10-00			195
3	THE ANATOMY OF DEFENSE	5/20/66	6	60	7-30			100
1	IN SEARCH OF MAN	5/23/66	2	60	10-00			166
2	MAKING OF THE PRESIDENT	10/19/65	3	90	9-30	11	19	284
1	TEEN-AGE REVOLUTION	10/29/65	6	60	10-00	9	17	166
1	THIS PROUD LAND	11/09/65	3	60	10-00	11	23	85
1	MAYHEM SUNDAY AFTERNOON	11/24/65	4	60	10-00	13	25	166
3	CONGRESS NEEDS HELP	11/24/65	4	60	10-00			284
1	A VISIT TO WASHINGTON	11/25/65	5	60	10-00	9	13	
3	WORLD OF JAMES BOND	11/26/65	6	60	10-00	27	50	185
1	IN SEARCH OF MAN	12/13/65	2	60	10-00	11	21	166
1	THIS PROUD LAND	12/18/65	7	60	9-30	14	25	85
3	VIETNAM--DECEMBER, 1965	12/20/65	2	60	10-00			26
2	NATIONAL GEOGRAPHIC SHOW	12/22/65	4	60	7-30			4
3	MICHELANGELO--LAST GIANT	12/22/65	4	60	9-00			14

SPEECHES

1	STATE OF THE UNION SPEECH	1/12/66	4	60	9-00
2	STATE OF THE UNION TALK	1/12/66	4	60	9-00
3	STATE OF THE UNION SPEECH	1/12/66	4	60	9-00
2	A REPUBLICAN APPRAISAL	1/17/66	2	30	10-30
2	VIETNAM PERSPECTIVE	2/23/66	4	40	9-30

NEWS AND NEWS ANALYSIS

3	NEW YORK TRANSIT STRIKE	1/06/66	5	30	9-30	113
3	VIETNAM--TURNING POINT	1/31/66	2	30	8-00	113
3	THE HAWAIIAN CONFERENCE	2/08/66	3	30	8-00	113
2	VIETNAM PERSPECTIVE	2/18/66	6	60	10-00	68
3	THE WAY TO GENEVA	2/18/66	6	60	7-30	
1	GEMINI VIII COVERAGE	3/16/66	4	120	8-00	
2	GEMINI VIII COVERAGE	3/16/66	4	210	7-30	
3	GEMINI EIGHT COVERAGE	3/16/66	4	210	7-30	
2	VIETNAM PERSPECTIVE--RUSK	4/18/66	2	30	7-30	277
2	VIETNAM PERSPECTIVE--RUSK	5/09/66	2	30	9-30	154
2	VIETNAM PERSPECTIVE	5/11/66	4	30	8-30	154

1	THE SPACE FRONTIER	12/04/65	7	30	10-30			
3	THE FLIGHT OF GEMINI	12/16/65	5	30	9-30			113
1	THE SPACE FRONTIER	12/18/65	7	30	10-30			
1	YEAR OUT--YEAR IN	12/26/65	1	45	10-15			

PANEL TALKS

1	GARY MOORE'S PEOPLE POLL	2/04/66	6	60	10-00			
2	THE U.S. AND CHINA	5/27/66	6	60	9-00			

POLITICAL PROGRAMS

3	ELECTION NIGHT IN BRITAIN	3/31/66	5	30	9-30			113

SPORTS AND SPORTS NEWS

3	ORANGE BOWL FOOTBALL GAME	1/01/66	7	195	7-45			
3	MAJOR LEAGUE BASEBALL	5/30/66	2	90	7-00			123

CIRCUS VARIETY

3	RINGLING BROS. CIRCUS	4/07/66	5	60	7-30	23	40	257
2	MARINELAND CARNIVAL	4/10/66	1	30	7-00	24	49	23
3	RINGLING BROS. CIRCUS	11/18/65	5	60	7-30	24	37	257

COMEDY VARIETY

3	BOB HOPE CHRISTMAS SHOW	1/19/66	4	90	9-00	35	55	64
2	CAROL PLUS TWO	3/22/66	3	60	8-30	33	48	20
3	A FUNNY THING HAPPENED	5/19/66	5	60	8-30			50
2	ANDY GRIFFITH SPECIAL	10/07/65	5	60	8-00	27	44	20
3	JACK BENNY SPECIAL	11/03/65	4	60	9-00	19	31	82
3	THE DANNY THOMAS SHOW	11/08/65	2	60	9-00	22	34	69
3	THE DANNY THOMAS SHOW	12/08/65	4	60	9-00	27	41	69

MUSICAL VARIETY

2	YOUNG PEOPLE'S CONCERT	1/05/66	4	60	7-30	9	15	39
3	THE ROGER MILLER SHOW	1/19/66	4	30	10-30	23	45	68
3	PERRY COMO'S MUSIC HALL	1/24/66	2	60	9-00	20	29	140
1	THE DAVE CLARK FIVE	1/28/66	6	30	7-30			
1	SAMMY AND FRIENDS	2/01/66	3	60	8-30			
3	THE DANNY THOMAS SHOW	2/06/66	1	60	7-30	25	38	69
2	NEW YORK, NEW YORK	2/14/66	2	60	10-00			10
2	CAROL CHANNING	2/18/66	6	60	8-30	28	45	101
2	THE STROLLIN' TWENTIES	2/21/66	2	60	10-00			22
2	YOUNG PEOPLE'S CONCERT	2/22/66	3	60	7-30			39
3	PERRY COMO'S MUSIC HALL	2/28/66	2	60	9-00			140
3	BALLET FOR SKEPTICS	3/11/66	6	60	7-30			284
3	THE DANNY THOMAS SHOW	3/13/66	1	60	9-00	29	45	69
3	THE JULIE ANDREWS SHOW	3/23/66	4	60	9-00			14
3	PERRY COMO'S MUSIC HALL	3/28/66	2	60	9-00			140
2	COLOR ME BARBARA	3/30/66	4	60	9-00	21	33	61
3	MARY MARTIN AT EASTERTIME	4/03/66	1	60	7-30			14

1	JACK JONES ON THE MOVE	4/05/66	3	60	10-00	16	32		56
3	PERRY COMO'S MUSIC HALL	4/25/66	2	60	9-00				140
1	HOLIDAY ON ICE	5/14/66	7	60	9-30				66
3	SINATRA AND HIS MUSIC	5/15/66	1	60	10-00				25
3	PERRY COMO'S MUSIC HALL	10/18/65	2	60	9-00	19	31		140
2	MY NAME IS BARBARA	10/20/65	4	60	10-00	15	31	+	61
1	JIMMY DURANTE	10/30/65	7	60	9-30	16	28		134
3	PERRY COMO'S MUSIC HALL	11/22/65	2	60	9-00	22	34		140
3	SINATRA AND HIS MUSIC	11/24/65	4	60	9-00	17	28		25
3	MUSIC BY COLE PORTER	11/25/65	5	60	7-30	12	23		168
3	THE JULIE ANDREWS SHOW	11/28/65	1	60	9-00	28	43		14
2	YOUNG PEOPLE'S CONCERT	11/29/65	2	60	7-30	12	19		39
2	ICE CAPADES	12/01/65	4	60	9-00	30	45		83
2	YOUNG PEOPLE'S CONCERT	12/14/65	3	60	7-30	8	14		39
3	A CHRISTMAS SING ALONG	12/17/65	6	60	8-30	18	31	+	12
3	PERRY COMO'S MUSIC HALL	12/20/65	2	60	9-00				140
3	HOME FOR THE HOLIDAYS	12/24/65	6	60	8-30				12

VAUDEVILLE VARIETY

3	LONDON PALLADIUM	5/26/66	5	60	7-30				
3	LONDON PALLADIUM	6/03/66	6	60	8-30				49
2	SALUTE TO STAN LAUREL	11/23/65	3	60	8-30	28	43		61

NON-CLASSIFIABLE

3	TESTING--ANYBODY HONEST	1/23/66	1	60	10-00				125
3	TESTING--HOW QUICK IS EYE	2/28/66	2	60	10-00				125
3	TESTING--POLITICS	4/20/66	4	60	10-00				26

SUMMER 1966

DRAMATIC READINGS

3	THE ANGRY VOICES OF WATTS	8/16/66	3	60	7-30

FAIRY TALE/CARTOON DRAMA

1	KING KONG	9/06/66	3	60	7-30

AWARDS AND PAGENTS

2	MISS UNIVERSE PAGEANT	7/16/66	7	60	10-00	198
3	MISS AMERICA PAGEANT	9/10/66	7	60	10-00	180

DOCUMENTARY

3	THE UNDECLARED WAR	6/15/66	4	60	9-00	26
1	THE BAFFLING WORLD OF ESP	6/16/66	5	60	10-00	43
3	SIBERIA--A DAY IN IRKUTSK	7/20/66	4	60	9-00	26
1	THE GOLD RING	8/05/66	6	60	9-00	
3	AMERICAN WHITE PAPER	8/25/66	5	210	7-30	
2	WONDERFUL WORLD OF WHEELS	9/08/66	5	60	7-30	85

	NEWS AND NEWS ANALYSIS					
2	CHICAGO RIOTING REPORT	7/15/66	6	30	9-00	
2	MISSION OF GEMINI TEN	7/20/66	4	30	7-00	98
3	GEMINI TEN FLIGHT REPORT	7/20/66	4	30	7-00	113
2	WHITE HOUSE WEDDING PREVU	8/05/66	6	60	10-00	
3	WHITE HOUSE WEDDING NEWS	8/06/66	7	60	7-30	68
	PANEL TALKS					
2	THE AMERICAN ECONOMY	9/09/66	6	60	10-00	
2	YOUNG MR. EISENHOWER	9/13/66	3	60	10-00	297
	SPORTS AND SPORTS NEWS					
1	U.S. OPEN GOLF	6/19/66	1	30	6-00	
3	MAJOR LEAGUE BASEBALL	7/04/66	2	120	7-00	107
1	ALL-AMERICA FOOTBALL GAME	7/09/66	7	90	9-30	
2	PROFESSIONAL FOOTBALL	8/12/66	6	90	9-30	
2	PROFESSIONAL FOOTBALL	8/19/66	6	90	9-30	
2	PROFESSIONAL FOOTBALL	8/26/66	6	90	9-30	
2	PROFESSIONAL FOOTBALL	9/02/66	6	60	10-00	
3	MAJOR LEAGUE BASEBALL	9/05/66	2	120	7-00	
1	ART OF FOOTBALL WATCHING	9/07/66	4	60	10-00	166
3	PROFESSIONAL FOOTBALL	9/09/66	6	150	7-30	
2	PROFESSIONAL FOOTBALL	9/10/66	7	90	9-30	
	MUSICAL VARIETY					
3	UP WITH PEOPLE	8/30/66	3	60	7-30	225
3	CLASS OF '67	9/10/66	7	60	9-00	257
	VAUDEVILLE VARIETY					
3	LONDON PALLADIUM	6/30/66	5	60	8-30	
3	LONDON PALLADIUM	7/15/66	6	60	8-30	
3	LONDON PALLADIUM	7/31/66	1	60	10-00	
3	LONDON PALLADIUM	8/12/66	6	60	8-30	

APPENDIX B

This appendix simply lists the sponsors of prime time special programs on the national networks. The number preceeding each advertiser's name is the code number assigned to identify that sponsor. Corresponding numbers appear as the final one-, two-, or three-digit figure listed for sponsored special programs in Appendix A.

001	Abbott Laboratories
002	Academy of Motion Picture Arts and Sciences
003	Admiral Corporation
004	Aetna Life and Casualty Company
005	Alberto Culver
006	Alcoa Aluminum
007	Allied Chemical
008	Allstate Insurance
009	Aluminum Ltd.
010	American Airlines
011	American Cancer Society
012	American Chicle
013	American Child Guidance
014	American Gas Association
015	American Home Products Corp.
016	American Honda
017	American Luggage
018	American Machine and Foundry
019	American Medical Association
020	American Motors
021	American Telephone and Telegraph
022	American Tobacco Co.
023	Anderson, Clayton and Co.
024	Andrew Jergens
025	Anheuser-Busch Brewing Co.
026	Armour
027	Armstrong Cork
028	A. Saagner and Sons
029	ASR Products
030	Atlantic Refining
031	Autolite Division of Ford Motor Company
032	Avco Manufacturing Company
033	Babbitt

034 Ballantine Ale
035 Bayuk Cigars
036 Beecham Products
037 Beechnut
038 Bell and Howell
039 Bell Telephone Company
040 Benrus Watch Company
041 Berkshire
042 Better Vision Institute
043 B. F. Goodrich
044 Block Drug Company
045 Breast O' Chicken Tuna
046 Brillo Manufacturing Company
047 Bristol-Myers
048 Brown and Williamson Tobacco
049 Buick Division of General Motors
050 Bulova Watch Company
051 Burgermeister Brewing Company
052 Bymart
053 Campbell Soup Company
054 Canada Dry Beverages
055 Carling Brewing Company
056 Carnation Company
057 Carter Products
058 CBS Columbia
059 Champion Sparkplug
060 Chanel, Inc.
061 Chemstrand
062 Chesebrough-Ponds
063 Chevrolet Division of General Motors
064 Chrysler Corp.
065 Cities Service
066 Clairol
067 Coca Cola
068 Colgate-Palmolive Company
069 Consolidated Cigar
070 Continental Oil Company
071 Corn Products
072 Corning Glassworks
073 Coty, Inc.
074 Cowles Magazines
075 Cracker Jacks
076 Disabled American Veterans
077 Dodge and Plymouth Division of Chrysler Corp.
078 Douglas Fir Plywood
079 Dow Chemical
080 Drackett Company
081 Dr. Pepper Company
082 Eastern Airlines
083 Eastman Kodak Company
084 Edsel Division of Ford Motor Company

085 E. I. DuPont de Nemours and Company, Inc.
086 Electric Companies of America
087 Elgin Watch Company
088 Encyclopedia Britannica
089 Equitable Life Assurance Company
090 Exquisite Form
091 Falstaff Brewing Company
092 Fedders Corp.
093 Field Enterprises
094 Firestone Tire and Rubber Company
095 Florsheim Shoe Company
096 Ford Motor Company
097 Frigidaire
098 Fritolay Snack Foods
099 General Cigar Corp.
100 General Electric Corp.
101 General Foods
102 General Mills
103 General Motors
104 General Tire and Rubber Company
105 Georgia-Pacific Company
106 Gibson Greeting Card Company
107 The Gillette Company
108 Glenbrook
109 Goodyear Tire and Rubber Company
110 Green Giant
111 Greyhound Bus Company
112 Gulf American Land Corp.
113 Gulf Oil Company
114 Hallmark Greeting Cards
115 Handmacher Vogel Company
116 Hartford Insurance
117 Heileman Brewing Company
118 Helena Rubenstein
119 Helene Curtis
120 Hi C Fruit Drinks
121 Hills Brothers Coffee
122 Hoover Vacuum Cleaners
123 Humble Oil Company
124 Hunt Foods
125 Institute of Life Insurance
126 International Telephone and Telegraph
127 Interstate Bakeries
128 J. B. Williams Company
129 John H. Breck Company
130 Johnson Motors
131 Johnson's Wax
132 J. Oster Manufacturing Company
133 Kaiser-Frazer Corp.
134 Kellogg Foods
135 Kelvinator Division of Nash Motors

136 Kemper Insurance
137 Kitchens of Sara Lee
138 Kiwi Polish Company
139 Knomark Manufacturing (Esquire Boot Polish)
140 Kraft Foods
141 Lanvin
142 Lehn and Fink
143 Lever Brothers
144 Libby-McNeil-Libby
145 Liberty Mutual Insurance
146 Life Magazine
147 Lifebouy Soap
148 Lincoln-Mercury Division of Ford Motor Company
149 Lincoln National Life Insurance
150 Longines-Wittnauer Watch Company
151 Look Magazine
152 Maclean's Toothpaste
153 Marck, Sharp and Dohme
154 Marlboro Cigarettes
155 Mars Candy, Inc.
156 Martin Marietta Company
157 Maybelline Company
158 Maytag
159 Mead, Johnson and Co.
160 Menley and James
161 Mennen
162 Metropolitan Life Insurance
163 Midas Flour
164 Miles Laboratories
165 Miller Brewing Company
166 Minnesota Mining and Manufacturing Company
167 Mobil Oil
168 Mohawk Carpet Mills Division of Mohasco Industries
169 Motorola
170 Mutual of Omaha
171 National Carbon Company
172 National Dairy Association
173 National REA
174 Nestle Company
175 North American Phillips Company
176 Norwich Pharmacal Company
177 Noxema
178 Ocean Spray Cranberry Juice
179 Old Gold Cigarettes
180 Oldsmobile Division of General Motors
181 Olin Mathieson Corp.
182 Pabst Brewing Company
183 Pan American World Airways
184 Parker Pen Company
185 Pepsi Cola
186 Pepto Bismol

187 Pharmacraft
188 Philco Corp.
189 Phillip Morris
190 Pillsbury Mills
191 Pittsburgh Plate Glass
192 Plymouth Division of Chrysler Corp.
193 P. Lorillard Company
194 Plough
195 Polaroid Camera Corp.
196 Political organizations of all types, all parties
197 Pontiac Division of General Motors
198 Procter and Gamble
199 Pty, Ltd.
200 Pure Oil Company
201 Purex
202 Quaker Oats
203 Quaker State Motor Oil
204 Ralston-Purina
205 Rayette
206 RCA, RCA Victor
207 RCA Whirlpool-Seeger Corp.
208 Red Cross Shoes
209 Remington Rand
210 Renault
211 Retail Clerks
212 Revlon
213 Reynolds Metals
214 Rexall Drugs
215 R. J. Reynolds Tobacco Company
216 Roto Broil
217 Royal McBee
218 Salada Foods
219 Sandran
220 S and H Green Stamps
221 Sandura
222 Sauter
223 Savings and Loan Foundation
224 Schaffer Brewing Company
225 Schick Razor Company
226 Schlitz Brewing Company
227 S. C. Johnson
228 Scott Paper Company
229 Scripto
230 Sealtest Dairy Products
231 Sears Roebuck Company
232 Sheaffer Pen Company
233 Shell Oil Company
234 Sherwin-Williams Paint Company
235 Shulton, Inc.
236 Sinclair Refining Company
237 Singer Sewing Machine Company

238 Smith Corona
239 Smith, Kline and French Laboratories
240 Socony Mobil Oil Company
241 Sperry Rand Corp.
242 Speidel
243 Standard Brands
244 Standard Oil
245 State Farm Mutual Insurance
246 Steel Companies of America
247 Stephen F. Whitman Candy Company
248 Sterling Drug
249 Sunbeam Corp.
250 Sun Oil Company
251 Sunshine Biscuit Company
252 Swift and Company
253 Sylvania Electric Products
254 [unassigned]
255 Texaco (The Texas Company)
256 Thomas J. Lipton
257 Timex Watches
258 Timken Roller Bearings
259 Toni Company
260 Top Value Enterprises
261 Travelers Insurance Company
262 Tupperware
263 Twentieth Century Fox
264 Union Carbide
265 Union Central Life Insurance Company
266 United Motors Service and Delco Remy Div. of Gen. Motors
267 United States Borax and Chemical Corp.
268 United Vintners
269 Upjohn Company
270 U. S. Brewers Foundation
271 U. S. Rubber Company
272 U. S. Steel
273 Vick Chemical Company
274 Warner-Lambert Pharmaceutical
275 Watchmakers of Switzerland
276 Westclox
277 Westinghouse Electric
278 Whitehall Laboratories
279 William Wrigley Jr. Company
280 Willy-Overland Company
281 Winston Cigarettes
282 Wolverine
283 WTS Pharmaceuticals
284 Xerox
285 Youngstown Kitchens
286 Yuban Coffee
287 Zenith
288 Liggett and Myers Tobacco Company
289 Co-Op sponsorship with local stations

290 7-Up Bottling Company
291 United Airlines
292 Newsweek Magazine
293 DuMont TV Corp.
294 American Oil Company
295 Nash Kelvinator (see also number 135; same company)
296 Time, Inc. Publications
297 General Telephone and Electronics
298 Institute for Cancer Research
299 Minute Maid

APPENDIX C

Following is a list of firms, arranged by network and special program type, which have sponsored prime time special programs by the single-sponsorship method.

ABC-TV

Drama

Action/adventure drama

Pontiac Division of General Motors
Procter and Gamble

Crime, mystery, spy, detective drama

Alberto Culver
Xerox

Fairy tale, puppet/cartoon drama

Coca Cola

Musical drama

General Electric
Mars Candy
Texaco
Westinghouse

Western drama

General Foods

Unclassified drama

Electric Companies of America
Xerox

Talks

Awards and pageants

Clairol
Eastman Kodak
Handmacher Vogel Co.
Mutual of Omaha
Philco
Procter and Gamble
Thomas J. Lipton Co.
Twentieth Century Fox
Zenith

Documentary

Alberto Culver
Alcoa Aluminum
Bell and Howell
B. F. Goodrich'
Clairol
DuPont
Gillette Safety Razor Company
Institute of Life Insurance
Mead, Johnson
Minnesota Mining and Manufacturing
Olin Mathieson
Philco
Procter and Gamble
Purex
Upjohn
Whitehall Laboratories
Xerox

News and news analysis

Beechnut
Gillette Safety Razor Company

Panel discussions

American Medical Association
Mutual of Omaha
Xerox

Political programs

Admiral Corporation
Brown and Williamson Tobacco Company
Buick Division of General Motors
Clairol

Kaiser-Frazer Corporation
P. Lorillard Tobacco Company
Philco
Political Organizations of all Types
Purex
Schaffer Brewing Company
Xerox

Sports and sports news

American Machine and Foundry
Florsheim Shoe Company
Gillette Safety Razor Company
Minnesota Mining and Manufacturing
National Carbon Company
Union Carbide

Variety

Circus variety

Lincoln-Mercury Division of Ford Motor Company
Timex

Comedy variety

Consolidated Cigar
Electric Companies of America
Oldsmobile Division of General Motors
Pharmacraft
Pontiac Division of General Motors
Purex
Revlon
Timex
Westinghouse

Musical variety

American Machine and Foundry
Beecham Products
Bristol-Myers
Bulova
Chevrolet Division of General Motors
Chrylser Corporation
Coca Cola
Consolidated Cigar
Electric Companies of America
Firestone Tire and Rubber Company
General Foods
J. Oster Manufacturing Company
Kellogg Foods

Oldsmobile Division of General Motors
Pharmacraft
Pontiac Division of General Motors
Procter and Gamble
Purex
Renault
Timex
Westinghouse
Youngstown Kitchens

Vaudeville variety

American Cancer Society
Philco

Non-classifiable

Bell Telephone System
Disabled American Veterans
Eastman Kodak Company
General Motors
Procter and Gamble

CBS-TV

Drama

Action/adventure drama

Buick Division of General Motors
DuPont

Comedy drama

Carling Brewing Company
DuPont
Ford Motor Company
General Foods
John H. Breck
Procter and Gamble
Westinghouse

Crime, mystery, spy, detective drama

Buick Division of General Motors
DuPont
Procter and Gamble

Dramatic readings

Anheuser-Busch

Fairy tale, puppet/cartoon drama

Coca Cola
John H. Breck
Procter and Gamble

Historical/biographical drama

DuPont

Motion Picture drama

Ford Motor Company
Procter and Gamble

Musical drama

Carling Brewing Company
DuPont
General Foods
John H. Breck
Pontiac Division of General Motors
Scheaffer Pen Company
Thomas J. Lipton
Westclox

Prestige drama

DuPont
John H. Breck
Westinghouse
Xerox

Western drama

Westinghouse

Unclassified drama

DuPont
Procter and Gamble
Revlon
R. J. Reynolds Tobacco Company
Westinghouse

Talks

Awards and pageants

Maybelline
Philco
Procter and Gamble
Willys-Overland

Documentary

Aetna Life and Casualty Insurance Company
American Airlines
American Home Products
American Machine and Foundry
Anheuser-Busch
Bell and Howell
B. F. Goodrich
Delco Remy Division of General Motors
DuPont
General Electric
General Foods
General Motors
Goodyear
International Telephone and Telegraph
Longines-Wittnauer
Metropolitan Life Insurance Company
Phillip Morris
Polaroid Camera
Procter and Gamble
Savings and Loan Foundation
Shulton, Inc.
Time, Inc., Publications
United Motors Service
U. S. Rubber
U. S. Steel
Xerox

Instructional programs

Bell Telephone System

News and news analysis

Allstate Insurance
Fedders Corporation
Firestone Tire and Rubber Company
General Foods
Goodyear
Marlboro Cigarettes
Metropolitan Life Insurance Company
P. Lorillard Tobacco Company
Savings and Loan Foundation
Smith, Kline, and French Laboratories
U. S. Rubber Company
Westinghouse

Panel talks

Firestone Tire and Rubber Company
General Telephone and Electronics

Liggett and Myers Tobacco Company
Mead, Johnson
Polaroid Camera
Smith, Kline, and French Laboratories
Westinghouse
Xerox

Political programs

American Home Products
Institute of Life Insurance
Kemper Insurance
Longines-Wittnauer
Nash Kelvinator
Political Organizations of all Types
Shell Oil Company
Westinghouse

Speeches

Steel Companies of America

Sports and sports news

A Saagner and Sons
Ballantine Ale
Carter Products
General Mills
Gillette Safety Razor Company
Renault
William Wrigley Company

Variety

Circus variety

Coca Cola
General Foods
Hi C Fruit Drinks
Remington Rand
Top Value Enterprises

Comedy variety

American Motors
American Tobacco Company
Carling Brewing
General Electric
General Foods
General Motors
Pontiac Division of General Motors

Procter and Gamble
Shulton, Incorporated
Thomas J. Lipton
Timex
Travelers Insurance Company
U. S. Steel

<u>Musical variety</u>

American Airlines
American Gas Association
Anheuser-Busch
Bell Telephone System
Bulova
Carling Brewing
Chemstrand Corporation
Corning Glassware
Eastman Kodak
Edsel Division of Ford Motor Company
Ford Motor Company
General Electric
General Foods
General Motors
Lever Brothers
Pontiac Division of General Motors
Procter and Gamble
Revlon
Shell Oil Company
Shulton, Incorporated
Texaco
Thomas J. Lipton
Timex
Westinghouse

<u>Vaudeville variety</u>

Carnation Company
Chemstrand
Coca Cola
Ford Motor Company
Martin Marietta Company

<u>Non-classifiable</u>

Autolite Division of Ford Motor Company
Bell Telephone System
Bymart
Chevrolet Division of General Motors
General Motors

NBC-TV

Drama

Action/adventure drama

Hallmark Greeting Cards

Comedy drama

American Gas Company
Consolidated Cigar
Hallmark Greeting Cards
John H. Breck
Miller Brewing Company
Rexall Drugs
Swift and Company

Crime, mystery, spy, detective drama

American Gas Company
Dow Chemical
Hallmark Greeting Cards
Purex
Rexall Drugs

Fairy tale, puppet/cartoon drama

Hills Brothers Coffee
Revlon
Timex

Historical, biographical drama

Equitable Life Assurance Company
Hallmark Greeting Cards
John H. Breck
Knomark Manufacturing
Purex
Swift and Company

Musical drama

Bell Telephone System
Buick Division of General Motors
Hallmark Greeting Cards
Liggett and Myers Tobacco Company
Longines-Wittnauer
Pontiac Division of General Motors

Prestige drama

Hallmark Greeting Cards
Steven J. Whitman Candy Company

Western drama

Hallmark Greeting Cards
Scott Paper Company

Unclassified drama

Electric Companies of America
Hallmark Greeting Cards
Purex
Toni Company

Talks

Actuality

U. S. Steel

Awards and pageants

Academy of Motion Picture Arts and Sciences
Buick Division of General Motors
Chesebrough-Ponds
Clairol
Colgate-Palmolive
Ford Motor Company
Frigidaire
General Motors
Look Magazine
National Carbon Company
Oldsmobile Division of General Motors
Pharmacraft
Procter and Gamble
R.C.A. and R.C.A. Victor
Schick Razor
Scott Paper Company
Timex
Watchmakers of Switzerland

Documentary

American Gas Company
American Telephone and Telegraph
Armour
Armstrong Cork
Bell Telephone System

Breast O' Chicken Tuna
Bristol Myers
Clairol
DuPont
Eastern Airlines
Eastman Kodak
Elgin Watch Company
Frigidaire
General Electric
Glenbrook
Gulf American Land Corporation
Gulf Oil Company
Humble Oil Company
Institute of Life Insurance
Life Magazine
Lincoln-Mercury Division of Ford Motor Company
Lincoln National Life Insurance
Mead, Johnson and Company
Merck, Sharpe, Dohme
North American Phillips Company
Ocean Spray Cranberry Juice
Pepsi Cola
Procter and Gamble
Purex
Reynolds Metals
Savings and Loan Foundation
Smith, Kline, and French Laboratories
Sterling Drug
Timex
Timken Roller Bearing
Thomas J. Lipton
U. S. Steel
Union Central Life Insurance Company
Westinghouse
Xerox

<u>News and news analysis</u>

Abbott Laboratories
American Motors
A.S.R. Products
Bell and Howell
Brown and Williamson Tobacco Company
Colgate-Palmolive
Eastern Airlines
Gulf Oil Company
Lincoln-Mercury Division of Ford Motor Company
Miles Laboratories
North American Phillips Company
Norwhich Pharmacal Company

Panel discussions

American Medical Association
General Cigar Corporation
Gulf Oil Company
Kraft Foods
Steel Companies of America
Union Central Life Insurance Company
Xerox

Political programs

Bayuk Cigars
General Cigar Corporation
General Tire and Rubber
Gulf Oil Company
Mennen
Philco
Pittsburgh Plate Glass
Political Organizations of all Types
Roto Broil

Sports and sports news

Buick Division of General Motors
General Foods
Gillette Safety Razor Company
Gulf Oil Company
Hartford Insurance
Humble Oil Company
National Carbon Company
P. Lorillard Tobacco Company
Union Carbide

Variety

Circus variety

Timex

Comedy variety

Beechnut
Buick Division of General Motors
Bulova
Chrysler Corporation
Eastern Airlines
General Foods
General Motors
Johnson Motors
Oldsmobile Division of General Motors

Pharmacraft
Plymouth Division of Chrysler Corporation
Pontiac Division of General Motors
Procter and Gamble
Renault
Revlon
Rexall Drugs
Texaco
Timex
U. S. Brewer's Foundation
Warner-Lambert Pharmaceutical

Musical variety

American Gas Company
Anheuser-Busch
Bell Telephone System
Benrus Watch Company
Buick Division of General Motors
Bulova
Chevrolet Division of General Motors
Chrysler Corporation
Cities Service
Colgate-Palmolive
Exquisite Form
General Foods
General Mills
General Motors
General Tire and Rubber Company
Gillette Safety Razor Company
John H. Breck
Kraft Foods
Liggett and Myers Tobacco Company
Lincoln-Mercury Division of Ford Motor Company
Mohawk of Mohasco
National Carbon Company
Pepsi Cola
Pharmacraft
Pontiac Division of General Motors
Procter and Gamble
Red Cross Shoes
Revlon
R. J. Reynolds Tobacco Company
S and H Green Stamps
Schick Razor
Sinclair Refining Company
Speidel
Standard Oil
Texaco
Timex

Top Value Enterprises
U. S. Brewer's Foundation
Westinghouse
Xerox

<u>Vaudeville variety</u>

American Child Guidance
Ford Motor Company
General Motors
Hallmark Greeting Cards
Institute for Cancer Research
Liggett and Myers Tobacco Company
Pontiac Division of General Motors
Rexall Drugs

<u>Non-classifiable</u>

American Medical Association
Bell Telephone System
General Motors
Gulf Oil Company

<u>DuMONT</u>

<u>Drama</u>

<u>Unclassified drama</u>

Electric Companies of America

<u>Talks</u>

<u>Documentary</u>

DuMont TV Corporation

<u>News and news analysis</u>

American Oil Company
Newsweek Magazine
United Airlines

<u>Political programs</u>

Political Organizations of all Types
Westinghouse

Sports and sports news

Admiral corporation

Variety

Musical variety

General Foods

Non-classifiable

Bell Telephone

BIBLIOGRAPHY

Articles

"ABC's $75-Mil Specs Splurge," Variety, March 29, 1967, p. 33.

"A Boost from Nielsen," Variety, April 26, 1967, p. 164.

Albig, William. "The Content of Radio Programs, 1925-1935," Social Forces, 16:3 (March, 1928), p. 338.

"Are Specials Only for Special Viewers?" Broadcasting, September 11, 1961, p. 94.

"Are Sponsors Disenchanted by Specials?" Printer's Ink, June 24, 1960, p. 12.

"As We See It," TV Guide, Wisconsin Edition, May 29, 1965, p. 4.

Baker, Kenneth. "An Analysis of Radio's Programming," in Lazarsfeld, Paul F. and Frank N. Stanton, eds., Communications Research, 1948-1949. New York, Harper and Brothers, 1949, p. 51.

Barcus, Francis. "A Bibliography of Studies of Radio and Television Program Content, 1928-1958," Journal of Broadcasting, 4:4 (Fall, 1960), p. 335.

Bartlett, Kenneth. "Trends in Radio Programs," The Annals, Vol. 213 (January, 1941), p. 15.

"Behind Those Gulf News Specials," Printer's Ink, May 26, 1961, p. 40.

Broadcasting-Telecasting and Broadcasting magazines, all issues from September, 1948 through 1960, plus quarterly "Special Show-sheets" in issues from 1961 through 1966.

"Bull Market for TV Specs," Variety, April 26, 1967, p. 167.

Christopher, Maurine. "Honeymoon Over for TV Specials," Advertising Age (September 12, 1960), p. 114.

Day, Fay. "Content Analysis in Mass Communication," in Nafziger, Ralph, ed., An Introduction to Journalism Research. Louisiana State University Press, 1949, p. 86.

"FCC Filing Signifies End of DuMont TV Network," Broadcasting-Telecasting, September 5, 1955, p. 7.

"FCC Hits NBC Sat. Plan," Broadcasting-Telecasting, February 20, 1950, p. 68.

"Fifty-Five Advertisers Set TV Specials for '59-'60," Advertising Age, August 3, 1959, p. 1.

"Ford Foundation to Cover 1968 Political Events for NET," Variety, April 19, 1967, p. 68.

Friendly, Fred W. "World Without Distance," NAEB Journal, 26:1 (January-February, 1967), p. 9.

"Gulf's $10-Million Buy," Broadcasting, May 1, 1967, p. 23.

Head, Sydney W. "Content Analysis of Television Drama Programs," Quarterly of Film, Radio, and Television, Vol. 9 (1954), p. 175.

Hettinger, Herman S. "Broadcasting in the United States," The Annals, Vol. 77 (January, 1935), p. 1.

Kingson, Walter. "The Second New York Television Survey," Quarterly of Film, Radio and Television, 6:4 (Summer, 1952), p. 317.

Lichty, Lawrence. "Who's Who on Firsts: A Search for Challengers," Journal of Broadcasting, 10:1 (Winter, 1965-66), p. 78.

Lichty, Lawrence W., Joseph M. Ripley II, and Harrison B. Summers. "Political Programs on National Television Networks: 1960 and 1964," Journal of Broadcasting, 9:3 (Summer, 1965), p. 217.

Lundberg, George. "The Content of Radio Programs," Social Forces, 8:1 (September, 1928), p. 58.

McClinton, H. L. "Radio Entertainment Since 1935," The Annals, Vol. 213 (January, 1941), p. 26.

"NBC Falls in Step on Rates," Broadcasting, December 19, 1966, p. 34.

"NBC's Hedonistic Show Loses Sponsor," Broadcasting, May 8, 1967, p. 46.

"NBC-TV 'Revue'," Broadcasting-Telecasting, March 6, 1950, p. 65.

"NBC-TV Revue Plans," Broadcasting-Telecasting, April 10, 1950, p. 66.

"Network Views Vary on Convention Coverage," Broadcasting, April 17, 1967, p. 92.

Postman, Neil. "The Literature of Television," in Steinberg, Charles, ed., Mass Media and Communication. New York, Hastings House, Publishers, 1966, p. 257.

"Radio-Television-Film Audience Studies," Department of Speech, University of Wisconsin, No. 2, June, 1966.

"RCA Victor to Sponsor 'Oscar' Awards Simulcast," Broadcasting, February 16, 1953, p. 38.

"RX for Ailing Video: Specs," Variety, May 17, 1967, p. 27.

"'Sat. Revue' Starts," Broadcasting-Telecasting, February 27, 1950, p. 62.

"Saturday Night on NBC-TV," Broadcasting-Telecasting, January 2, 1950, p. 45.

Smythe, Dallas W. "An Analysis of Television Programs," Scientific American, Vol. 184 (1951), p. 15.

________. "Commercial TV Programming in Champaign-Urbana, 1955," Audio-Visual Communication Review, 3:2 (Spring, 1955), p. 144.

________. "The Content and Effects of Broadcasting," in Nelson, Harry B., ed., Mass Media and Education. The Fifty-Third Yearbook of the National Society of Education, Part II. Chicago,

________. "Reality as Presented by Television," Public Opinion Quarterly, Vol. 18 (Summer, 1954), p. 143.

"Specs-Happy Webs Could Program Fourth Network with '67-'68 Rosters," Variety, February 22, 1967, p. 31.

Sponsor magazine, all issues from 1954 through 1962.

"Strategy for a Program Battle," Broadcasting, August 17, 1959, p. 27.

"Telestatus," Broadcasting-Telecasting, January 28, 1952, p. 74.

"The New Season," TV Guide, September 25, 1954, p. 4.

"The Ratings: A Photo Finish," Broadcasting, October 17, 1966, p. 66.

"The TV Special: It's No Gamble," Sponsor, September 11, 1961, p. 36.

TV Guide magazine, all issues from 2:7, February 12, 1954 to 14:37, September 10, 1966.

"TV Networks Differ on Specials Count," Printer's Ink, July 31, 1959, p. 10.

"Webs Getting More Statesmanlike in Answering Specs with Specs . . .," Variety, January 18, 1967, p. 31.

Books and Pamphlets

Berelson, Bernard. Content Analysis in Communications Research. Glencoe: The Free Press, 1952.

Bluem, A. William. Documentary in American Television. New York: Hastings House, Publishers, 1965.

Budd, Richard. An Introduction to Content Analysis. Iowa City, Iowa: State University of Iowa, 1963.

Chester, Giraud, et. al. Television and Radio, 3rd edition. New York: Appleton-Century-Crofts, 1963.

Committee on Local Television Audience Measurement. Standard Definitions of Broadcast Research Terms. New York: National Association of Broadcasters, January, 1967.

Ewbank, Henry L. and Sherman P. Lawton. Broadcasting: Radio and Television. New York: Harper and Brothers, 1952.

Head, Sydney. Broadcasting in America. Boston: Houghton-Mifflin Co., 1956.

Hettinger, Herman S. A Decade of Radio Advertising. Chicago: University of Chicago Press, 1933.

Horton, Donald, Hans O. Mauksch, and Kurt Lang. Chicago Summer Television, July 30-August 5, 1951. Chicago: National Opinion Research Center and the University of Chicago, 1951.

________. Chicago Television, January 4-10, 1952. Chicago: National Opinion Research Center and the University of Chicago, 1952.

Janda, Kenneth. Data Processing: Applications to Political Research. Evanston: Northwestern University Press, 1965.

Lazarsfeld, Paul F., and Frank N. Stanton. Communications Research 1948-1949. New York: Harper and Brothers, 1949.

Remmers, H. H. Four Years of New York Television, 1951-1954. Urbana: National Association of Educational Broadcasters, 1954.

Roper, Burns. Emerging Profiles of Television and Other Mass Media: Public Attitudes 1959-1967. New York: Television Information Office, 1967.

Selltiz, Claire, et. al. Research Methods in Social Relations, revised edition. New York: Holt, Rinehart and Winston, 1962.

Smythe, Dallas W. New Haven Television, May 15-21, 1952. Urbana: National Association of Educational Broadcasters, 1952.

________. Three Years of New York Television, 1951-1953. Urbana: National Association of Educational Broadcasters, 1953.

Smythe, Dallas W., and Angus Campbell. Los Angeles Television, May 23-29, 1951. Urbana: National Association of Educational Broadcasters, 1951.

Summers, Harrison B. Radio Programs Carried on National Networks, 1926-1956. Columbus: Speech Department, Ohio State University, 1958.

Summers, Robert E. and Harrison B. Summers. Broadcasting and the Public. Belmont, California: Wadsworth Publishing Company, 1966.

Dissertations and Theses

Hess, Gary Newton. "An Historical Study of the DuMont Television Network," unpublished Ph.D. dissertation, Northwestern University, 1960.

Lichty, Lawrence W. "The Nation's Station, a History of Radio Station WLW," unpublished Ph.D. dissertation, Ohio State University, 1964.

Silverman, Fred. "An Analysis of ABC Television Network Programming from February 1953 to October 1959," unpublished Master's thesis, Ohio State University, 1959.

Smith, Don C. "A Study of Programming of the Three Major Radio Networks Between October, 1931 and July, 1935," unpublished Master's thesis, Ohio State University, 1949.

Stewart, Robert H. "The Development of Network Television Program Types to January, 1953," unpublished Ph.D. dissertation, Ohio State University, 1954.

Unpublished Material

ABC-TV News and Special Events Department. List of News, Political, and Instant Specials for the Years 1958 Through 1962, New York no date. Mimeographed.

ABC-TV Program Research Department. "ABC-TV Specials [1957-1959]," New York, no date. Typewritten.

________. "Musical Specials, 1958-1959 Season," New York, April 2, 1959. Typewritten.

________. "ABC [Specials] 1961," New York, no date. Handwritten.

________. "CBS [Specials] 1961," New York, no date. Handwritten.

________. "NBC [Specials] 1961-2 Season," New York, no date. Handwritten.

________. "ABC [Specials] 1962," New York, no date. Handwritten.

________. "CBS [Specials] 1962," New York, no date. Handwritten.

________. "NBC [Specials] 1962-1963 Season," New York, no date. Handwritten.

________. "ABC [Specials] 1963," New York, no date. Handwritten.

________. "1963, CBS [Specials]," New York, no date. Handwritten.

________. "1963-1964, NBC [Specials]," New York, no date. Handwritten.

________. "ABC [Specials] 1964," New York, no date. Handwritten.

________. "Awards Specials, Beauty Contests [1964]," New York, no date. Handwritten.

________. "CBS [Political Specials, 1964]," New York, no date. Handwritten.

________. "News-Political, ABC [1964]," New York, no date. Handwritten.

________. "Sports, ABC [1964]," New York, no date. Handwritten.

________. "ABC-TV Specials, Goodrich Specials [1965]," New York, no date. Handwritten.

________. "ABC-TV Specials, Minnesota Mining and Mfg. Specials [1965]," New York, no date. Handwritten.

ABC-TV Sales Development. "ABC-TV Specials January-December, 1959," New York, no date. Mimeographed.

________. "Specials [July 19, 1959-June 5, 1960]," New York, July 17, 1959. Mimeographed.

________. "Specials on ABC-TV, 1959-60," New York, July 17, 1959. Mimeographed.

________. "ABC-TV Specials January-December, 1960," New York, no date. Mimeographed.

________. "ABC-TV Specials January-December, 1961," New York, no date. Mimeographed.

________. "ABC-TV Specials January-December, 1962," New York, no date. Mimeographed.

________. "ABC-TV Specials January-December, 1963," New York, no date. Mimeographed.

________. "ABC-TV Specials January-December, 1964," New York, no date. Mimeographed.

________. "ABC-TV Specials January-December, 1965," New York, no date. Mimeographed.

A. C. Nielsen Company. "Network Specials January-December 1964," Chicago, 1965. Mimeographed.

________. "Network Entertainment Specials, 1954-1963," Chicago, no date. Mimeographed.

CTN Research Department. "CTN Special Shows 1957-1958," New York, no date. Mimeographed.

________. "National Nielsen NBC Specials, 1957-1958," New York, no date. Mimeographed.

________. "NTI-National, Specials April-September, 1958," New York, no date. Mimeographed.

________. "NTI-National, Special Programs--All Networks, October 1958-April 1959," New York, no date. Mimeographed.

________. "NTI-National, Specials April-September, 1959," New York, no date. Mimeographed.

________. "Specials, All Networks, 1959-1960 season," New York, no date. Mimeographed.

________. "NTI-National, Specials April-September, 1960," New York, no date. Mimeographed.

________. "NTI-National, Entertainment Specials, October 1960-April 1961," New York, no date. Mimeographed.

________. "NTI-National, News, Public Affairs and Sports Specials, October, 1960-April, 1961," New York, no date. Mimeographed.

________. "NTI-National, Specials, April-September, 1961," New York, no date. Mimeographed.

________. "NTI-National, Entertainment Specials, October 1961-April 1962," New York, no date. Mimeographed.

________. "NTI-National, News, Public Affairs, and Sports Specials, October 1961-April 1962," New York, no date. Mimeographed.

________. "NTI-National, Specials April-September, 1962," New York, no date. Mimeographed.

________. "NTI-National, Entertainment Specials, October 1962-April 1963," New York, no date. Mimeographed.

________. "NTI-National, Specials, April-May 1963," New York, no date. Mimeographed.

________. "NTI-National, News and Public Affairs, October 1963-April 1964," New York, no date. Mimeographed.

________. "NTI-National, News, Public Affairs and Sports Specials, October 1963-April 1964," New York, no date. Mimeographed.

________. "NTI-National, Entertainment Specials Series, October 1964-April 1965," New York, no date. Mimeographed.

________. "NTI-National, News and Public Affairs, October 1964-April 1965," New York, no date. Mimeographed.

________. "NTI-National, Entertainment Specials, October-December [1965]," New York, no date. Mimeographed.

________. "NTI-National, Entertainment Specials, October 1965-January 1966," New York, no date. Mimeographed.

CTN Research, Program Records Division. "CBS Television Network One-Time Sustaining Programs Other then News 2/12/46 to Date," New York, May 10, 1960. Mimeographed.

________. "CBS Television Network One-Time Commercial Programs, April 7, 1958-December 31, 1948," New York, no date. Mimeographed.

________. "CBS Television Network One-Time Sustaining Programs, April 16, 1948-December 31, 1948," New York, no date. Mimeographed.

________. "CBS Television Network One-Time Commercial News and Public Affairs Programs (Except Paid Political and Sports) 1948-Date," New York, no date (about September, 1959). Mimeographed.

________. "CBS Television Network One-Time Sustaing [sic] New Programs 1948 to Date," New York, May 10, 1960. Mimeographed.

________. "Selected CBS Television Programs, 1948-1961," New York, December 1, 1961. Mimeographed.

________. "CBS Television Network One-Time Commercial Programs, 1948-1953," New York, January 9, 1962. Mimeographed.

________. "CBS Television Network One-Time Commercial Programs, January 1, 1950-December 31, 1950," New York, no date. Mimeographed.

________. "CBS Television Network One-Time Sustaining Programs, January 1, 1950-December 31, 1950," New York, no date. Mimeographed.

________. "CBS Television Network Commercial One-Time Special Programs, January 1, 1954 thru December 31, 1954," New York, no date. Mimeographed.

________. "CBS Television One-Time Commercial Programs January 1, 1955 thru November 6, 1956," New York, November 7, 1956. Mimeographed.

________. "CBS Television Network One-Time Commercial Programs, January 1, 1956-December 31, 1956," New York, no date. Mimeographed.

________. "CBS Television One-Time Sustaining Programs, January 1, 1956-December 31, 1956," New York, no date. Mimeographed.

________. "CBS Television Network One-Time Commercial Programs, January 1, 1957-December 31, 1957," New York, no date. Mimeographed.

________. "CBS Television Network One-Time Sustaining Programs, January 1, 1957-December 31, 1957," New York, no date. Mimeographed.

________. "CBS Television Network One-Time Commercial Programs, January 1, 1958-December 31, 1958," New York, no date. Mimeographed.

________. "CBS Television Network One-Time Commercial Programs, January 1, 1960-December 31, 1960," New York, no date. Mimeographed.

________. "CBS Television Network One-Time Sustaining Programs, January 1, 1960-December 31, 1960," New York, no date. Mimeographed.

________. "CBS Television Network One-Time Commercial Programs, January 1, 1961-December 31, 1961," New York, no date. Mimeographed.

________. "CBS Television Network One-Time Sustaining Programs, January 1, 1961-December 31, 1961," New York, no date. Mimeographed.

________. "CBS Television Network One-Time Commercial Programs, January 1, 1962-December 31, 1962," New York, no date. Mimeographed.

________. "CBS Television Network One-Time Sustaining Programs, January 1, 1962-December 31, 1962," New York, no date. Mimeographed.

________. "CBS Television Network One-Time Commercial Programs, January 1, 1963-December 31, 1963," New York, no date. Mimeographed.

________. "CBS Television Network One-Time Sustaining Programs, January 1, 1963-December 31, 1963," New York, no date. Mimeographed.

________. "CBS Television Network One-Time Commercial Programs, January 1, 1964-December 31, 1964," New York, no date. Mimeographed.

________. "CBS Television One-Time Sustaining Programs, January 1, 1964-December 31, 1964," New York, no date. Mimeographed.

________. "CBS Television One-Time Commercial Programs, January 1, 1965-December 31, 1965," New York, no date. Mimeographed.

________. "CBS Television One-Time Sustaining Programs, January 1, 1965-December 31, 1965," New York, no date. Mimeographed.

________. "CBS Television One-Time Commercial Programs, February 1, 1966-February 28, 1966," New York, no date. Mimeographed.

NBC Program Analysis. "Special Programs (not regularly scheduled) 1948," New York, December 13, 1961. Typewritten.

________. "1955-1956 NBC-TV Spectaculars and OTO Programs," New York, no date. Typewritten.

________. "1956-1957 NBC-TV Spectaculars and OTO Programs," New York, no date. Typewritten.

________. "NBC Specials 1959-1960," New York, no date. Typewritten.

________. "NBC Specials 1959-1960 Season," New York, no date. Typewritten.

________. "NBC-TV Public Service Programs, 1959-1960 Season, Aug. 27, 1959 thru July 10, 1960," New York, January 22, 1960. Typewritten.

________. "News Specials Feb. 1960 On," New York, no date. Typewritten.

________. "News and Public Affairs Specials, 1960," New York, no date. Typewritten.

________. "NBC Specials Summer 1960," New York, no date. Typewritten.

________. "Special Programs, September 3, 1960, thru August 11, 1961," New York, December 11, 1961. Typewritten.

________. "Specials Season of 1961-1962 News and Public Affairs, Entertainment, Informative and Cultural," New York, no date. Typewritten.

________. "NBC News Specials and Special Events, Including Religious Programs, 1960-1961," New York, no date. Typewritten.

________. "News Specials--Etc. [sic], 1960-1961," New York, no date. Typewritten.

________. "Special Programs 1960-1961," New York, no date. Typewritten.

________. "Specials Season of 1961-62, News and Public Affairs--Entertainment, Informative and Cultural," New York, no date. Typewritten.

________. "Specials 1962-1963 Season, News and Public Affairs--Entertainment, Informational, Cultural," New York, no date. Typewritten.

________. "Specials 1963-1964 Season, News and Public Affairs--Entertainment, Informational, Cultural," New York, no date. Typewritten.

________. "Special Programs September 3, 1960 thru August 11, 1961," New York, December 1961-January 1962. Typewritten.

________. "Specials 1964-1965 Season, News and Public Affairs--Entertainment, Informational, Cultural," New York, no date. Typewritten.

________. "Specials, 1965-1966 Season, News and Public Affairs--Entertainment, Informational, Cultural," New York, no date. Typewritten.

DISSERTATIONS IN BROADCASTING

An Arno Press Collection

Bailey Robert Lee. **An Examination of Prime Time Network Television Special Programs, 1948 to 1966.** *(Doctoral Thesis, University of Wisconsin, 1967)* 1979

Burke, John Edward. **An Historical-Analytical Study of the Legislative and Political Origins of the Public Broadcasting Act of 1967.** *(Doctoral Dissertation, The Ohio State University, 1971)* 1979

Foley, K. Sue. **The Political Blacklist in the Broadcast Industry:** The Decade of the 1950s. *(Doctoral Dissertation, The Ohio State University, 1972)* 1979

Hess, Gary Newton. **An Historical Study of the Du Mont Television Network.** *(Doctoral Dissertation, Northwestern University, 1960)* 1979

Howard, Herbert H. **Multiple Ownership in Television Broadcasting:** Historical Development and Selected Case Studies. *(Doctoral Dissertation, Ohio University, 1973)* 1979

Jameson, Kay Charles. **The Influence of the United States Court of Appeals for the District of Columbia on Federal Policy in Broadcast Regulation, 1929-1971.** *(Doctoral Dissertation, University of Southern California, 1972)* 1979

Kirkley, Donald Howe, Jr. **A Descriptive Study of the Network Television Western During the Seasons 1955-56 to 1962-63.** *(Doctoral Dissertation, Ohio University, 1967)* 1979

Kittross, John Michael. **Television Frequency Allocation Policy in the United States.** *(Doctoral Dissertation, University of Illinois, 1960)* 1979

Larka, Robert. **Television's Private Eye:** An Examination of Twenty Years Programming of a Particular Genre, 1949 to 1969. *(Doctoral Dissertation, Ohio University, 1973)* 1979

Long, Stewart Louis. **The Development of the Television Network Oligopoly.** *(Doctoral Thesis, University of Illinois at Urbana-Champaign, 1974)* 1979

MacFarland, David T. **The Development of the Top 40 Radio Format.** *(Doctoral Thesis, University of Wisconsin, 1972)* 1979

McMahon, Robert Sears. **Federal Regulation of the Radio and Television Broadcast Industry in the United States, 1927-1959:** With Special Reference to the Establishment and Operation of Workable Administrative Standards. *(Doctoral Dissertation, The Ohio State University, 1959)* 1979

Muth, Thomas A. **State Interest in Cable Communications.** *(Doctoral Dissertation, The Ohio State University, 1973)* 1979

Pearce, Alan. **NBC News Division:** A Study of the Costs, the Revenues, and the Benefits of Broadcast News and **The Economics of Prime Time Access.** *(Doctoral Dissertation, Indiana University, 1972)* 1979

Pepper, Robert M. **The Formation of the Public Broadcasting Service.** *(Doctoral Dissertation, University of Wisconsin, 1975)* 1979

Pirsein, Robert William. **The Voice of America:** A History of the International Broadcasting Activities of the United States Government, 1940-1962. *(Doctoral Dissertation, Northwestern University, 1970)* 1979

Ripley, Joseph Marion, Jr. **The Practices and Policies Regarding Broadcasts of Opinions about Controversial Issues by Radio and Television Stations in the United States.** *(Doctoral Dissertation, The Ohio State University, 1961)* 1979

Robinson, Thomas Porter. **Radio Networks and the Federal Government.** 1943

Sadowski, Robert Paul. **An Analysis of Statutory Laws Governing Commercial and Educational Broadcasting in the Fifty States.** *(Doctoral Thesis, The University of Iowa, 1973)* 1979

Schwarzlose, Richard Allen. **The American Wire Services:** A Study of Their Development as a Social Institution. *(Doctoral Thesis, University of Illinois at Urbana-Champaign, 1965)* 1979

Smith, Ralph Lewis. **A Study of the Professional Criticism of Broadcasting in the United States. 1920-1955.** *(Doctoral Thesis, University of Wisconsin, 1959)* 1979

Stamps, Charles Henry. **The Concept of the Mass Audience in American Broadcasting:** An Historical-Descriptive Study. *(Doctoral Dissertation, Northwestern University, 1956)* 1979

Steiner, Peter O. **Workable Competition in the Radio Broadcasting Industry.** *(Doctoral Thesis, Harvard University, 1949)* 1979

Stern, Robert H. **The Federal Communications Commission and Television:** The Regulatory Process in an Environment of Rapid Technical Innovation. *(Doctoral Thesis, Harvard University, 1950)* 1979

Tomlinson, John D. **International Control of Radiocommunications.** 1945

Ulloth, Dana Royal. **The Supreme Court:** A Judicial Review of the Federal Communications Commission. *(Doctoral Dissertation, University of Missouri-Columbia, 1971)* 1979